THE ILLUSTRATED ENCYCLOPEDIA OF
WILDLIFE

VOLUME 10

The Fishes

Wildlife Consultant

MARY CORLISS PEARL, Ph. D.

Distributed by Encyclopaedia Britannica
Educational Corporation

Grey Castle Press

Published by Grey Castle Press, 1991

Distributed by Encyclopaedia Britannica Educational Corporation, 1991

THE ILLUSTRATED ENCYCLOPEDIA OF WILDLIFE
Volume 10: THE FISHES

Library of Congress Cataloging-in-Publication Data
The Illustrated encyclopedia of wildlife.
     p.   cm.
     Contents: v. 1−5. The mammals—v. 6−8. The birds —
v. 9. Reptiles and amphibians — v. 10. The fishes —
v. 11−14. The invertebrates — v. 15. The invertebrates
and index.
     ISBN 1−55905−052−7
     1. Zoology.
QL45.2.I44 1991   90−3750
591—dc20   CIP

ISBN 1−55905−052−7 (complete set)
     1−55905−046−2 (Volume 10)

Printed in Spain

Photo Credits

Photographs were supplied by *Archivio IGDA*: (Bertinetti) 1812b; (C. Rives) 1813; *Ardea*: (P. Morris) 1920, 1925, 1951; (B. & V. Taylor) 1825; *H. Chaumeton*: 1804, 1805, 1808b, 1817, 1831, 1859, 1860p, 1862, 1864, 1865, 1871, 1880, 1881, 1895−1998, 1900−1909, 1912−1915t, 1919, 1933, 1936−1939, 1944, 1947, 1952, 1953, 1961b, 1962, 1963, 1975, 1977−1980, 1982−1984, 1986, 1987, 1990, 1994, 1995, 1997, 2001, 2002, 2008−2010, 2013, 2015, 2016, 2020, 2021t, 2024, 2025, 2027, 2030, 2034b, 2038, 2046t, 2047t, 2049, 2050, 2051, 2053, 2057, 2058, 2060, 2061, 2062, 2066, 2067, 2073, 2074, 2075, 2087, 2092, 2093; (Bassot) 1945, 1946, 1959, 1966, 1998b; (Breit) 2028; (Hellio) 1812t; (Lanceau) 1830, 1834, 1840, 1845, 1857, 1858, 1954, 1985, 2011, 2023, 2029, 2031, 2032; *Bruce Coleman*: 1821; (J. Burton) 1876, 1877, 1967; (M.P. Kahe) 1829; (D. & M. Plage) 2041; (A. Power) 1843, 1887, 2004b, 2044; (H. Reinhard) 1817, 1867, 1878, 2045b; (F. Sauer) 1891; (M.Timothy) 1844; (Bill Wood) 2065; *S. Giacomelli*: 1846; *D. Hosking*: 1815, 1823; *ICP*: 1921; *IGDA*: (C. Rives) 2096, 2097; *Jacana*: 1847, 1853, 1974b; (B. Atiegler) 2045t; (H. Chaumeton) 1820, 1850, 1855, 2000, 2046b; (A.R. Devez) 1848; (J.L.S. Dubois) 1828; (Gillon) 1974t; (A. Kerners) 1851; (R. Konig) 1808t, 2006; (Laboute) 2086; (Noailles) 1992; (Tercafs) 1849; (Varin-Visage) 1808c, 1856, 1948, 1958, 1998, 2056, 2072, 2080b; (Yoff) 1964, 1969l; *A. Margiccio*: 1842t; *Marka*: (F.W. Lane) 1928; *G. Mazza*: 1819, 1841, 1842b; *NHPA*: (ANT) 2088, 2089; (Agency Nature) 1943; (H. Ansloos) 2047t; (G.I. Bernard) 1923; (Karl Switak) 1971; (Roy Waller) 2033, 2040; (Bill Wood) 2021b, 2065; *OSF*: (Mike Birkhead) 2063; (Sarah Cunliffe) 2086; (Frederick Ehrenstrum) 2036; (Laurence Gould) 2078; (Breck P. Kent) 1935; (Rudie H. Kuiter) 2080t; (David Shale) 1961tr; *Planet Earth Pictures*: (Martin Coleman) 2034t; (Peter David) 1809, 1960; (Georgette Douwima) 1991, 2059; (Jim Greenfield) 2017; (N. Greaves) 1916, 1917; (Jim Green) 1957; (Lutjanus Kasmira) 1810, 1811; (Jon Kenfield) 1803, 2042; (K. Lucas) 1807, 1822, 1837, 1854, 1869, 2005, 2014; (J. Lythgoe) 1875; (David Maitland) 2079; (D. Perrine) 1835t, 1836; (C. Petron) 1852; (Mike Potts) 1929; (C. Roessler) 1801, 1802, 1833, 2085; (R. Salm) 1915b; (F. Schulke) 1832; (P. Scoones) 1872, 1885, 1998b, 2043; (H. Voightmann) 1873, 1998t; (Warren Williams) 2018, 2019; (Bill Wood) 2098; *Seaphot*: 1889; (P.M. David) 1956; (W. Deas) 1989; (C.C. Hemmings) 1950; (J. Kenfield) 1892; (J. Lythgoe) 2035; (J.I. Mackinnon) 1888, 2003; (C. Petron) 1965, 1999.

FRONT COVER: A blue surgeonfish (Planet Earth Pictures/K. Lucas).

CONTENTS

FISHES
SEA SQUIRTS AND LANCELETS

INTRODUCTION

There are over 22,000 known species of living fishes, and zoologists estimate that there may be several thousand more awaiting discovery, particularly among those that dwell in the deep sea. Many species occur in vast numbers in the fresh and marine waters of the world—and some, such as the mudskippers, climbing perch and walking catfish, even occur out of them (for some of the time, at least). Fishes account for more than half the vertebrates alive today, and every backboned animal on Earth is ultimately descended from the fishes.

Despite their scientific and economic importance, the fishes are among the least understood of all animals. The reason for this is simple: they live in an alien environment that can often be penetrated only by trained divers using special equipment, and for only short periods at a time. Such fleeting visits offer few opportunities for the patient, detailed observations that form the basis of all that we know about land animals. Some fishes are easier to study than others; small species with a limited range that live in shallow lagoons, lakes or rivers can be visited day after day, allowing naturalists to piece together a complete picture of their lives. But large, wide-ranging species spend most of their time in waters not easily accessible to humans. The little we know of the behavior of such fishes has been based on brief sightings, or deduced from specimens trawled up in fishing nets.

A scientific approach

The commercial needs of the fishing industry have stimulated a lot of research into the habits of economically important species such as the cod fishes, salmon and herring. At one time fishing was not carried out scientifically, but increasing costs—and the depletion of stocks

through overfishing—have made a more precise approach essential. Today, the fishing fleets know exactly where to find their quarry throughout the year—the result of an intensive, well-funded study of the fishes' habits that has benefited biologists as well as dealers in frozen food. But, inevitably, the more that we know about such species, the more vulnerable they are to exploitation by humans.

Aquarium life

One option open to researchers is to capture fishes alive and to study them in the controlled environment of the aquarium. For the smaller species, natural habitats can be reproduced with some degree of accuracy. A naturalist can study the life history of a small fish (such as a three-spined stickleback) in detail, confident that the captive fish's behavior is representative of its activities in the wild.

With large or deep-sea species it is a different matter. An aquarium cannot accommodate the life history of one of the larger sharks, for example; nor can it effectively reproduce the natural habitat of the deep-sea angler fish, which lives in the lightless, high-pressure conditions of the deep ocean, some 3200 feet below the surface.

Some species may appear to act normally in captivity, and may even breed. But an interesting habit displayed by a captive fish may be no more than a form of neurosis, or a response to an imbalance in its environment. Such problems beset all studies of animal behavior, but with fish the difficulty is increased because we often have no idea how a particular species behaves in the wild and therefore have no basis for comparison. Although our knowledge of fishes still has a long way to go before it matches our understanding of mammals, birds, reptiles and amphibians, a vast amount is known about numerous species. In these pages, we will provide some idea of the extraordinary diversity of forms and adaptations to be found among the fishes— arguably the most successful of all vertebrates.

FAR LEFT Many of the world's most colorful fishes are inhabitants of coral reefs. The parrot fishes not only live among the corals, but feed on them. Their front teeth are fused together to form a strong "beak" that they use to bite off pieces of living coral. Teeth inside their throats grind the coral down, and the fishes then swallow the edible parts.

ABOVE Sea squirts live either as separate individuals, as in these bright purple animals from the Philippines, or in dense colonies, in which groups share the same excretory opening.
PAGE 1801 Groupers are thick-set, predatory fishes with large mouths and needle-sharp teeth. Some reach a great size, the largest weighing up to half a ton and measuring 10 feet in length.

Sea squirts and lancelets

Sea squirts and lancelets are small, unfamiliar marine animals that form a link between the vertebrates and the invertebrates. Although they do not possess a proper backbone—unlike mammals, birds, reptiles and fishes—sea squirts (at least in the larval stage) and lancelets do have a notochord, a rod of cells in a tough connective tissue that supports the trunk and the tail. While a sea squirt bears no resemblance to a true fish, the lancelet's long, flattened shape begins to look like the fishes on the next rung of the evolutionary ladder.

THE
FISHES

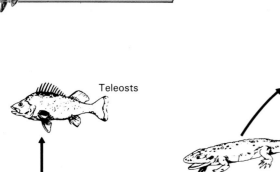

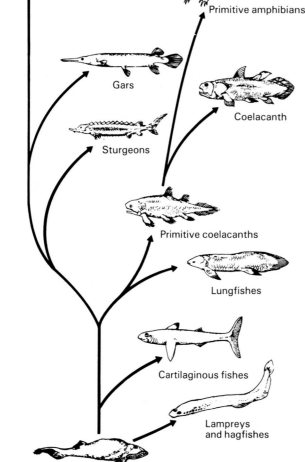

Teleosts

Primitive amphibians

Gars

Coelacanth

Sturgeons

Primitive coelacanths

Lungfishes

Cartilaginous fishes

Lampreys
and hagfishes

Primitive fishes

ABOVE The hagfishes, lampreys and cartilaginous fishes branched off from the mainstream of fish evolution very early on. A later branch led to the lungfishes, the coelacanth, amphibians and ultimately the reptiles, birds and mammals. Bony fishes, such as the sturgeon, gars and perch, were the last to develop.
PAGES 1804-1805 Two young lumpsuckers cling to a rock with paired pelvic fins that have been modified to form a single suction disk. Lumpsuckers are sometimes called sea hens because the male guards the eggs—he may go for several weeks without eating.

RULERS OF THE WATER

The four classes of fish that exist today are the hagfishes; the lampreys; the cartilaginous fishes (such as the sharks and rays); and the bony fishes (such as the trout, herring and mackerel). They have little in common except their ability to extract oxygen from the water, their skill as swimmers and the fact that they have internal skeletons.

The hagfishes and the lampreys, known as the jawless fishes, do not have proper skulls with jawbones, and they feed by rasping at their prey with their rough tongues. The skeletons of these eel-shaped animals are even less well developed than those of sharks and rays: the lamprey has a row of arch-like pieces of cartilage in place of a backbone, while the hagfish has only a simple, flexible rod called a notochord (from the Greek *noton* meaning "back," and *chorde*, meaning "a string"). In most other vertebrates, the notochord has developed into a backbone.

The skeletons of cartilaginous fishes are built up of flexible cartilage instead of bone. They do not have ribs, and their fins are also quite different from those of bony fishes. Both bony and cartilaginous fishes, however, have well-developed skulls with jawbones that have flexible joints.

The structure of the bony fishes is based on the backbone—a row of short, spinal bones or vertebrae, linked together into a flexible vertebral column that supports the ribs and skull. These elements are common to all bony fishes, amphibians, reptiles, birds and mammals, and as a result, all these creatures are classified together as vertebrates—animals with backbones. The other three classes of fish are also classified as vertebrates because they have a notochord.

There are about 32 species of hagfishes and about 41 species of lampreys. The cartilaginous fishes are much more abundant, with some 790 species of sharks, rays and chimaeras, but the most numerous by far are the bony fishes, with over 21,000 species.

Origin of the fishes

The hagfishes, lampreys and cartilaginous fishes are survivors from an earlier era before the bony fishes appeared in the seas. Jawless fishes provide the oldest identifiable fossils of fishes, and were laid down some 500 million years ago. Their bodies were wholly or partly armor-plated, and they probably spent their

lives on the seabed, feeding through their jawless mouths that were on the undersides of their heads. Their mouths probably contained small, movable plates with ridges of tough dentine (the substance from which teeth are composed) that acted like pairs of flexible lips, enabling the fish to suck or scoop up food particles from the mud or sand. These were the first true vertebrates—the ancestors of all the fishes, amphibians, reptiles, birds and mammals that flourish on Earth today.

Three hundred and eighty million years ago, there existed a bewildering diversity of jawless fishes. Their body armor ranged from massive, heavy plates to hard, bony lumps or nodules reinforcing the skin. One branch of the jawless fishes eventually led to the lampreys; their earliest fossils date from about 300 million years ago. No definite remains of early hagfishes have been discovered—probably because they do not have hard skeletons, and they decay too quickly to be preserved.

The arrival of jaws

The era that saw the great diversification of the jawless fishes also saw the appearance of the first jawed fishes. The oldest of these fossils have been found in rocks laid down about 430 million years ago at the beginning of the Silurian period. Known as the acanthodians, they had large eyes, scales and bony

ABOVE The pike is a voracious freshwater predator with a wide distribution—it haunts rivers and lakes across much of Europe, Asia and North America. A solitary hunter, it preys mainly on other fish, but also catches frogs and even drags birds from the surface of the water. Its dorsal and anal fins are positioned far back on its body near the tail. The cluster of fins at the rear can propel it rapidly forward out of vegetation to snatch passing fish.

skeletons as well as fully functioning jaws. Measuring less than 12 in. long, their bodies were streamlined and muscular with prominent fins, suggesting that they hunted for active prey such as crustaceans and other fishes. Unable to compete effectively with the early bony fishes, the acanthodians became extinct about 270 million years ago.

Armor plating

Another group of jawed fishes, the placoderms, were far more primitive in appearance than the acanthodians. Like their jawless counterparts, they were protected by plate armor that covered the front half of their body. In some cases, this armor was jointed like the upper shell, or carapace, of a lobster. Some species even had plates encasing their pectoral fins (the "forearms" of a fish), so that they formed bony limbs that looked similar to crabs' legs. These may have been used to raise their bodies off the muddy sea floor.

The first sharks

By the time the placoderms had died out in the early Carboniferous period (some 360 million years ago), the first sharks had appeared in the oceans. In many respects, these resembled modern sharks, with cartilaginous skeletons and powerful, muscular bodies well suited to a life spent preying on other fish. Indeed, the sharks were so successful that they had no reason to evolve further.

The other main group of cartilaginous fishes, the skates and rays, did not appear until about 200 million years later, in the early Jurassic period. Essentially flattened sharks, they became specialized for lives spent lying flat on the seabed.

The bony fishes

Bony fishes seem to have developed in freshwater habitats, but they moved into the seas during the Devonian period, some 350-400 million years ago. One group, known as the dipnoi, were able to breathe atmospheric oxygen through a sac-like organ that, in other fishes, later became a swim bladder. The dipnoi eventually gave rise to the lungfishes, famous for their ability to survive out of water for several months during dry summers.

Another group of early bony fishes, the lobe-finned fishes, could also breathe air by means of lungs. Instead of having flexible fin rays (the bones supporting the fin), these fishes had leg-like fins with jointed bones that could rotate. The lobe-finned fishes became, in time, the ancestors of the first land-dwelling vertebrates, the amphibians—and they, in due course, gave rise to all the reptiles, birds and mammals. A fish of this type, the coelacanth, still occurs in the Indian

TOP LEFT The bony fishes are a class numbering 42 orders. Seven of these can be grouped together as the "primitive" bony fishes—they are distinct from the other, more advanced orders in the class (the teleosts). The alligator gar belongs to the primitive group and is a sleek, heavily armored predator.
CENTER Sturgeons (primitive bony fishes) are famous for the market value of their eggs, which are processed into caviar. The Russian sturgeon shown here is one of the most valuable of all sturgeon and lives in rivers in the USSR, particularly those from the Black and Caspian seas.
BOTTOM The red-tailed shark, a member of the carp family, belongs to the teleosts—the advanced bony fishes. Despite its name, it is unrelated to the sharks and is a popular aquarium fish.

Ocean off the East African coast, and is almost identical to the fossil coelacanths found in rocks of the Devonian period.

The lungfishes, coelacanths and their allies seem to have split off from the mainstream of fish development during the Devonian period, and evolved along a route of their own that reached its highest point in the land vertebrates. As fish, they have almost all died out.

Rise to dominance

A quite different future lay ahead of a third group of bony fishes—the ray-finned fishes—that were to diversify into most of the species alive today. The evolution of this group began in the late Silurian period, some 410 million years ago, with the heavily scaled palaeoniscids. Its development gained pace during the Mesozoic era (from about 225 to 65 million years ago), when the palaeoniscid line gave rise to sturgeons, gars and most of the rest of the fishes (the teleosts). The teleosts appeared in the Cretaceous period (130-65 million years ago) and quickly overtook the others to assume the dominant position that they maintain today. The scale of this evolutionary achievement can be measured by the fact that they account for over half the vertebrates on Earth—including all the other fish, amphibians, reptiles, birds and mammals put together.

In waters everywhere

Fishes are found in every type of aquatic environment on the planet, with the exception of very hot springs, highly polluted waters and lakes with a naturally high salt concentration. They occur in the deepest waters on Earth, thousands of feet below the surface, where there is no sunlight, the pressure exerted by the water is enormous, and there is nothing to eat except each other. They are also found at high altitudes, in mountain lakes over 1600 feet above sea level. Between these two extremes, they occupy waters of all kinds, encompassing a wide range of temperature, salt content, light level, organic richness, oxygen content, depth, volume and turbulence.

Multitude of shapes

In size, fishes range from the tiny dwarf goby that inhabits the Philippines to the mighty whale shark. The dwarf goby grows to 0.3 in. in length, microscopic in comparison to the massive and aptly

ABOVE More than a thousand species of fishes can generate their own light. Lantern fishes have special organs that create light as a communication signal and to lure prey. PAGES 1810-1811 Many fishes, such as these blue- banded snappers, swim in dense shoals. By grouping together, they are better able to detect food and keep watch for enemies. If they are attacked, the swirling movements of the shoal can confuse a predator.

FISHES CLASSIFICATION

Well over 22,000 species of fishes have so far been discovered, and they are broken down into four separate classes. Two of these are small: the first, the Myxini, contains only the hagfishes, while the second, the Cephalaspidomorphi, contains only the lampreys. These two classes are often combined in a superclass, known as the Agnatha. The third class of fishes is the Chondrichthyes, which contains the cartilaginous fishes—the sharks, rays and chimaeras. It is divided into six orders.

The vast majority of fish species belong to the fourth class, the Osteichthyes or bony fishes. Classification within this class is complicated, and differs considerably from one authority to another. It contains a total of 42 orders. The first seven of these—which include the lungfishes, the sturgeons and the freshwater gars—are regarded as the most primitive (they are grouped together on pages 1847-1856). The remaining 35 orders are collectively known as the teleosts (see pages 1857-2087). The teleosts are the most advanced of the fishes, and include most species alive today.

TOP LEFT When humans learned to use nets to surround shoals of fish, they were able to catch greater numbers than had been possible before. **BOTTOM LEFT** The same principle is used to net salmon on a commercial scale. The technique is so successful that, in some waters, the salmon population has been severely depleted.

ABOVE Fish farms, where stocks of fish are bred in captivity, may be an answer to the worldwide problem of overfishing. However, fish farms have their own problems — waste from the captive animals and excess food given to them can pollute the sea, and the overcrowded fish are more susceptible to diseases.

named whale sharks that usually measure 39 ft. in length, but can reach an astonishing 59 ft. Variations in the shapes of fishes are almost infinite. Fast-swimming fishes are typically streamlined and cylindrical in shape. Others are spherical, disk-shaped, flattened, ribbon-like, cuboid and elongated, adorned with crests, ridges, nodules, barbels, enlarged fins and dramatic colors. Some species consist of millions of individuals—others teeter on the brink of extinction.

Despite their huge variety of shapes, the basic body structure of fishes remains fairly constant. A fish typically has one or more dorsal fins on its back and a pair of pectoral fins that lie low on its flanks behind its head. These pectoral fins correspond to the forelimbs of land-based animals. It also has two pelvic fins that normally occur farther back beneath the body (although not always), an anal fin beneath the hind part of the body (often balancing the dorsal fin), and a tail fin.

The range of foods that fishes eat is as great as that of terrestrial animals. But the proportion of plant-eating species is far smaller, mainly because many marine fishes do not have access to suitable plant food. In the seas, most large plant life occurs in coastal shallows, where it can anchor itself to rocks on the seabed while still benefiting from the sunlight that penetrates the shallow water. Generally, in deeper water, anchored plants are unable to develop on the ocean bed because they cannot absorb energy from sunlight. In most parts of the world, the only plants that occur on the surface are the microscopic plants floating in plankton.

These minute, planktonic plants are eaten by tiny floating invertebrates, which in turn fall prey to small fish. In the food chain of fishes, the small fish are hunted by larger fish that form the main food of big predators, such as sharks. On the seabed, crustaceans and shellfish sift the bottom debris for organic material, and themselves fall prey to bottom-living fish, such as the skates, rays and flatfishes.

Breeding strategies

There are two basic reproductive strategies among fishes. They may produce enormous numbers of larval offspring and abandon them after ovulation in the hope that enough will survive to adulthood to ensure the perpetuation of the species. The other strategy is to produce relatively few, well-developed young and to provide parental care to ensure their survival.

Bony fishes produce large numbers of young, particularly in those species that live in open water. The cod, for example, produces two or three million eggs at a time and can lay as many as nine million. Currents scatter the eggs widely over the seabed and they gradually float upward to the surface where the young hatch. By the time they hatch into tiny, tadpole-like larvae, the young are able to feed on the microscopic plants floating near the surface—but they, in turn, are devoured by other fish. Only a tiny proportion survive to breed.

Cartilaginous fish (sharks and rays) are at the other end of the reproductive scale. Sharks, such as the tope, retain their 20 eggs inside their bodies until they have developed into fully formed young sharks, each about 16 in. in length. The young are able to take care of themselves, and a comparatively high proportion reach adulthood and breed.

Between the two extremes of bony fishes and sharks, fishes have adopted a variety of techniques for safeguarding their young and so reducing the number of eggs they have to produce. Many conceal their eggs—the salmon, for example, buries them in the gravel of a riverbed. The male lumpsucker defends his clutch against other fish and even "broods" them by fanning water over them with his fins to aerate them. Some species take parental care even further. The mouth-brooding cichlids of central Africa accompany their young as they feed, and if danger threatens, the adults scoop up their offspring in their mouths to protect them. Because a larger proportion of young survive to maturity, mouth-brooding fishes need to produce far fewer young than other, less protective cichlids.

Hunting for fish

Early humans quickly developed the techniques of spearing and hooking fish. Excavations of Stone Age remains reveal that early humans used hooks of stone and bone. These comparatively inefficient methods did not affect the size of the fish populations. But the development of nets foreshadowed the commercial fishing of deep-sea fish. Fishing became an industry, and the economic foundation of several nations. Modern fishing techniques offer larger and more efficient yields, but threaten fish stocks that are unable to renew themselves. The inexhaustible supply of fish that has lasted for centuries is now under threat.

Drift-net fishing

Until quite recently, the reproductive rate of the main food species, such as herring and cod, enabled the fish populations to compensate for the losses inflicted by the fishing fleets. In the North Sea, herring were traditionally caught in drift nets—curtains of netting that the fishing boats suspended from the surface to a depth of 20 feet. In the 1930s, some 932 miles of drift nets were set each night in the North Sea, but because the herring shoals swam at different depths, a large proportion of the adult fish escaped. The massive quantity of eggs that they produced was enough to replenish the stocks.

Echo sounding

The introduction of echo-sounding devices upset this natural balance, enabling the fishing fleets to establish the exact location of shoals in the water. By adjusting the depth of their nets accordingly, they caught far more fish—but because far fewer adults escaped, the numbers of eggs produced each season dropped drastically. The fish stocks were rapidly eroded, and the fishing industry responded by turning to yet more efficient methods. The "purse seine" net can encircle an entire shoal (located by an echo sounder) and, when pulled tight with a drawstring, forms a vast netting bag from which escape is impossible. The result is inevitable—the herrings in the North Sea have been almost wiped out, and those that remain require the protection of a total ban on herring fishing.

Governments all over the world now control fishing rights by imposing internationally agreed quotas. But pollution of the seas with chemicals, oil spills and dumped industrial waste, including radioactive waste from nuclear reactors, is just as serious a threat to the survival of the fishes. The poisons and radioactivity released into the water by these waste materials inevitably find their way into the sea creatures. Humans must act immediately, if we are to safeguard the future of fishes.

JAWLESS PARASITES

Lampreys and hagfishes are the survivors of the most ancient line of fishes. Though they lack jaws, they are voracious feeders, rasping through live and dead prey using their sharp teeth

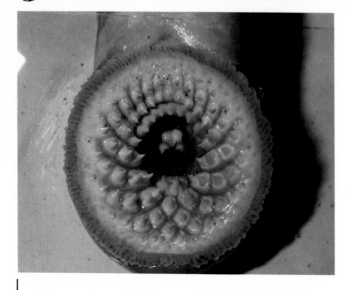

ABOVE The circular mouth of a sea lamprey is ringed by horny teeth that enable the fish to bite a hole in its victim.
BELOW Adult sea lampreys swim into rivers to breed (A), placing their eggs on the riverbed. The larvae that develop live in burrows at first (B), but when they reach maturity (C), they become parasites, attaching themselves to other fishes (D) with their sucker-like mouths (E), and feeding on their victims' flesh and blood.
FAR RIGHT Brook lampreys have a short adult life. They cease to feed once they have reached maturity, and die soon after the migration to their spawning grounds.
PAGE 1815 Brook lampreys use their mouths to cling onto rocks, and adults use them to carry stones to their breeding nests.

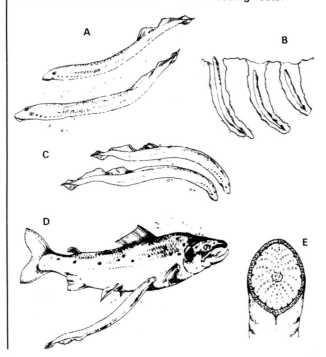

Lampreys and hagfishes are the last survivors of a group of extremely primitive fishes, most of which became extinct more than 200 million years ago. Eel-shaped, slimy-skinned and seldom measuring over 24 in. long, they are the most primitive of living vertebrates. Since they do not have jawbones, they are known as jawless fishes, and they belong to the superclass Agnatha (from the Greek *a* meaning "without" and *gnathos* meaning "jaw"). However, since lampreys and hagfishes are also quite different in their internal structure, they are placed in separate classes. They comprise a total of 73 species and are greatly modified descendants of the jawless fishes of the distant past—and therefore of the first fishes to appear on Earth.

Armored ancestors

Fossils recently discovered in rocks dating from 500 million years ago proved to be the remains of creatures an inch long, with bodies encased in bony shields. They were quite unlike anything living today. Close analysis revealed that they were fishes, with body muscles grouped around a central core resembling a backbone, but without jaws. They are the earliest known remains of animals with true vertebral columns—that is, the first vertebrates—and as such they may be the ancestors of all modern vertebrates: fish, amphibians, reptiles, birds and mammals.

Superficially, these armor-plated fish have little in common with the scaleless lampreys and hagfishes, which are supported by skeletons completely lacking in bony tissue. Despite this, certain anatomical features provide overwhelming proof that they are relatives, albeit distant ones. Both the present-day fishes and the ancient fossils lack jaws, both have a hooked nostril on the top of the head, and both have the same inner ear structure. As final proof of their common ancestry, both groups have a series of large gill pouches on each side of the head, linked to the outside through a row of holes.

It is possible that the primitive Agnatha lost their armor because they developed a more free-swimming way of life, and the protective value of the armor became less important than its weight. Whatever the reason, with its loss, the fishes became much more vulnerable to total decay when they died, and the immediate ancestors of the modern hagfishes and lampreys did not fossilize well. Some fossil lampreys

AGNATHA CLASSIFICATION

The superclass Agnatha (or Cyclostomata) contains two separate groups of fishes: the hagfishes of the class Myxini and the lampreys of the class Cephalaspidomorphi. Only a few species of hagfishes and lampreys have been given common names—the remainder are referred to just by their scientific names.

Hagfishes

The hagfishes all belong to the order Myxiniformes and the family Myxinidae. There are about 32 species (the number depending on the system of classification used) grouped in two subfamilies. They range through much of the Atlantic, Pacific and Indian oceans with most species occurring in temperate waters. Twelve species are grouped in the subfamily Myxininae. Nine of these belong to the genus *Myxine*, including the Atlantic hagfish, *M. glutinosa*. The other species are *Notomyxine tridentiger*, *Neomyxine biplinicata*, and *Nemamyxine elongata*. The 20 or so species that make up the subfamily Eptatretinae belong to the genera *Eptatretus* and *Paramyxine*.

Lampreys

There are about 42 species of lampreys (the exact number depending on the classification system), all belonging to the order Petromyzontiformes and the family Petromyzontidae. They occur mainly in the cooler waters of the Northern and Southern hemispheres, both in the sea and in freshwater habitats. There are three subfamilies, the smallest of which, the Geotriinae, contains just one species, *Geotria australis*. The subfamily Mordaciinae comprises three species, all in the genus *Mordacia*. The largest subfamily, the Petromyzontinae, contains four genera. The genus *Lampetra* comprises the majority of the lampreys—some 30 species in all, including the parasitic river lamprey or lampern, *L. fluviatilis*, and the brook lamprey, *L. planeri*. The genus *Petromyzon* contains only the sea lamprey, *P. marinus*, while the genus *Caspiomyzon* contains only *C. wagneri*. Six species belong to the genus *Icthyomyzon*.

have been found, dating from about 300 million years ago, but so far no fossil hagfishes have been traced.

Filtering animals

The diet of adult lampreys may shed no light on the habits of their ancient forebears, but a study of their juvenile stages provides a clue. Lampreys spend several years as blind, worm-like larvae, living in a very different manner to adults. (The larvae were called ammocoetes by 19th century naturalists who considered them to be an entirely separate species.) Instead of swimming freely, the lamprey larvae burrow into the mud or sand on the beds of streams and rivers. Anchored by their tails, they protrude from their burrows and feed by taking in water through their mouths and filtering it through their gills in order to trap food particles. Since their armored ancestors were probably bottom-dwelling animals during the peak of their evolution, about 415-400 million years ago, and were well equipped with gill pouches and openings, it has been suggested that they too were filter feeders, living on organic debris and microscopic, floating animals.

Strange survivors

Lampreys and hagfishes lack many structures common to all modern fishes. Not only do they lack jaws, but they do not have bones, scales, paired fins, a sympathetic nervous system or a spleen. They also have only one nostril—in hagfishes, it can be found at the forward tip of the body; in lampreys, on the top of the head.

Hagfishes have no external eyes and they look similar at both ends. However, close inspection reveals differences: they have several thick, fleshy barbels at the head end and a vague tail fin at the hind end. Lampreys do not have a recognizable head with large eyes, dorsal fins and a tail fin. In both groups, a single rod of fibrous material, studded with pieces of cartilage, serves as a backbone. The fins, such as they are, are weakly supported by cartilage.

In spite of such primitive features, both hagfishes and lampreys are highly specialized and remarkably well adapted to their way of life. Both groups of fish have thin, horny, replaceable teeth mounted on the tongue: in the hagfishes, these horny teeth bite against a single tooth in the roof of the mouth; the lamprey has one or more circular rows of teeth.

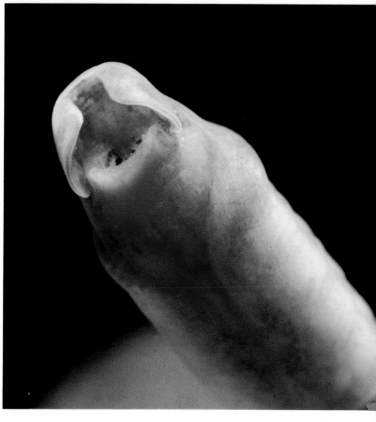

Parasites and scavengers

Jawless fishes feed by attaching themselves to the bodies of other fish. Most lampreys are parasites, sucking the blood and body fluids of living prey, whereas hagfishes are scavengers that feed on the flesh of dead and dying fishes—as well as some worms and crustaceans. Using its teeth, the hagfish rasps a hole in the side of its prey, then eats its way right through it, leaving only skin and bones.

Lampreys and hagfishes cannot breathe and feed at the same time and therefore do not take in oxygen-laden water through their mouths like other fishes. Instead, the water enters their bodies through their single nostril and flows into several internal pouches lined with gills. Here, the fishes take the oxygen from the water and lose their carbon dioxide. The water then flows out through external openings. The whole system is supported by an intricate cage of elastic cartilage. Lampreys have seven pairs of gill pouches; hagfishes have five to fifteen pairs with similar openings, except that in some species a single exit far back on the body provides the only outlet.

When lampreys use their mouths to feed or to attach themselves to the bottom, they breathe by pumping water back and forth. The muscles in the wall of the gill pouches contract, forcing water out, and then relax, sucking fresh water in through the nostril. The suction is helped by the cartilage cage, which is put under tension when the lamprey breathes out, and springs back into shape when the muscles relax, opening the gill pouches. Hagfishes also pump water in and out. The front part of the hagfish gut, its gill pouches and gill ducts all contract to force water out over the gills, and then relax to draw more in through the single nostril.

Senses for hunting

Lampreys and hagfishes use different senses to detect food. Hagfishes have a keen sense of smell, but extremely weak eyes that are hidden beneath the skin. Lampreys have prominent, large eyes—a necessary adaptation for finding their living prey. It is in their life histories, however, that the most marked differences between these similar, but unrelated, classes of primitive fish occur. The hagfishes seldom stray from one area, and have no known larval stage. Their 0.8-inch-long eggs, laid in batches of 20 to 30, hatch directly into miniature adults. By contrast,

ABOVE The head and mouthparts of a lamprey larva are quite unlike those of an adult. Instead of a toothed sucker, the larva has a mouth fringed with filaments that strain the water for tiny particles of food. The mouth is protected by a hood that extends down from the upper lip.

BELOW Lampreys undergo a visible transformation as they mature. The most obvious change is in the conversion of the mouthparts from a filtering device into a rasping sucker, and in the growth of fins that permit a free-swimming, rather than a burrowing, life-style.

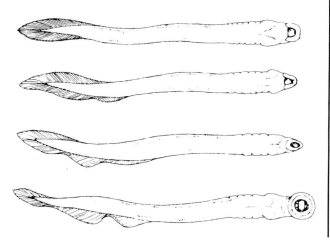

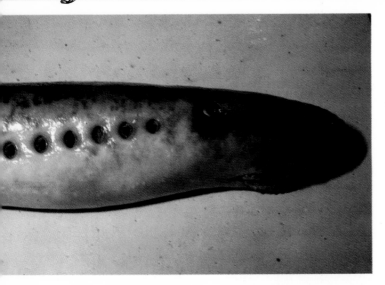

the lampreys are migratory, and have a distinctly different form when young. As many as 200,000 0.04-inch-long eggs hatch into larvae that are blind, worm-like, filter-feeding burrowers.

Hagfishes

In appearance, feeding habits and defense mechanisms, hagfishes must be among the least attractive of fish. There are about 32 species, inhabiting cold, deep, salty waters. They range from sub-Arctic to temperate waters in the North Atlantic, and also inhabit the Mediterranean, the coastal waters of California, southern South America, South Africa and Japan; and the Gulfs of Panama and Mexico. They all look very similar, and only close examination can distinguish the different species.

The Atlantic hagfish is typical of the group. It is a grayish, eel-shaped creature with six thick, fleshy barbels at the front and a single fin outlining the belly and part of the tail. It grows to 24 in. or more long in the western Atlantic Ocean and up to 12 in. long in the eastern, with females generally larger than the males. The species is found over soft, muddy seabeds at depths of between 66 and 2620 feet. Where conditions are favorable, it is quite common.

Hagfishes spend much of their time buried in the mud with only the head showing, waiting for their keen sense of smell to alert them to the presence of food. They are most active at night. Deepwater species have lost the use of their eyes. Their pinkish brown skin on the uppersides of their bodies blends in with the color of the muddy seabed. Species living in lighter, shallower waters have an identifiable retina and colorless skin above the eyes, perhaps allowing limited vision.

Tied in knots

When a hagfish finds a dead or dying fish to feed on, it first chooses its point of entry—usually a wound or a natural opening in the body. Then, by a combination of biting, wriggling and tying itself into knots up and down its body as a method of leverage, the hagfish eats its way into its prey. It consumes nearly all of the softer tissues, turning the whole fish into a slimy bag of bones. Commercial fishermen, who set thousands of hooks over muddy ground off the coasts of Northumberland (England) and Brittany (France) detest hagfish, since the fish they catch are perfect

ABOVE The parasitic river lamprey or lampern has seven circular gill openings on each side of its body. These are lined with fleshy filaments that absorb oxygen from the water and pass it into the animal's bloodstream.

BELOW When lampreys mate, the male attaches himself to the female (A), while she grips a rock with her sucker (B). The male entwines his body around hers (C-D), and sheds his sperm over her eggs as they emerge (E).

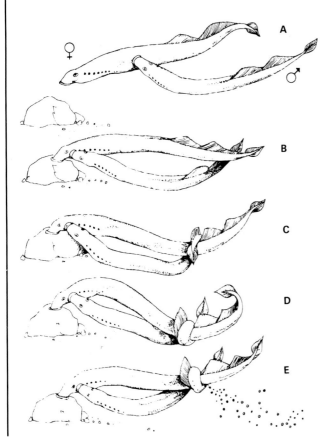

targets for this kind of feeding, especially if the weather prevents the line from being picked up for a couple of days. When the fishermen haul up their catch, all that appears on the deck is a nearly empty bag of bones.

The hagfish has a row of 70-200 slime glands on its flanks. These glands produce a slimy mucus and threads that probably strengthen it. The purpose of this reinforced slime is uncertain, but it may clog the prey's gills, preventing it from breathing. The hagfish is capable of producing an extraordinary amount of slime over its body in a very short time. A hagfish placed in a 2-gallon bucket of water can convert the contents to a solid mass of slime in a matter of seconds—and then do it again a short while later if the water has been changed.

Hagfishes breed throughout the year, laying horny eggs anchored by clusters of threads to muddy ground. Although each hagfish possesses the organs of both sexes, only one of them develops at a time.

Lampreys

Some 41 species of lamprey live in both salt and fresh water, mainly in the cooler regions of the Northern Hemisphere. There are no parasitic species in the Southern Hemisphere. Silvery and eel-shaped, lampreys are easily recognized by their round, sucker-

ABOVE A parasitic lamprey clamps itself onto a rainbow trout, rasping the fish's flesh away until it reaches the bloodstream. It will stay attached until it has eaten its fill of blood and tissue, and then drop off. The large, deep wound that the lamprey leaves behind is likely to become infected by bacteria or fungus and the trout will probably die.

like mouths, lack of paired fins, and the seven holes along the sides of their bodies that lead to the gill pouches. They grow to a maximum of about 35 in. in length, and most species migrate. Some feed at sea and breed in fresh water; others move between lakes and streams. Three species inhabit the waters of northern Europe, the Mediterranean, northwest Africa and eastern North America. Of the three, the sea lamprey and the river lamprey (or lampern) move between rivers and the sea, while the brook lamprey—the most common of the three—matures, breeds and dies in its home stream without feeding.

Stone-moving nest builders

In spring and early summer, adult sea lampreys move from the sea to clean rivers to find a nesting site. They prefer a shallow part of the river with a gravel bed, preferably in the shade, with a muddy backwater nearby where the larvae can hatch. As they move

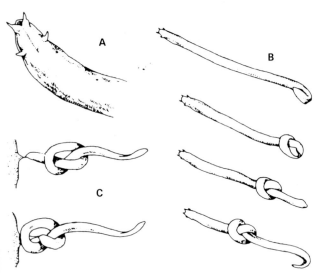

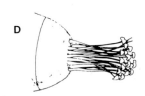

ABOVE A hagfish has no eyes, but parts of its body around the head and the cloaca can detect the presence of light.

LEFT The head of a hagfish ends with a slit-like mouth surrounded by several paired barbels (A). A hagfish can throw a living knot down the length of its body (B), enabling it to clear the large amount of slime produced by special glands in its skin. The knot also helps the animal to force its way through the skin of its victim (C). Each hagfish egg has a bunch of tiny hooks (D) that anchors it to the sea-bed, or to one another (E).

FAR RIGHT The map shows the world distribution of the lampreys.

upriver, they use the clinging ability of their sucker mouths to attach themselves to weirs and boulders in fast water, alternately resting and worming their way onward. The male and female build a nest—often picking up and moving pebbles together until they have formed a hole about 6 in. deep and 24 in. wide.

Other species of lamprey have very different nest-building methods. In one American species, as many as fifty adults cooperate to dig a nest 20 ft. long and 3 ft. wide. In another species, an individual lamprey simply hangs onto a stone and lashes its tail to create a shallow depression.

To mate, the female attaches herself to a rock on the upstream end of the nest. The male winds himself around the female, probably squeezing the tiny eggs (perhaps more than 200,000) out of the female, and fertilizes them. Exhausted from their efforts, the parents die soon after spawning.

Blind and toothless

The eggs hatch after a week or two, and the blind, toothless larvae—worm-like but quite different in appearance from their parents—burrow into the mud or silt of the stream bottom. For the next four or five years, depending on the temperature of the stream, they filter minute organic matter from the water and avoid the light. Known as ammocoetes or prides, they lack teeth and feed using a hood equipped with filtering structures.

Once the larvae reach a length of approximately 6 in., they begin to change into true lampreys. Their eyes start to function, and the digestive tract alters in structure. More obviously, much of the mouth turns into a sucker armed with 112-125 horny teeth arranged in concentric rings around the small mouth opening. The young lampreys move downstream to the sea, ready to start life as parasites on a wide variety of fishes.

Once at sea, the lamprey finds it prey and clings fast to it with its teeth, rasping away the fish's skin to gain access to its bloodstream. The lamprey secretes chemicals that help it to digest the prey's muscle tissue and prevent the prey's blood from clotting, enabling it to continue feeding until its victim dies, or until it has eaten enough and drops off. Once wounded by a lamprey, even a large fish has a slim chance of survival, since the smallest of wounds that breaks the mucus layer on the skin of a fish is open to fungal and bacterial infection.

After one or two years at sea, the lamprey matures at a length of 24-32 in. and returns to shallow river waters to complete its cycle. Unlike salmon, lampreys do not seek out the stream of their birth—all that they require are non-polluted, breeding conditions.

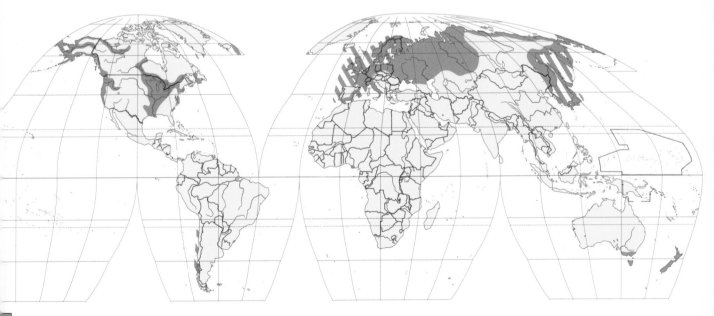

Lampreys

ABOVE **Glands in the skin of lampreys secrete a layer of mucus that is toxic to many animals, and is probably a defense against attacks from other, larger fish. The mucus can also be harmful to people who catch and eat lampreys, often causing severe stomach pains.**

BELOW **A lamprey builds its nest on the riverbed by shifting stones around to form a shallow, oval depression. A view from above shows the lamprey putting a large stone into place (A); a side view shows stones graded according to size, with the largest facing upstream (B).**

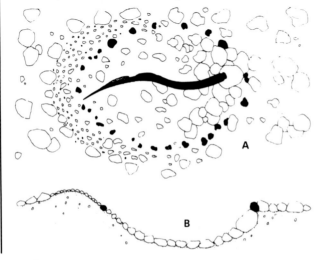

Invasion of the Lakes

One of the greatest disasters caused by lampreys occurred in the Great Lakes area of North America during the 1920s and 1930s. The event had its origin in 1829, with the opening of the Welland Canal, which linked Lake Ontario to Lake Erie. Oceangoing ships were able to sail for the first time from the St. Lawrence River through Lake Ontario and into Lake Erie (bypassing the powerful and obviously non-navigable Niagara Falls). However, ships were not the only users of the canal. Sea fishes now had an easy route into the Great Lakes, and soon appeared in increasing numbers.

Within a few years, it became obvious that something was disturbing the lake trout. Less and less were caught, and many were found dead with scars on their flanks. They were the victims of the parasitic sea lampreys. Over the next hundred years, the sea lampreys became well established throughout the Great Lakes. The trout population dwindled, and the once-thriving and profitable trout fisheries were almost destroyed. Whitefish populations were also affected.

Fishing declined from an annual catch of 14.3 million pounds of trout in the 1930s to less than 440,000 pounds in 1961. Mechanical and electrical traps were devised to fight back against the lampreys, and weirs—enclosures built of stakes—were set up to trap the lampreys as they migrated upriver. During the 1960s, biologists succeeded in developing chemicals that killed the lamprey larvae in their home streams. The operation cost millions of dollars, but was successful. As soon as the lampreys were under control, lake trout were reintroduced.

Sea lamprey side effects

Between 1931 and 1954, a bony fish called the alewife also migrated from the open ocean into Lake Erie and the other upper lakes (Huron, Michigan and Superior). The alewife faced little competition and predation from other fishes, which had been drastically reduced in numbers by the sea lampreys, and they soon became the most abundant fish species in the lakes. Unfortunately, not only are alewives of little commercial value, but they also die in the millions periodically and are washed ashore to rot on the beaches. To combat the cost of having to clear up the dead fish, chinook and coho salmon were introduced to the lakes to control the alewives (and to provide sport for fishermen).

ROVING PREDATORS

Sharks and rays are cartilaginous fishes that have changed little in the last 150 million years. Although sharks are deadly hunters, their fearsome reputation for uncontrolled ferocity is largely unfounded

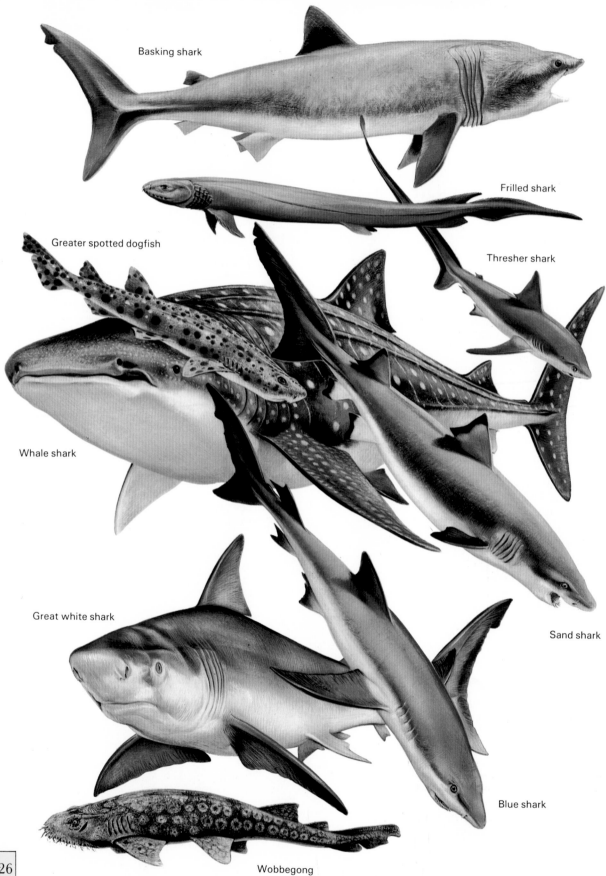

Basking shark

Frilled shark

Greater spotted dogfish

Thresher shark

Whale shark

Great white shark

Sand shark

Blue shark

Wobbegong

Sharks, rays and chimaeras together make up a class of fishes known as the cartilaginous fishes. Although they constitute only some three percent of the total number of fish species, they have received a great deal of attention. The fearsome image of the predatory shark, and the sheer elegance of the giant rays as they fly through the water, fascinate humans. Only the chimaeras—slow, blunt-headed relatives of the sharks—remain little known.

The sharks

More than 340 species of sharks inhabit the tropical, temperate and polar oceans of the world at all depths. Not all are the giant killers of popular mythology: they range in size from the 6-in.-long dwarf shark to the enormous whale shark, which can grow to an adult length of 59 ft.

Modern sharks are the descendants of a group of fishes that dominated the oceans during the Carboniferous period. They have changed relatively little in the last 400 million years and now inhabit every freshwater and saltwater environment. However, whole groups of species became extinct because of competition with the bony fishes and changing environmental conditions. The largest ancestor of the sharks was the *Carcharodon megalodon*, very distantly related to today's great white shark. It had 7-in.-long teeth, and its body grew to a length of 39 ft.

Half of the modern species of sharks measure from 6 to 39 in. in length, and only four percent of sharks grow larger than 13 feet. In shape, they show a wide variation across the range, from the ray-like angel fish to the grotesque, flabby megamouth. Bottom-

ABOVE The spotted eagle ray inhabits the shallow waters of the tropical and subtropical seas, where it forages for shellfish that lie hidden in the sand. Sharks and rays, which have skeletons made of cartilage, belong to an entirely separate class from the bulk of the world's fishes, which have bony skeletons.

PAGE 1825 The great white shark is one of the most powerful of all aquatic predators, and is one of the few sharks that regularly attack humans. However, its reputation as a man-eater has been greatly exaggerated—sharks feed by instinct, and there is little chance that they could develop a "taste" for human flesh.

dwelling sharks have flattened bodies and are sluggish in behavior. Open-sea sharks, such as the mackerel sharks, have muscular, streamlined bodies that enable them to reach underwater speeds in excess of 29 mph.

According to the different species, sharks' teeth are pointed for gripping prey, serrated for cutting and tearing, and blunt for crushing their victims. They have about 3000 teeth that lie in 6 to 20 rows stretching back from the rim of their crescent mouths. However, they only use the first two rows, keeping the remaining rows as replacement teeth that move forward as the original teeth decay. During an attack, predatory sharks use their large, razor-sharp teeth to shred their prey into small pieces.

Although sharks have pectoral fins behind their heads that stabilize and direct their attacks, they strike in a series of wild, swerving lunges, terminating in an upward tilt of the mouth that enables them to grip their prey. Sharks are reported to attack humans about 100 times each year, of which only 30-40 prove fatal. There is about as much chance of being attacked by a shark as there is of being struck by lightning.

CHONDRICHTHYES CLASSIFICATION: 1

The cartilaginous fishes make up the class Chondrichthyes. The class is divided into two subclasses: the Elasmobranchi, the sharks and rays, with five orders and 22 families; and the Holocephali, the chimaeras, with one order and three families. Together these fishes have a worldwide distribution, occurring in polar, temperate and tropical seas, and with some species occurring in freshwater habitats.

CHONDRICHTHYES CLASSIFICATION: 2

The frilled shark and the cow sharks

Two families of sharks belong to the order Hexanchiformes. The family Chlamydoselachidae contains only the frilled shark, *Chlamydoselachus anguineus*, which occurs off the coasts of Europe, southern Africa, Australia, Japan, Chile and California. The family Hexanchidae, the cow sharks, comprises four species in three genera that range throughout the oceans. The most well-known is the six-gilled shark, *Hexanchus griseus*.

Bullhead sharks

The order Heterodontiformes contains just one family, the Heterodontidae, which comprises the six species of bullhead or horn sharks. They inhabit the tropical waters of the Indian and Pacific oceans. All members of the genus *Heterodontus*, they include the Port Jackson shark, *H. portjacksoni*.

ABOVE Six-gilled sharks— the individual seen here is a young one—usually rest on the bottom of the sea during the day. They become more active at night, hunting a wide variety of fishes, squid and crabs. The species typically inhabits the deep water of the temperate Mediterranean Sea and Atlantic, Pacific and Indian oceans. It usually lives at depths of down to 6000 ft.

Sensory detectors

Sharks detect prey using various senses. Their eyesight is generally poor, and they hunt primarily by smell. Two large olfactory lobes in the brain enable a shark to smell and detect prey over a distance of 1300 ft. Sharks, rays and chimaeras also have a system of canals running the length of their bodies (called the lateral line). The canals are full of a jelly-like substance that functions as a sensory receptor, detecting the pressure waves caused by movements of other animals. They also have a series of electroreceptive pits on their snouts to detect the natural electric output of animals.

Fertilization in sharks takes place internally. The different species either lay eggs or develop the young internally. The eggs are large and well supplied with nutrients. Some species lay flat, cushion-shaped eggs with tendrils on the corners that tangle with seaweed and anchor them to the seabed.

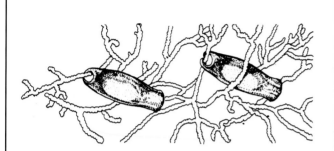

RIGHT The tasseled wobbegong is a member of the carpet shark family and occurs in the shallow waters off the coast of Australia. Its curious, flattened shape, mottled coloration, and the strange, seaweed-like growths at the front of its body allow it to lie perfectly camouflaged against rocks, corals and vegetation on the seabed. ABOVE The carpet sharks lay eggs that are enclosed in horny cases. The tendrils at the corners of the eggs become entangled with weed and coral and prevent the cases from floating away.

The most primitive sharks

The frilled shark is the most primitive of living sharks. It is a long-bodied, slender fish that grows to a maximum length of 6 ft. 6 in. It has dark brown upperparts and paler brown underparts. Frilled sharks are distinctive because of the six gill flaps that form a frill around their heads. The arrangement of these long, floppy flaps gives the sharks their common name.

The frilled shark inhabits the deep, cold waters of the continental shelf at depths of 650-3300 ft. and, though rare, it is widespread. It lives in waters off the coasts of Europe, South Africa, Australia, New Zealand, Namibia and Japan. It also occurs in the Pacific Ocean off California and Chile. The frilled shark is armed with some 300 sharp, three-cusped teeth that it uses to catch small fish and squid. Usually, it swallows its prey whole.

The cow sharks

The six-gilled and seven-gilled sharks belong to the cow shark family. Although a typical modern shark has five gill openings, these species have one or two extra gill flaps. The six-gilled shark grows to a length of over 16 ft. and weighs about 1765 lbs. Inhabiting most of the world's oceans, the six-gilled sharks occur primarily in the North Atlantic and the Mediterranean. They cruise near the seabed, feeding on a wide variety of fishes and crabs that they swallow whole. They have long, tapered teeth in the upper jaw, but the lower jaw has finely serrated teeth similar to those of a comb. Six-gilled sharks are among the most prolific of all sharks—the female develops her young internally, and produces about 40 eggs (although one female that was captured contained 108 embryos).

A shark with horns

The shallow waters of the Indian and Pacific oceans are the home to an unusual family comprising the bullhead sharks. Also known as horn or Port Jackson sharks, there are only six species in the family. Unlike the large, streamlined sharks, bullhead sharks have stout, stocky bodies that seldom grow to more than 5 ft. in length. Prominent brow ridges above the eyes give them the appearance of having horns. All species have spotted or patterned markings on their skins.

The gentle giants

Despite the fearsome reputation of sharks as man-eaters, the two largest sharks in the world are harmless to humans. The whale shark and the basking shark cruise through the upper waters of the sea at speeds of 2 to 2.5 miles per hour, opening their huge mouths to take in great quantities of water. They filter minute plankton and small, schooling fishes from the water across cartilage-cored, sieve-like plates that bridge their internal gill openings—these are known as gill rakers. Although the whale shark and the basking shark are not closely related, they have similar life-styles.

ABOVE A nurse shark investigates the crevices in a reef rock pile, accompanied by a remora, or suckerfish, stuck to its skin. Nurse sharks have a specialized way of feeding: they suck their prey from crevices by sealing holes with their muscular lips and opening their throats. These sharks generally have placid natures, but divers who try to play with them do so at their own risk, since nurse sharks are large fish—up to 13 feet long—and are quick to bite when annoyed.

The whale shark inhabits the tropical waters of the world. It usually grows to about 39 ft. in length and weighs over 22 tons. It is easily distinguished by the striking color pattern that adorns its body—it has gray to brown upperparts and is white underneath; the head and body have a covering of white spots. The whale shark has a long, cylindrical body, a broad head and a cavernous mouth—wide enough to allow two humans to crouch inside. Since it has no commercial value, it remains unmolested by humans, but as a result, little is known about its life-style. Indeed, a chance encounter resulted in what little zoologists know about the whale shark's breeding habits. A pregnant female whale shark that was caught was found to contain eight eggs with embryos developing inside. The embryos had the characteristic shape and coloration of the adults.

Basking sharks spend considerable periods of time idling at or near the surface of the water with their huge mouths gaping open as they filter food. They inhabit the temperate oceans of the world, particularly the Atlantic Ocean. Apart from a long, bulbous nose in younger specimens, the basking sharks resemble more predatory, oceanic sharks. But they are exceptional in reaching a recorded length of 36 ft. Basking sharks feed on shrimp-like copepods, the eggs of other fish and arrowworms. One shark can sieve 1980 gallons of water across its gill rakers each hour while cruising, allowing it to consume huge quantities of plankton. In late autumn, when water in temperate seas cools down and plankton becomes scarce, basking sharks disappear into hibernation in deeper water.

Carpets, nurses and wobbegongs

Many of the 28 species that make up the carpet shark family have striking markings across the color range—brown, yellow and black. They are warm-water sharks, occurring in the Indian and Pacific oceans and in the Red Sea. Although the group varies widely in size and coloration, characteristic features include their rounded fins, heavy bodies, and a pair of grooves that connect the mouth to the nostrils. At the front end of these grooves they have a fleshy barbel—a

ABOVE The greater spotted dogfish is a small shark measuring about 3 feet long. Here, one of them cruises above some lesser spotted dogfish, a species once sold in English fish-and-chip shops under the name of "rock salmon."
RIGHT Sharks have an extremely keen sense of smell, and are receptive to changes of electrical fields that may indicate food. The sequence shows the feeding responses of a dogfish when various objects are buried under sand. Solid arrows show the fish's movements; broken arrows indicate water flow. The dogfish is seen responding to: a fish (A); a fish in an agar chamber (B); pieces of fish in a chamber (C); a fish in a plastic-covered chamber (D); active electrodes (E); and an active electrode and a piece of fish (F).

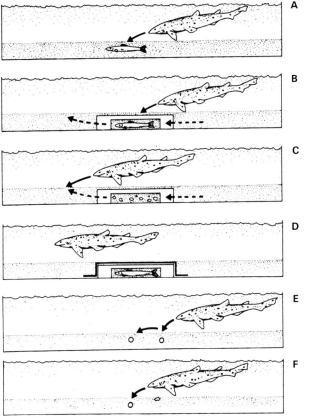

feature that is more pronounced in the wobbegongs from Australian waters. Wobbegongs have a seaweed-like fringe around the mouth.

Most species of wobbegongs are small in size and prefer inshore waters. But certain species, such as the Atlantic nurse shark, grow to a length of 13 feet. They mainly feed on crabs, fish and other creatures of the seabed. The Atlantic nurse shark employs a novel method of extracting prey from holes and crevices. Sealing the hiding place with its thick lips, it expands its muscular throat and sucks out the prey—creating a suction pressure roughly equal to atmospheric pressure.

ABOVE The jaws of a great white shark show how parallel rows of teeth fit behind one another in the fish's mouth. Some sharks have up to 20 rows of teeth, although only the first two rows are used to tear up prey. The remainder are replacement teeth that gradually move forward to take the place of those that have broken or worn down.

Flattened in body shape with wide pectoral fins, wobbegongs are masters of camouflage and ambush. They lurk among rocks and weeds, perfectly hidden by their ornate body markings of brown or green spots. They are usually small in size, although the largest of the six species grows to a length of 10 feet. Wobbegongs are sluggish in behavior—they draw in water through holes behind the eyes (known as spiracles) and force it over the gills, thus avoiding the need to move in order to maintain a breathing current. They have long, sharp teeth but are usually harmless to humans. A few attacks do occur when divers try to pull them from holes or play with them.

If looks could kill

The sand sharks or sand tigers have long, thin teeth that give them a ferocious appearance. Otherwise known as the ragged-tooth sharks, the five species of sand tigers inhabit shallow waters in all warm temperate and tropical seas. They are large sharks,

growing to a length of 10-12 ft. and they hunt on the bottom, eating bony fishes, rays, other sharks, and various large shellfish. They have a reputation for being man-eaters in certain parts of the world. The gray nurse (which, despite its name, is one of the sand shark family) has launched attacks on people in Australian waters, while the Atlantic sand shark is considered harmless in America but is a dangerous man-eater in Africa.

Closely related to the sand sharks, and arguably the most unattractive shark of all, is the goblin shark. Growing to a length of 14 ft., it is a translucent white color, becoming very dark brown soon after death. Its long snout projects from its forehead and resembles a dagger. It also has tiny, needle-like teeth that it uses to eat fish. Although it occasionally appears in shallow water, it is generally a deep-sea species, occurring off Japan, India and Portugal.

The megamouth

The megamouth is the most exciting shark discovery of recent years. The 15-ft.-long shark first came to light in 1976, when a specimen became entangled in the parachute anchor of a US research vessel 26 miles northwest of Oahu (one of the Hawaiian Islands). It has a heavy body, a short, rounded snout and a cavernous mouth used for filter-feeding. Many of the organs of the mouth are thought to be luminous. A second specimen, measuring 14 ft. long, was caught in 1984 off California and taken to the Los Angeles Museum of Natural History for study. The megamouth eats tiny shrimps and jellyfish, and lives at depths of up to 550 ft.

The mackerel sharks

The great white shark, the makos and the porbeagles are all members of the mackerel shark family and are known to be dangerous to man—the great white has made more proven attacks on man than any other species. They are all oceanic predators, and they travel vast distances in search of water that is both a comfortable temperature and also contains the fish, marine mammals, crabs and squid that make up their normal diet. Mackerel sharks, together with the killer whale, are probably the ocean's best-equipped predators.

Mackerel sharks are superbly streamlined; their body shape enables them to conserve energy when cruising and ensures the lowest possible water

resistance when sprinting for prey. The long pectoral fins on the side of the body, and the high, triangular dorsal fins along the back, are all set around the fishes' center of gravity for maximum effect.

The powerful tail

The mackerel sharks, although large, are relatively fast swimmers. The mako sharks, for example, can reach speeds of over 59 mph. As a means of propulsion, the mackerel shark's tail is one of the most well adapted in the fish world. It has an unusual caudal or tail fin that is rigid and crescent-shaped. The lobes are nearly equal in length, but the upper lobe is slightly longer. Caudal keels on either side of the tail enable the shark to turn at low speed and provide extra leverage for the tendons that support the tail. Power to drive the tail comes from enormous blocks of muscle—as much as 60 percent of a mackerel shark's weight is pure muscle.

Mackerel sharks, like the tunas, are homeothermic—they have a complicated blood system that allows them to maintain a body temperature at least 10.8°F above that of the surrounding water. The warmth of the blood speeds up all the body processes; it has been estimated that an 18°F rise in temperature triples the power output of vertebrate muscle.

The most feared shark

The great white shark is the largest and most feared species of the mackerel shark family. The largest reported specimen was caught almost a century ago off the coast of Australia. It measured 38 ft. 6 in., but the evidence was only hearsay and 21 ft. 6 in. is a more acceptable maximum length for the great white sharks of today. An adult great white matures at an average length of 11-14 ft. Despite its name, the great white is generally slate gray above and off-white below, and has dark-edged fins. Some individuals have darker upperparts, in some cases almost black, and others have dark spots behind each pectoral fin. Although it ranges across most of the world's oceans, it prefers warmer water and is commonly found in the Mediterranean. Usually a fish of the open seas, the great white comes inshore with some regularity. Warm, shallow waters near to ocean depths are favorite spots. It also ventures to great depths; one individual was caught off Cuba at a depth of 4200 ft. Females give birth to as many as nine live young.

ABOVE The great white shark is the only shark that preys mainly on sea mammals, with seals, sea lions and dolphins providing the bulk of its food. It has been suggested that the similarity in shape between a seal and a surfboard has led to many attacks on windsurfers in recent years, especially off the coast of California.

The great white has a large mouth with broad, serrated teeth that are well suited to biting large chunks of flesh from whales and seals. It will also pick up carrion. It feeds mainly on marine mammals, including seals, dolphins and sea otters, and it shares with the killer whale the habit of "spy-hopping"— poking its head vertically out of the water, possibly to frighten prey from rocks.

Spectacular leaps

Although big-game fishermen hunt the great white, the mako sharks are more highly prized since their flesh is regarded as a delicacy. A slimmer, smaller version of the great white, the makos have a deep blue back and are white below, and they grow to about 12 ft. in length. Mako sharks make some spectacular leaps into the air—probably to dislodge skin parasites—an impressive sight in a fish that can weigh up to 880 lbs.

Mako sharks occur in the Atlantic, Pacific and Indian oceans, and are occasionally caught off the

ABOVE **The white-tipped reef shark derives part of its name from the prominent white tips on the two dorsal fins and upper tail fin. A common occupant of warm, shallow** water, **the white-tipped reef shark ranges from the Red Sea to the Indian and Pacific oceans. About 5 ft. long, it is inquisitive by nature, but poses no threat to humans.**

weather they seek deeper waters. The females bear from one to five live young, which measure around 20 in. long and are often bloated with the yolk of the unfertilized eggs that they have eaten inside their mother before birth.

The fox or thresher sharks live in all but the coldest oceans. They grow to a length of 20 ft. in the warmer parts of their range, considerably less where the water is cooler, and occur quite frequently in northern European waters. Thresher sharks, although similar in appearance to other oceanic sharks of the upper waters, can be distinguished by their unusual tails. The upper lobe of the tail is very long—often more than half the length of the body. Females bear two to four live young that often measure as much as 5 ft. long at birth. Thresher sharks use shallow water as a nursery area.

A blow from the tail

Threshers hunt alone or in pairs, usually far out at sea. Having found a shoal of small fish, they circle it, lashing their powerful tails to concentrate their prey into a tight, disorganized ball. Then they charge at them, snapping to the right and left for mouthfuls of fish, and lashing their tails to stun those they miss.

The cat sharks

The cat sharks form a large family containing 94 species. Most cat sharks are small, inshore fish. Their dorsal fins are set well back, and they have long upper lobes on their tails. Cat sharks tend to live near the bottom, feeding on a variety of marine life including shrimps, shellfish, crabs and fish. Many of the cat sharks are brightly marked with mottles, stripes and patterns.

Around British shores, the two most common cat sharks are the lesser and greater spotted dogfishes. A dogfish seldom weighs more than 9 lbs. or grows over 3 ft. in length. It has rough skin that is sandy brown with darker brown spots. The dogfishes live over sand, gravel and mud at a depth of about 180 ft.

The tope, another member of the cat shark family, is a slender-bodied cat shark that comes quite close inshore. It inhabits waters to a depth of 330 ft. and feeds on small flatfish.

Most of the cat sharks lay eggs. The oblong, leathery cases have tendrils at the corners and are known as mermaids' purses. Those of the greater and lesser spotted dogfishes often wash up along the tideline.

southwest coast of England as they follow shoals of spurdog or mackerel (hence their name). The mako shark that inhabits the Pacific and Indian oceans has unusually long pectoral fins and is probably a separate species. Mako sharks are considered dangerous and have been implicated in a number of attacks on people.

The porbeagle sharks are the only mackerel sharks that enter northern European waters regularly. Porbeagles resemble the makos, but have thicker, more deep-set bodies. They have blue-gray backs and cream underparts and grow to a length of 11 ft. 6 in. Porbeagles occur in the Atlantic, from Iceland to Africa and from Newfoundland to South Carolina, and they also inhabit the Mediterranean. The porbeagle sharks prefer the open ocean, but do occasionally come inshore. They feed on a wide variety of fish, including bottom-dwelling creatures such as flounders, squid and cuttlefish. In cold

Requiem sharks and smooth hounds

The smooth hounds occur in shallow water to a depth of 656 ft. and are found in most of the world's oceans. The main distinguishing feature of the smooth hounds is their blunt, flat teeth that they use to crush the shells of crabs and other shellfish. The smooth hounds are not dangerous to humans, and most do not exceed 4 ft. long. They all bear live young, some of them developing a placenta, others simply hatching their eggs internally. The leopard shark, of the smooth hound group, occurs off the Pacific coast and is noteworthy for its spectacular coloring—large black blotches on a light tan background.

The requiem sharks are abundant in tropical oceans, and present in all the others. Requiem sharks have a distinctive notch and lobe on the upper curve of the tail. The blue shark is a slim open-sea (pelagic) species of the requiem shark group. It reaches a maximum of 10 ft. in tropical waters, but seldom exceeds 5 ft in British waters. It weighs between 40 and 60 lbs. The blue shark is a vivid blue in color, and has very long, slender pectoral fins. It is a late arrival among summer fish around British coasts, appearing in late June and leaving in October. While in British waters, the blue shark is found off the west coasts of Ireland, Scotland and Wales. It is a voracious eater of herring, mackerel and spurdog, sometimes taking squid and cod.

Bulls and tigers

Bull sharks, found worldwide, commonly enter fresh water. The Ganges, Zambesi and the Nicaraguan bull sharks all swim upriver, the Zambesi bull shark has been found more than 620 miles from the ocean, in the Zambesi River. The Ganges bull sharks grow to 12 ft. and combine triangular, serrated teeth in the upper jaw with pointed, serrated teeth in the lower. They often live in close proximity to humans, and attacks can cause serious injury or be fatal.

The tiger shark, named for its distinctive barred coloration, is the largest of the requiem sharks, reaching a length of 18 ft. It occurs in all the tropical and subtropical seas and eats almost anything, from turtles, conch shells, crabs, porpoises and fish to a wide variety of marine trash, including tins, rolls of copper wire and empty oil cans. It is the only requiem shark to hatch eggs inside the body. The other species nourish their young through a placenta.

TOP The bull shark reaches over 11 ft. in length and is one of the few large sharks to live in both freshwater and seawater habitats. It occurs in tropical American rivers as well as in the tropical western Atlantic Ocean.
ABOVE The black-tipped shark is common in tropical reefs and often moves in quite large shoals. Although not dangerous to humans, it is curious, and many divers have suffered nervous moments when, on entering a lagoon, they have been surrounded by inquisitive groups of black-tipped sharks.

ABOVE The dark, barred markings that give the tiger shark its name fade with age and are clearly visible only on young animals. Adult tiger sharks can measure well over 16 ft. in length and are aggressive creatures, responsible for many of the 100 or so shark attacks on humans that are reported each year.

The hammerhead sharks

There are nine species in the hammerhead shark family. They range from 5 to 16 ft. 6 in. in length. The family takes its name from the lateral projections on each side of the shark's head; the tips of each projection bear an eye and a nostril that may be as much as 3 ft. apart. It has been suggested that their hammer-shaped heads act as a stabilizer to aid maneuverability. The eyes, set far apart, give hammerhead sharks a wider range of vision, and the distance between the nostrils may provide the shark with a more sensitive detection system enabling it to locate a scent more accurately.

Hammerhead sharks are inhabitants of the warm seas, from the surface to 1300 ft. in depth.

Spiny dogfish sharks

The spiny dogfish sharks make up a large and diverse family that occurs in all oceans, from the shallows to great depths. Most spiny dogfishes have two dorsal fins preceded by a sharp spine. The spine is associated with a poison gland that produces a venom that is painful to humans but not fatal. All spiny dogfishes develop eggs internally (they are ovoviviparous), and produce up to 12 young per litter. In size, the spiny dogfish sharks range from 12 to 24 in. Many, especially the deepwater species, feed on squid and octopus.

The bramble sharks (a genus of the spiny dogfish family) lack the spines, but instead have overdeveloped "tooth scales" on the skin, making them very prickly to handle. They live on the continental slopes to a depth

of 3000 ft., but occasionally enter quite shallow water. The bramble sharks grow to 10 ft. long, while the related Pacific prickly shark may grow up to 13 ft. in length.

Spiny dogfishes are commercially exploited by most European countries. The spurdog or bone dog is a common species. A dull gray fish decorated by white spots on the back, it grows to 4 ft. and is widely distributed in the North Atlantic. Spurdogs live in quite shallow waters, down to depths of 3000 ft., and move in enormous packs. The shoals usually contain fish of the same sex and of similar size. They migrate constantly, and cover great distances. Apart from the females moving inshore to bear young, the movements of spiny dogfishes are unpredictable.

The spurdog is an important food source, and because of its long breeding cycle it is in danger of being overfished. Males do not mature until they are 11 years old, and females mature when they are

ABOVE The bonnethead shark is one of the nine species of hammerhead sharks, all of which have curious, flattened heads that extend sideways. Like all sharks, they have long pectoral fins that extend sideways like aircraft wings; these give the shark support and enable it to steer. The fins are relatively inflexible and cannot be used as brakes—an attacking shark cannot stop or back away, but must simply veer to the side.

19 or 20. The female's gestation period takes 18-22 months, and she gives birth to only 3 to 11 young. All these delays, combined with small litters, mean that the stocks are easily overfished—particularly in the North Sea.

The smallest shark

Most of the spiny dogfishes live near the coasts, but about 20 species inhabit deep water. The velvet bellies, named for the feel of the very fine denticles (small toothlike projections) embedded in their skins, have

Lantern shark

Chimaera

Eagle ray

Hammerhead shark

Angel shark

Cuckoo ray

Roughshark

Manta ray

Guitarfish

Ocellated electric ray

Stingray

Smalltooth sawfish

1838

light organs on their undersides enabling them to glow in the dark. The pygmy shark is another member of the spiny dogfish family that glows in the dark. It reaches only 10.4 in. in length. The dwarf or midwater shark of the western Pacific, whose black body measures only 6 in. in length, is considered to be the world's smallest shark.

Saws and angel sharks

Two shark families—the saws and the angel sharks—show some similarities to the rays, the second major group of cartilaginous fishes. Although saw and angel sharks resemble rays with their large pectoral fins,

flattened bodies and bottom-dwelling habits, they differ from them in two distinct ways. The pectoral fins are separate from the head in saw and angel sharks, and their gill slits are not situated under the pectorals as they are in the rays.

The saw sharks—not to be confused with the sawfish, which are rays—live in shallow coastal areas, and at least one of the five species penetrates high into fresh water. For example, one population of small-toothed saw sharks lives in Lake Nicaragua. The saw from which they take their name is a gross elongation of the snout, with teeth set unevenly in both sides. They also have sensitive, fleshy filaments (barbels)

CHONDRICHTHYES
CLASSIFICATION: 3

The large order Lamniformes contains a total of 239 species of sharks with a distribution throughout the seas of the world. They are grouped into 66 genera and eight families.

The whale shark and carpet sharks

The whale shark, *Rhincodon typus*, which ranges mainly through tropical waters, is the sole member of the family Rhincodontidae. The carpet or nurse sharks make up a group of 28 species in the family Orectolobidae. Most inhabit the warm waters of the Indian and Pacific oceans. They include the wobbegongs of the genus *Orectolobus* and the nurse sharks of the genus *Ginglymostoma*.

Sand sharks and the megamouth

The family Odontaspididae includes the five species of sand sharks or sand tigers from the genera *Odontaspis* and *Pseudocarcharias*, which inhabit shallow, warm and tropical waters, and the goblin shark, *Mitsukurina owstoni*, which is a deepwater species. The megamouth, *Megachasma pelagias*, of the Pacific Ocean is placed in a family of its own, the Megachasmidae.

Mackerel sharks and cat sharks

The family Lamnidae, the mackerel sharks, contains nine species that occur throughout

the temperate and tropical seas. They include the great white shark, *Carcharodon carcharias*; the two species of mako sharks of the genus *Isurus*; the two species of porbeagle sharks from the genus *Lamna*; the basking shark, *Cetorhinus maximus*; and the three species of thresher sharks of the genus *Alopias*. The family Scyliorhinidae, the cat sharks, contains a total of 94 species. They range throughout the oceans, and include the lesser spotted dogfish, *Scyliorhinus caniculus*; the greater spotted dogfish, *S. stellaris*; the soupfin shark, *Galeorhinus zyopterus*; and the tope, *G. galeus*.

Smooth hounds, requiem sharks and hammerhead sharks

The family Carcharhinidae contains both the smooth hounds and the requiem sharks, fishes that are distributed throughout the tropical and temperate seas. The smooth hounds or smooth dogfishes number 41 species, and include the leopard shark, *Triakis semifasciata*, and the smooth hound, *Mustelus canis*. The 50 or so species of requiem sharks include the bull sharks and reef sharks of the genus *Carcharhinus*; the tiger shark, *Galeocerdo cuvier*; and the blue shark, *Prionace glauca*. The family Sphyrnidae contains only one genus, *Sphyrna*, with nine species of hammerhead sharks. They range through all the oceans, though they are most common in warm, coastal waters. They include the great hammerhead shark, *Sphyrna mokarran*, and the bonnethead shark, *S. tiburo*.

ABOVE The coloration of the European monkfish provides good camouflage when it lies on the seabed. It is an active hunter, taking flatfish, whelks and crabs as it swims with sculling motions of the tail. Its unusual way of moving distinguishes the European monkfish from the rays, with which it shares similarities of appearance and anatomy. It is common in the Atlantic waters of Europe. BELOW The sideways swimming motion of the sharks (A) is quite different from the undulating, flying motion used by the rays (B).

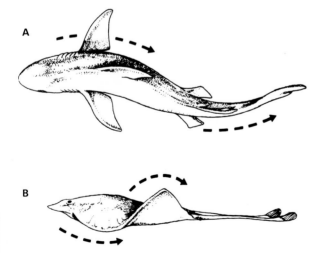

under the snout, used for feeding. Saw sharks dig around in the soft seabed with their saws—sometimes in water so shallow that their dorsal fins show above water—and eat a wide variety of invertebrates and small fish. They also use the saw like a swordfish's sword, thrashing it through fish shoals and returning to pick up the dead and crippled prey. Most saw sharks are small, seldom growing over 5 ft. long, but the greater saw shark may be very large—the largest saw shark reliably measured was 25 ft. 3 in. in length, but a specimen of 35 ft. has been recorded, weighing up to 5000 lbs. Saw sharks do not usually pose a threat to people, but their saw can injure fishermen when they are netted. Various species of saw sharks inhabit most of the inshore tropical waters, and they are particularly common around estuaries.

Similarities to the rays

The angel sharks or monkfish are even closer to the rays than the saw sharks, both in appearance and internal anatomy. They are squat fish, with large pectoral fins, flattened heads, and large spiracles (blow holes) behind each eye. About 11 species of angel sharks inhabit most of the warm temperate and tropical seas, occasionally coming quite close inshore. The European monkfish reaches a maximum

length of 71 in. and a weight of 70 lbs. 8 oz. Angel sharks feed on bottom-dwelling fishes and invertebrates and, despite their cumbersome shape, are active swimmers. They give birth to litters of 9-16 live young that are born in summer. Like many other sharks, angel sharks are not dangerous to people unless they are provoked or handled carelessly, when their rough skin, strong muscles and many fine, pointed teeth, can cause severe injury.

Sawfishes

The six species of sawfishes make up a small family within the order of skates and rays. They are immediately recognizable by their elongated, blade-shaped snouts armed with sharp teeth that project sideways. The greater sawfish reaches over 26 ft. in length and has 24-32 pairs of teeth on its "saw." Its body resembles that of a shark, though the snout, the enlarged pectoral fins and the positioning of the gills beneath the body are different.

Living in shallow water, including estuaries, the greater sawfish uses its saw to probe in and stir up the mud where it finds the small animals on which it feeds. It also catches food by swimming into a shoal of fishes and slashing its saw from side to side, killing and wounding fish as it goes. The teeth that line the saw are not its true teeth; small, blunt-crowned teeth in the jaws crush and grind up the sawfish's prey.

Electric rays

The electric ray family consists of about 38 species. They probably evolved from similar ancestors to the sharks, but most of them developed flat, disk-shaped bodies adapted to living on the bottom of shallow water.

Electric rays have loose, soft, smooth skin. Their two pectoral fins have expanded enormously so that their leading edges join up with the front of the head, creating the fish's rounded outline. They usually have two dorsal fins, and the tail fin is well developed. The Atlantic torpedo is one of the giants of the electric ray family, measuring up to 6 ft. in length and over 110 lbs. in weight. It is uniformly dark green, brown or black above and creamy white below. The electric shock delivered by the Atlantic torpedo is very powerful—up to 220 volts—and is easily capable of knocking over a human. Fortunately, the Atlantic torpedo rarely swims at depths of less than about 26 ft., so casual swimmers are not at risk.

ABOVE Electric rays, such as the blue-spotted electric ray of the Mediterranean Sea and the eastern Atlantic, can emit a powerful shock from the "batteries" of modified muscles on each side of their heads. The electric rays can discharge a shock of over 300 volts. It is used to kill prey and also as a defense against predators. Fortunately, electric rays tend to live in deep water and rarely come into contact with people.

CHONDRICHTHYES CLASSIFICATION: 4

Spiny dogfishes, saw sharks and angel sharks

The order Squaliformes contains three families of sharks. The family Squalidae, with its 71 species of spiny dogfishes, is grouped into 18 genera. They have a worldwide distribution, and include the bramble sharks of the genus *Echinorhinus*; the cigar sharks of the genus *Isistius*; the Greenland shark, *Somniosus microcephalus*; and the spurdog, *Squalus acanthias*.

The family Pristiophoridae consists of five species of saw sharks, grouped in two genera, *Pristiophorus* and *Pliotrema*. They occur in coastal shallows around South Africa and in the seas from Australia to Japan. The family Squatinidae contains the 11 species of angel sharks, which all belong to the genus *Squatina*. They range worldwide in tropical and temperate waters, and include the European monkfish, *S. squatina*, and the Pacific species, *S. californica*.

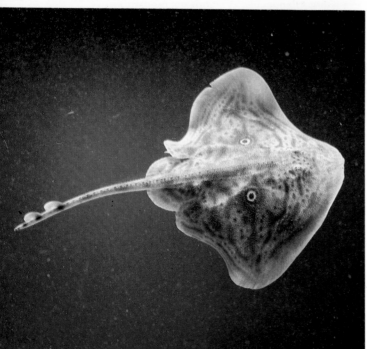

The electric rays use their electric shock to stun attackers, but more commonly to shock prey so that they can be eaten more easily. The electric cells are located in two bulky organs under the skin on either side of the head. Each organ is composed of many hexagonal (six-sided) columns formed from hundreds of fine plates filled with a jelly-like substance. The separate plate-shaped units are connected via a nerve directly to the brain—and each one acts as a battery, with the top side of the plate being positive and the lower side negative. When stimulated, all the units discharge together in one large pulse.

CHONDRICHTHYES CLASSIFICATION: 5

The large order Rajiformes contains the rays and their relatives. They range throughout the oceans of the world and a few species are found in freshwater habitats. There are 424 species in total, grouped into 51 genera and nine families.

Sawfishes and electric rays

The family Pristidae contains the six species of sawfishes. All members of the genus *Pristis*, they mainly inhabit the tropical seas and are sometimes found in estuaries. The largest species is the greater or smalltooth sawfish, *P. pectinata*. The electric rays make up the family Torpedinidae. They occur in all tropical, subtropical and temperate seas. There are about 38 species, including the Atlantic torpedo, *Torpedo nobiliana*; the blue-spotted electric ray, *Torpedo torpedo*; and the marbled electric ray, *Torpedo marmorata*.

Guitarfishes, rays and skates

The guitarfishes of the family Rhinobatidae occur in tropical and warm temperate waters. There are about 48 species, the most well known of which is the European guitarfish, *Rhinobatus rhinobatus*. The large family Rajidae, the skates and rays, contains about 190 species. They occur in all the oceans, and include the common or blue skate, *Raja batis*; the cuckoo ray, *R. naevus*; and the thornback ray or roker, *R. clavata*.

TOP The European guitarfish spends most of its time on the sea bottom, feeding chiefly on mollusks and crustaceans. When swimming, it uses its broad pectoral fins for maneuvering and its powerful tail for propulsion.

ABOVE The cuckoo ray has a large eyespot on each wing. Like all rays, it hunts mainly by scent and feeds on shrimps, ragworms and sand eels. It lays rectangular, amber-colored egg capsules during the spring.

RIGHT The ribbontail ray is a colorful member of the stingray family that can grow to over 6 ft. 6 in. in length, much of which is composed of its long, flattened tail. It lives on reefs and in shallow coastal waters in the tropics, feeding on small invertebrates.

BELOW RIGHT The drawings show the swimming movements of a ray. It flaps its large pectoral fins like wings to propel itself forward. The tail is hardly used for locomotion.

Guitarfishes constitute a family of about 48 species and occur in the tropical and warm temperate waters of the Atlantic, Indian and Pacific oceans. Measuring from about 24 inches to 10 feet long, they have flattened heads and bodies, long, strong tails and large pectoral fins. Guitarfishes take their name from their shape, which loosely resembles a guitar. The European guitarfish is a typical member of the guitarfish family. It lives on the bottom of shallow waters and is a rather sluggish fish, spending much of its time buried in the mud and sand. It feeds on small crustaceans and mollusks, crushing them with small, densely packed teeth.

Skates and rays

Some 190 species make up the skates and rays family (stingrays, eagle rays and manta rays belong to different families). Their flattened bodies are roughly diamond-shaped, and their tails are long and thin with very small or no tail fins. All the species have electric organs, though they are much weaker than those of the electric rays and are situated toward the base of their tails. Most skates and rays have prickly skin, and a row of spines often runs along the middle of their backs.

There is no biological difference between skates and rays; the larger species are usually referred to as skates, while the smaller are called rays. They all breed by internal fertilization, and all lay eggs. Each egg is enclosed in a square, horny case with stiff, pointed tendrils at the corners. These egg cases—known as mermaids' purses—often wash onto the shore and can be seen along the tideline.

Many skates and rays are a valuable source of food for humans. The common or blue skate is one of the most important commercial species in European fisheries and is caught by deep-sea trawlers in great numbers. A long-snouted species, its upper surface is brownish or grayish with light or dark spots, and the lower surface is bluish gray with dark markings. It grows up to 9 ft. long and 6 ft. wide and can weigh over 200 lbs.

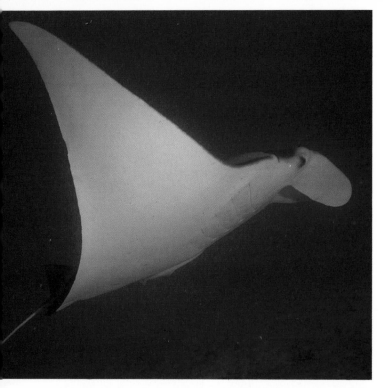

The mature male common skate has spines all over its upper surface, but the female only has them on the front half of her body, while the young common skate has a smooth body. The common skate feeds on a variety of fish, including other species of rays, flatfish, dogfish, herrings and pilchards. It also takes lobsters and crabs.

The thornback ray—called the roker in East Anglia, England—is more abundant in inshore waters at depths of 6 ft. 6 in. to 164 ft., and is an important commercial species. It is a mottled pale brown or gray in color, and grows to about 33 in. long.

Stingrays

The 90 species of stingrays form a family that lives mainly in the warm tropical or subtropical waters of the Atlantic, Pacific and Indian oceans. Their flattened bodies may be disk-shaped or slightly rectangular in

ABOVE **Manta** rays are the largest living rays—some have a "wingspan" of over 20 feet—but in spite of their huge size they feed mainly on plankton. They swim in the upper layers of the sea, and sometimes bask on the surface.

BELOW A manta ray with its train of remoras (A)—fish that attach themselves to the ray with their sucker heads—and pilot fish (B). The remoras and pilot fish dart out to pick up scraps of food when their host feeds.

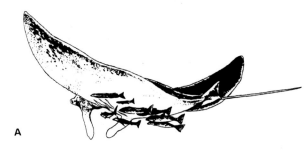

A

B

CHONDRICHTHYES CLASSIFICATION: 6

Stingrays and river stingrays

The stingrays of the family Dasyatidae comprise about 90 species. They are marine animals of the Atlantic, Pacific and Indian Oceans, and a few occasionally occur in brackish and freshwater. They include the ribbontail ray, *Taeniura lymma*; the common stingray, *Dasyatis pastinaca*; and the smooth butterfly ray, *Gymnura micrura*. The family Potamotrygonidae contains the 14 species of river stingrays. They are grouped into two genera—*Potamotrygon* and *Disceus*—and are all freshwater species that inhabit Atlantic-draining rivers of South America.

Eagle rays and manta rays

The eagle rays make up the family Myliobatididae. There are about 24 species, and they occur in most tropical and warm temperate seas. The most well-known species is the eagle ray, *Myliobatis aquila*. The manta or devil rays form the family Mobulidae, with 10 species. They include the Atlantic manta or giant devil ray, *Manta birostris*, and the European manta ray, *Mobula mobular*.

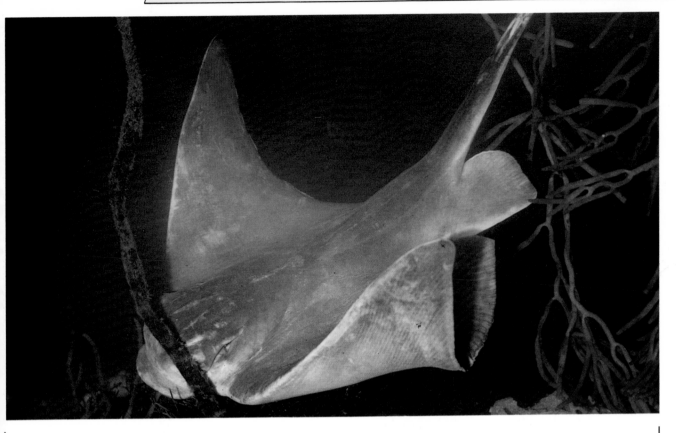

outline, with their tails reduced to slender whips. Although the tail has no fins, it bears the stingray family's most unpleasant feature: one or two sharp, serrated, erectile spines that may measure up to 15 in. long. The spines have a groove along their lower side containing venom-producing tissue. When the stingray is trodden on by a bather, or attacked, it lashes its tail from side to side or over its body until the spines (or spine) penetrate its tormentor.

A stingray's poison has various effects on a human: inflammation around the puncture spot, sharp, shooting pains and a throbbing sensation. Severe gashes can cause paralysis and even death. Because of this, stingrays are notorious wherever they occur. The common stingray is one of the several stingrays found in the Mediterranean Sea. Growing to about 8 ft. long, its skin is mainly smooth, and colored gray or brownish above and pale below. Like all the stingrays, it is ovoviviparous—the eggs develop in the female's oviducts and the young are born live. It prefers shallow waters and eats crustaceans and some fish.

Eagle rays

The eagle ray family has about 24 species, of which the eagle ray is the most familiar. Occurring in warm seas throughout the world, they have abandoned their

ABOVE The eagle ray feeds on the ocean floor. It finds buried prey by digging into the sand or mud with its nose or by disturbing the bottom with its flapping wings. Though it browses on the bottom, it is a strong swimmer, and has even been observed leaping right out of the water.

life on the seabed for a more mobile existence in the water. Unlike skates and other rays, the eagle rays' heads are quite distinct from the rest of their diamond-shaped bodies, since their pectoral fins do not extend to their snouts. In addition, their eyes and breathing holes (spiracles) are on the sides of their heads, rather than on the top.

The eagle ray itself spends much of its time on the seabed; it is, however, a fast swimmer, seeming to fly through the water with graceful flapping motions that resemble the flight of an eagle. Eagle rays sometimes break clear of the water surface and skim across the waves. Like many members of the family, the eagle ray has a long, poisonous tail spine that it uses for defense.

Manta rays

The manta or devil rays are graceful giants among fish. They have abandoned the bottom-living habits of their fellow rays to live at or near the surface of the great oceans. Manta rays have wide, disk-shaped

ABOVE The Atlantic ratfish — one of the chimaeras — takes its name from its thin, rat-like tail. Together with its close relatives, it is also known as a rabbitfish because of its large front teeth. The **Atlantic ratfish spends most of its life in deep waters, but moves inshore to breed, migrating in single-sex shoals. The female lays her long, tapering egg capsules in spring and summer.**

bodies with broad pectoral fins that are pointed at the ends. Their eyes and spiracles are located on the sides of their heads, and their mouths are situated between two movable lobes—the cephalic fins—which are forward extensions of the pectoral fins. It is these horn-shaped features that give the group the name of "devil fish." Their tails are long and lack fins, but they have a dorsal fin and some species have a tail spine.

The Atlantic manta ray (or giant devil ray) reaches about 20 feet in width and weighs well over a ton. It has rarely been captured, and some individuals may well grow larger. Its diet, like that of the rest of the family, consists of plankton and tiny schooling fish. It feeds by swimming through the water with its immense mouth wide open, taking in and filtering food by means of special horny outgrowths on the gill arches. The manta rays, like the great whales and the giant sharks, are examples of enormous marine vertebrates that feed on the smallest organisms in the sea.

Chimaeras

Most cartilaginous fishes can be distinguished from bony fishes by the presence of several external gill slits. The three families of cartilaginous fishes known as the chimaeras are the exception. Commonly known as ratfishes (named for their long, rat-like tails) or rabbitfishes (from the long, rabbit-like teeth), they have gills that are covered by a single flap of skin. (In the bony fishes, this flap is composed of three plates of skin.) Other features that place the chimaeras among the cartilaginous fishes include their cartilaginous skeletons, the presence of claspers in males, and the absence of lungs or swim bladders.

Despite similarities with sharks and rays, chimaeras show distinct differences. Usually less than 3 feet long, chimaeras are smooth-skinned with massive heads. The bodies taper off toward the rear and end in slender tails. The short, first dorsal fin is placed high on the fish's back and a strong, sharp poison spine projects in front of it. The long, low, second dorsal fin merges into the tail fin.

Single-sex shoals

The Atlantic ratfish or rabbitfish occurs in relatively deep water, usually at depths of 656-1640 ft., though it moves to shallower waters during the spring and summer breeding season. The female, which is larger than the male, grows to about 5 ft. long. It is mottled with white and brown above and cream beneath with a metallic sheen. The Atlantic ratfish feeds on crustaceans, starfish and mollusks and appears to migrate in single-sex shoals.

CHONDRICHTHYES CLASSIFICATION: 7

Chimaeras

The order **Chimaeriformes** contains the three families of chimaeras, also known as the ratfish or the rabbitfish. The family **Chimaeridae**, the shortnose chimaeras, contains **13 species** from two genera that range through the Atlantic, Pacific and Indian Oceans. One of the best-known species is the Atlantic ratfish or rabbitfish, *Chimaera monstrosa*. The family **Rhinochimaeridae** comprises the six species of longnose chimaeras. They are grouped in two genera, and occur in the Atlantic and Pacific oceans. The family **Callorhynchidae** contains the four species of ploughnose chimaeras from the genus *Callorhynchus*. They are confined to the seas of the Southern Hemisphere.

BONY PRIMITIVES

Although they belong to the class of bony fishes, the lungfishes, bichirs, sturgeons and the prehistoric-looking coelacanth each retain certain primitive features—heavy skull bones, smooth, bright scales or simple lungs

ABOVE **The close similarities between the South American lungfish and the African lungfishes lend support to the view that long ago the continents of Africa and South America were joined. As the continents drifted apart over millions of years, the lungfishes became separated.**

BELOW **The Australian lungfish has stronger fins than the African and South American lungfishes, and uses them to push itself forward on the riverbed.**
PAGE 1847 **Bichirs are well-armored fishes, with thick, hard scales. They are native to lakes and slow-flowing rivers in Africa.**

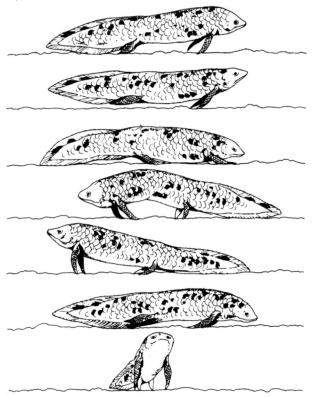

Bony fishes comprise by far the largest of the three groups of marine creatures. There are about 21,000 species, in both sea and freshwater habitats, including such familiar fish as cod, carp, perch, tuna and plaice.

Bony fishes vary enormously in appearance and habits, but most possess a number of characteristics that distinguish them from cartilaginous fish. Apart from having a skeleton consisting of bone rather than cartilage, they usually have overlapping rounded scales on their skin, complex and bony jaws with little cartilage, gills covered by a bony plate (operculum) and paired flexible fins that are not modified into claspers. Most bony fishes also have an air-filled swim bladder that makes them weightless in water so they can remain motionless without sinking.

Non-teleosts

Although most bony fish are teleosts, about 50 of the rarer and more primitive-looking species are not. The non-teleost group of bony fishes comprises the lungfishes, the coelacanth, bichirs, sturgeon, paddlefish, gars and the bowfin. They are distinguished from teleosts by their unusual appearance. For example, sturgeons' tail fins are different lengths, bichirs are snake-like with shiny scales, and the coelacanth has limb-like fins. The primitive appearance of non-teleosts is no coincidence, since they are the last survivors of species that flourished tens or even hundreds of millions of years ago.

Lungfishes

There are two orders of lungfishes, found in South America, Africa and Australia. As their name suggests, they use their lungs to breathe. Also called fringe-finned fishes, lungfishes have fibrous, leathery scales;

paired fins with fleshy lobes at the bases; dorsal, anal and caudal fins that form a continuous fold around the rear of their bodies; and fan-shaped toothplates that they use to crush their food.

The South American and African lungfishes grow to about 5-6 ft. 6 in. respectively. They have paired lungs that they use as their primary method of breathing, eel-like bodies with small, round scales and very small pectoral fins. The Australian lungfish (in an order of its own) is similarly elongated in shape, and about the same length as the South American species, but it has larger scales and more developed pectoral and pelvic fins. It can breathe air through its single lung, but mainly breathes through its gills.

All species of lungfishes occur in freshwater habitats, but while the Australian species lives in permanent waters that do not dry out, the African and South American species live in habitats that often lack oxygen and dry up completely in the hot sun—for example, in slow-moving rivers, swamps and marshes. When oxygen is low, these species breathe through their lungs, and when there is no water at all, they lower their metabolic rate to survive until conditions improve.

The South American lungfish of the Amazon Basin buries itself in mud, at first rising up to the surface of the water to breathe and then, when the water has evaporated, sealing itself in with blobs of mud. It secretes an envelope of mucus and surrounds itself with it, reemerging only when the rains arrive. The African species connect their mucus-lined cocoons to the surface with a narrow tube through which they breathe. In this condition, they have been known to survive dry conditions for up to four years.

ABOVE The African lungfishes are sometimes regarded as "living fossils"—they are very similar to species of fishes that were abundant hundreds of millions of years ago. African lungfishes are dependent on their lungs for breathing. They have to swim to the surface of the water every few minutes to take in air.

BELOW During the dry season, when the water it inhabits dries up, the African lungfish survives by burrowing into the mud. There, it curls up inside a cocoon of mucus that hardens to prevent the fish from drying out. It continues to breathe through a small hole in the cocoon.

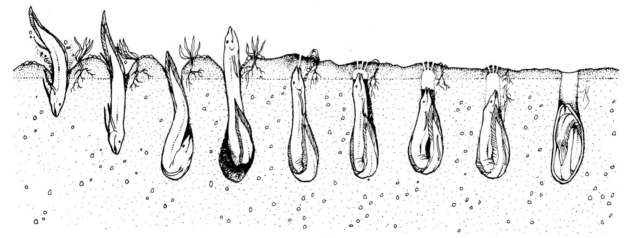

LEFT The coelacanth, thought to be extinct until 1938, has fleshy pectoral and ventral fins that are mounted on muscular lobes. These enable it to maneuver, while its tail is used for fast swimming. Close relatives of the coelacanth (now extinct) may well have been the forerunners of all amphibians, reptiles, birds and mammals.

PRIMITIVE BONY FISHES CLASSIFICATION: 1

The bony fishes that make up the class Osteichthyes number 42 orders. Seven of these, which are termed the "primitive" bony fishes, are distinct from the other, more advanced orders within the class (collectively known as the teleosts).

Lungfishes, the coelacanth and bichirs

There are two orders of lungfishes, both confined to freshwater habitats. The order Ceratodontiformes contains the family Ceratodontidae, the only member of which is the Australian lungfish or Burnett River salmon, *Neoceratodus forsteri*, of the Burnett and Mary rivers in Australia. The second order, the Lepidosireniformes, comprises two families. The Lepidosirenidae contains only the South American lungfish, *Lepidosiren paradoxa*, of the Amazon Basin, while the family Protopteridae has the four species of African lungfishes from the genus *Protopterus*, which live in west and central Africa. The coelacanth, *Latimeria chalumnae*, lives in the Indian Ocean, and is the only member of the family Latimeriidae, which, in turn, is the only family within the order Coelacanthiformes.

The order Polypteriformes contains only the family Polypteridae, the bichirs and the reedfish. Found in freshwater habitats in Africa, they comprise the reedfish or ropefish, *Calamoichthys calabaricus*, and the 10 species of bichirs from the genus *Polypterus*, including the Nile bichir, *P. bichir*.

The South American lungfish spawns early in the rainy season, in a burrow that the male digs and defends energetically once the female has laid her eggs. At this time, the male's pectoral fins undergo a remarkable change, developing a gill-like web well supplied with blood vessels. The function of these temporary structures is unknown, but they may increase the male's oxygen intake so that he does not need to leave the eggs in order to breathe at the surface. Alternatively, they may allow the male to transfer oxygen to the developing eggs or young.

When just hatched, the young South American lungfish cling to vegetation with adhesive glands that disappear after 6-8 weeks. They also have gills on their heads and bear a distinct resemblance to tadpoles.

The coelacanth

The coelacanth is one of our most remote ancestors, and was widespread in sea and freshwaters 300-90 million years ago. It was considered to be extinct until a single specimen was discovered in a trawl off the South African coast in 1938.

Like lungfishes, the coelacanth has fibrous, leathery scales. Its second dorsal, pectoral and pelvic fins are on stalk-like muscular lobes, giving the fish considerable dexterity. Close relatives of the coelacanth, now extinct, had an internal fin skeleton that was remarkably similar to that of an amphibian or other early land vertebrate, into which they may have evolved.

Only about a hundred coelacanths have been captured, mostly at depths of 492-1310 ft. and all in the Comoro Islands group to the northwest of Madagascar. The coelacanth is dark metallic bluish in color, with occasional irregular cream or whitish blotches on its slimy scales and brownish fins. It is a carnivore, and the female lays eggs that remain inside her body until they are ready to hatch.

Bichirs

The bichir family comprises 10 species of bichirs and a single species of reedfish (also known as ropefish).

ABOVE The Russian sturgeon is an important commercial fish, exploited for both its flesh and for its caviar (caviar is the female roe or eggs, that are pickled in brine and pressed). Like all sturgeons, it is susceptible to pollution and changes in river flow, and stocks have to be carefully managed. In some parts of Russia, it is raised on fish farms.

BELOW The map shows the world distribution of the bichirs, the sturgeons, the bowfin, the gars and the lungfishes.

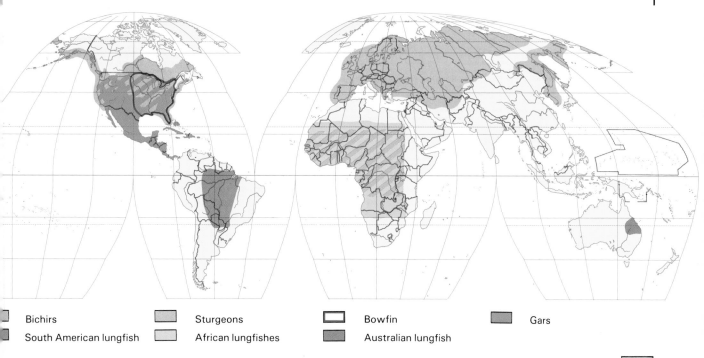

▫ Bichirs	▫ Sturgeons	▫ Bowfin
▫ South American lungfish	▫ African lungfishes	▫ Australian lungfish

▫ Gars

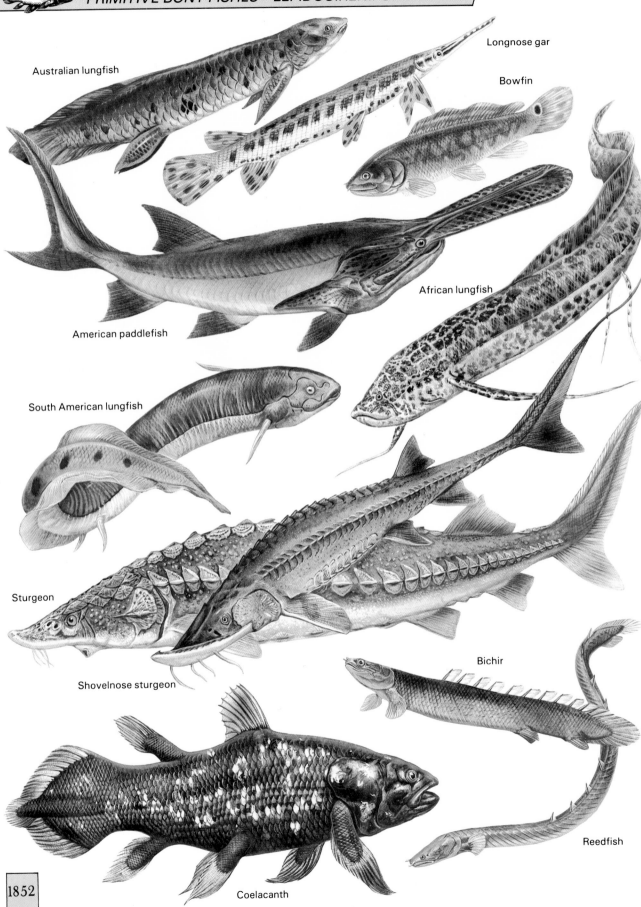

Australian lungfish

Longnose gar

Bowfin

American paddlefish

African lungfish

South American lungfish

Sturgeon

Bichir

Shovelnose sturgeon

Reedfish

Coelacanth

Bichirs inhabit weedy, still and slow-moving waters in the lakes and rivers of Africa. Ancient in origin, they resemble fish known only from fossils. All have snake-like bodies, reaching a maximum of 3 ft. 3 in. in length in the Nile bichir but no more than 20 in. in the reedfish. Their bodies have square scales with glistening enamel-like surfaces, and their pectoral fins are fan-like, with fleshy stalks. Bichirs use their double-chambered lungs to breathe, particularly in hot conditions, when oxygen levels fall in their still waters.

The Nile bichir is olive-green on top and yellowish below. It has a dorsal fin divided into a series of small, sail-like portions, each composed of a stiff ray and attached membrane. A predatory fish, it catches and eats other fish and amphibians. Prior to reproduction, the male's anal fin increases in size and becomes fleshy, a characteristic that may have a courtship or mating function. At birth, the offspring have external gills on each side of their heads, giving them a strong likeness to newt tadpoles.

The reedfish is an eel-like fish, producing larvae that also resemble newt tadpoles. Like other members of the bichir family, it lives in still and slow-moving waters where its lungs are valuable when oxygen levels fall. Its dorsal fin is composed of one or several smallish spines, with soft rays.

ABOVE The Atlantic sturgeon is principally a bottom feeder, pushing its jaws into the mud to catch the variety of invertebrates on which it feeds. It has poor eyesight but a highly developed sense of touch—four sensitive barbels hang from its mouth and feel the ground for food. Atlantic sturgeons have been known to reach 10 ft. in length and 600 lbs. in weight, but overfishing means that sturgeon of this size are now very rare.

Sturgeons and paddlefishes

Sturgeons are large fishes, with 23 species all in the Northern Hemisphere. The white sturgeon, which inhabits rivers along the Pacific coast, is the largest North American freshwater fish, reaching 15 ft. in length (one specimen measured up to 20 ft. long). Sturgeons possess several distinguishing characteristics. They have five rows of bony plates arranged along their bodies by their tails. They also have vertebral columns that turn upward at the tip and extend into the upper lobes of their tail fins (the upper lobes are much longer than the bottom lobes). In addition, their long, bill-like snouts have four sensory barbels beneath them.

Sturgeons start their lives in freshwater, where they reproduce. Later on, some move to the sea. The Atlantic sturgeon grows to 10 ft. in length and can weigh over 600 lbs. Feeding on bottom-living

ABOVE The American paddlefish has a bill that accounts for about one third of its total length. It swallows water with its huge gape, and filters out plankton as the water is sieved through its long, densely packed gill rakers. The two species of paddlefishes live in freshwater and haunt the murky depths of the Mississippi River in North America and the Yangtze River in China.

invertebrates, it lives for much of the year in coastal waters, but swims upriver to breed during the spring, selecting areas with gravelly bottoms. The adults return to the sea, but the young remain river fish for at least two years.

The Atlantic sturgeon is a slow-growing fish that does not become sexually mature until it is several years old. Overfishing in the breeding rivers has affected the populations badly. Obstructions in breeding rivers (dams and weirs) have also reduced their numbers by preventing the fish from reaching their breeding grounds. Pollution has taken its toll, too. The Atlantic sturgeon was once found in many western European rivers in the breeding season; now it occurs in only a handful. The white sturgeon, caught in the thousands in the Sacramento River in the 19th century, became extremely rare there early in the 20th century, but has now begun to recover well due to a conservation program.

One of the largest freshwater fish alive today is the beluga, a species of sturgeon. It grows to 16 ft. 6 in. in length and weighs over 2500 lbs. Typical of the sturgeons, it spawns in rivers and produces large numbers of eggs—estimated at up to 7 million in a mature female. It can be very long-lived, reaching over 75 years of age. The beluga is a carnivore with a large mouth. The young feed on invertebrates, graduating to fish as they develop. Fully grown fish have been known to catch and eat small seals.

The paddlefish family contains two species—the American paddlefish (or spoonbill) of the Mississippi and the Chinese paddlefish of the Yangtze and Huang Ho rivers in China. They resemble sturgeons in their basic shape, but have no plates along their sides. Their distinguishing feature—which sets them apart from both the sturgeons and any other fish—is the shape of their bills, which are very long and broader at the tip than at the base. It is this paddle shape that earns the fish their name.

Both species of paddlefish live in large freshwater rivers and feed by opening their huge mouths wide and taking in food as they swim along. They strain it out on their long gill rakers. The American paddlefish feeds on plankton. The narrower-snouted Chinese

species, with far fewer gill rakers and a protruding mouth, feeds mainly on tiny shoaling fishes and other small animals.

Gars

There are seven species of gars, inhabiting the Americas from the Great Lakes down to Costa Rica. They are carnivorous and live almost exclusively in freshwater habitats.

Gars have thick, four-sided, shiny, hard scales arranged tightly together like a mosaic. Their bodies are large and long, and most species have long, crocodile-like snouts equipped with pointed teeth. Their dorsal and anal fins lie on top of one another, immediately in front of the tail fin. Their fin arrangement gives gars the general appearance of the unrelated pikes—hence their alternative name, garpikes. Gars and pikes are an example of convergent evolution—occurring when different groups of animals evolve to look alike because they have adapted to similar life-styles.

The longnose gar is a typical species. Generally about 3 ft. in length, it is brownish above and white with dark blotches below and on its fins. It inhabits lakes and slow-moving rivers with dense vegetation, as well as brackish waters in the south of its

ABOVE The longnose gar is such a voracious predator that it often causes severe damage to freshwater fish stocks. It hangs still in the water before pouncing on its prey, which it catches with a sideways movement in its well-toothed jaws. The female lays her eggs during the spring, when large numbers of the fish congregate in shallow water to breed.

range and, occasionally, the sea. It has a considerable appetite and lies completely immobile among vegetation, waiting for prey. When it sees a passing fish, it launches a surprise attack—just as the unrelated pikes do. All gars have lungs, so they can breathe easily when the level of oxygen in the water is low—a frequent occurrence in summer. The longnose gar displays the unusual habit of sticking its long snout out of the water to take in air.

The bowfin

There is just one species of bowfin, inhabiting the warm, fresh waters of the eastern parts of North and Central America. It lives in slow-moving and densely vegetated ponds and other waters, where it is a voracious predator of all fish species, as well as aquatic invertebrates and amphibians.

Like the gars, the bowfin has lungs, but unlike them it has scales that are thin, rounded and overlapping. It

PRIMITIVE BONY FISHES — CLASSIFICATION: 2

Sturgeons and paddlefishes

The order Acipenseriformes contains two families. The sturgeons make up the family Acipenseridae, with 23 species grouped in four genera. All occur in the Northern Hemisphere, in both freshwater and saltwater habitats. They include the white sturgeon, *Acipenser transmontanus*; the Atlantic sturgeon, *A. sturio*; the Russian sturgeon, *A. gueldenstaedti*; the beluga, *Huso huso*; and the shovelnose sturgeon, *Scaphirhynchus platorhynchus*. The two species of paddlefishes make up the second family, the Polyodontidae. The American paddlefish, *Polyodon spathula*, lives in the Mississippi River in the USA, while the Chinese paddlefish, *Psephurus gladius*, occurs in the Yangtze and Huang Ho rivers in China.

Gars and the bowfin

The order Lepisosteiformes contains only the family Lepisosteidae, the freshwater gars or garpikes. All seven species belong to the genus *Lepisosteus*, and they inhabit rivers and lakes in the New World, from the Great Lakes south to Central America. One of the best-known species is the longnose gar, *Lepisosteus osseus*. The bowfin *Amia calva*, from warm freshwaters in eastern North America is the only member of the family Amiidae, which, in turn, is the only family within the order Amiiformes.

ABOVE The bowfin lives in the warm freshwaters of the eastern USA, in habitats that sometimes become depleted of oxygen. At such times, the bowfin uses its lungs rather than its gills for breathing. BELOW During the mating season, bowfin males prepare a saucer-shaped nest (A). They then await the arrival of a female, fertilize her eggs and guard them jealously. They watch over the young for some time after they hatch, often swimming around with them (B).

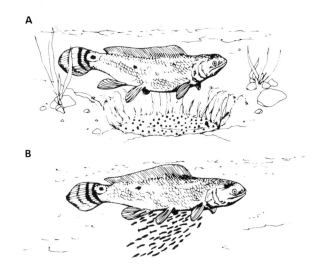

A

B

is usually about 24 in. in length, but can be over 3 ft. long, with a long dorsal fin and a rounded tail. The bowfin has an olive-green body, with a distinctive black spot just in front of the rounded tail fin. The male, which is slightly smaller than the female, has a bright orange-red circle around his black tail spot.

At the end of the summer, the male moves to shallow waters where plants grow thickly. He clears and excavates a roughly circular area on the bottom in which the female lays her eggs. She produces up to 70,000 eggs, which the male defends against predators. The eggs hatch about two weeks later. The young remain in the nest, being guarded by the male, until they are about 4 in. long, when they swim free.

SUPERIOR SWIMMERS

The great majority of fishes belong to the advanced
bony fishes known as teleosts. Streamlined, fast and agile,
they have reached the peak of development
for life underwater

ABOVE Surgeons take their name from the sharp, scalpel-like spines on the sides of their tails. They belong to the spiny-finned group of teleosts, and are among the most highly evolved of all the fishes. PAGE 1857 The huge variety of fishes that comprise the teleosts include species that range over vast stretches of ocean, and others that are confined to small seas or river basins. The Red Sea butterfly fish is an abundant species around coral reefs in the Red Sea, but occurs nowhere else in the wild.

TELEOSTS CLASSIFICATION

The teleosts comprise most of the bony fishes, covering 35 of the 42 orders within the class, and all but about 50 of its 21,000 species. The remaining chapters in the fishes section of the encyclopedia describe the teleost orders. These include the Anguilliformes, the true eels; the Clupeiformes, the herrings and their relatives; the Cypriniformes, the carps and their relatives; the Siluriformes, the catfishes; the Salmoniformes, the salmons and their relatives; the Myctophiformes, the lantern fishes; the Gadiformes, the cods; the Perciformes, the perch-like fishes; and the Pleuronectiformes, the flatfishes.

Most species of fishes within the bony fishes class belong to one group—the teleosts. The teleosts have achieved great evolutionary success by adapting to many different habitats and ways of life. They present an enormous range of forms and colors, and include most of the fishes familiar to man. There are over 21,000 known species of bony fishes—over 40 percent of all living vertebrates.

The teleost group of fishes first appeared 200 million years ago, evolving from ancient ancestors of other bony fishes—the gars and the bowfins. During the Cretaceous period, the teleosts spread rapidly throughout salt and freshwaters.

Body fluids

Fishes survive in aquatic environments by balancing the level of body fluids and salts with the level in the surrounding water (a process called osmoregulation). In the sea, the salts in the water are more concentrated than in the body of a bony fish. As a result, the water is drawn out of the body of the fish and salts from the sea are drawn in (in a process called osmosis). Osmosis is the movement of water molecules from an area of high salt concentration to one of lower salt concentration.

In freshwater, the situation is reversed—the bodies of the bony fishes have a higher level of salt than the surrounding water. Consequently, the salts move out of the fish and the fish takes in water through the gills, but not through the mouth. In order to avoid dangerously high levels of water in their bodies, the freshwater fishes continually excrete large quantities of water out of the body through the kidneys, thereby preventing excessive dilution of their body fluids and tissues.

Extraordinary diversity

Teleosts range throughout the waters of the world, inhabiting almost every aquatic habitat. They come in a variety of forms, from the fascinating and grotesque species of the cold, dark ocean beds to the highly specialized fishes that survive in warm springs. Eels, another unusual group of teleosts, occupy weedy, silted rivers of lowland Europe, but launch themselves out across the Atlantic to the Sargasso Sea to breed. Teleosts also occur as the colorful, darting fish of coral reefs, and the rare species of tropical streams, familiar in the bubbling living-room aquarium. They are an important source of food for humans too, some

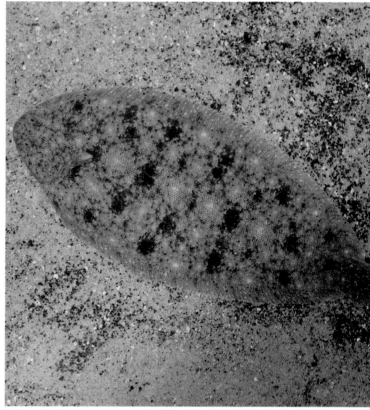

of the more familiar being the cods, plaice, haddocks and herrings that inhabit cool northern seas.

Buoyant fishes

Apart from efficient osmoregulation, the bony fishes display a number of additional adaptations that have enabled them to live successfully in diverse habitats. Fish float by maintaining the same specific gravity as the surrounding water—their weight must equal the weight of an equal volume of water. Because the specific gravity of their tissues is greater than that of water, teleosts would have difficulty floating. As a result, they have an adaptation called the swim bladder, which originally evolved from the lungs. By adjusting the gas pressure in the swim bladder, the teleosts alter the specific gravity of the whole body, enabling them to float at any chosen depth in the water without effort.

The higher concentrations of dissolved salts in seawater give it a higher specific gravity than that of freshwater. Consequently, sea fish only need a small swim bladder—it comprises 5 percent of the body size in sea fishes and about 10 percent in freshwater species. Primitive fishes, which do not have swim bladders, achieve buoyancy by depositing oil from their body tissues.

ABOVE LEFT AND ABOVE The various orders of teleosts differ greatly in appearance. An eel (above left) is snake-like in shape, with two sets of paired fins—pectorals at the front, behind the gill openings, and pelvic fins toward the rear. The sole (above) has a flattened body, with one side twisted around to form its back and the other its belly.

Streamlined tails

Many bony fishes have symmetrical (or homocercal) tails in which the upper and lower lobes of the tail fins are the same size. Together with their relatively short, compressed bodies, the tails enable the fishes to swim quickly with great maneuverability. The fastest swimmers, such as the mackerel and tuna, have deep, elegant, streamlined tails. The shape of their tail fins enables their tails to project above and below the backwash of their bodies as they move through the water. In sluggish fish like the gobies, the tail is blunter and more rounded in shape—rather than being divided into two deep, sharp lobes. The speed at which fishes swim varies considerably—while the goby moves slowly at only 2.5 mph, the superbly powerful and streamlined swordfish can reach 45 mph. Needless to say, the swordfish is a predator that few fish can outpace.

In contrast to the thick, hard scales of the bichirs and other more primitive bony fishes, the scales of the

Vivid colors

Teleosts have adapted a wide range of colors that act as camouflage in their natural habitats. Usually, color variation is a result of pigments produced by special cells (chromocytes) that mainly lie in the surface layer of the skin. Different chromocytes produce different colors—melanocytes contain black, dark red and brown pigments, xanthocytes contain yellow pigments and erythrocytes contain red pigments. The pigments are not wholly responsible for different body colorations. The silvery color of many fish, noticeable particularly when they twist and turn in the water, is caused by the reflection of light from guanine crystals in cells known as iridocytes.

Fishes that live in warm, clear waters are often very brightly colored—especially where different species are abundant—since coloration plays a crucial role in the recognition of potential breeding partners. But it is wrong to assume that all teleosts are brightly colored. The familiar flatfishes, for example, are dull on their upperparts so that they blend in with sand, pebbles or mud. They can change color rapidly to camouflage themselves from predators as they lie on the bottom. Fish that feed near the surface have dark upperparts and light underparts to provide camouflage.

Feeding and digestion

Teleosts have developed a wide range of feeding adaptations. In species that obtain their food from the bottom, the mouth is often extendible, and may have sensory barbels on it. The mouths of predatory fishes are well armed with sharp teeth for tearing at flesh or for grabbing prey before swallowing it whole.

At the point where the fish's stomach joins the intestine there are a series of finger-like structures (pyloric caeca). These greatly increase the surface area of the intestinal lining, improving the rate at which the food is digested and absorbed. The structures vary in number and arrangement according to species. The structure of the liver also varies greatly from one species to another. In some fishes it is a single, compact organ; in others, it is divided into a number of lobes. Some species have livers that are made up of several sections spread out between the other organs. In many fishes the pancreas, which produces digestive juices, consists of strings of cells distributed along blood vessels inside the liver, in the fat around the intestine and beneath the outer layer of the spleen.

ABOVE **The teleosts have a varied range of diets in their marine and freshwater habitats. Some teleosts, including some of the largest of the species, are vegetarian and feed on plankton that they filter** from the water. Others, **such as the member of the perch family shown here, feed on invertebrates such as worms and insect larvae, and some hunt fish that they tear apart with their sharp teeth.**

teleosts are thin and flexible. They vary greatly in shape, but divide into two basic types—cycloid or ctenoid. The cycloid scales of fishes such as perch have smooth surfaces and smooth, exposed edges. In comparison, the ctenoid scales that cover the body of the carp and spiny-finned fish families are rough, and have projections on their trailing edge.

Scales (not present in all teleosts) grow at a rate directly proportional to the overall rate of growth of the fish itself. In fishes that occur in seasonal habitats, zoologists can estimate when the overall growth of a fish has slowed down or stopped (for example, in the cold season) by examining its fins.

A film of mucus covers the body surface of the teleosts. It protects the underlying tissues from invasion by unwanted bacteria, fungi and other pests. Skin infections quickly occur in fishes deprived of this protective layer.

SUPERIOR SWIMMERS

Keeping afloat underwater

A cartilaginous fish, such as a shark, is not very buoyant, and has to keep swimming in order not to sink. Many teleost fishes have developed a device—known as the swim bladder—that makes constant swimming unnecessary (see p.1859). The swim bladder is basically an internal balloon filled with air. By adjusting the amount of air it contains, a fish can become more or less buoyant, rising or falling through the water at will. If necessary, it can hang in one place, quite motionless.

The swim bladder lies on top of the other internal organs and is fairly large, accounting perhaps for more than 10 percent of the fish's total body volume in freshwater species. Since it is a flexible sac, external pressure easily changes its shape; when a fish moves down to greater depths, the water pressure compresses the gas inside the swim bladder and reduces the degree of its buoyancy. To counter this effect, the fish has to increase the amount of gas in the bladder.

Some fishes fill their swim bladders by introducing gas from the digestive tract through an air duct; others inflate their swim bladders with gas released from the blood. To reduce the buoyancy of the swim bladder enabling the fish to sink, the gas is reabsorbed by a dense network of blood capillaries covering either a large or small part of the swim bladder wall.

The gases in the swim bladder are the same as those in the atmosphere—mostly oxygen, nitrogen and carbon dioxide. But the proportions of the mixture differ from that found in the atmosphere and also differ from species to species. The gas supply is

BELOW The trunk barb or flying fox is a member of the carp family and a popular tropical aquarium fish. The carps have excellent hearing. A chain of small bones links the inner ear to the swim bladder (known as the Weberian mechanism). Sound waves traveling through the water penetrate the fish's body and vibrate its swim bladder. The swim bladder amplifies the sound and transmits it down the chain of bones to the ear. In most fishes, a simple air duct links the swim bladder to the ear, a much less efficient arrangement.

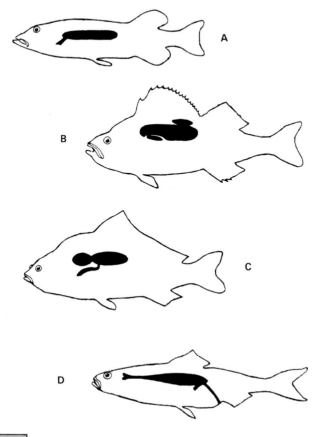

ABOVE The "lateral line" of this young perch is visible as a curved line along its flanks. It consists of external pores connected to a fluid-filled canal that acts as a pressure-sensitive device, detecting the movement of water and passing the information to the fish's brain.

LEFT The shape and location of the swim bladder vary between different species. The drawings show its position in a pike (A), a perch (B), a carp (C) and a dace (D).

tailored to each fish's needs, and varies according to its way of life. Among some deep-sea fishes, the contents of the swim bladder may range from almost pure nitrogen to pure oxygen.

Some teleost fishes, such as flatfishes, do not have swim bladders, since they live on the sea bottom and do not need to keep buoyant. Other fishes without swim bladders include certain fast-swimming fishes such as mackerel. As with the sharks, mackerel keep at the correct level in the water by swimming at speed (they cruise at up to 30 mph). It is likely that mackerel spend their whole lives swimming and never rest; if they did, they would sink to the seabed.

Sound signals

Several fishes produce sounds. Gurnards, for example, produce grunting noises by vibrating their swim bladders. The sounds they make can be surprisingly loud: during World War II, the noise of the gurnards was enough to confuse several underwater listening stations set up to detect enemy activity. Many of the drums—a family of mainly tropical fish—twitch special muscles to vibrate the walls of their swim bladders, producing loud, resonating sounds like drumbeats. Porcupine fish and horse mackerels grind their teeth to produce sounds that are then amplified by their swim bladders.

Fishes have good hearing, picking up sound waves as they enter the semicircular canals in the skull. The hearing of several thousand fish species is greatly improved because it is linked to their swim bladders. These organs of buoyancy are highly sensitive to the smallest change in pressure produced by underwater vibrations. A fish without a swim bladder can detect only the most powerful pressure variations, and as a result it cannot detect sounds from any distance away. A fish with a swim bladder can detect the tiniest pressure changes, allowing it to perceive high-frequency sounds from some distance. In these fishes the swim bladder is connected to the inner ear, either via an extension to the bladder itself, as in the herring, or via a series of small bones, as in the carp. The carp's hearing is so acute that it can hear treble tones with frequencies of up to 5000Hz (well above the top note on a piano).

Pores for detection

Teleost fishes make use of pressure waves in an echolocation system that helps them find their way, detect prey and evade predators. The system is based on the lateral line, a row of minute pores in the scales that run along the fish's flanks. These pores are connected to a fluid-filled channel that extends from head to tail. The channel itself is equipped with numerous tiny sensory receptors called neuromasts.

A pressure change in the fish's surroundings compresses the water in each pore, and this is detected by the neuromasts, which pass the message via nerve

cells to the brain for analysis. Such pressure changes occur when another animal comes near, or the fish swims past an obstacle. Minute variations in the pressure detected in each pore enable the fish to locate the source of the change precisely and assess its size and shape. It is this ability to sense nearby objects that allows fishes to navigate in the dark, and to move in perfect unison in a shoal.

Sight and smell

The eyes of a fish are basically similar to those of other vertebrates. Each eye has a transparent shield in front, an iris, a lens and a receptive retina well supplied with sensory cells and nerve endings at the back. The focusing mechanism is different, though. In a human eye, small muscles provide long-range and short-range focusing by changing the shape of the lens

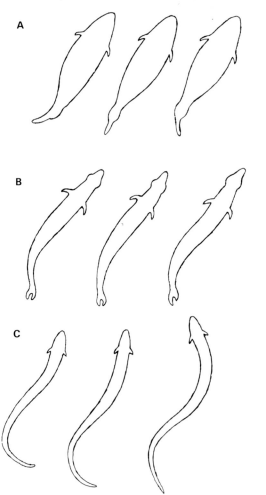

RIGHT Most fishes use their body fins as rudders and stabilizers, and they propel themselves through the water by flexing their bodies and tails. In some species, such as the tunas, only the tail moves (A). A mackerel flexes the rear end of its body to accentuate its tail-fin movement (B), while an eel drives itself along by undulating its whole body (C).

ABOVE Many bony fishes have fleshy barbels attached to their lips. These act rather like a cat's whiskers, detecting vibrations and enabling the fish to feel its way about in dark or cloudy water. The stone loach, a freshwater fish, feeds at night and uses its six long barbels to detect its prey (such as small shrimps). The barbels are well equipped with taste organs, enabling the fish to sample its food before taking it into its mouth.

itself. In a fish's eye, the whole lens moves in and out in relation to the retina, like the lens of a camera. The range of movement is restricted and most fishes are rather near-sighted.

Almost all fishes that have been studied have a good sense of smell. The nostrils are located on the fish's snout and open into a pair of olfactory pits lined with scent detectors. In fishes that detect their food mainly by smell, folds or finger-like structures increase the surface area of the lining. A flap of skin divides each nostril into two. The fish takes in water through the front opening, analyzes the chemical composition of the water with the scent detectors, and passes it out through the rear opening. When the fish is swimming, this water flow occurs automatically, but when it hangs motionless in the water—as a lurking pike might do, for example—the fish uses muscles to pump the water through its nostrils.

The fish's scent detectors are restricted to the inside of the olfactory pits, but its taste buds are more widely distributed. They occur inside and around the mouth, on the lips and whisker-like barbels, as well as on the head, gill arches and fins. In certain species, such as blind, cave-dwelling fishes, the taste buds cover most of the body.

Glands and hormones

The various glands that make up a fish's endocrine system, and the substances they produce, are of enormous importance to all the vital functions of the animal. Despite this, many of the glands are small or deeply embedded in body tissues, making them difficult to identify.

The pituitary gland is located in the fish's head, just below its brain. It secretes two types of hormones: those that trigger the activity of other glands, and those that regulate body processes, such as the activity of the chromatophores that are responsible for changes in the fish's skin color. It is these hormones that enable many fishes to change color to match their environment.

The thyroid gland is made up of a number of structures distributed in the area of the pharynx (the back of the mouth cavity). Its main function is to absorb iodine and other elements from the bloodstream in order to make thyroxin—the hormone that regulates the fish's metabolic rate. The thyroid gland also has some effect on growth.

Making adrenalin

The tissue that corresponds to the adrenal glands found in higher vertebrates is usually very extensive in fishes. Part of it, the adrenal cortex, is located in front of the kidneys, as in other animals. It produces substances that help break down food and maintain water balance. The remainder, the medulla, is scattered throughout the body and is responsible for producing adrenalin, the hormone that surges into the fish's veins when it is alarmed and gives it the ability to act quickly in an emergency.

Of the remaining endocrine glands, the most important are the ultimobranchial glands, arranged in a string under the gullet, which regulate the calcium content of the blood; the pancreatic cells, known as the islets of Langerhans, which are spread throughout the body and produce insulin for regulating the sugar level in the bloodstream; and the pseudobranchia,

ABOVE Gouramis, such as these pearl gouramis, have long, touch-sensitive antennae that have evolved from modified pelvic fin rays. Gouramis are freshwater fish, occurring mainly from India to the Malaysian Archipelago and Korea.

RIGHT Three spot or blue gouramis indulge in elaborate courtship rituals during the mating or spawning season. The males drive rival suitors away to ensure that they will not fertilize any of the female's eggs.

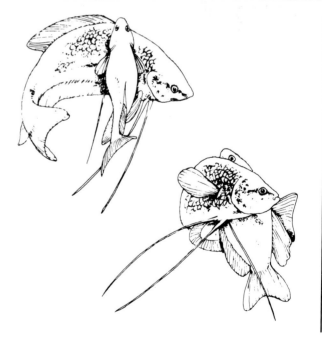

found on the internal surfaces of the gill covers, which control the blood circulation in the eyes.

Reproductive system

The male and female sex organs—the testes and ovaries—produce hormones that govern the many behavioral and anatomical changes that occur as the fish becomes sexually mature. They also produce the sperm cells of the male and the eggs of the female. When sperm and egg meet at the moment of fertilization, they fuse to form a fertile cell that develops into the embryo; this eventually becomes a young fish.

The reproductive organs (or testes) of male teleost fishes are mostly paired, usually whitish in color, and are suspended in the body cavity beside or below the swim bladder. In sexually mature individuals, they grow steadily larger throughout the year as the breeding season approaches. When fully grown, they can account for 10 percent of total body weight. The testes are formed from a mass of small tubes whose walls produce the sperm cells. These are carried in a milky fluid, called milt, that is ejected into the water through a sperm duct.

Paired ovaries

The female fish's ovary or ovaries vary in structure. The most complex occur in species that produce live young, since they are used not only for egg formation, but also to store the sperm introduced by the male and to act as a womb for the developing embryos. Most female fishes have two ovaries, shaped like elongated sacs, although they may be fused to form a single unpaired organ. Like the testes of the male, they change in size according to the season: immediately before egg-laying, they account for up to 50 percent of the female's body weight.

As with most other animals, the majority of teleost fishes are either male or female, but in several species the individual fishes are hermaphrodites, with both testes and ovaries. Usually, such fishes breed by fertilizing each other, but self-fertilization does, occasionally, occur.

Strange breeders

Certain fishes have developed extraordinary methods of reproducing. In some deep-sea angler fishes, the male is tiny (about 0.4 inch long) compared with the female, which may measure up to 39 in. long. When the male becomes mature, he latches onto the female with his teeth. In due course, the bodies and bloodstreams of the two animals fuse, so that food eaten by the female nourishes both animals. The male, meanwhile, becomes merely a sperm-producing appendage for the female. She uses his sperm to fertilize her own eggs, and becomes, in effect, a self-sufficient hermaphrodite. Some females may carry 5 to 10 males in this way.

Two other methods of reproduction have been observed among fishes, both in the laboratory and in the wild. One is known as parthenogenesis, in which the embryo develops from an unfertilized egg. In the other method, called gynogenesis, the sperm penetrates the egg and triggers its further development but does not actually fuse with it. In both cases, the male contributes nothing to the genetic makeup of the new individual and, as a result, the young are exact genetic copies, or clones, of their mother. The lack of variation means that each generation is identical with the last, and such species evolve very slowly, if at all.

Watery fertilization

Among teleost fishes that reproduce sexually, fertilization generally occurs externally: when the male and female mate, they eject eggs and sperm into the water where they mingle. Many eggs remain unfertilized, but females lay so many eggs that their loss is not significant.

In many species, the fishes leave the eggs to float freely, while others lay them on rocks or plants. In some species, the fishes lay eggs in nests and leave them to develop either unattended or watched over by one or both parents (usually the male). Those species that guard their eggs also often protect the young after they have hatched. Fishes that do not protect their eggs, such as cod, will produce up to several million eggs.

Internal fertilization is also relatively widespread (notably in cartilaginous fishes, such as the sharks and rays). The male introduces the sperm into the female's body during mating, as mammals do. Since far fewer eggs are lost this way, the fishes do not have to produce so many eggs. In many species, internal fertilization allows the females to keep the eggs inside their bodies until they hatch, so that the young are born live.

Classification

At first sight, the classification of the teleost fishes seems to be a haphazard affair, with many apparently dissimilar fishes grouped together. The order Salmoniformes for example, contains species as diverse as the pike and the rainbow trout. They are grouped together because they have small but significant similarities in their skeletons and internal organs. These similarities indicate a common ancestry that has become masked by later developments in shape, size and habits. The classification of fishes is under continual revision as more and more discoveries are made.

A TELEOST TRIO

The first three orders of teleost fishes include the 8 ft. 2 in.-long arapaima of South America—perhaps the largest freshwater fish in the world—the ocean-living tarpon and the scaled, deep-sea spiny eels

Between them, the bony-tongued fishes, the tarpons, and the notacanths (the first three orders among the teleosts) occupy most of the world's marine and freshwater habitats. They vary widely in appearance and habits.

The bony tongues

The bony-tongued fishes are a diverse order that includes some of the more unusual freshwater species—the immense arapaima, the flying butterfly fish and the curious featherbacks that must rise to the surface regularly to gulp in air. They are generally tropical, freshwater fishes that have toothed jaws. Bony-tongued fishes all exert the main bite on their prey by pressing the bones in their tongues against teeth on the roof of their mouths.

Bony-tongued fishes are large in size measuring up to 8 ft. 2 in. in length, and have prominent eyes and scales. They have long bodies with dorsal and anal fins placed well back on the trunk. One of the largest freshwater fish in the world is a bony-tongued species—the arapaima. Ranging throughout South America, Central Africa, the Malay Archipelago and Australia, it has several common names, depending on its distribution—it is known as the paiche in Peru and the pirarucu in Brazil. Despite claims that the arapaima grows to a length of 15 ft. and a weight of 375 lbs., zoologists have never captured an individual that exceeded 8 ft. 2 in. in length and 220 lbs. in weight.

The arapaima is a graceful, sinuous predator with unpaired fins set well back toward a primitive, lobe-like tail fin. It has a long, cylindrical body, a small,

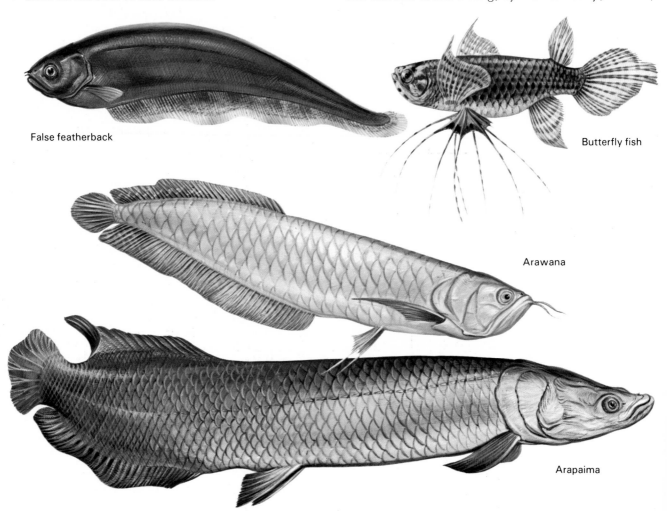

False featherback

Butterfly fish

Arawana

Arapaima

flattened head and a jutting lower jaw. The body color of the arapaima changes toward the tail. It is green in the front, but the rear half of the body becomes increasingly reddish before changing into crimson on the tail. Stout, bony scales cover the body, each containing canals that form a mosaic-like pattern.

Inhabiting shallow water, the arapaima usually cruises slowly but can produce a startling burst of speed. Occasionally, it rises to the surface to gulp air into its swim bladder, which opens by a duct into the back of the throat. The swim bladder is a large, rudimentary breathing apparatus that occurs above the alimentary canal and acts as a primitive form of lungs. It consists of cellular, lung-like tissue that is well supplied with blood vessels.

Although primarily a fish-eating predator, the arapaima will eat a wide range of aquatic creatures— water snails, shrimps, turtles, frogs and even snakes. It has developed adaptations to survive periods of drought when prey is scarce, using a modification in one gill raker to filter plankton.

The arawana, another bony-tongued fish, lives alongside the arapaima throughout its range. It is a smaller fish, seldom growing to more than 3 ft. in length, and often falls victim to its larger neighbor. The arawana is a mouth brooder and has a distinctive, acutely sloping jaw decorated with a pair of barbels.

The butterfly fish

At the other end of the size spectrum lies the small 4 in.-long butterfly fish, a high-leaping, bony-tongued fish that inhabits the rivers and swamps of the Congo and Niger basins in tropical West Africa. It is capable of leaping high out of the water, extending its large, wing-like pectoral fins to glide or fly for some distance. The shoulder girdle is broad and flattened to give support to a highly developed system of muscles.

The butterfly fish spends long periods of time swimming close to the surface of its freshwater habitat, trailing four long, separated rays from each pelvic fin as it hunts for surface prey. It is a small, flat-backed fish that lives in still, often stagnant waters.

The featherbacks

Named for their curious arrangement of fins, the six species of featherbacks inhabit slow rivers, swamps and canals in Southeast Asia and tropical Africa. Growing to a maximum length of 3 ft. 3 in., the

ABOVE The 8-ft.-2 in.-long arapaima is one of the largest species of freshwater fishes. It lives in shallow waters in South America where it occasionally surfaces to gulp in air.

PAGE 1867 Although only 4 in. long, the butterfly fish of West Africa can leap high out of the water with its wing-like pectoral fins extended, and can skitter over the surface.

___ OSTEOGLOSSIFORMES ___ CLASSIFICATION

The order Osteoglossiformes contains six families, with a total of 206 species in 26 genera. Freshwater fishes, they range over North and South America, Africa, southern and Southeast Asia and Australia. The family Osteoglossidae, the bony tongues, contains six species, including the arapaima, *Arapaima gigas*, and the arawana, *Osteoglossum bicirrhosum*. The butterfly fish, *Pantodon buchholzi*, is the sole member of the family Pantodontidae. It lives in parts of west and central Africa.

There are six species of featherbacks or knifefishes in the family Notopteridae. Occurring in tropical Africa and southern and Southeast Asia, they include the false featherback, *Xenomystus nigri*, and the species *Notopterus chitala*. The elephant snouts form by far the largest family in the order, with some 190 species distributed over most of sub-Saharan Africa and along the Nile Valley. They include the species *Marcusenius longianalis*; *Campylomormyrus curvirostris*; and *Gnathonemus petersi*. The Nile electric eel, *Gymnarchus niloticus*, is the only member of the family Gymnarchidae. It occurs in many parts of tropical Africa and along the Nile Valley.

Elephant snout (Marcusenius longianalis)

Nile electric eel (Gymnarchus niloticus)

Elephant snout
(Campylomormyrus curvirostris)

Elephant snout
(Mormyrus kannume)

Elephant snout (Gnathonemus petersi)

bodies of the featherbacks are long and flattened from side to side and usually brown in color. Their mouths are large with many small teeth, and they have a tentacle beside each nostril.

Featherbacks have distinctive anal fins that run along the underside of the fishes to join up with their small tail fins, forming a continuous curtain around the bottom of their bodies. The anal fins undulate to provide propulsion as the featherbacks swim.

Featherbacks are solitary fishes, resting by day among thick stems or under overhanging banks. While at rest, they float with their heads sloping downward. They are active at night, prowling the bottom in search of invertebrates and small fishes, including smaller members of their own species.

An electrical sense

The elephant snouts and the Nile electric eel use electricity as a means of assessing their immediate surroundings. The elephant snouts are large, bottom-dwelling fishes that range through the lakes, rivers and floodpools of Africa. Growing to a maximum length of 5 ft., they have slimy, thick-skinned bodies with elongated lips that form down-curved snouts for rooting in the river or lake bed.

The elephant snouts have deeply forked tail fins with long, narrow tail stalks. The tail stalks consist of muscle cells in a mass of clear, jelly-like tissue. These are modified to form electric organs that generate a continuous field of weak electrical discharges, creating a radar field around the fish. Distortions in the electric field allow the elephant snouts to interpret their surroundings, and detect approaching prey and potential mates among the sediment and mud of their murky habitat.

The electroreceptors in the brain of the elephant snouts are very large, giving it the largest brain of lower vertebrate animals. Large brains do not necessarily mean that the animals have greater intelligence, but aquarium keepers often report that elephant snouts are unusually playful, occupying themselves for hours with a leaf or a ball of tinfoil.

The Nile electric eel is closely related to the elephant snouts but has a different appearance. Growing to 35.5 in. in length, it has a distinctively long dorsal fin and lacks a tail fin. It swims by graceful undulations of the dorsal fin, and can reverse with the same speed and accuracy that it uses to move forward.

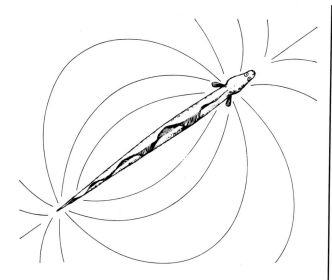

TOP The elephant snouts are bottom-dwelling fishes with long, downward-pointing snouts. When swimming in murky water, they send out electrical discharges from their muscles, creating weak electrical fields around themselves. Their brains then pick up disturbances in the field, enabling them to detect approaching prey or predators.
ABOVE The Nile electric eel creates an electrical field around itself that enables it to detect disturbances from nearby objects.

ELOPIFORMES AND — NOTACANTHIFORMES — CLASSIFICATION

The order Elopiformes contains three families: the Megalopidae, the tarpons; the Elopidae, the tenpounders; and the Albulidae, the bonefishes. There are 12 species, grouped in four genera, and they are found in most tropical waters. They include the Atlantic tarpon, *Tarpon atlanticus*; the Pacific tarpon, *Megalops cyprinoides*; the tenpounder, *Elops saurus*; and the bonefish, *Albula vulpes*.

There are also three families within the order Notacanthiformes, including the Halosauridae, the halosaurs and the Notacanthidae, the spiny eels. The order contains about 20 species placed in six genera, and they are distributed throughout the oceans of the world. They include the blunt-snouted spiny eel, *Notacanthus chemnitzii*, and *Halosauropsis macrochir*, one of the halosaurs.

ABOVE Atlantic tarpons migrate to coastal areas to spawn, and the young (or fry) remain in shallow water in swampy areas, including swamps and shallow lagoons, until they have completed their metamorphosis into mature adults. The gleaming silver scales of the adults are sometimes used to make unusual jewelry.

Glittering shoals

Tarpons are large, powerful, torpedo-like fish, covered with gleaming silver scales. They are found in tropical and subtropical waters along the Atlantic coast of America and tropical West Africa, and are remarkable in that they can live equally well in either fresh- or saltwater. The Atlantic tarpon is a valuable food source and weighs up to 353 lbs.

Tarpons often swim in large shoals. Females lay their eggs from late June to September in shallow seas. The young tarpons look completely different from the adults. The larvae are transparent, leaf- or ribbon-shaped and are called leptocephali (from the Greek *lepto* meaning "slender" and *cephalus* meaning "head"). The leptocephali are carried to the shore by the currents, where they metamorphose into young tarpons. Juvenile tarpons are often found in mangrove swamps or lagoons. When they reach maturity, they move out of the lagoons into the open sea where they can grow to over 6 ft. 6 in. in length.

The notacanths

The notacanths—the spiny eels and halosaurs—form a separate order of fishes. They are all deep-sea creatures, feeding on invertebrates that live on the ocean bed. Notacanths have elongated bodies that become gradually more narrow along their length, and end in thin, pointed tails. Some species have a tiny fin on the end of their tails. They have rounded or pointed snouts, and their mouths are located on the underside of their heads—an ideal position for foraging on the seabed.

The spiny eels have a row of spines on their backs that take the place of the dorsal fin. One species, the blunt-snouted spiny eel, lives in the seas around northern Europe, and is occasionally trawled up from the fishing grounds off Iceland. It can grow to 47 in. in length and lives at a depth of about 984 ft., where it feeds on sea anemones and other creatures attached to the seabed. It browses in a slanting, head-down posture to obtain a strong grip on its food.

The halosaurs are more slender in shape than the spiny eels, with longer snouts and a small dorsal fin instead of spines. Many species have conspicuous scales. They occur in deeper water than the spiny eels, usually being trawled up from depths of 1650-3300 ft. In the North Atlantic, they have been caught at depths of over 16,500 ft.

SERPENTINE MIGRANTS

Eels are renowned for their cylindrical, snake-like shape. They include the fiercely territorial moray eels and the European eel, whose tiny larvae make an epic 3000-mile journey from the Sargasso Sea to feeding grounds in Europe

Long, supple and slippery, the eels form an order called the Anguilliformes (a name derived from the Latin *anguis*, for snake). They lack pelvic fins and have fused dorsal, anal, and tail fins that form a continuous ribbon around their elongated bodies—differing in length according to the species. Their pectoral fins have lost the skeletal and ligament connection with their heads, as found in many other fishes, and their gills and gill chambers extend unusually far backward to small gill openings. Eels inhabit most waters throughout the world (they live in both fresh- and seawater), and they grow to a maximum length of 10 ft.

Most eel species are smooth and lack scales completely, although close inspection of some (the European freshwater eel, for example) reveals small, scattered, smooth (cycloid) scales deeply embedded in the skin. The long bodies of eels are extremely flexible, a feature often associated with bottom dwellers. Many species of eel spend their lives hiding in burrows and crevices, and are well practiced in backing into tiny spaces, burrowing headfirst in soft mud, or burrowing backward using their hardened tails.

Eels are formidable predators, either striking from the security of their lairs, or venturing out to hunt actively. Some are excellent swimmers, capable of making long migrations that may involve overcoming obstacles as hazardous as weirs or water meadows.

All eels pass through a larval stage, when they are thin and willow-leaf-shaped. Known as leptocephali, the larvae are so different to the adults that they were once thought to be a separate species. The larvae usually have the same number of vertebrae and muscle segments as the adults, so careful examination can reveal the species to which they belong.

Freshwater or marine

There are nearly 600 species of eels, contained in 19 families. Most of them live permanently at sea, with a few species entering freshwater to feed. Most of the 16 species in the freshwater eels family feed and develop in freshwater, migrating back to the sea many years later to breed. Other species, such as the snake eels, visit freshwater seasonally to feed in rivers and flooded areas. Most eels prefer to live in warm water. The species belonging to the two largest families (the moray and the worm eels) live in waters that may reach up to 68°F. However, the freshwater eels and the conger eels (which are totally marine) penetrate temperate waters. In some northern areas, congers live in shallow coastal waters, and thousands die if a sudden, large drop in temperature occurs in winter.

Variations in color and form

Eels change color during different stages of their lives—their backs may be black, brown, green or gray. Young eels or elvers of the freshwater eel family are usually dark on their backs and sides, with yellow bellies. Commonly known as "yellow eels" at this stage, they have blunt snouts with small eyes and large mouths. The elvers grow steadily in the freshwater rivers to which they traveled as larvae. The females can reach as much as 3 ft. 3 in. in length. Males tend to

ANGUILLIFORMES CLASSIFICATION

The eels of the order Anguilliformes form a large group with 597 species in 147 genera and 19 families. They range throughout the oceans, and some also occur in freshwater habitats. The family Anguillidae, the freshwater eels, contains 16 species, including the European eel, *Anguilla anguilla*, the American eel, *A. rostrata*, and the Japanese eel, *A. japonica*. The moray eels of the family Muraenidae comprise 110 species, including the Mediterranean moray, *Muraena helena*, the green moray, *Gymnothorax funebris*; and the zebra moray, *Echidna zebra*. The conger eels that make up the family Congridae number 109 species. Among these are the conger eel, *Conger conger*, and the garden eels, which belong to several genera, including *Gorgasia* and *Heteroconger*.

The large family Ophichthidae contains 236 species of snake eels, such as *Myrichthys oculatus*, while the 28 species of cutthroat eels in the family Synaphobranchidae include the snubnose parasitic eel, *Simenchelys parasiticus*. The family Nemichthyidae contains the nine species of snipe eels, including the snipe eel, *Nemichthys scolopaceus*. The swallowers make up the family Saccopharyngidae, with four species in the genus *Saccopharynx*, while the gulper eel, *Eurypharynx pelecanoides*, is the sole member of the family Eupharyngidae.

be smaller, rarely measuring more than 20 in. in length. As they reach sexual maturity, the elvers turn silver in color. At this stage in their development they are commonly known as "silver eels." Their bodies become very fatty, and they command high prices in fish markets. Although freshwater eels may reach a weight of 20 lbs., they generally weigh less.

Hunting and habitat

Eels live in nearly every type of freshwater habitat, from swift streams to the muddiest ditch and farm pond. They favor areas with muddy bottoms, or rocky areas full of nooks and crannies. Large numbers of eels can often be found in the thick weedbeds of warmish waters. Around the coast, eels favor estuaries and the mud holes that litter sand beaches between the tides and immediately below the low tide mark. Here, they establish their territories.

Eels rest by day and hunt by night. In freshwater, they feed on a wide variety of prey and have developed

ABOVE **A European eel wriggles over a flooded meadow in the course of its breeding migration to the sea. Because its gill openings remain firmly closed during the journey, the eel survives by absorbing oxygen through its wet skin. Migrating eels usually travel by night during the autumn months,** moving overland only for short distances.
PAGE 1873 **Garden eels spend most of their lives rooted to the seabed with the lower part of their bodies hidden in burrows in the sand, snatching food that is carried by the current. When not feeding, the eels retreat fully into their burrows.**

adaptations to suit their diet. There are two distinct types of young eel: some have pointed snouts and feed on small creatures such as worms, shrimps and insect larvae; those with broader snouts eat larger prey, such as crabs, bottom-dwelling fishes (such as loach, gudgeon and bullhead), sticklebacks, crayfish and frogs.

Male European eels reach sexual maturity after 7 to 12 years, while the females can take as many as 19 years to mature. Once mature, their

1875

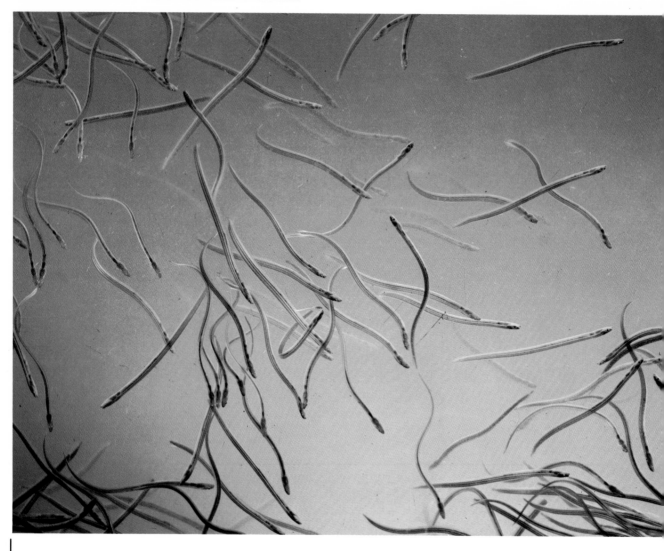

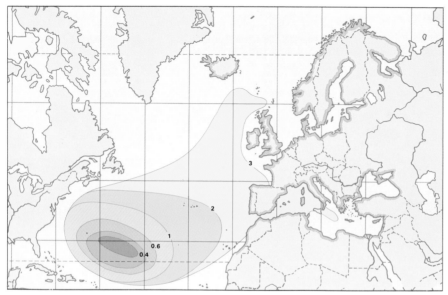

ABOVE AND LEFT The larvae (or leptocephali) of the European eels hatch in the Sargasso Sea in the west Atlantic where the waters are warm—up to 68°F—to great depths. The young eels drift toward the coast, which they reach after about three years. At this stage in their development, they are known as "glass eels," and can measure up to 6 in. in length. They are carried along the Gulf Stream from their breeding area (orange) to their home coastline around Europe (blue). The numbers indicate the length in inches of the larvae at various stages of their journey.

backs become a dark gray-black in color, while their sides and bellies turn bright silver. The eyes, normally quite small, enlarge greatly, their snouts become more pointed and their mouths decrease in size. "Silver eels" do not feed and, as a result, their lower jaw weakens. Gradually their stomachs shrink, making room for their developing sex organs.

In late summer, the European eels leave their freshwater ponds, pools and streams and make their way downstream to the sea to breed. Eels are capable of closing their small gill openings and obtaining as much as 60 percent of their oxygen requirements through their skin. Because of this, they are able to move overland through wet grass by night.

Breeding grounds

Scientists have only a limited knowledge of eel activity once they return to the sea, but it is thought that they swim in midwater, using up the stored fat in their bodies to swim and to form reproductive organs. They mate in deep water some 3100 mi. from the European coast, in an area of the western Atlantic known as the Sargasso Sea. After mating, the adult eels die. The eggs—which to date have not been seen—hatch into leptocephali, the small, transparent, blade-shaped larvae that drift with the ocean currents all the way to the shores of Europe, taking up to three years.

European eels are not alone on the Sargasso breeding grounds. A close relative, the American freshwater eel, also breeds there. The breeding grounds have not yet been traced for all the eel species. The Japanese eel has an unknown spawning ground, but it is known, however, that eels from the eastern part of southern Africa breed to the east of Madagascar.

Growth and metamorphosis

The leptocephali, or eel larvae, grow steadily and become distinctly more leaf-shaped. When they reach the continental shelf, they change shape and form. The larvae shrink in size as they metamorphose into the adult shape, and when they appear around the coasts, they are tiny, transparent creatures, commonly called "glass eels" or elvers. The elvers congregate in the thousands near estuaries, where they gradually acquire pigment in their skin and turn black. At this stage, they are miniature replicas of the adult eels.

The brackish water at river estuaries induces a change in the elvers' behavior. Instead of drifting

ABOVE Using pebbles to secure themselves against the current, a pair of elvers (young adult eels) pause in their migration upstream. As the elvers develop, they become blacker in color. A popular and highly nutritious food, many thousands of elvers are caught as they migrate and are taken to farms where they mature more quickly than in the wild.

passively, they start to swim upriver, against the current, and few natural obstacles can stop their progress. They exploit every tiny crack, rock crevice or damp "back route" to overcome areas of fast current. Males usually remain in the lower reaches of the river, in estuaries and coastal waters, while the females move higher up and may even migrate overland to lakes and ponds.

Male or female?

In the early 1970s, a Japanese research team discovered that the sex of an eel depends on the population density. Immature eels contain the organs of both sexes, and pass through successive stages of sexuality and neutrality prior to becoming male or female. The final sex of an eel is determined by environmental factors. In an overpopulated estuary, or in the overcrowded conditions of a commercial rearing tank, eels turn into small males.

THE EUROPEAN EEL
— MYSTERIOUS ORIGINS —

European freshwater eels have been creatures of mystery for over 2000 years, and it was not until the start of the 20th century that important discoveries were made concerning the location of their breeding grounds. Even today, much of their life cycle remains to be studied.

Theories from the past

Eels in the days of the ancient Greeks and Romans were plentiful, thriving in all but the coldest, fastest streams. They were thought to be different from all other fish because there was no evidence that they produced eggs and sperm at the start of the breeding season. Millions of eels had been caught and gutted for food, but no one had ever seen a recognizable baby eel of less than 6 in.

in length, or even an eel that contained roe, which would identify it as a female.

The ancient natural historians offered various suggestions as to where the eels might have come from. Aristotle (384-322 B.C.) maintained that eels were miraculously formed out of mud. Pliny the Elder (A.D. 23-79) wrote that eels were created from pieces rubbed from the skin of adults as they passed over sharp rocks. Some said that eels originated from horsehairs, others that they were the offspring of silver beetles.

The search for evidence

No progress was made in solving the mystery until 1777, when a Professor Mondini of Bologna University claimed to have found the ovaries along

the top of an eel's abdominal cavity. In 1788 a biologist by the name of Spallanzani stated that no freshwater eel he had ever seen showed these structures, but he recorded that eels instinctively tried to escape from traps and to head for the sea at certain times. Nearly a century later, the Polish biologist Syrski found male reproductive organs in an eel. The discovery was made in a fairly large specimen. The search then moved in the direction of large eels, but since males are seldom larger than 20 in., it was a fruitless investigation. In 1903 a typical male and female were caught and positively identified at sea, thus confirming that eels bred and laid their eggs at sea.

The larval stages of the eels, however, had still not been recognized for what they were, although one had been discovered in 1763 by a zoologist named Theodore Gronovius. It had been identified as a separate fish species, and named Leptocephalus morrisii. The transparent, willow-leaf-shaped creature, caught off Holyhead, bore little resemblance to an eel.

In 1896 two researchers named Grassi and Calandruccio caught two leptocephalus larvae and put them in a tank. Before long, the larvae turned into eels. The thin, leaf-like larvae have been called leptocephali ever since.

Discovery of the breeding grounds

The eels' breeding grounds at sea remained unknown. Constant sampling by ships in the Mediterranean and Atlantic revealed that the leptocephali were smaller toward the western Atlantic. The spawning grounds of the European eel were finally traced by a Dane, Johannes Schmidt, who spent years painstakingly plotting larva sizes. He finally found a specimen that measured only 0.4 in. long in an area south of Bermuda known as the Sargasso Sea. Subsequent research has established that the European eel probably breeds at moderate depths, where the water temperature is about 68°F. The Sargasso Sea is one of the few areas where such a high temperature is maintained at some depth.

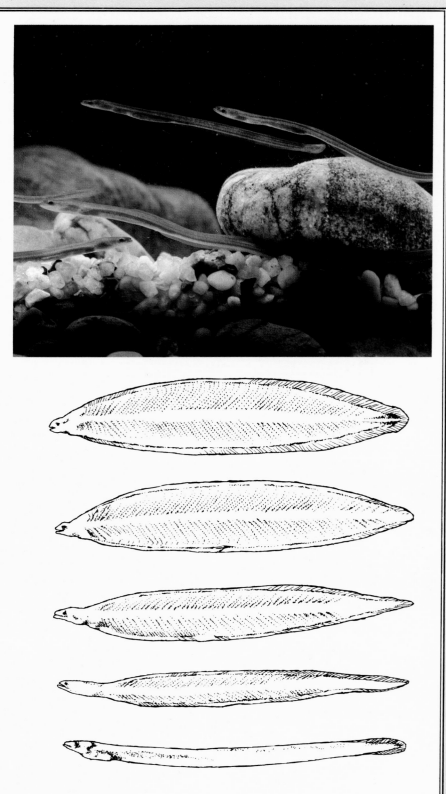

RIGHT During metamorphosis, the leaf-shaped leptocephalus (top) progressively shrinks to form the slimmer elver or young adult (bottom).

ABOVE RIGHT Small, transparent elvers instinctively move upstream in search of places to feed and grow before they return to the western Atlantic on their own breeding migration.

LEFT As the time for the breeding migration to the Sargasso Sea approaches, the upperparts of the eel turn a dark gray-black in color and the sides become silvery-gray.

ABOVE Moray eels, such as this species *Echidna nebulosa*, are carnivorous and highly territorial. They are quick to defend their homes in the coral reefs against intruders.

RIGHT Although non-venomous, moray eels have sharp teeth and a powerful bite. They are voracious feeders, and will eat almost any animal that they can swallow whole.

The moray eels

Found in the Mediterranean and all tropical seas, the family of moral eels are the most abundant and widespread of all the eels. There are around 110 species, ranging from 6 to 118 in. in length. They have thick, leathery skins, a distinct shoulder hump behind their heads, and large mouths armed with teeth that vary from blunt crushers to needle-sharp, piercing fangs, so long that the eels' mouths cannot close.

Many species of moray eel are patterned and brightly colored, ranging from the body-wrapping stripes of the zebra moray from the Indo-Pacific to the map-like mottlings of the Mediterranean moray. They are also known as painted eels. The green moray has a blue-gray skin, but the yellowish algae that covers it gives the eel a variable greenish hue. Sometimes the green moray appears brown, due to colonization by another species of algae. Many morays lack obvious fins, making them look more like snakes than fish.

Moray eels live in fairly shallow water (down to 14 ft. in depth) and are active by night. They spend their days lying in holes, tunnels, and crevices, with only their heads showing. They are not strong swimmers, and are rarely found in the open sea. Morays eat a wide variety of prey, such as crabs, fishes and octopus; their favorite prey, however, is the shellfish, abalone. As long as their bodies are secured against something solid, they are capable of a very swift and snake-like downward strike with the first third of their bodies. Morays do not appear to migrate to breed, although they do pass through a leptocephali or larval stage.

Dangerous eels: fact and fable

Morays have an aggressive appearance. They have large heads, watchful eyes and open, tooth-lined jaws that emit a territorial warning to any passers-by. Although the display of teeth serves as a warning, their open mouths also function in their respiratory system—they pump water over their gills quite energetically.

When attacking, morays bite once and release their victim. Although their bite is reputed to contain venom, they do not actually have venom glands. However, rotting particles of past meals that remain on their teeth may cause poisoning or infection. There are many tales of persistent morays holding people underwater—but the tales are unlikely to be true since morays take food in one bite-sized piece. They are unable to breathe and grip with their mouths at the same time. Moray eels should, however, be treated with the respect any well-armed predator with a territory deserves. There have been incidents when morays have been openly aggressive. For example, when the exploration raft *Kon-Tiki* was wrecked on a coral atoll in the Pacific, its occupants were driven from the lagoon by morays.

The conger eels

The conger eel family comprises 109 species. They are large creatures with pectoral fins and stout, muscular bodies. Although found at most levels in tropical and temperate oceans, they prefer shallower water. The conger eel is the best known of the conger eel family. It is a muscular eel, brown above and gold to white underneath in shallow water, and lighter brown above and gray below in deeper water, with a partial black border on its dorsal fin. It grows to impressive dimensions and can reach up to 9 ft. long, weighing up to 145 lbs.

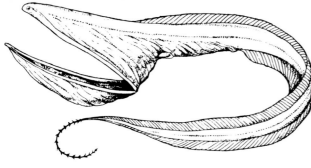

TOP **The Mediterranean moray eel commonly has a gaping mouth since it needs to pump water over its gills during breathing. As a result, the eel appears to be either threatening or panting.**
ABOVE **The gulper eel grows to about 34 in. in length and inhabits the depths of the Pacific, Indian and** Atlantic oceans. **The fish is adapted to eating whatever it can find in the inky waters: its enormous mouth may be a quarter of its body length, it can unhinge its jaws, and its belly can expand to several times its normal size, allowing the gulper to swallow prey larger than itself.**

Conger eels live from the tidal zone to a depth of approximately 400 ft. They prefer to settle on the seabed in areas of rough ground where they can establish a territorial hole or lair. The artificial habitats created by piers and sunken ships are ideal, presenting a multitude of places in which to live, at the same time as attracting plenty of prey. Congers eat a wide variety of fish (especially bottom dwellers), as well as taking crabs, lobsters and octopus. Shallow-water congers move by night, but those that live in deeper waters or around shipwrecks are more dependent on tidal movements, and usually feed around slack water by day or night.

Mating in captivity

Conger eels migrate to deep water to breed in distinct breeding grounds. One of these exists between Gibraltar and the Azores at depths of 10,000-13,000 ft. Other breeding areas occur in the Mediterranean and serve local populations of congers. There are few records of migrating congers, but studies of those kept in captivity indicate that they degenerate greatly before breeding. The teeth soften and fall out, the skeleton decalcifies and becomes soft, the muscles waste away, the body fat is used up and the skin ulcerates. Known as "rubber eels," they seem barely capable of mating. Because of their weak condition, it is thought that they breed before the extremes of degeneration have set in. The eggs hatch into larvae, and their journey to inshore waters takes one to two years. Before assuming adult shape, the larvae are 5 in. long. By the time they appear as tiny eels, they are only 3 in. long.

The conger family also contains bathymyrinid eels, pike congers and garden eels. The best known of the bathymyrinid eels is *Ariosoma bowersi*, a 16-in.-long silver inhabitant of the sandy shallows around Hawaii. It has developed transparent tissue to protect its eyes while it burrows. The pike congers grow to over 6 ft. 6 in. long, and have large fangs in their jaws. Pike congers are widely distributed in shallow, warm waters, entering rivers occasionally.

The garden eels are notable for their curious colonial life-style. Groups of these 20-in.-long eels build burrows at regular intervals in the sand, and spend much of their lives with the upper two-thirds of their bodies waving above the sand, the lower third concealed. They feed on the small, floating animals and plants that are carried by the current, and they retreat into their burrows if disturbed. Their coloration reflects their life-style—the front parts of their bodies are dark, and their tails are pale.

Garden eels dig their burrows tail-first, using a hard point at the end of their tails to break through the sand. They line the burrows with mucus from their skin that makes it easier for them to slide in and out of their holes. The security provided by the burrows is so important that the animals may not even leave them when they mate. Studies of a garden eel colony in the Red Sea revealed neighboring males and females stretching across toward one another and intertwining the top halves of their bodies with their tails still anchored in the sand. A small number of eggs

ABOVE Inhabitants of the Atlantic Ocean, conger eels are a nocturnal species that hide beneath rocks and in crevices during the day. Males grow to about 31 in. long, but the females usually measure 47-59 in. and may weigh over 154 lbs. They can be distinguished from freshwater eels by their lack of scales. Conger eels have powerful, toothed jaws with which they catch their prey, including flatfish, herrings and dogfish, as well as some crustaceans.

RIGHT A colony of garden eels sways in the current, feeding on planktonic organisms. Garden eels inhabit sand beds in the warmer oceans. If a predator, such as a ray, approaches, the whole colony slips down into their burrows as the enemy passes across the sand.

were fertilized each time the animals linked together, and a pair of eels would repeat the process up to 20 times in one day.

The snake eels

The snake or worm eels make up a family comprising 236 species. They are small, slim-bodied eels, many are brightly colored, and they have an unusual habit of burrowing backward into the soft mud. Many snake or worm eels have sharp, pointed tails that lack fins. Their size and habits make them exceptionally difficult to catch and study, so little is known about these fishes except that they live in the warm oceans of most of the world.

Eels of deep water

Several eel families live in deep water, both in the mesopelagic (800-3500 ft. in open ocean) and

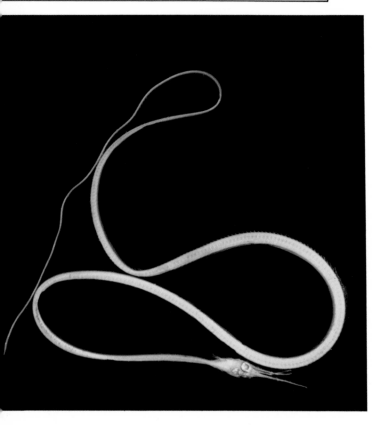

ABOVE The snipe eel is a large-eyed, extremely elongated creature that occurs in warm waters at depths of 1150-6600 ft. It can measure as much as 48 in. in length. Only the females and young of both sexes have the distinctive long jaws. The males have short jaws and were, until recently, regarded as a separate species of deep-sea eel.

bathypelagic (deeper) zones. Members of the cutthroat eel family are small—they seldom exceed 3 ft. in length—sharp-headed and have long jaws. They live at depths of 3300-13,000 ft. Most of them lead predatory life-styles, but one species has taken to parasitism in a manner similar to the primitive hagfishes (see pp. 1815-1824). The snubnose parasitic eel grows to about 24 in. and lives at depths of 1650-4500 ft. off the American Atlantic coast, the Azores and Japan. It cuts its way into the bodies of dead and dying fish (especially halibut), then eats its way through the organs of the body.

Snipe eels and sawtooth eels

The snipe eels are deep-sea eels. They are long and thin, growing to about 47 in., and have bird-like heads. The females and young fish have long, thin jaws lined with fine teeth, while the males have short jaws. Snipe eels live between 1148 and 6600 ft. deep and are so fragile that the few specimens taken are of little help to research. Although not closely related, the 10 species of sawtooth eels are similar in appearance. They live from 3300 to 10,000 ft. deep in the Atlantic, Pacific and Indian oceans. They appear to move in groups, feeding on shrimps and lantern fishes, and are themselves consumed by larger species. They have been found in the stomachs of cods in the North Atlantic.

The gulper

The gulper eel—the only member of its family—has the largest mouth in a large-mouthed group. Its long, whip-like tail starts almost where the mouth stops and the gills open nearer to the vent than the snout.

The gulper is most common in the Atlantic Ocean at depths of 1800-13,000 ft. It swims in midwater, rather than on the bottom. A 24-in.-long predator, it eats small fishes, shrimps and worms. Its hunting method is a mystery, since its tail lacks the power to propel it forward at any speed, and the tissues of its mouth appear far too flimsy to withstand a struggle. The tip of its tail is luminous, so the gulper may use it to lure its prey.

The swallowers

The four species of swallowers are larger fishes with comparatively small mouths. They make up for this, however, by having jaw hinges that allow an enormous gape and they have expandable stomachs that enable them to swallow a fish a third longer than their own body length. Large specimens may reach 71 in. in length, placing them among the larger deep-sea fishes. They live as deep as 10,000 ft.

Swallowers have a number of unusual anatomical features. Their lateral-line sense organs are not embedded in the sides of their bodies—instead, each lies at the end of a short stalk that protrudes into the surrounding water. Such an arrangement is thought to make it easier for the fish to detect vibrations in the water, enabling them to detect the presence of their prey in the darkness. Like the gulper, the swallowers have luminous tail organs that give off a steady pinkish light, although it it not known what purpose these serve. Their gill chambers are also unusual in that they are partially covered by skin. Rows of curved teeth line the jaws of eels, making it difficult for victims to escape once they have been caught.

SILVERY SHOALS

Herrings and anchovies are among the most familiar marine fishes in the world. Easily trawled because of their shoaling habits, their numbers have greatly declined through overfishing, leading to the collapse of the fishing industry in many regions

The order Clupeiformes contains four families, including the herrings and anchovies, and comprises some 330 species. The herrings form by far the largest family—about 200 species varying in size, growth rate and migration habits. Some of the herrings are among the most primitive of the teleosts. Herrings are mainly small, shoaling fish that occur in vast numbers in the surface waters of almost all the oceans of the world. As such, they provide food for a wide variety of marine predators, such as the various species of tuna.

The herring (of which there are several races) is fairly typical of the herring family. It is built for speed, with a slender, streamlined body covered with a smooth layer of large, fragile scales. Each of the scales—which are easily displaced during handling—contains growth rings that indicate the fish's age. Mature fish have rounded bellies, but young fish have a blade-like keel with a serrated edge formed from shield-shaped scales. These are particularly noticeable in other members of the family, such as the shads, where they occur on older fish as well as juveniles.

Coloring and camouflage

The herring's back is deep greenish-blue, fading to silvery-white on its belly. Its silvery flanks and gill covers are shot with green, violet and rose tints. (The lateral line cannot be detected visually, although it is present beneath the skin.) Such a color scheme is typical of surface-living species that spend their lives in open water off the coast. In the upper layers of the deep sea, the sunlight from above lights up the back of the fish, leaving its sides and belly in the dark. When lit from above, the dark upperside of the herring appears the same tone as the pale but shadowed underside. As a result, it appears to have no shading and its rounded shape is masked. Its camouflage is enhanced by the greenish blue color of its back. The effect of the camouflage depends on the fish maintaining its normal upright swimming position. If the herring rolls onto its side, owing to illness or weakness, it immediately loses its disguise and becomes an easy target for predators.

The herring's single, short dorsal fin, like its other fins, is supported only by soft rays, and is situated near the center of the fish's back. Its tail is symmetrical—the two lobes of the tail fin are the same size and shape. The anal fin is located near the tail, the pelvic fins are beneath the dorsal fin, and the pectoral fins are low down, immediately behind the gills.

The herring has large eyes and a fairly small mouth, with its lower jaw projecting beyond the upper. Inside its mouth, it has small teeth and a dense fringe of long, fine spines on each gill arch. These form a net that it uses to catch small floating organisms, such as fish larvae, algae, shellfish larvae and tiny shrimp-like crustaceans. These minute creatures occur in enormous drifting clouds known as plankton. The herring swim through the clouds, sieving the water through their gills to filter out the edible items.

Shoals of silver

Plankton is a rich food source capable of feeding extremely large animals, and many plankton feeders are giants. The basking shark and baleen whales are examples. Although herrings are fairly small fish (rarely longer than 16 in.), they take advantage of the riches available by congregating in vast shoals, sometimes containing several thousand tons of fish. (These huge shoals are now often depleted due to overfishing.) The individuals in the shoal swim in unison, all turning at once and accelerating away from danger in perfect formation. They are able to do so because their lateral-line organs monitor the position of adjacent fish by continually assessing the pressure waves they create; the slightest change in the pattern is transmitted to the nervous system and causes the fish to make an immediate correction.

Herrings have a keen sense of hearing. The fine-walled swim bladder in a herring has a pair of narrow sacs that extend forward and surround its inner ear. Any vibrations picked up by the swim bladder are transmitted directly to the eardrum, enabling an individual fish to orientate itself within the shoal.

All these features are typical of the other herring-like fishes, such as the sprat, pilchard, sardine, shad and anchovy. The wolf herring (which belongs to a separate family of its own) has rather different feeding habits. As its name suggests, it is a predator, and it has long fangs and a large appetite. The wolf herring is by far the largest member of the order, growing to more than 11 ft. long, but it is of little commercial value.

Collective reproduction

The shoaling habit of most of the herring-like fishes is maintained and even strengthened during the

breeding season. As a result, the fish have no need to resort to elaborate ways of attracting a mate, since their future mates are already swimming alongside them.

Most species in the herring family lay their eggs during the warmer months of the year in open water, although spring-spawning herrings move inshore. The females shed their sticky eggs close to the bottom, where they fall to the seabed and form a dense mat, often several eggs thick. The newly hatched larvae measure about 0.2 in. in length. They are attracted to the surface by the light, and feed on microscopic floating animals and plants in the plankton. The young herrings form part of the shoals of plankton themselves, and are in some danger from other plankton-feeding fishes, sea birds, seals and dolphins. As they grow, they form large shoals.

The spawning of herrings

The spawning of the thousands of fish in each shoal is so well synchronized that it suggests they lay their eggs in response to stimulants emitted into the water. Experiments have been carried out on the Pacific herring, both in captivity and in the wild along the coasts of British Columbia in Canada. The experiments show that when herring sperm are introduced into a

ABOVE A trio of gold spot herrings—named for the yellow spots near their gill openings—show the silvery scales and streamlined body shape typical of members of the herrings and anchovies order.
PAGE 1885 Herring swim in vast shoals containing millions of fish. All the fish in the shoal swim in the same direction and change course at the same instant. They can do this because their lateral-line organs give each fish an instant awareness of the movements of its neighbors. In the same way, they can detect predators and take evasive action.

tank of fish during the spawning season, fish of both sexes start to spawn almost immediately. They have no courtship ritual, and in the Pacific the spawning takes place well inshore, in the intertidal zone between the high and low tidelines. Each female rolls over on one side, extends her fins and starts to beat her tail with increasing frequency as she rubs her genital region over rocks, water plants and other submerged objects. The eggs appear in strings and stick to the rocks and plants. The male swims beside or behind the female while she is laying, and releases his sperm over the eggs to fertilize them. When a large shoal is spawning, the milky sperm turns the water thick and cloudy.

Shads

Some of the herring-like fishes—for example, the shads—have abandoned coastal waters as a breeding ground, exchanging them for the gravel beds of rivers. Shads are large-headed, heavily built fishes with deep, laterally flattened bodies. The twaite shad and the allis shad are both European varieties. They grow to maximum lengths of 22 in. and 24 in., respectively. The allis and the twaite shad are similar in appearance, but can be distinguished by the number of gill rakers on the first gill arch. The twaite has 40-60, while the allis shad has as many as 80-130. Both species enter rivers in the spawning season. The twaite shad migrates to the brackish tidal reaches, but the allis shad swims upriver to freshwater where it spawns in fast-flowing currents, usually at night. Once the eggs have been laid and fertilized, the adult fishes return to the sea.

The scarcity of shads

Both the twaite and allis shads have become scarce in recent years, owing to the problems they encounter when trying to reach their spawning grounds in rivers. Pollution is a particular problem in the lower reaches of rivers, while canals, locks, weirs and dams all present barriers that can prevent many fish from achieving the upper reaches of the rivers. The allis

**ABOVE Like all the herring-like fishes, the North American anchovy of the eastern Pacific is very prolific: the female of this small (7 in. long) fish can produce up to 20,000 eggs a year and is capable of breeding during the first year of life. Despite this, the numbers of all these fishes have declined due to overfishing.
FAR LEFT A dense shoal of thread herrings winds through a coral reef off the coast of the Bahamas.**

shad is the more vulnerable of the two and has almost disappeared from British waters.

Dwarf races of the twaite shad live in the Lakes of Killarney in southwest Ireland (where it is known as the goureen) and in several large, deep, glacial lakes in northern Italy and Switzerland such as Lakes Garda, Como, Lugano and Maggiore. Since they are landlocked, the shad never return to saltwater.

Freshwater shad

The Lake Maggiore shad has been studied in some detail. Like the twaite shad, it has a series of prominent black spots along its silver flanks and no visible lateral line. It becomes sexually mature at two years old, when it is about 7 in. long. It breeds in July along sand or gravel shores, in very shallow water. Lake Maggiore shad often spawn together in great numbers—particularly at night. Immediately before spawning their sexual organs account for 14 and 16 percent of the total body weight in males and females, respectively. At the end of their second year, the fish measure about 8 in. long, reaching an average maximum length of 11 in. at three years old. Their life spans are quite short, and they rarely live longer than four years. Older specimens may grow to 20 in. long, but this is unusual.

Outside the breeding season, Lake Maggiore shad congregate in shoals in the upper layers of the lake. The depths at which they occur vary according to the season, but the shoals rarely swim deeper than 98 ft. They are filter feeders like herrings, and feed almost exclusively on planktonic crustaceans such as copepods and water fleas. However, large specimens may abandon this diet in favor of other prey, including small fish such as young bleak (a member of the carp family found in slow-moving rivers and lakes in Britain and mainland Europe).

CLUPEIFORMES CLASSIFICATION

Fishes of the order Clupeiformes are classified in four families that occur in most seas, with some species inhabiting freshwater. There are a total of 331 species in 68 genera. The largest family is the Clupeidae, the herrings, with 190 species. Worldwide in their distribution, they include the herring, *Clupea harengus*, which has a number of different races such as the Norwegian herring and the Baltic herring; the sprat, *C. sprattus*; the pilchard, *C. pilchardus*, which is sometimes known as the sardine; the Atlantic menhaden or mossbunker, *Brevoortia tyrannus*; the allis shad, *Alosa alosa*; the twaite shad, *A. fallax*; and the Pacific sardine, *Sardinops sagax*.

The anchovy family, the Engraulidae, also has a worldwide distribution. It contains 139 species, including the anchovy, *Engraulis encrasicolus*, and the anchovetta, *E. ringens*. The other two families in the order have only one species each. The denticle herring, *Denticeps clupeoides*, is the sole member of the family Denticipitidae, and is restricted to rivers in southwest Nigeria. The wolf herring, *Chirocentrus dorab*, forms the family Chirocentridae, and is found in the western Pacific and the Indian Ocean.

The historic herrings

Few other fish have made such a mark on history as the herring. The vast shoals that once occurred in the North and Baltic seas were the basis of fisheries that supported the economies of nation states. International rivalry for rights to fish herrings led to wars that redrew the map of northern Europe.

The vast shoals of herrings and anchovies are preyed on by a range of predators, including other fishes, birds, dolphins, seals—and humans. With some 340 species distributed worldwide, the members of the herring and anchovy families account for a third of the total world fish catch. Half of this enormous tonnage is processed for oil or ground into fish meal for use as fertilizer and animal feedstuffs. Of the rest, the Atlantic and Pacific herrings are still important as a food fish. In the Mediterranean, the pilchard (known as the sardine) and the anchovy make up most of the catch.

The importance of anchovies

The 140 or so anchovy species are distributed widely throughout tropical and temperate seas in both the Northern and Southern hemispheres. Although relatively small—usually no more than 6 in. in length—they are an important food fish, often sought for their oil. One of the most exploited species is the anchovetta, which is caught in huge numbers in the southern Pacific Ocean, off the west coast of South America. Natural fluctuations in the populations of these fish have on occasions all but destroyed the South American fishing industries. Despite this, their exploitation continues on a scale that threatens not only the anchovetta itself—and the fishery based on it—but also the many other animals that eat it.

The anchovetta is the main food of many sea birds, chiefly guaney, cormorants, Peruvian boobies and the Peruvian pelican. The quarrying of guano (accumulated bird droppings), an important industry in Peru and Chile, has been badly hit by a fall-off in the bird population—a decline that can be directly traced to the increasing scarcity of the anchovetta.

The species of herrings found in landlocked lakes have also supported thriving—if smaller—fishing industries. For example, the shad found in the lakes of northern Italy have been an important part of the diet of local lakeside communities for centuries, owing to the fish's abundance and suitability for preservation by drying and salting.

FINS IN FRESHWATER

Carps, characins and catfishes belong to a huge order that comprises almost three-quarters of the world's freshwater fishes. Often large fish, they have conquered most rivers and lakes

LEFT Milkfish thrive in captivity because they are able to withstand extremes of temperature and are not cannibalistic. As a result, they are farmed for food in many parts of Southeast Asia. From March to May, the milkfish run into shallow water to lay their eggs. The young are then caught and placed in coastal ponds to breed.

PAGE 1891 Having been introduced into many parts of the world outside its natural range, the carp is now one of the most widespread of all freshwater fishes. It is prized by anglers, and in ideal conditions can grow to over 3 ft. in length.

Freshwater habitats—lakes and rivers—constitute less than one-thousandth of the world's water, yet they provide homes for more than a third of all living fish species. Moreover, nearly three-quarters of all freshwater fishes belong to a single superorder that includes the familiar carps, characins and catfishes. These fishes share two important sensory features. With only a few exceptions, they can communicate by means of chemicals, and they have a sophisticated hearing system that can detect the smallest vibrations in the water.

The carps and their relatives use chemicals mainly as a defense mechanism. Their skins have specialized cells that contain chemical substances known as pheromones that induce fear. If a fish is injured, its pheromones are released into the surrounding water and nearby fishes detect it and scatter for cover. Fishes possess pheromones in their cells from the moment they hatch, but they have to learn their responses to them. An injured young fish, for example, provides a warning to adults, but not to other young. However, the young quickly learn to associate warning scents with the need to escape from danger.

Acute sense

Fish pick up vibrations in the water through two sets of organs—their ears and their lateral lines. Carps, catfishes and characins possess a system of amplification that links their swim bladders with the liquid-filled chambers of their inner ears, giving them acute hearing. In this system, known as the Weberian mechanism, the first four vertebrae immediately behind the skull of the fish have developed into a series of levers that transmit sound waves received by the swim bladder to the middle ear. The exact function of the Weberian mechanism is not known, although it may provide an early warning system against predators and a means of communication.

Fishy sounds

The satinfin shiner, a North American minnow, produces at least two kinds of sounds—a high-pitched purr as it releases bubbles (probably from the swim bladder) and a sharp knocking when males are fighting. Male blacktails and red shiners, close relatives of the satinfin shiner, can distinguish between the calls of their respective mates (demonstrating that sound enables different species to identify each other).

Catfishes also have a repertoire of sounds and responses. One species has extensions to its vertebrae that are connected to the swim bladder and are controlled by powerful muscles. By moving these muscles, the fish can generate sounds in the swim bladder. Another species of catfish makes grunts that can be heard out of the water over 98 ft. away. Fishermen in the Danube River exploit the European wels because of its responsiveness to sound. Using

GONORYNCHIFORMES CLASSIFICATION

The order Gonorynchiformes contains four families with a total of about 27 species in seven genera. They occur in the Indian and Pacific oceans and in freshwater habitats in tropical Africa. The milkfish, *Chanos chanos*, is the most well-known species, and the sole member of the family Chanidae. Another single-species family is the Gonorynchidae, which contains only *Gonorynchus gonorynchus*. Most members of the order belong instead to the family Kneriidae, including fishes of the genera *Cromeria* and *Kneria*.

a specially shaped stick, they make hollow glugging noises to attract the fish. It is not known whether the wels is drawn to the sound intending to chase an imaginary intruder or to join it in feeding.

A large proportion of freshwater habitats are murky, preventing proper communication among fishes. The catfishes are among the species most well adapted to muddy conditions. They have sensory barbels, sometimes of considerable length, that enable them to explore their habitat.

A resolute survivor

The milkfish and its relatives constitute a diverse order of fish placed between the herrings and the carps. The milkfish, the only member of its family, is a hardy inhabitant of coastal, brackish, and occasionally freshwater habitats in the Indian and tropical Pacific oceans. It is a remarkable creature, able to live in water that is low in oxygen, heavily salinated and extremely warm (as high as 105°F).

Similar to the herring in appearance, the milkfish grows to a length of 6 ft., has a long body flattened from side to side and is covered with small, silvery scales. The tail fin is deeply forked, and the single dorsal fin is high and sharply pointed. The upperparts of the milkfish are blue to bluish olive, the head is yellow and the flanks and underparts are white.

Milkfish are of considerable commercial importance in Southeast Asia as a source of food, particularly in the Philippines and Indonesia where they are reared in extensive fishpond nurseries. Between March and May, the milkfish enter shallow, sandy bays and estuaries to breed. The female lays up to 6 million floating eggs in clear water; they hatch after 24 hours, but the shoals of 0.4 inch-long fry remain inshore, making them easy to catch in scoop nets. The fry are often then transferred to brackish rearing pools where they are cultivated by artificial feeding. The ability of the milkfish to withstand high water temperatures makes them easy to farm. As their small pools dry up in summer (often finding a second use as salt evaporation sites), farmers transfer the fish to larger ponds, where they graduate to a diet of plants.

Familiar food fish

Carp, tench, barbel and roach—fish that are well known among anglers and aquarium keepers alike—belong to one of the six families that comprise the

TOP An inhabitant of the muddy bottoms of rivers and lakes, the carp uses the sensory barbels on its snout and its protruding mouth to rummage in the mud for insect larvae and freshwater shrimps. ABOVE Foraging for food in a cloud of silt, a carp plows the bottom of its home lake.

order Cypriniformes. Many of the Cypriniformes species are especially important for the ease with which they can be reared for human food. One of the commonest is the minnow, which inhabits lakes and rivers in shoals of up to a hundred fish. The males are famous for their bright colors during the breeding season.

The goldfish is one of the most familiar species in the order, and has been kept as a household pet for hundreds of years. The wild form of the goldfish is dull green or brown in color, though red or reddish gold individuals sometimes occur as a result of mutations in their genes. The ancient Chinese collected these strikingly colored individuals and bred them to bring beauty to their ornamental pools. The suckers belong to a family that are recognizable by the large, fleshy lips that surround their mouths. They use these to suck up invertebrates when feeding.

There are almost 2500 species in the order, the majority of which are freshwater, egg-laying fish—although a few species do venture into brackish estuaries and coastal areas. They range throughout the world, with the exception of South America, Madagascar and Australia. Although the introduction of Cypriniformes into new environments is increasing, it is not always to the advantage of native fish populations. The Cypriniformes vary most widely in Southeast Asia, especially China, where there are almost 580 species.

Although they lack teeth in their mouths, most Cypriniformes have a pair of teeth in their throats. They also have jaws that they can thrust forward. In size, the Cypriniformes vary from small, agile and narrow-bodied minnows to the enormous mahseer of the Himalayan and Indian rivers, which grows to a length of 6 ft.

CYPRINIFORMES
CLASSIFICATION: 1

The large order Cypriniformes contains about 2500 species of fish in 256 genera and six families. They occur mainly in freshwater habitats, and range over North America, Africa and Eurasia.

Carps and minnows

The family Cyprinidae, the carps, minnows and their relatives (also known as the cyprinids), form one of the largest of all the fish families, with about 2070 species. They occur in most parts of North America, and are widespread through the Old World, from the far north of Europe to the southern tip of Africa, and from the British Isles east to Japan. Many have been introduced into areas outside their natural range. They include several familiar species such as the carp, *Cyprinus carpio*; the goldfish or gibel carp, *Carassius auratus*; the tench, *Tinca tinca*; the gudgeon, *Gobio gobio*; the barbel, *Barbus barbus*; the striped barb, *B. lineatus*; the minnow, *Phoxinus phoxinus*; the nase, *Chondrostoma nasus*; the chub, *Leucistus cephalus*; the dace, *L. leucistus*; the roach, *Rutilus rutilus*; the rudd, *Scardinius erythrophthalmus*; the bleak, *Alburnus alburnus*; the bitterling, *Rhodeus sericeus*; and the giant danio, *Danio malabaricus*.

Cleaner fishes and suckers

The family Gyrinocheilidae contains just three species of cleaner fishes or algae eaters from the genus *Gyrinocheilus*. They live in Southeast Asia, and include the cleaner fish, *G. aymonieri*. The suckers belong to the family Catostomidae. There are about 61 species, living in North America and Asia. Two-thirds of these belong to the genus *Catastomus*, including the longnose sucker, *C. catostomus*, and the white sucker, *C. commersoni*. The smallmouth buffalo, *Ictiobus bubalus*, is another member of the family.

Loaches and hillstream loaches

The family Cobitidae, the loaches, contains about 175 species. They are found in Europe, Asia and part of northeast Africa. Some of the more well-known species are the spined loach, *Cobitis taenia*; the stone loach, *Noemacheilus barbatulus*; the coolie loach, *Acanthophthalmus kuhlii*; and the clown loach, *Botia macracantha*. The family Homalopteridae, the hillstream loaches, is restricted to Southeast Asia and Indonesia. It comprises about 110 species, including the Bornean hillstream loach, *Gastromyzon borneensis*.

Sensory barbels

Most species in this order will eat almost anything—algae, mollusks, insects, arthropods and sometimes aquatic vegetation. The loach hides under stones and uses its barbels to hunt for food at night. Similarly, the barbel and the gudgeon that inhabit the murky bottoms of rivers and ponds overcome the problem of poor visibility by using sensory barbels around their mouths to probe the bottom before feeding. The bream, a narrow, deep-bodied fish, has a curious habit of standing on its head to root for insects, larvae, worms and mollusks in the muddy bottom. In contrast, the rudd is a voracious eater that mainly feeds on plants.

The carp is typical of the carp family and is tolerant of a wide range of conditions. Selective breeding in Southeast Asia has resulted in a slimmer, more athletic fish that inhabits faster water. In Japan, aquarists cultivate the carp as an object of beauty. Several hundred years of intensive breeding has improved the color range of the carp, and many are sold to ornament ponds and gardens.

Europe's national fishes: a wasted resource?

The order Cypriniformes contains the fishes that occupy the warmer freshwaters of Europe. Although they are commonly recognized as important food fish,

ABOVE **The goldfish is most familiar as an ornamental fish, and has been bred domestically in China for over 2000 years. Goldfish were first brought to Europe in the 17th century. Some were introduced into warm lakes and slow-flowing rivers where wild populations became established. Wild goldfish are greenish brown, and the offspring of the introduced golden varieties usually revert to this color, although from time to time they may still produce golden young.**

attitudes toward them vary from country to country. In Britain, for example, very few people eat carp, but are prepared to pay high prices for farmed trout. In much of eastern Europe, however, carp are fish-farmed and remain a commercially valuable source of food.

The roach, rudd, tench, bream, carp, barbel and other so-called "coarse fish" are the target of "coarse" angling, the largest participation sport in Britain. After catching "coarse" fishes, the anglers always weigh them and return the captured specimens to the water. In contrast, "game" anglers pay enormous sums for the right to fish salmon or trout in breeding ponds for food. The opposite situation exists in Scandinavia where, in spite of large stocks of Cypriniformes (and other "non-game" species), the majority of anglers fish for salmon and trout while ignoring "coarse" fish completely.

ABOVE **The tench is often reared and caught for food in areas where sea fish are not readily available. It occurs in still lakes, ponds and occasionally in slow-moving lowland rivers with soft, muddy bottoms.**

Tench avoid severe weather conditions by burying themselves in the mud where they remain until the conditions improve. Secretive fish, they will disappear from sight if disturbed.

The carps

The carp family contains over 2000 species and is restricted almost entirely to freshwater. The different species occur naturally in most areas throughout the world, but have been introduced into Australia, New Zealand, South America, Madagascar and the far north of North America. Their habitats range from lakes and weedy ponds to clear, fast-flowing streams.

Carps have toothless jaws, a set of grinding throat (pharyngeal) teeth and large swim bladders that are divided into two or three segments. Modified vertebrae connecting their swim bladders to their inner ears form a system known as the Weberian mechanism. The mechanism provides an efficient hearing system that detects predators and maintains contact with others in the shoal. Some members of the family can make sounds that can function as a primitive form of communication; minnows, for example, make noises by blowing air bubbles from their mouths.

The carp, now one of the most widespread of freshwater fishes in the world, may have originated in the warm rivers of southeast Europe and Asia Minor, and may have been introduced into Britain and western Europe by the Romans. It is a deep-bodied fish, flattened from side to side with a symmetrical, forked tail and a long, dorsal fin. It has a large mouth that can be protruded to grab food and a set of four sensitive barbels—a pair of shorter ones on the upper lip and another, longer pair, on the corners of the mouth—that enable the carp to detect food in murky waters. Carp have yellow or brown flanks and a lighter belly, and their anal and pelvic fins are often tinged with red.

Breeding for the table

The scales in the carps are varied as a result of centuries of breeding. Carps have always been a food fish, and breeders have attempted to produce a carp that lacks scales and is easy to prepare for the table. There are three principal forms of carp: the leather carp has few or no scales; the mirror carp has one or two lines of large scales running along its lateral line; and the scaled carp has a full set of scales and is similar to the original form. The original carp is a rare fish in the wild and needs protection.

The carp's natural habitat is shallow, still or slow-moving water with a muddy bottom and abundant vegetation. It often lives in waters where oxygen is scarce, yet it survives with ease by rising to the surface and gulping in oxygen—some of which it stores in its blood vessels. Carp can adapt to a wide range of temperatures (reflected by their wide distribution), though in cooler waters, such as those of Britain, they often find it too cold to breed. Here, the young only survive in warm years.

Carp breed in late spring or early summer in shallow, thickly vegetated water. They generally spawn in water that has stayed at 62.6°F for at least 14 consecutive days, although in Britain, carp will only spawn if the water temperature has reached 73.4°F. Breeding is accompanied by much splashing about in the shallows. The female may lay more than a million eggs in a single season. They stick to the aquatic vegetation and hatch after a week. The newly hatched fry measure about 0.2 in. in length. At first they feed on their yolk sacs, and when these are exhausted the young carp start eating plankton, graduating onto bottom-living invertebrates. Mature

fish eat larger invertebrates, including shellfish, as well as much vegetation during the summer. Carp can reach over 3 ft. in length and 40 lbs. in weight. They can live as long as 50 years in captivity.

Oriental origins

The goldfish, a common prize in fun fairs in many parts of the world, are descended from the gibel carp, a fish that swims in the rivers of eastern Europe and Asia. The ornamental goldfish may have originated from a race of gibel carp living in China and other parts of eastern Asia. Goldfish and gibel carp lack barbels and have long dorsal fins. Coloration varies from the familiar gold through pale yellow and white to dull brown. In the ornamental goldfish, the coloration may be plain or variegated, and the body shape ranges from the standard carp shape to the flamboyant varieties with double fins and other exaggerated features produced by breeding. The gibel carp occurs in ponds, lakes and slow rivers, usually where there is abundant vegetation, and it tolerates thick, muddy water and low oxygen levels. Most adult goldfish are about 8 in. long, although some grow to about 12 in. or more rarely 20 in. Like carp, they are long-lived, and in captivity individuals have survived for over 30 years.

The tench

Tench live in still or slow-moving water and can be identified at a glance by the thick, rounded profiles of their moderately long bodies, their rounded, almost spoon-shaped fins and slimy skin. In general, tench have small scales, although some specimens have none at all. The tench's coloring varies from one population to another depending on the habitat, and ranges from dark brown to bronze-green, dark green and yellowish green. Their bellies are a little lighter with a distinct yellow sheen, and their eyes are red. Some ornamental varieties are colored gold.

ABOVE RIGHT The gudgeon has a wide range of habitats in Europe. It lives on the bottom of rivers, streams, lakes, flooded gravel pits and marshy pools. Gudgeon are small in comparison to most members of the carp family, seldom growing to more than 8 in. in length, with the largest specimens often found in gravel pits.
RIGHT The striped barb is a popular aquarium fish, sought for its attractive colors and its lively habits. Although the barb is easy to keep, it has proved very difficult to breed in captivity.

ABOVE LEFT Minnows inhabit clean, unpolluted streams and pools. They occur in large shoals and consume great quantities of aquatic invertebrates. However, they, in turn, are an important food for large predators, such as pike, otters and herons.

ABOVE RIGHT Barbels live in shallow, stony stretches of rivers, where they feed on invertebrates, such as mollusks or the larvae of caddis flies. They frequently turn over stones and uproot plants with their long snouts in the search for prey.

Tench feed mainly on aquatic invertebrates that they find by probing the mud and hunting among the aquatic plants. They prefer lakes, gravel pits and slow-moving rivers with dense vegetation (especially dense clumps of water lilies) on soft, muddy beds. Young tench eat algae, but mature specimens eat little plant material. Tench can tolerate low levels of oxygen and spend most of their time swimming slowly around near the bottom of the water. It is thought that in winter they shoal in deep water, and if the weather becomes severe, they bury themselves in mud.

Tench begin to breed after the first long hot spell of early summer. However, in colder climates or in particularly deep or heavily shaded waters, tench may not breed at all. Their greenish yellow eggs are 0.4 in. in diameter, and stick in clusters to the aquatic vegetation. They hatch in six to eight days. In British waters, the young grow slowly, reaching about 1.5 in. by the end of their first year, and 6 in. when they are about four years old. In warmer, more favorable conditions, tench can reach 4 in. in length by the end of their first year and 16 in. by the time they are five years old. Mature tench can grow to nearly 24 in. in length.

Male and female tench can be identified by differing features. In the male, the second ray of the pelvic fin is thicker than it is in the female, and the male's pelvic fin is wider and longer. During the breeding season, the male develops small bumps (tubercles) on his skin known as nuptial pads.

The gudgeon

The gudgeon rarely grows to more than 8 in. in length and 4 oz. in weight. A gregarious fish, it occurs in closely packed shoals and occupies ponds, lakes and rivers. Its favorite habitat, however, consists of fairly fast-flowing clear water with gravelly bottoms. It also lives, especially in Britain, in flooded gravel pits. (Such habitats do not have fast-flowing water, but they do have gravel beds.) Gudgeon always swim near the bottom and often hide beneath stones. As a result, they have flattened undersides as an adaptation to a bottom-dwelling life-style.

Gudgeon are long fish, green-gray on their backs and yellowish on their sides, becoming paler beneath with dark patches of varying sizes on their flanks, backs and fins. A gudgeon is distinguished from the larger but otherwise similar barbel by having two sensory barbels, rather than four, at each side of its thick-lipped mouth. Gudgeon feed mainly on invertebrates, but insect larvae are particularly important in the warm months, and mollusks and crustaceans in the winter.

The barbels

The barbels are among the most widely distributed members of the carp family, occurring in both the temperate waters of Europe and Asia and the tropical waters of Asia and Africa. The barbel itself, a European fish, is large and powerful with a long, rounded body and a short, high dorsal fin. It can grow to over 31 in. and weigh 13 to 18 lbs. Barbels vary in color, but their backs tend to be greenish brown or bronze. Their flanks have a golden-yellow tint, and their bellies are yellowish white. Their pectoral and pelvic fins and their rounded anal fins are orange, while their other fins are grayish brown.

Barbels prefer deep, fast-flowing rivers with sandy or stony bottoms, but will tolerate muddier and slower-moving rivers. In England, they were once mainly found in the Trent and Thames rivers, but since they are such popular fishes with anglers, they have been widely introduced and are now found in most of the lowland rivers in southern England. During the day, barbels often gather in shoals, facing upstream and moving only short distances from time to time. When twilight comes, they separate, moving off to hunt for food on their own.

Jutting jaw

The barbel's mouth is well adapted for bottom feeding. The upper jaw juts out beyond the lower one, so that its mouth is well positioned to root about on the riverbed for prey. The four fleshy barbels are richly supplied with taste cells, enabling the fish to find insect larvae, worms and other invertebrates. Barbels sometimes uproot and eat water plants. They also have flattened undersides as an adaptation for life on the beds of fast-flowing rivers.

Barbels spawn from May to July. They migrate upstream to sandy spawning grounds where they lay their eggs. The sticky, yellow eggs are 0.08 in.

ABOVE The nase is a long, slender species with silvery scales that catch the light as the fish turns through the water. It lives in large shoals in deep, strongly flowing rivers, and moves to the upper reaches of the rivers for the spring breeding season. It feeds on a variety of water plants, and uses the tough, horny lips on its mouth to scrape algae from the surface of stones.

in diameter and become attached to water plants and rocks. One female may produce over 100,000 eggs. The eggs hatch within two weeks and are believed to be poisonous to humans.

Numerous barbel species are found in Africa, India and Southeast Asia. Some of these, such as the Rippon Falls barbel, are of considerable size and therefore of interest both as food and as sporting fish. The rest are very small and many, such as the rosy barb and the striped barb, are kept as aquarium fish because of their bright markings.

Tiny and colorful

The minnow—the familiar "tiddler"—rarely grows more than 3-4 in. long, and never exceeds 4.7-5 in. It makes up for its small size with its attractive appearance. Minnows are quite variable in color; their backs and sides are deep olive-green, with a metallic bronze sheen on their flanks, blending into

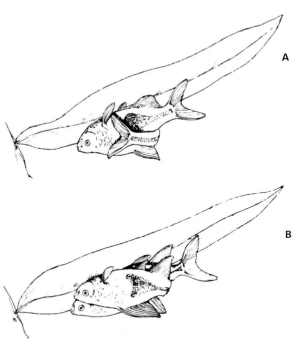

A

B

ABOVE The chub preys on many small fishes such as minnows, gudgeon, young dace and roach, as well as frogs and newts. It has a double row of curved teeth in the back of its throat and a hard plate at the top to crush its food.

RIGHT Harlequin rasboras place their eggs on the undersides of leaves. After a brief courtship display the male wraps himself around the female (A), positioning himself so that he can fertilize the eggs as they emerge (B).

in summer, but the shoals break up in colder weather when they live and feed nearer the bottom.

The nase is a silvery fish that reaches a maximum length of 20 in. It lives in large shoals and breeds in the spring in the upper reaches of rivers. Its mouth has sharp, horny lips that scrape algae and plankton off the stones on the riverbeds.

A robust omnivore

The chub is a river fish that reaches about 24 in. in length when mature. In Britain, it weighs up to 10 lbs., and on mainland Europe up to 18 lbs. It is an omnivore, feeding on invertebrates that range in size from small worms to crayfish, as well as on small fish, vegetable matter and debris. Chub are robust fish with gray or greenish brown backs, greenish or bluish sides with a metallic sheen on their large scales, and silvery, whitish or yellowish bellies; their single anal fins are orange-red. The chub's head has distinctive thick lips.

Young chub are sociable fish, but they become solitary when adult. Only during the breeding season, in spring and early summer, do sexually mature specimens form shoals. After being pursued by several males, the female lays her sticky, yellowish eggs onto plants or stones in a sheltered location. She may

pale yellow or whitish bellies with dark markings over their backs and sides. In the breeding season, the male takes on bright colors—its belly becomes bright red and its tail, pectoral and pelvic fins become pale orange. As with many other breeding male fish in the carp family, numerous little white lumps, or tubercles, develop around its head.

Although minnows live in rivers and lakes with muddy bottoms, they do need well-oxygenated, clean water. (The presence of minnows in the Thames River during the 1970s showed that there had been an improvement in the cleanliness of the river.) Minnows are highly gregarious fish, and may form shoals numbering thousands of individuals. They eat mainly small aquatic invertebrates, such as insect larvae and crustaceans, although they will also eat water plants, including algae. They sometimes feed near the surface

produce as many as 100,000 eggs over the course of the season. The eggs—each of them approximately 0.06 in. in diameter—hatch in about a week.

The dace is closely related to the chub. A slender, dark-backed and silvery-sided shoaling fish, the dace is common in many of the rivers of Europe, where it feeds on both plant and animal matter. Not only does it eat algae, waterweed and aquatic invertebrates such as crustaceans, but it will also take flying insects trapped on the water's surface film—they only have to be there a moment for the dace to seize them. Dace measure 6-12 in. long and breed in spring in clear stretches of rivers that have stone or gravel beds. The most immediate difference between the dace and the chub is that the dace's dorsal fin is concave, while the chub's is convex.

Pinkish fins

The roach is widely distributed and abundant north of the Alps where it lives in lakes, flooded gravel pits, reservoirs and slow-moving rivers. It prefers water with plenty of weed, and feeds on both plant and animal matter. It is an attractive and elegant fish, measuring about 10 in. in length (though it occasionally grows to as much as 20 in.). Roach rarely weigh more than 4 lbs. and anglers regard even a specimen weighing 2 lbs. as a prize catch. The fish has a dark, greenish back, silvery sides and a white belly. All the fins apart from the dorsal are warmly tinged with pink.

Roach spawn between April and June, during which time the fish do not feed at all. The females lay their 0.04-inch-diameter eggs among the dense vegetation. A female produces 200,000-400,000 eggs for every kilogram of her body weight. Once laid, the eggs stick to underwater plants and hatch after about 10 days. The fish mature after about three years and can live for over 10 years.

Roach are gregarious fish and live in shoals together with closely related species such as bream and rudd. The spawning sites are such a frenzy of activity that cross-breeding often takes place and hybrids between these species are not unknown.

The tolerant rudd

The rudd is another member of the carp family that prefers weedy, still water. It tolerates mildly polluted water and survives in poorly oxygenated waters, though the populations there often consist

TOP The roach is a highly adaptable species and can survive in poorly oxygenated and mildly polluted water. It is one of Europe's most common fish, occurring in lakes, ponds, lowland rivers and estuaries. It normally eats both invertebrates and plant matter, but ceases to feed entirely during the spawning period.

ABOVE The giant danio lives in clear, swift-flowing streams in India and Sri Lanka. It reaches 5 in. in length and is a popular aquarium fish that breeds easily in captivity.

of rather stunted individuals. The rudd looks superficially similar to the roach, but it differs in several ways: the rudd has golden-yellow irises to its eyes while those of the roach are red; the front edge of the rudd's dorsal fin is farther back than the base of the pelvic (belly) fins, while in the roach the dorsal fin is in line with the pelvic fins; the rudd's fins are more red than those of the roach. The rudd measures 8-12 in. in length and averages 8-9 oz. in weight. Its diet is varied, and includes invertebrates and some plant material. The rudd's mouth slants steeply downward, enabling the fish to snatch insects from the surface of the water with ease.

The rudd travels in shoals throughout the year. It spawns between April and June in smallish shoals and in similar places to the roach. The transparent yellow eggs stick to water plants and hatch after a few days. At first, the larvae depend on their yolk sacs for food, but later move on to tiny aquatic animals. Rudd usually grow more slowly than roach and may take four or more years to reach maturity.

Shoals in freshwater

The bleak is one of the most common freshwater fish in Europe; in Britain it occurs mostly in eastern England and parts of Wales. Rarely exceeding 7 in. in length, it is a slender fish that forms shoals so large and dense that they call to mind those of marine fish such as anchovies and sardines. Indeed, if a weakened bleak loses contact with its shoal, it is unlikely to survive, soon falling victim to larger, predatory fish.

The bleak lives in the open waters of clear rivers and lakes, where it eats mostly small insects, taking them from the water and from the surface. It may also feed on the bottom. During the breeding season, which lasts from May until August, bleak come in closer to the shore. The females spawn in shallow waters, attaching their pale yellow eggs (about 0.06 in. in

ABOVE LEFT The rudd has an upwardly angled mouth that enables it to snatch aquatic insects both from the middle depths and from the surface film of the water. Because of the shape and the position of their mouths, however, rudd find it difficult to feed off the bottom.

LEFT The bleak is a gregarious fish that lives in open freshwater habitats, avoiding overgrown or heavily silted stretches of water. In the 19th century a substance called guanin was extracted from its silvery scales and used to make artificial pearls.

diameter) to water plants. The eggs hatch in two to three weeks. The bleak plays an important role in the food chain, since it provides a staple diet for many predatory fish species.

A mollusk maternity home

The bitterling lives in muddy lakes, ponds and slow-moving rivers and feeds mainly on small invertebrates, though it also eats some plant matter. It grows no more than 4 in. in length. It has large scales and is gray-blue on its back, silvery on its sides and white beneath. A bright, blue-green stripe runs from the middle of each flank to the base of its tail fin. In the breeding season the male's sides turn pinkish, its dorsal and anal fins become red, and white tubercles develop on its head. At the same time, the female develops an ovipositor or egg-laying tube that measures about 2.5 in. long. The male takes up residence in a territory containing a large freshwater mussel or clam and defends it from all comers. He attracts a passing female to the mollusk, and she points her ovipositor between the two shells of the mollusk so that she can lay her eggs directly in its gill chamber.

After the female has withdrawn her tube and left, the male releases his sperm near the mollusk's intake siphon (the tube that draws water in and over the gills). The sperm is drawn into the gill chamber where it fertilizes the eggs. Once the eggs have hatched, the young develop inside the mollusk—not, apparently, doing it any harm. When the young are three to four weeks old and only 0.08 inch in length, they leave the mollusk, swept out on water through the mollusk's outlet siphon (the tube taking water out of the mollusk). Since the male may attract several females to his mollusk, and each female may lay up to 100 eggs, the mollusk may contain large numbers of eggs during the course of the breeding season—all of them at different stages of development.

ABOVE RIGHT A silver bream turns, revealing the high-sided but narrow body that is typical of species from slow-flowing, lowland waters. Growing to a length of 12 in., the silver bream retains its gleaming appearance even when it reaches old age.

RIGHT The bream feeds by sucking up mud into its mouth, swallowing any edible morsels and spitting out the waste. As a shoal of bream feed in deeper water, they often send up small clouds of muddy water that reveal their presence to anglers.

The relationship between the bitterling and the mollusk is not all one-sided: the mollusk's larvae dig themselves into the skin of the young fish when they are developing inside them and feed on their body fluids and blood, without harming them. The young mollusks later drop from the fish to begin their lives on the river bottom.

Unmistakable mouths

The suckers belong to a family that is fairly closely related to the carps. They are restricted mainly to North America, though a few species occur in northern Asia. Similar in many respects to the carp-like fishes, they differ in the arrangement of the pharyngeal bones (in the upper part of the gullet) and teeth. None of the suckers have barbels. Thick lips bearing numerous bristles surround their mouths; they can be thrust forward and are one of the fish's most striking features. Suckers feed by using their powerful mouths to draw in material. When they take food from the bottom, they remove the edible portion by sifting it out in their gill rakers, and then spit out the remainder. Some species move stones aside with their snouts to reach invertebrates hidden beneath.

Some suckers occur in still or slow-moving water rich in vegetation. The bigmouth buffalo, the largest of the American suckers, is a carp-like fish that reaches 3 ft. or more in length and is a bottom dweller. Other members of the family prefer fast-flowing waters that are clear and well oxygenated, with stony or sandy bottoms. One such species is the longnose sucker, although this fish will live in deep lakes as well.

The longnose sucker breeds in swift, gravel-bottomed streams that have begun to warm up with the retreat of the winter snows. The eggs settle onto the streambed or become lodged in cracks on the bottom, and the young fish stay hidden among the stones for some days after hatching. Longnose suckers are gray along their backs and sides and white below, but in the breeding seasons the males are distinguished by the presence of a red stripe along their sides, and tubercles on the heads and fins. The fish's diet consists mainly of bottom-dwelling invertebrates, though young longnose suckers also eat plankton.

Bottom-dwelling fishes

The loaches are small fish, with rather elongated bodies—some are almost eel-shaped. Their mouths

ABOVE AND BELOW The bitterling is native to northern and eastern Europe, and has the remarkable habit of laying its eggs in the gill chambers of mollusks. A male bitterling guides a female—her egg-laying tube trailing in the water— to a freshwater mussel (A). The female finds the mussel's outlet siphon (B), inserts her egg-laying tube (C) and passes her eggs down it into the mussel's gill chamber. After she has removed the tube (D), the male discharges his sperm (E). When the mussel takes in water, it draws the sperm into the gill chamber and fertilizes the eggs.

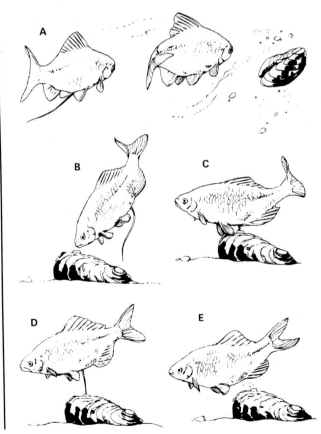

ABOVE Like all loaches, the spined loach is well adapted for a bottom-dwelling life-style, and spends most of the time buried among weeds or in the mud, with only its head exposed. The spined loach takes its name from the tiny spines underneath its eyes. These are usually buried in the skin, but they can be erected for defense against predators.

bear a number of pairs of barbels, or whiskers, that they use as feeling organs. They have no teeth, and their scales are small or absent. The loaches are well adapted to a bottom-dwelling existence. Some do not live on the bottom but actually in it, spending long periods buried almost completely in the mud or sand. Members of the loach family are particularly abundant in Southeast Asia.

Some loaches have thread-like external gills during the juvenile stages, enabling the young fish to breathe in oxygen-poor conditions, but the fish lose them as they mature. Adults cope with oxygen shortage in a different way: they rise to the water surface and gulp in air. As some of the air passes into the intestine, the oxygen enters the rich system of blood vessels in the intestine walls, where it can be stored.

One of the European species of loach is the spined loach. Reaching about 5 in. in length at most, it has a brownish back marked with dark blotches, a yellowish belly and six pairs of barbels. The fish takes its name from the double-pointed spines that lie underneath each eye. Normally buried in folds in the skin, the spines can be erected to give a nasty injury if the fish is handled. The spined loach lives in lakes and slow-moving rivers, mainly those with muddy or sandy bottoms. It is a secretive fish, hiding most of its body under sand, mud or waterweed, and leaving only the head showing. It feeds at night on small, bottom-dwelling crustaceans.

Victim of pollution

The stone loach is less secretive than the spined loach, and lives in streams and lake margins where the water is clear and the bottom pebbly. Unfortunately, it has become noticeably less common in many of its haunts in recent years as a result of increasing water pollution. It grows to a maximum length of 6 in., and spends much of the time hidden among rocks or vegetation. It is generally sluggish, although it will swim quickly for cover if disturbed. Its diet consists of small, bottom-dwelling aquatic invertebrates, such as insect larvae, crustaceans and worms, and it feeds mainly at night. It becomes more active when the weather is gray and damp. The stone loach spawns in spring, and the female lays up to 25,000 eggs either on plants or on the stream or lake bed.

1905

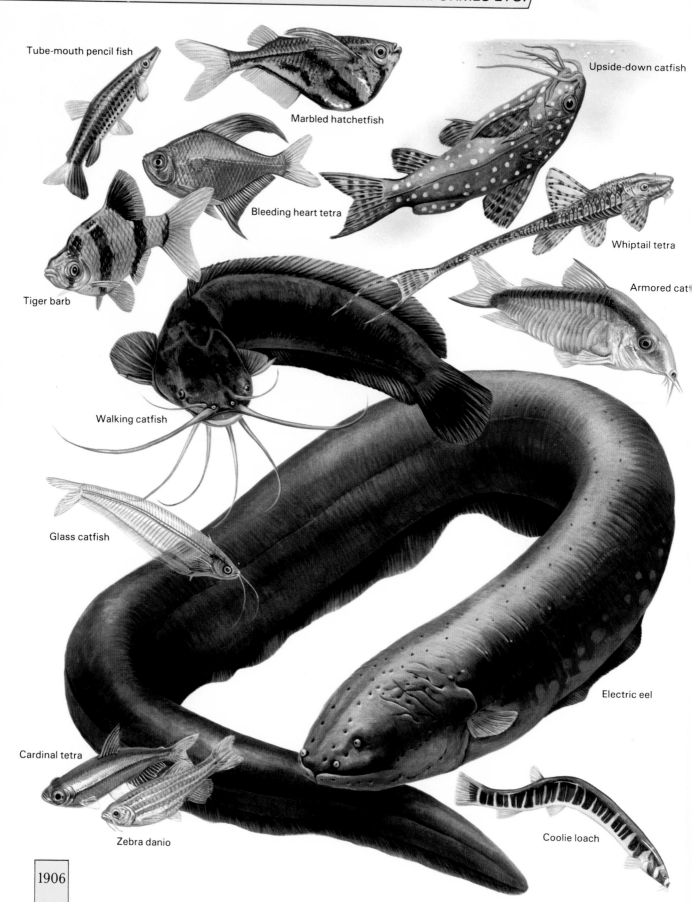

Tube-mouth pencil fish

Marbled hatchetfish

Upside-down catfish

Bleeding heart tetra

Whiptail tetra

Tiger barb

Armored cat

Walking catfish

Glass catfish

Electric eel

Cardinal tetra

Zebra danio

Coolie loach

1906

The mountain streams of Southeast Asia contain members of the hillstream loach family. Their bodies are flattened from top to bottom in the front, and they are equipped with greatly expanded pectoral and pelvic fins that serve as suckers. The suckers enable the fish to hold onto rocks and stones even when the current is extremely strong. The Bornean hillstream loach is a typical member of the family. Just 3.5 in. long, it uses its mouth—situated underneath its head—to graze on the algae growing on the rocks. A curved arrangement of bones protects its head while the fish feeds on the rocks.

The characins

Some 840 species of characins constitute the largest family within the order Characiformes. The majority of species live in the tropics of Central and South America, but there are about 200 species in Africa.

Most characins resemble carps. However, unlike members of the carp family, characins usually have a fleshy (adipose) fin set far back between their dorsal (back) and tail fins. They also have a set of replacement teeth behind the ordinary teeth in their mouths. Characins do not have barbels and cannot extend their mouths to grab prey.

Many African characin species are predators; they include the largest of all the characins, the tiger fishes. One species of tiger fish from Zaire, West Africa, grows to about 5 ft. in length and can weigh more than 99 lbs. Silvery in color, with some of its fins tinged with red, it catches other fishes in powerful jaws that are armed with sharp, interlocking teeth. Tiger fishes are built for speed, having elegant, streamlined bodies with powerful tails and pointed fins.

Frenzied feeders

South American characins include the most infamous of all aquatic predators—the piranhas. There

ABOVE RIGHT The clown loach reaches up to 6 in. in length, and, like many of the tropical loaches, is a popular aquarium fish. It is a hardy species renowned for uprooting vegetation.
RIGHT The cleaner fishes or algae eaters are related to the carps but are distinguished by their strange, rasping lips, with which they can remove algae from almost any surface, including pebbles and fish-tank glass. The lower part of their mouths are modified into sucking organs that allow the fish to hold tightly onto the surfaces from which they are feeding.

LEFT The red piranha occurs in many parts of the Amazon Basin and grows to 12 in. in length. Like most piranhas, it is a fierce predator and has large, flat triangular teeth with very sharp points. Piranhas feed mainly on small fish, especially weak and sick individuals, but will also attack injured land animals that become stranded in the water. Some species of piranhas are mainly vegetarian and feed on seeds and fruit that fall into the water.

CHARACIFORMES CLASSIFICATION

The order Characiformes comprises 10 families of freshwater fishes, with a combined total of more than 1330 species grouped in 252 genera. Over 90 percent of these are found in the New World, the remainder occurring in Africa.

Characins

The family Characidae, the characins, is by far the largest in the order, with 841 species. They are distributed over South and Central America and Africa. They include the tiger fish, *Hydrocynus vittatus*; the piranha or piraya, *Pygocentrus piraya*; the red piranha, *Serrasalmus nattereri*; the wimple piranhas of the genus *Catoprion*; the cardinal tetra, *Cheirodon axelrodi*; the neon tetra, *Paracheirodon innesi*; the beaconfish, *Hemigrammus ocellifer*; the black tetra, *Gymnocorymbus ternetzi*; the penguinfish, *Thayeria obliquua*; and the swordtail characin, *Corynopoma riisei*.

Freshwater hatchetfishes and other families

The freshwater hatchetfishes make up the family Gasteropelecidae. There are just nine species, and all occur in South America. They include the silver hatchetfish, *Gasteropelecus levis*, and the marbled hatchetfish, *Carnegiella striata*. The family Lebiasinidae comprises about 60 species of South American fishes, including the tube-mouth pencil fish, *Nannostomus eques*, and the splashing tetra, *Copeina arnoldi*. Several other large families within the order Characiformes do not have common family names and contain few well-known species. South America is the home of the family Curimatidae, with 138 species, and the family Anastomidae, with 105 species. The African family Citharinidae contains some 77 species.

are several species of piranhas, all of which are stocky and quite small, averaging 12 in. long. Although they grow quickly, the largest species only just measures 24 in. in length. Piranhas have deep heads and bodies and short, powerful jaws. Their most feared features are their triangular, razor-sharp, interlocking teeth that take precise bites—enough for one swallow at a time—out of their prey's flesh.

Piranhas are group predators, and there are strong bonds between members of local piranha communities. They live in shoals and make up for their small size by attacking in a frenzied mass. In general, they feed on smaller fishes, efficiently cleaning the rivers by eating those fishes that are sick, wounded or dead. They also attack larger, injured animals, such as capybara, that stray into the calm, deep waters that piranhas haunt. Piranhas often eat other piranhas that have been caught in nets or on hooks—but only those that do not belong to their community.

Once piranhas have spilled their victim's blood, they become increasingly frantic, tearing off mouthfuls of its flesh. The blood attracts other piranhas, which join in the attack, and together, the shoal can strip an animal down to its skeleton within minutes.

Although piranhas have attacked people bathing or wading in rivers, their danger to humans has been exaggerated. They are more of a nuisance, hindering

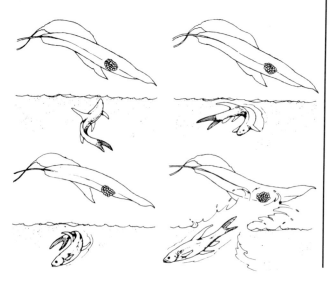

fishing operations by tearing open nets to free themselves when captured or to remove and eat other fishes. Amazonian Indians have long used the piranhas' sharp teeth for cutting and slicing.

Wimple piranhas feed on the scales of other fishes. Their lower jaws jut out beyond the upper ones, and their teeth can scrape off the scales of an unwary victim in a single, upward movement. When fish scales are not available, the wimple piranha lives on insects and other small invertebrates.

Silver dollars are omnivorous or vegetarian fishes that are close relatives of the piranhas. Lacking their relatives' sharp teeth, they feed on seeds and fruit. The pacu is another vegetarian characin. Resembling a giant piranha, it reaches 27.5 in. or more in length and feeds on fruits that fall into the rivers.

The tamer tetras

Some South American characins, notably the tetras, are far less fearsome than the piranhas. Many have become popular aquarium fishes because of their striking colors. (The name, tetra, is a shortened form of the genus *Tetragonopterus* into which many of these small, colorful fish were placed.) The cardinal tetra is a peaceful and gentle species, reddish in color, that reaches about 1.6 in. in length.

ABOVE LEFT Beaconfishes take their name from the bright spots at the base of their tails. Male beaconfishes are almost transparent—against strong light it is possible to see their swim bladders. ABOVE The black tetra is one of many tetras kept as aquarium fishes. In the wild, black tetras are sociable when young, but become solitary with age. BELOW Splashing tetras lay their eggs out of water to keep them safe from other fish. To keep the eggs moist, the male regularly comes to the surface and uses his tail to splash them with water.

The neon tetra takes its name from the two luminous stripes—one red and the other blue-green—that run along its sides. The related Buenos Aires tetra is one of the larger tetras, reaching about 3 in. in length. It is brightly colored with a striking, red anal fin. The penguinfish is remarkable for its habit of swimming with its head pointing upward and its ability to leap high out of the water.

The swordtail characin has been well studied for its unusual method of reproduction. The male initiates the breeding cycle with a display. He approaches the female and attempts to attract her with the long, spoon-shaped appendages on each of his gill covers. (The female's gill covers bear a much shorter spine.) He strokes her with his gill-cover extension, and she snaps at it, presumably because it reminds her of small items of food. Then the male produces a small package of sperm (a spermatophore), similar in appearance to the tip of his gill-cover extension. The female takes it with her mouth and transfers it to her cloaca, where internal fertilization takes place. Later, she lays her eggs, places them on a leaf and then guards them. The eggs hatch after a couple of days.

Leaping and laying

The splashing tetra is a much-studied member of the characin order. A long-finned fish measuring about 3 in. long, it lives in hot, marshy places where there is often little or no oxygen in the water. The male has much larger fins than the female.

To breed, the male splashing tetra entices the female to his chosen territory, which lies beneath a low, overhanging branch. Both fish then swim to the surface and leap into the air with their flanks held closely together. When they reach the undersurface of a leaf, the female deposits a few eggs on it and the male fertilizes them before falling back into the water with the female. They repeat these leaps, which can measure 2.7-4 in. in height, until the female has laid all her eggs—usually about 60. The male keeps the eggs moist by splashing water on them with his tail several times an hour. After each bout of splashing, he swims off quickly to avoid revealing the location of the eggs by his presence. The eggs hatch after two or three days, and the fry fall into the water.

Freshwater hatchetfishes

The characins include the only fishes in the world that truly fly—the nine species of freshwater hatchetfishes. They have strong pectoral muscles that enable them to flap their pectoral fins in genuine, powered flight—as opposed to passive gliding. Their bodies are narrow and their breasts are deep to hold the powerful muscles needed for flying. They use their

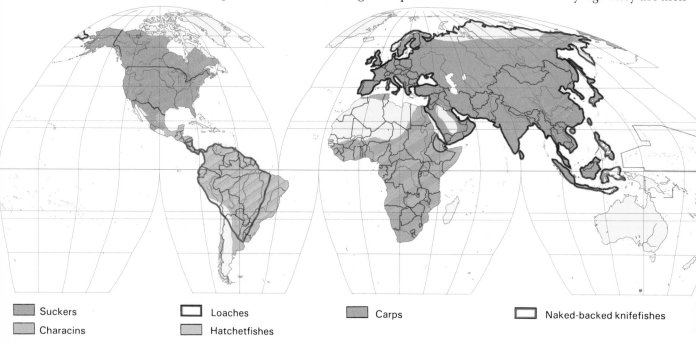

Suckers	Loaches	Carps	Naked-backed knifefishes
Characins	Hatchetfishes		

flying ability either to escape from predators or to capture insects flying just above the water surface.

First, they travel some distance above the river, brushing the water with their tails and bellies. Then they leave the water entirely for several feet, flapping their pectoral fins rapidly so that they make a buzzing noise.

The catfishes

There are more than 2000 species (and 31 families) of catfishes inhabiting most freshwater habitats in Africa, the Americas, Australia, Europe and Asia. Members of two families—the sea catfishes and the eeltail catfishes—live in tropical and subtropical seas. Catfishes vary from small species that are only about an inch long to large freshwater species that can grow to about 5 ft. long and weigh as much as 100 lbs.

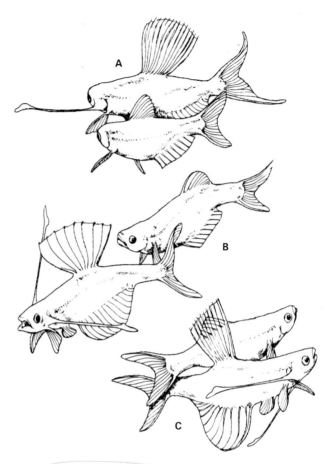

RIGHT The mating ritual in a pair of swordtail characins; the female approaches the male, attracted by his long, thin gill-cover extensions (A); the male and female swim close together (B); and the male releases his spermatophore to fertilize the female's eggs (C).

BELOW LEFT The map shows the geographical distribution of six families: the suckers, the loaches, the carps, the characins, the freshwater hatchetfishes and the naked-backed knifefishes. BELOW The map shows the world distribution of five of the catfish families.

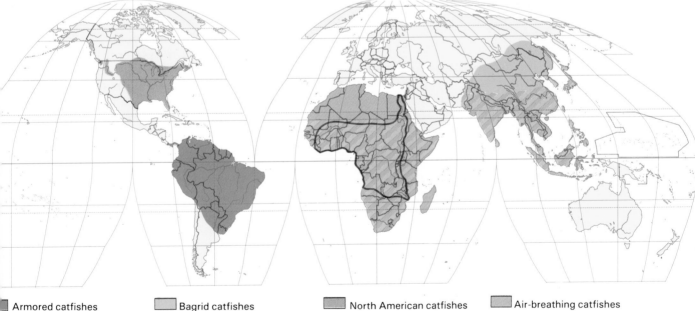

■ Armored catfishes   ■ Bagrid catfishes   ■ North American catfishes   ■ Air-breathing catfishes

■ Electric catfishes

ABOVE **Several species of catfishes live in tropical pools that are prone to drying up. Members of the armored catfishes family have an armor of bony plates on each flank that resist the loss of body fluids if the pool water evaporates completely in the dry season. Armored catfishes are popular with aquarium owners since they feed on organic debris that collects in the bottom of the tank.**

Catfishes are recognized by their long, sensory barbels that superficially resemble cats' whiskers and give catfishes their name. They have long anal fins, a single fatty (adipose) fin between their dorsal and tail fins, flattened heads and scaleless skins. Some catfishes have bony, armor-like plates instead of skin.

Some catfishes of China, Indonesia and southern Japan are known as torrent catfishes. Living in swift mountain streams, they have evolved ways of clinging tightly to the riverbeds and even climbing steep rock-faces under waterfalls. To do this, some species make combined use of their modified pelvic fins and smooth, muscular bellies that they use like suckers, clamping them onto the rocks. Other species use their mouths as suckers. Since these catfish cannot then breathe in the normal way (drawing oxygen-laden water through their mouths and over the gills), they have to draw the water in through their gill openings and pump it out the way it came. Torrent catfishes have flattened bodies—an adaptation that both reduces the effect of water pressure and makes use of it to thrust the fish down onto the streambed.

In contrast, other catfishes live in slow-moving or still waters that are often almost stagnant—that is, they contain very little dissolved oxygen. To survive, the catfishes can breathe atmospheric oxygen when necessary by using a type of primitive lung. Air-sac catfishes of India, Sri Lanka and Burma, for example, possess a long air sac that extends backward from the gill chamber and occupies a large proportion of the fish's body. The air sac serves as a lung from which the fish can extract oxygen.

Species of air-breathing catfishes of Africa and southern and western Asia have a similar but much smaller extension to the gill chamber. It is equipped with a branching structure densely supplied with blood vessels, enabling the fishes to absorb oxygen more efficiently. Air-breathing catfishes are capable of living out of water, and native fishermen often carry them alive in baskets to markets many miles from where they were caught.

Certain catfishes live in the permanent darkness of underground streams and lakes. Some American species are known only from deep wells bored in the

SILURIFORMES CLASSIFICATION

The catfishes

The catfishes belong to the large order Siluriformes. Classification within the order is still under debate, but there are probably over 2200 species grouped into some 400 genera and 31 different families. Two families contain marine species, but the majority of catfishes live in freshwater habitats around the world, with more than half the species occurring in the Americas.

The family Ictaluridae, the North American freshwater catfishes, contains 45 species, including the brown bullhead, *Ictalurus nebulosus*. The Eurasian catfishes or sheatfishes make up the family Siluridae, with 70 species such as the European catfish or European wels, *Silurus glanis*, and the glass catfish, *Krytopterus bicirrhus*. The five species of torrent catfishes form the Asian family Amblycipitidae. They belong to the genera *Amblyceps* and *Liobagrus*. There are about 100 species of air-breathing catfishes in the family Clariidae. Inhabitants of Africa and Asia, they include the walking catfish, *Clarias batrachus*. The African family Malapteruridae contains the two species of electric catfishes from the genus *Malapterurus*.

Most of the sea catfishes in the family Ariidae live in tropical and subtropical seas, but some occur in freshwater. There are about 120 species, including the gafftopsail catfish, *Bagre marinus*. There are 150 species of upside-down catfishes in the African family Mochokidae, including those from the genera *Chiloglanis* and *Sinodontis*. The long-whiskered catfishes of Central and South America form another large family, the Pimelodidae, with about 290 species from genera such as *Calophysus* and *Pimelodus*.

The parasite or pencil catfishes from South America make up the family Trichomycteridae. There are about 175 species, including the candirus of the genera *Vandellia* and *Branchioica*. The armored catfish family, the Callichthyidae, comprises 110 South American species, more than half of which belong to the genus *Corydoras*. The largest of all the families is the Loricariidae, the suckermouth armored catfishes. Inhabitants of Central and South America, they include the whiptail catfish, *Loricaria parva*.

ABOVE Catfishes are named for the whisker-like barbels that sprout from their lips and snouts. In the dark and often murky conditions of the river or seabed, catfishes use their barbels to feel their way around and locate food. The catfishes shown here belong to the eeltail family—a group of marine fishes that have poisonous spines on their pectoral fins.

ground. The species *Trogloglanis* and *Satan* were collected in Texas from artesian wells some 984 ft. deep, and have never been found anywhere else. It is believed that they live in long, narrow, water-filled openings deep beneath the surface. Their extraordinary way of life has left its mark: the subterranean catfishes have lost the use of their eyes, and their skin is colorless.

The vast majority of catfishes live in freshwater, but the sea catfishes and some species of catfish eels occur in tropical and subtropical seas.

Breeding strategies

Since catfishes look after their eggs and care for their offspring, they produce, on average, rather fewer eggs than their relatives, the carps and their allies. The protection catfish give to their young greatly reduces the death toll of young catfish during the first few weeks of life—the most critical stage of their life cycle.

Most sea catfishes practice mouth brooding, a system whereby the male fish carries the eggs in his

mouth to keep them safe. The male gafftopsail catfish of North America, for example, collects between 15 and 30 fertilized eggs in his mouth, each egg measuring 0.6-1 in. in diameter. One particular male 1 ft. 7 in. long was found to have 55 eggs in his mouth. Before the male picks up the eggs, his large mouth grows even larger, expanding at the bottom and sides to provide extra room. His parental care does not end when the eggs hatch, since the live offspring remain in his mouth until they are ready to fend for themselves, after a period of several weeks. Once the young have absorbed their yolk sacs, they begin to feed themselves by filtering water from their father's mouth and trapping any minute plants and animals that it contains. Occasionally, they leave their shelter to find food outside, but rush back at the least hint of danger.

The catfish's parental care reduces the chance of losing eggs and young to almost nothing, but it has its drawbacks. With his mouth full of eggs, the male cannot eat, and has to go without food for up to two months.

Caring catfishes

Most catfishes are not so selfless. The numerous freshwater catfishes display many different levels of parental care. The Eurasian catfishes, a group that includes the European wels, display comparatively little care. The European wels is one of the largest European freshwater fishes with a maximum length of about 10 ft. The female lays some 100,000

ABOVE **The glass catfish of Southeast Asia has evolved a remarkable form of camouflage. Its body is almost completely transparent, so that when it weaves in and out of the underwater vegetation it is barely visible to its enemies.**

BELOW **The female European wels lays her eggs on water plants (A) and the male guards them until they hatch (B). The young offspring feed on insects and small fishes (C), but a fully grown wels attacks and eats waterfowl and mammals (D).**

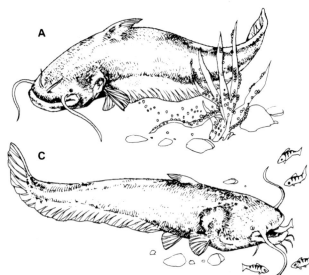

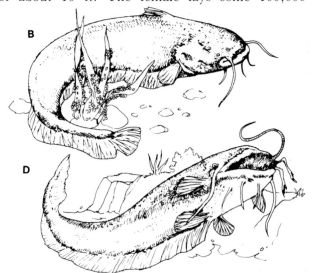

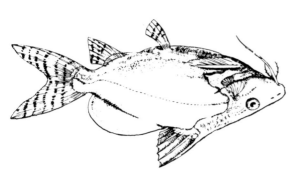

ABOVE AND TOP RIGHT Some members of the upside-down catfishes family habitually swim on their backs in order to feed on the invertebrates and algae that live on the underside of floating vegetation.
BELOW RIGHT Some of the armored catfishes of South America can move short distances across dry land, supported by their strong pectoral and ventral fins.

PAGES 1916-1917 A wriggling mass of barbel catfish become stranded as the water evaporates from their breeding pool at the onset of the dry season. Barbel catfish belong to the air-breathing catfish family—another group renowned for their ability to walk over dry land; many of the stranded fish will be able to escape from the dried-up pool to the safety of a river.

sticky eggs. After they have attached themselves to waterweed, the male watches over them.

North American freshwater catfishes construct more advanced nests. The behavior of one of them, the brown bullhead, has been studied in detail. Occurring in central and eastern areas of North America, it has been introduced into New Zealand and Europe.

The brown bullhead breeds in late spring and summer when the water temperature reaches 69.8°F. One or both members of the pair dig a shallow hollow in a muddy or sandy bottom with a diameter that is slightly larger than their body length. They usually choose an area near submerged branches, the roots of water plants or rocks.

Spawning among the brown bullheads takes place during the day. The male and female begin by brushing one another with their barbels, as if they were caressing. They then lie alongside one another in the nest with their heads facing in opposite directions. The female produces a clutch of sticky eggs covered in jelly-like mucus, and the male immediately fertilizes them. They then repeat the sequence several times until the female has laid all her eggs—up to 13,000 in a 9-in.-long individual.

Scavengers and predators

Many catfishes are scavengers, scouring the bottom of rivers and lakes for debris; others eat mainly bottom-dwelling animals or plants. The largest catfish family—the armored catfishes with about 410 species—have comb-like teeth that they use to scrape algae from rocks. They search for food using the taste cells that are concentrated in the barbels but are also distributed over most of their bodies.

Some large catfish are voracious predators, gulping down any animal that will fit in their huge mouths. The European catfish eats not only fishes but waterfowl and small mammals that venture into the water. Reports tell of it attacking dogs swimming in rivers. One South American species of the long-whiskered catfish family has been seen eating monkeys that have fallen into the river.

THE BROWN BULLHEAD
— COMMUNICATION BY CHEMICALS —

An inhabitant of small lakes, ponds and slow-moving rivers, the brown bullhead is a freshwater species of North American catfish (though it was introduced into Europe at the beginning of the 20th century). It is nocturnal, hiding in hollows during the day and searching for food in the evenings. Much of its diet consists of mud-dwelling worms and insect larvae, although it will eat larger animals.

The brown bullhead relies on its sensitive barbels both to locate its prey and to find its way through the murky waters of the riverbed. As it moves along, the fish brushes the long, sensitive barbels over the bottom of the water, using them as tongues and antennae to taste and feel its way.

For social communication, brown bullheads use their sense of smell—sending and receiving chemical messages. Experiments have revealed the complexity and importance of a "chemical language" in the bullheads' social organization. Two bullheads placed in a tank will divide the space between them, each creating its own territory and not crossing into the other's. Even when one fish is removed for several hours, the second one does not enter its territory.

However, if a different fish is placed in the vacated area, the other one attacks it immediately. When the intruder is removed and the first one replaced in the tank, the two fish resume their original relationship.

The behavior of bullheads under experimental conditions suggests that they can both identify other fishes and also retain a memory of them. The memory is basically chemical, processed by the fish's sense of smell.

Bullied by a bullhead

On one occasion, also under laboratory conditions, a large bullhead jumped out of its tank and into a nearby one containing smaller fish. The bullhead immediately began to create havoc, causing several of the small fish to leap out of their tank and onto the floor. When the intruder was removed, only two small fish remained in the tank, obviously scared by the incident. Afterward, when water was taken

from the bullhead's tank and poured into the tank of the smaller fish, the small fish abandoned their individual territories and hid together. The two fish continued to react in this way for four months, demonstrating that they had retained a perfect memory of their enemy's chemical signal.

In bullhead communities with only a few members, hierarchies are based on the recognition of territorial rights. The highest-ranking fish controls the most extensive and sheltered territory. Subordinate fish are left with smaller, more exposed areas.

Bullheads are physically aggressive only toward strangers. They can be vicious, mauling one another and causing serious injuries. If their smelling apparatus is immobilized, individuals of the same community behave like strangers and fight openly, since they are no longer able to recognize each other's chemical identity. When their smelling apparatus is restored to normal, the fish are able to recognize one another again.

In a crowded community with hundreds of individuals, brown bullheads are not territorial, swimming freely and coming into contact with one another without fighting. In laboratory experiments, bullheads densely packed into a tank also lead a collective life.

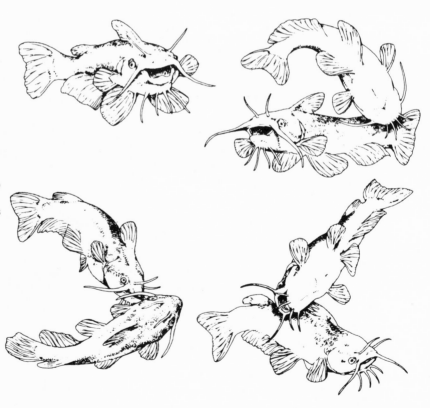

FAR LEFT AND LEFT The brown bullhead is native to central and eastern North America, but has been introduced into parts of Europe and New Zealand. One of the most well-known members of the North American catfish family, it grows to 7.5-12 in. in length and has long barbels and sharp, barbed spines on its pectoral fins.
ABOVE RIGHT The barbels of the brown bullhead act both as feelers and as taste organs. By using them to "taste the water," the fish can locate prey and detect the presence of enemies.
RIGHT With barbels spread and jaws gaping, two neighboring brown bullheads wrestle with one another during a dispute over a territorial boundary.

1919

TOP AND ABOVE The electric eel of South America has powerful electric organs along its sides, composed of modified muscle tissue. The animal lies on the bottom of rivers and pools waiting for prey to come within reach. As soon as a small fish draws close, the eel stuns it with an electric shock and snatches its victim before it has a chance to recover.

The large South American catfishes are the unwitting hosts of much smaller catfishes known as the parasite or pencil catfishes. These have elongated, scaleless bodies. They live by penetrating the gill chambers of larger fish and feeding on their blood. One species, the candiru, is notorious for the occasions when it has swum up the urine streams of mammals urinating in the water, mistaking the flow of liquid for the water pumped out of the catfishes' gill chambers.

The upside-down catfishes constitute an African freshwater family that is interesting for two reasons. They can produce noises by rubbing their pectoral spines against their bodies, and some species have the remarkable habit of swimming upside-down to gather food from the water surface. The normal camouflage pattern of a fish (a dark back and pale belly) is useless when the fish is swimming upside-down, and in some cases the pattern is reversed as the fish matures, so that its belly is darker than its back.

If attacked, many catfishes rely on an armor of bony plates and spines, sometimes augmented by fearsome

GYMNOTIFORMES CLASSIFICATION

The order Gymnotiformes contains six families in all, with about 55 species in 23 genera. They are all freshwater species, and are confined to Central and South America. There are three species of naked-back knifefishes in the family Gymnotidae, including the banded knifefish, *Gymnotus carapo*. There are just two species in the family Rhamphichthyidae, the most well known of which is the bandfish, *Rhamphichthys rostratus*, while the family Electrophoridae consists solely of the electric eel, *Electrophorus electricus*.

spiny rays that are connected to poison glands (the marine catfishes of the eeltail family are particularly dangerous in this respect).

A self-propelled battery

Naked-backed knifefishes are members of the Gymnotid family, and include three species—all inhabiting murky waters in South America. They have long bodies ending in a pointed tail, and greatly elongated anal fins that run the length of their bodies.

Since they have poor vision, knifefishes rely on their electrical ability to navigate and detect food. They emit slow pulses of low-voltage electricity that bounce off objects in a similar manner to radar. One species, the banded knifefish, reaches about 24 in. in length. It has small teeth and feeds at dawn and dusk—the adults preying on crustaceans and small fish. The young feed on crustaceans and insect larvae. The bandfish, another South American species, can grow to over 3 ft. in length. It has weak electrical abilities, too, but its shock is not a great threat to humans.

By contrast, the electric eel—the sole member of the Electrophorid family—produces a powerful shock that it uses to stun predators and prey as well as to navigate and detect food. Its electric organs, which are modified muscles, lie along the sides of its body and consist of columns of thin plates arranged in rows that resemble the electric organs of electric ray fish. An electric eel only 20 in. in length can produce electrical discharges of 40-300 volts, and larger specimens—up to 8 ft. long—produce shocks of 600 volts or more.

ROBUST AND SPIRITED

Respected by anglers for their vigorous fighting spirit, many salmon and trout overcome enormous obstacles on their journeys back to their breeding grounds. In the sea depths, the lightfishes and lantern fishes give off ghostly lights in the inky depths of the sea

Twaite shad (order Clupeiformes

Mooneye (order Clupeiformes)

Pacific salmon

Grayling

Powan

Northern pike

Alaska blackfish

Atlantic salmon

1922

Gizzard shad (order Clupeiformes)

The unrivaled position of the salmon as a sporting and food fish has ensured that the salmon family is one of the most well-known of all the fish groups. In fact, these fish are only part of a larger group, the order Salmoniformes, that includes fish as diverse as the predatory pike of freshwater, the slender, delicate smelts found in brackish and coastal waters, and the silvery, deepwater argentines.

Majestic migrants

Many of the Salmoniformes are distinguished by a small, fleshy extra dorsal fin that occurs well back on the spine just in front of the fish's tail. The "adipose fin," as it is called, occurs on all the fishes of the salmon family, and also on some other families of Salmoniformes. The salmon and many of its immediate relatives are migratory between freshwater and the sea.

Migration has several advantages. Predators are relatively scarce in freshwater, so more eggs and larvae are likely to survive and less have to be laid. The sea, on the other hand, has much richer food resources, and by migrating to the sea, the fish can grow quickly.

But there are also drawbacks to migration. The fish take time to become accustomed to the changes in conditions. Swimming upstream to spawn often involves surmounting obstacles such as rapids and

ABOVE When salmon fry hatch from their eggs, the yolk sacs remain attached to their bodies and continue to provide them with food for several months. As the yolk supply finally runs out, the young start to feed on small invertebrates.

PAGE 1921 A salmon leaps a waterfall during its upstream migration to its spawning ground. Salmon will travel thousands of miles, overcoming many obstacles on the way, to return to the stream in which they were hatched.

waterfalls—a problem that the salmon species overcome in spectacular fashion at the many well-known "salmon leaps." Another much more serious problem has arisen as a result of human interference with the environment. Not only have many rivers become blocked by barriers, such as dams, that defeat the most determined fishes, but rivers are also often polluted to such an extent in the lower reaches that the fish cannot pass through to reach the headwaters where they breed. The result is that many species have disappeared from rivers where they were once numerous, and several have become rare.

Some species, such as the brown trout, exist in both migratory and non-migratory (or sedentary) forms. These may be distinguished from each other by color or size. After a season of feeding at sea, the so-called "sea trout" are nearly twice the size of the brown trout that remain in the rivers. The sea trout acquire a silver coloration (although they are genetically the same species as the brown trout). Some of the freshwater forms occur in landlocked lakes and so cannot migrate. Others could migrate, but they choose not to—it is not yet known why.

Territorial fish

Salmon and their allies feed exclusively on small animals such as fish and invertebrates, but almost all species tend to become mainly fish feeders when conditions permit. In the open sea, their diet of fish enables them to reach their maximum size.

In freshwater, individual salmon occupy their own territory, defending it actively against intruders. The fishes maintain fixed positions with their heads facing into the current. They leave these positions only to grasp food from the bottom or the surface. The territories vary in size according to the available food and the size of the fish. If there is plenty of food, a small territory will be sufficient. A large fish usually occupies more space, or a more favorable position in the stream where it can obtain as much food as possible and grow to its maximum size. It flourishes at the expense of its smaller neighbors, ensuring that at least some individuals of each generation grow large enough to survive and breed in their turn.

The salmon

The Atlantic and Pacific oceans, along with some extensive inland water systems, are home to various species of salmon. Most of them are anadromous (feeding at sea, migrating up freshwater rivers to breed). The landlocked species migrate within their home river and lake systems. The group of Pacific salmon are the most numerous in terms of species and total numbers.

Pacific salmon inhabit the coastal areas of the northern Pacific, from Japan to California, as well as areas of the Arctic as far north as Kamchatka. There are seven species of Pacific salmon, two of which have landlocked forms. The sockeye salmon, also called the red or blueback salmon, is found from southern Oregon to Japan, and averages about 7 lbs. in weight (with a maximum of 15 lbs.). Another species occurs in Lake Biwa in Japan. The largest species in the Pacific salmon group is the chinook, also known as the king salmon or quinnat. One chinook salmon was recorded as weighing 126 lbs. (although 55 lbs. is a more realistic maximum today, with an average size of 20 lbs. while migrating). The coho or silver salmon may reach 26 lbs., but is usually caught at around 9 lbs.; the chum or dog salmon varies between 7 lbs. and 18 lbs., with a maximum of about 35 lbs., while the humpback or pink salmon averages less than 3 lbs., with a maximum of 11 lbs. The latter only takes two years to mature.

The life cycle of most salmon is similar in pattern, in that they feed in the sea and return to the rivers to spawn. However, there are a few variations to this pattern. The humpback salmon, for example, has a two-year life cycle. The sockeye lives for about eight

SALMONIFORMES CLASSIFICATION: 1

There are 320 species contained within the order Salmoniformes, arranged in 15 families and 90 genera. Together, they range throughout the oceans and occur in freshwater habitats on every continent.

The salmon family

The family Salmonidae contains about 70 species that range throughout the Northern Hemisphere. They include the sockeye salmon, *Oncorhynchus nerka*; the chinook salmon, *O. tschawytscha*; the Atlantic salmon, *Salmo salar*; the brown, lake or sea trout, *S. trutta*; the rainbow trout, *S. gairdneri*; the brook trout or brook char, *Salvelinus fontinalis*; the arctic char, *S. alpinus*; the grayling, *Thymallus thymallus*; and the whitefish and ciscos of the genus *Coregonus*

Smelts and galaxiids

The smelts of the family Osmeridae occur both in rivers and in cold coastal waters of the Northern Hemisphere. There are 10 species, including the European smelt or sparling, *Osmerus eperlanus*, and the capelin, *Mallotus villosus*. The family Galaxiidae contains the 49 species of galaxiids—freshwater fishes of the Southern Hemisphere. The most widespread species is *Galaxias maculatus*.

ABOVE AND LEFT The chinook salmon is the largest Pacific salmon, weighing up to 126 lbs. When sexually mature, the male develops a bright coloration and a hooked jaw, with large teeth that he uses to defend his spawning territory.

PAGES 1926-1927 Pacific salmon return after several years to the shallow stream where they were hatched in order to spawn. They recognize the stream by the smell of the chemicals that reach the water from the rocks and surrounding vegetation.

years, and its migratory form gives rise to smaller, landlocked fishes known as kokanee, that were once considered a separate species. The Atlantic salmon is the only species to occur naturally in the Atlantic, and its life cycle typifies that of all the other species.

Spawning of the Atlantic salmon

Atlantic salmon spawn between October and January. High in the headwaters of the river of her birth, in clean, cool streams, the female salmon digs a nest—called the redd—by thrusting aside gravel with powerful lashes of her tail. The current carries away any small shingle, and the completed redd is a groove measuring 6-12 in. deep with large stones in the bottom. The female "crouches" in the nest, and the male adopts the same position beside her. The two fish then shed their eggs and sperm (milt) together. At the same time, young male salmon (called parr) that

have not yet been to sea, dart in and out of the redd shedding their own sperm. Up to 75 percent of these youngsters are fertile, and their behavior ensures that all the eggs are fertilized. The large male is fairly clumsy and sheds his milt in the scattering force of the current. By swimming into the sheltered water inside the redd, the parr make sure that milt penetrates all the gaps in the gravel into which the eggs have fallen.

Returning to the sea

The female repeats the nesting procedure several times, moving upstream a little so that dislodged gravel buries previous egg batches quite deeply. The eggs are covered in such a way that they are exposed to a good flow of well-oxygenated water. The oxygenated water serves two functions: it supplies the eggs with oxygen and removes metabolic wastes. The spawning period may last up to two weeks. Exhausted and

ABOVE AND BELOW An Atlantic salmon leaps through rapids on its upriver spawning migration (above). Its jumping technique depends on the flow of the water. If an obstruction is very steep, it will leap directly from its base (below, A), but if the angle allows, the fish will race upcurrent until it has almost lost momentum, and then leap (B). One of the main threats to salmon breeding occurs when man-made structures—for example, dams and hydroelectric barriers—block the path of the migrating fish.

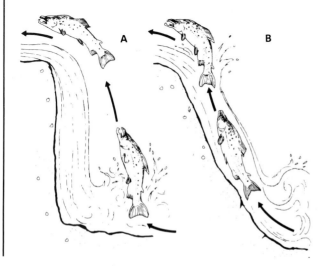

emaciated, having lost 30-40 percent of their pre-spawning weight, the salmon drop back downstream. At this stage they are known as kelts. The majority, particularly the males, will die after spawning. Due to their weakened physical condition, they succumb to disease and predators. On average, only 5-10 percent of these kelts will return to spawn again. The record is held by an eight-year-old female from the Add River in Ireland that spawned no less than five times.

Development of the young

The eggs hatch in April to May, and the young are known as alevins. For several months they live on the contents of their yolk sacs. With the exhaustion of the yolk supply, the brightly colored fry emerge from the gravel and begin feeding on insect larvae and other invertebrates. As they grow they develop into parrs. The dark blotches that appear on their bodies serve as camouflage. The length of time they spend in freshwater varies from five years in the north of their range to one year in the south. At 4-7.5 in. long, the parrs lose their spots and become silver all over. At this stage, they are ready to migrate to the sea and are called smolt. The young salmon pause briefly in estuaries to acclimatize themselves to the saltwater before they disappear to feed at sea. Once in the sea, the smolts feed on small fish, squid and shrimps in well-defined feeding grounds.

Determined travelers

After one to five years, the salmon return to freshwater to breed, covering thousands of miles at an average speed of 3-6 miles a day. The largest fish—those that have lived in the sea for up to four years without spawning—tend to arrive early in the season, while the small, one-year-old "grilse" appear in midsummer. During their time at sea, the fish build up large reserves of fat. Once in freshwater they do not feed. They simply swim upstream, resting and leaping over obstacles and up waterfalls and rapids until they reach the spawning grounds, sometimes hundreds of miles inland.

On this journey they undergo more changes of color and form. Their color changes from silver-blue to brown or green with orange mottling. The males develop a hook on their lower jaw, known as the kype, which they use for fighting other males during courtship and for defending their territories.

Following their noses

A remarkably high proportion of the fish can return to the exact tributary of their birth. For the salmon, each river has its own unmistakable "signature" scent that they can detect at great distances. The salmon are able to swim to the coastline containing the estuary of their native river. There are many theories about how the fish navigate on this part of their journey. The position of sun and stars, polarized light, and the salt content of the water and its temperature have all been suggested as guides.

Exploitation

The long migration and seasonal abundance of the Atlantic salmon have made it a target for exploitation for hundreds of years. In the days of cleaner rivers, salmon was an easily accessible and cheap fish food. The industrial revolution of the 19th century began a period when all but the most remote rivers became polluted. The salmon left the rivers or died, and became a luxury item.

During the 1960s fishermen of several nations discovered the salmon feeding grounds at sea, and overfishing of salmon became a serious problem. They have, however, been given a temporary reprieve

ABOVE Their frantic spawning period over, dead and dying silver salmon litter the bed of a river in Alaska. Breeding salmon do not feed while they are in freshwater, and can lose over a third of their body weight by the time they have finished spawning. If they do not immediately succumb to exhaustion or the injuries suffered during territorial battles, their weakened condition leaves them vulnerable to predators and diseases. Very few mature adults survive to return to the sea.

by the increased efficiency of fish farming. Recent years have seen the introduction of salmon reared in cages at sea. Salmon farming may well have helped to keep up the numbers of salmon, but it also has its own problems. Chemicals used to prevent diseases in the salmon population have caused many further diseases in the salmon and in other marine life.

Salmon farming has increased the numbers of salmon, and exploitation of the fishes has decreased. However, until effective measures are taken to control pollution and the blocking of rivers, the previously high numbers of salmon may never return.

When a salmon enters the river mouth on its breeding migration, it is a handsome, streamlined fish, silver in color, with hard X-shaped markings on its flanks. It may weigh anything from 11 to 77 lbs. The

ABOVE Because of their great popularity as game fishes, various species of trout have been introduced into areas outside their normal range. The picture shows a young brook char (commonly known as brook trout)—a species introduced to Europe from North America—dwarfed by a native brown trout. These two species occasionally interbreed to create a striped hybrid called the zebra trout.

salmon is easily confused with the sea trout, but several features distinguish them. The upper jaw of the salmon does not extend past its eye; a salmon's tail stalk is thinner than a trout's (a fresh salmon can be held by the tail, while a trout slips through the fingers); and the tail profile of a salmon is quite deeply notched, while the rear edge of a trout's tail is straight or only slightly concave.

A diversity of trouts

Trouts belong to the salmon family and occur in an extraordinary variety of sizes and colors, depending on the temperature and conditions of their surroundings. Their rate of growth varies from river to river and from river to sea (trout living in small streams grow more slowly than those in large rivers). The brown trout of Europe occurs in a variety of forms, and many new subspecies have been identified.

The brown trout of Europe occurs in three forms that vary in color, form and behavior—the brown trout, the lake trout and the sea trout. The brown trout and lake trout usually inhabit clean, well-oxygenated freshwater habitats. Unlike the sea trout, the brown trout and the lake trout are non-migratory, although the lake trout prefers to swim upstream to spawn. The sea trout is a large, silver-scaled fish that resembles the salmon in appearance. It usually feeds at sea and, like the salmon, swims upriver to breed in freshwater. When feeding at sea, it is covered in small, black spots, but its body darkens after returning to freshwater during the breeding season.

Because the sea offers a greater abundance of food than rivers, sea trout that feed in the mouths of rivers grow to a larger size than the non-migratory forms of brown trout. Indeed, size is a distinguishing factor among the three forms of brown trout. The brown trout rarely exceeds 2 lbs. 3 oz. in weight and generally grows to a length of 12-18 in. In contrast, the sea trout commonly reaches 11 lbs. in weight, since it has access to rich feeding grounds. The brown trout has a small, greenish brown body decorated with red and black spots, while the lake trout is a silver, marble-backed fish that feeds on the abundant food available in its natural habitat.

Fishing for rainbows

The rainbow trout is a native of North America west of the Rocky Mountains, and is particularly common along the Pacific coast from Alaska to southern California. It occurs in migratory and non-migratory (sedentary) forms, and derives its common name from the distinguishing pinkish, iridescent colors along its flanks. Another form of rainbow trout, known as the steelhead trout in Canada, occurs in the northern part of the range and migrates to the ocean.

The rainbow trout has a greater tolerance of low-oxygen conditions than the brown trout and feeds on a wider variety of invertebrates. As a result, it is more adaptable and competitive when sharing its habitat with the brown trout. Since it can be farmed easily, the rainbow trout has been introduced into several parts of Europe, often at the expense of the local fishes. Conversely, the brown trout has been introduced into western parts of North America and into most countries of the Southern Hemisphere.

The cutthroat trout is similar to the rainbow trout in its natural range and habits. Often rated as one of North America's finest sporting fishes, it derives its common name from the brilliant red markings around its chin that give the impression that its throat has been cut. It reaches a length of 8-14 in. and weighs 13-20 lbs.

ABOVE Like most members of the salmon family, the brown trout varies widely in size according to its habitat and the availability of food. Where food is plentiful, such as in the sea or in a large lake, brown trout can reach weights of over 22 lbs. **BELOW** The map shows the ranges of the salmons and their relatives, the pikes and the smelts.

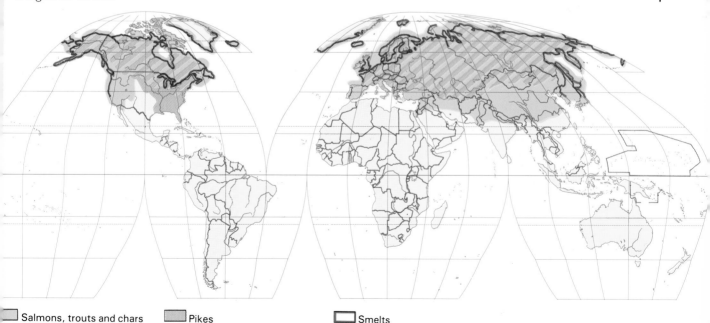

☐ Salmons, trouts and chars   ▨ Pikes   ☐ Smelts

THE BROWN TROUT
— CLEAN LIVING FISH —

The brown trout is an extremely variable fish that occurs in three different forms within the same species (and each form is subject to many local variations). The three basic forms of brown trout are the sea trout (sometimes known as the salmon trout), the brown trout and the lake trout. Each varies in size, color and migratory habits.

The sea trout is a large, silver-scaled fish that is similar in appearance to the Atlantic salmon. As a migratory fish, it mirrors the behavior of the salmon in swimming upriver from the sea to breed. However, while the Atlantic salmon will migrate far out to sea and often spawns only once in its lifetime, the sea trout never ventures far from the mouth of a river and will return to the upper reaches of the river several years in succession to spawn.

Because of the abundance of food in the sea, the sea trout is a large fish that weighs about 11 lbs. It feeds on a wide diet of sprats, young herring, sand eels and small crustaceans.

The brown trout and lake trout are non-migratory fish that remain in freshwater throughout their lives. The

brown trout weighs about 2 lbs. and has a small, greenish brown body with lighter flanks and yellowish underparts. A decoration of red and black spots covers its body. The brown trout prefers cold, fast-flowing, well-oxygenated streams and rivers that run over gravel beds. It needs a clean water environment since it is highly susceptible to pollution. The male brown trout begins to breed after two years, the female after three. They spawn between September and February after swimming a short distance upstream from their feeding territories.

The lake trout inhabits large lakes at depths of 400 ft. where it has access to a wealth of food that rivals the riches available in the sea. But since it does not embark on long migrations, the lake trout grows even larger than the sea trout. The lake trout does not breed in the lake itself, but prefers to swim up tributary streams to spawn, usually between the months of September and December.

The three forms of brown trout display almost identical mating, hatching and growth behavior. Once the female reaches the spawning grounds, she will defend it against other females. After securing her breeding area, she then digs a nest or "redd" in a gravel hollow by swimming on her side and brushing the stones aside with her tail. Each female is courted by a male who drives away any other suitors, sometimes with considerable violence. As the female lays her eggs in the redd, the male fish fertilizes them, positioning himself alongside her, slightly to the rear.

The female then covers the eggs with gravel and moves off to find another nest site. In total, she lays up to

10,000 eggs (the amount is always proportional to the weight of the fish).

Small fry

The period of incubation varies according to the water temperature, increasing as the water gets colder. The larvae or fry generally hatch after two or three months. During the first few days of their lives, the 0.8-in.-long fry are equipped with bulky yolk sacs that sustain them while they remain buried in the gravel.

Eventually they leave the nest, but stay out of the light until their yolk stores are empty. Three weeks later—or even three months if the water temperature is very low—they swim toward the surface where they begin to hunt for small crustaceans and insect larvae. Their diet broadens after a year to include small fish and even amphibians, mammals and small birds. After they reach the age of two, young sea trout migrate to the river mouth and spend the next three years feeding in the sea. When they are sexually mature, they show extraordinary homing instincts, returning to the same place where they hatched in order to spawn.

FAR LEFT With the benefit of abundant food and ideal water conditions, brown trout that inhabit lakes can grow to twice the size of their river-dwelling cousins.

TOP RIGHT The brown trout needs clean, well-oxygenated waters in which to live. It cannot cope with pollution in any form.

ABOVE RIGHT With their yolk sacs still attached, two brown trout fry emerge from their eggs. Brown trout lay their eggs in gravel, and the newly hatched young will remain among the stones until their yolk runs out and they can catch food for themselves.

RIGHT A spawning female brown trout digs a series of nests upstream from one another. Each time she digs a new one with upward scoops of her tail, the excavated gravel drifts downstream to cover the eggs laid in the previous nest.

Relics of the Ice Age

The chars are similar in shape and habit to the trouts. They inhabit cold, clean lakes and rivers in the far northern regions of the world. As with other salmonoids (members of the salmon family), chars are adaptable fishes, occurring in both land and sea-dwelling forms. In Europe, the lake chars have existed in upland lakes since the Ice Age glaciers retreated, hundreds of thousands of years ago. They are small, red fish, growing to a length of 8 in. In contrast, the seagoing, migratory forms of char might reach a length of 38 in. and a weight of over 26 lbs.

Populations of Arctic char have enjoyed long periods of isolation, leading to differences in form and behavior. Several species are members of the char group but have the inaccurate common name of trout. The brook trout, for example, is a char. Growing to over 35 in. in its migratory form, the brook trout inhabits eastern parts of North America. It has also been widely introduced into Europe where it rarely exceeds 18 in. in length. In Europe, the brook trout hybridizes with both the brown trout and the intro-duced rainbow trout to form the unusual "zebra trout."

A Dickensian char

The lake trout is an important commercial fish in North America and Canada. Until the introduction of lampreys into its natural habitat (which killed off large numbers of the trout), it was the mainstay of a profitable fishery in the Great Lakes. The 48-in.-long Dolly Varden trout is another sporting char of North America. It derives its common name from its conspicuous red spots that are thought to be reminiscent of the cherry ribbons worn by a like-named character in Charles Dickens' novel "Barnaby Rudge."

The whitefish: shoals of plankton eaters

Whitefish and ciscos are silvery salmonoids that inhabit the cold, deep lakes of northern Eurasia and North America. While whitefish are plain, ciscos are decorated with spots and patterns. Unlike the predatory trout, salmon and char, whitefish are plankton eaters with small mouths, heavy tails and fins less streamlined in shape than those of their predatory relatives. Whereas the other salmonoids are solitary in behavior and highly territorial, the ciscos and whitefish congregate in shoals to exploit their lakeland homes more efficiently. The whitefish

vary from species to species and are difficult to classify, especially since they hybridize, adapt to individual lakes and water systems and may be either landlocked or migratory.

Perhaps the most widespread whitefish in Europe is the vendace, or pollan, an 18-in.-long fish that bears a greater resemblance to the herrings than to the trout. Inhabiting lakes from Britain east through the Baltic to the USSR, the vendace spends most of the year in deeper water, feeding on planktonic crustaceans, insect larvae, mollusks and occasionally on fishes. On summer nights, shoals of vendace come to the surface to feed, and breeding takes place over gravelly shallows in autumn.

The Arctic cisco, an important source of food in Siberia and the northern parts of European Russia, is a migratory fish that visits coastal areas and may cover 600 miles of rivers in its breeding migration. In Lake Baikal in the USSR, it grows to a weight of 15 lbs. 7 oz. The least cisco is of great commercial importance in the USSR, and also forms the basis of a subsistence fishery in Alaska. It is a smaller fish than the Arctic cisco, growing to a length of 16 in. It moves between estuaries and lakes in immense shoals in the northern parts of its range, but is more sedentary in the south, where the winters are less severe.

Lake whitefish

The lake whitefish inhabits the lakes of North America, and can reach a weight of 42 lbs.—although 22 lbs. is a more usual weight. It is an extremely popular food fish, and has been hunted increasingly on a commercial scale in recent years. Since the lake whitefish leaves its tiny eggs on shallow gravel for the whole winter, they are particularly vulnerable to predation by crayfish, birds and egg-eating fish before hatching occurs in spring.

Britain is home to several species of whitefishes. The houting inhabits Loch Lomond and Loch Eck in Scotland, the skelly lives in England's Lake District, while the gwyniad occurs in Bala Lake in Wales. The migratory form of the skelly, which has a curious, pointed snout, was once common in the Baltic and the southern North Sea, but is now extinct in the latter.

The graceful graylings

Probably the most beautiful of northern freshwater fishes, the graylings are all similar in form. They have

tapered, streamlined bodies, large eyes, small mouths, and heavily forked tails. A distinguishing feature of the graylings is an unmistakable large, purple dorsal fin, decorated with various borders and spots. In color, the graylings range from greenish brown to blue green on the upperparts with flanks of silvery-gray and white underparts. Coloration varies according to species and breeding condition.

Graylings inhabit clear, cold swift-flowing streams with stony or rocky bottoms. They usually congregate in large shoals, often found in the deep runs below undercut banks or in the quieter pools below shallow streams. In warmer weather, shoals of grayling congregate in the shallows near the banks. They are migratory fishes, but are wholly freshwater.

Flexible diet

The European grayling is typical of the group, inhabiting streams and rivers throughout Europe from the Alps to the Ural and Volga rivers in the USSR. The cold waters of the north are not especially rich in food, so it is not surprising that European graylings will take almost any insect. When they are available, the fish eat freshwater shrimps, snails,

ABOVE Rainbow trout are native to North America, where they exist in two forms: the rainbow trout, which keeps to lakes and rivers; and the steelhead trout, which runs to the sea to feed, only returning to freshwater in the breeding season. Although many rainbow trout have been released in European waters, very few have bred, and so far there have been no confirmed reports of steelhead trouts surviving in the wild in Europe.

mayflies and caddis worms. In times of food shortage, they also take adult insects and spiders—they have even been known to eat shrews.

Graylings breed in spring from early March to mid-May. After competition among males, the shoals break up into pairs over gravelly shallows. During the mating season, the males' colors are heightened, and their dorsal fins become especially vivid. A clear, shallow stream alive with the protruding fins of competing males is a remarkable sight on a spring day. The female digs a shallow bed in the gravel, and the male lies alongside her, his dorsal tail wrapped over her back as he fertilizes the eggs. The female then buries her yellow eggs. The eggs take 18-20 days to hatch at a minimum temperature of 50°F. While the young are still carrying their yolk sacs, they hide

among stones, only emerging into the main current after they have absorbed these sacs. They grow rapidly, reaching a length of 6 in. in just a year.

Bad reputation

Although graylings may reach 4 lbs. 6 oz. in weight in some waters, and they fight well on the rod, they have a poor reputation among most trout anglers who consider that the introduction of grayling has reduced trout stocks. Consequently, anglers who manage their waters carefully will often net and kill graylings, placing the local population under threat. In fact, graylings only eat trout eggs and compete against trout in poor waters where food is scarce.

Although they share the same habitat as the trout, graylings differ in behavior and feeding habits. In reasonably rich, wide waters, graylings and trout occupy different parts of the stream, eat at different levels, and even spawn at different times. Shoals of graylings hang in the main current, while individual trout live near underwater outcrops; graylings feed on the bottom, while trout prefer to hunt the upper water; graylings breed in spring while most salmonoids breed in winter.

Originally freshwater fishes of the Arctic regions, graylings thrive in colder climates and their modern distribution tallies with the boundary of the last Ice Age. Stranded far south of their original home when the ice retreated, the graylings adopted the freshwater zones that most resembled Arctic conditions. These areas were also the domain of the trout, but the differences of diet and behavior prevented direct conflict and competition.

The smelts

Many tiny estuary and sea fishes have, mistakenly, been called smelts, but the true smelts are members of the salmon order. They can be identified by the small, rayless, fatty fin set on their backs, just forward of their

ABOVE LEFT **The Arctic char inhabits the open sea and rivers in northern regions of the world. In the far north, it can grow over 3 ft. in length and weigh over 15 lbs. Most populations of the fish are migratory, traveling from the food-rich northern** seas to spawn in gravel-bottomed rivers.
LEFT **The brook char or brook trout is native to North America. It was introduced to Europe in 1884, but does not breed with much success outside its natural range.**

tail fins. Some 10 species make up the smelt family and they inhabit cold, inshore waters in the Northern Hemisphere. Some (known as anadromous fish) migrate from the sea into freshwater to breed, some are landlocked in freshwater lakes, and others remain at sea permanently.

Most smelts measure about 8 in. long (few exceed 12 in.). They are slender, silver fish with large mouths and scales that can easily be removed. Wherever smelts occur, they are a vital link in local food chains. The capelin, for example, occur in vast numbers in the coastal waters of the Arctic, North Pacific and North Atlantic oceans. Measuring up to 8 in. long, these greenish smelts feature in the diets of seals, whales, porpoises, and nearly every species of fish-eating bird. They also provide food for salmon, char, cod, saithe (coalfish), halibut and many other commercially important fishes.

The most familiar smelt in European waters is the European smelt or sparling. Rarely reaching more than 8 in. long, it ranges from the river Seine in France to the Baltic Sea, although its distribution is quite patchy.

The pike

At the other end of the food chain from the smelts lie the pikes. They are specialized and efficient predators that inhabit all but the fastest-flowing freshwaters in the Northern Hemisphere. There are five species, all of them having the same distinctive body shape: the head has a flattened outline, and the dorsal fin lies far back on the body, above the anal fin and near to the deeply forked tail.

The concentration of fins at the rear of a pike's body allows the fish to accelerate fast as it darts out from its hiding place to snatch wary, often fast-moving prey. Pikes are mottled or marbled green and black on a light green or yellow background. Their coloring serves as excellent camouflage for their stalk-and-rush method of hunting. Pikes' mouths are armed with a formidable array of backward-pointing teeth for seizing and holding large, struggling prey.

The most widely distributed member of the pike family is the pike (called the northern pike in North America), which lives in freshwater throughout the Northern Hemisphere. Many of the myths and inaccuracies that attach themselves to large predators have inevitably built up around this fish. Although there are accounts of giant pike weighing up to a quarter ton and measuring almost 20 ft. long, pike of more than 45 lbs. in weight and 3 ft. long are extremely rare. Reliable reports from the USSR mention specimens weighing 75 lbs., and there are unconfirmed observations of pike at 145 lbs.

Pike usually live in the shallower, weedy parts of rivers and lakes. They eat a wide variety of aquatic creatures, including frogs, newts, small or young water birds and voles, as well as all kinds of fish, including smaller pike.

Other species of pike lead similar lives to the pike. The muskellunge (an American Indian name meaning "great fish") is the largest of the pike species. In the past, individuals were reported to have reached a length of 8 ft. and a weight of 100 lbs. Today muskellunge (also called musky) weigh a maximum of

SALMONIFORMES CLASSIFICATION: 2

Pikes and mudminnows

The family Esocidae contains the five species of pikes and pickerels, which occur in freshwater habitats in the Northern Hemisphere. They include the pike or northern pike, *Esox lucius*, the muskellunge, *E. masquinongy*, and the chain pickerel, *E. niger*. The family Umbridae comprises a further five species of freshwater fishes from the Northern Hemisphere, including the European mudminnow, *Umbra kraemeri*, and the Alaska blackfish, *Dallia pectoralis*.

Deep-sea families

The argentines or herring smelts from the family Argentinidae are one of several groups of deep-sea fishes within the order Salmoniformes. The 20 species in the family include the Atlantic argentine, *Argentina sphyraena*, and the two members of the genus *Xenophthalmichthys*. The 10 species of barreleyes or spookfishes belong to the family Opisthoproctidae, and include the little barreleye, *Opisthoproctus grimaldi*. The other families are the Bathylagidae, which contains the 27 species of deep-sea smelts, the Aleopcephalidae, with the 60 or so species of slickheads, and the Searsiidae, with the 29 species of searsiids.

60-70 lbs. They live in freshwater in eastern and central Canada, ranging south through the Great Lakes area and into the upper Mississippi and Ohio river valleys. Under pressure from pollution and sport fishermen, the muskellunge appear to be declining.

America is also home to the pickerels, smaller versions of the pike that live in weedy, slow-moving water. The grass pickerel lives mostly on the eastern side of the USA and grows to no more than 14 in. long. The chain pickerel ranges from southeast Canada to Texas and may reach 32 in. in length. Some fish experts regard these two pickerel species merely as subspecies of a single species, the redfin pickerel.

Life in mud and ice

Mudminnows and blackfish belong to a family closely related to the pikes. Although they do not bear an immediate resemblance to pikes, their single dorsal fins are—like those of the pike—set far back on their bodies. Three species of mudminnows live in North America, and one species occurs in southeast Europe. Seldom more than 5 in. long, they live in muddy, weedy ponds and swamps, in surprisingly large numbers. Unlike most other fishes, they can tolerate remarkably low oxygen levels in the water,

ABOVE A grayling remains stationary in the current with subtle movements of all of its fins. Fish of strong, deep, main currents, grayling tend to lie close to the bottom, often in large shoals, occasionally rising to the surface to catch flies. They feed on the bottom as well, making the best use of the often poor resources of the chilly northern streams in which they live.

RIGHT A study in concentration, a small pike edges out of the weeds toward a frog. With subtle ripples of the fins, the pike stalks to within striking range of its prey. Then, with an abrupt flick of the tail, it launches itself to the attack. Its teeth are sharp and backward-facing, so few creatures that the pike bites have a chance to escape.

and can increase their oxygen supply by taking air at the surface of the water and holding it as bubbles in their gill chambers. Mudminnows derive their name from their ability to survive days or weeks of drought by burying themselves in mud.

Although mudminnows have a reputation for surviving low temperatures, they cannot match the cold endurance of their American cousin the Alaska blackfish. A large-mouthed, round-finned fish measuring 8 in. long, it lives in the mossy pools, streams and marshes of the Alaskan and Siberian arctic tundra, feeding on the abundant insect larvae and snails that emerge in summer. In winter, it can withstand water temperatures near to freezing.

Herring (order Clupeiformes)

Tarpon (order Elopiformes)

Anchovy (order Clupeiformes)

Wolf herring
(order Clupeiformes)

Black dragonfish

Sloane's viperfish

Scaly dragonfish

Pearlfish

Bristlemouth

Deep-sea hatchetfish

1940

The twilight zone

Few animals of any kind can live deep in the ocean where the sunlight fades past the point at which plants can make use of it. Fewer still can survive in total darkness. In the oceans, photosynthesis in the plankton probably stops at about 500 ft. deep. In the clearest water, light still penetrates, to a maximum of perhaps 4300 ft. The area between the 500 ft. point and the 4300 ft. point is known as the mesopelagic (literally "middle ocean") zone, a twilight region that contains its own unique fish fauna, numbering perhaps 850 species.

Mesopelagic fishes belong to several different orders, but many of them have evolved parallel adaptations to the dim, cold conditions in which they live. Generating light and detecting it are two of their priorities. Luminous glands of various kinds signal across the gloom, sometimes to identify the species, sometimes to lure prey. Some of these signals may serve as subtle forms of camouflage or means of breaking up the fishes' outlines. Fishes in the mesopelagic zone have large eyes, many of them being strange barrel shapes. Besides increasing the fish's sensitivity—it has been estimated that a fish can tell the difference between night and day at about 4265 ft. in the Indian Ocean—the exact function of these adaptations is unknown, although barreleyes seem to be confined to the deepest layers.

Deep-dwelling Salmoniformes

The borders of the deeps are the home of some 18 species of argentines or herring smelts. Their name "argentine" has nothing to do with the country Argentina, but refers to their silvery sheen (*argentum* is the Latin for "silver"). They are large-eyed, small-mouthed fishes with large scales. The Atlantic argentine is common. A silvery-green to yellow fish that seldom exceeds 22 in. long, it occurs on both sides of the Atlantic at depths of around 300-3000 ft. It feeds on small fishes and other midwater organisms. Although argentines are taken in commercial nets, their flesh is not tasty enough for use as human food, but they are caught for processing into fish meal to feed farm livestock.

One of the two species from the genus *Xenophthalmichthys* is a slender and fragile little fish, also a member of the argentine family. Known from only a few specimens, it is notable for its tubular eyes. Its habits are not fully known and it may not swim horizontally. Instead, its structure suggests that it

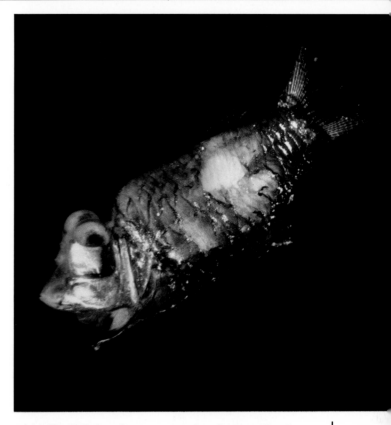

ABOVE The little barreleye, or spookfish, reaches a maximum length of approximately 4 in. and lives at depths of 650-2000 ft. It probably feeds on the stinging cells of jellyfish-like creatures known as siphonophores. The exact function of its tubular, upward pointing eyes is unknown.

hangs in the water, tail-down, with its eyes pointing upward so that it can spot prey or enemies against the more sunlit water above.

Visible brain

The barreleyes or spookfishes occur in the mesopelagic zone in most temperate and tropical oceans. The little barreleye of the North Atlantic is typical. A silvery, large-scaled fish measuring only about 4 in. long at most, it has a deep body in which the base is flattened into a broad, shallow, plate-shaped structure called the sole. The barreleye's skull is transparent—so much so that its brain can be seen easily, while its eyes are mounted in tubes that face forward or upward.

The slickheads are less spectacular but far more common than many other of these deepwater species, since trawlers, fishing for deep edible species such as hake, sometimes catch them. Slickheads are small and large-eyed, and most of them have scaled bodies; the scales are large and thin. Their heads lack scales and are smooth, hence their common name. Some of them have light cells, but these do not rival those of their close relatives, the searsiids. The 29 or more species are distinguished by a tube that opens at the shoulder just behind the gill cover. It contains a luminous mucus that the fish can squirt at will, creating a fiery, blue-green display.

The bristlemouths

The bristlemouths belong to an order of mesopelagic fishes with some 250 species grouped into nine families. Not unlike miniature herrings in shape, bristlemouths seldom exceed 3 in. in length. Many have large mouths with fine, bristle-like teeth and light-emitting organs on the sides of their bodies.

The bristlemouth species, *Gonostoma denudatum*, lives at mesopelagic depths in the Mediterranean Sea and the Atlantic Ocean. It grows to about one inch in length, has silvery flanks, a black back and a full set of prominent, light-emitting organs. Its eyes are large, and its jaws are strong and equipped with pointed teeth that vary in length. The parts of its brain associated with sight, smell and muscle control are well developed, and its firm muscles are contained inside a fairly rigid skeleton. It has a large swim bladder that offsets the weight of its muscles and skeleton.

Another bristlemouth species, *G. bathyphilum*, which lives at depths below 3250 ft. in the Atlantic, lacks nearly all the refinements of its shallower-water cousin. It is entirely black, with inconspicuous and underdeveloped light-emitting organs. Its jaw is long, and opens to a wide angle. Its eyes are small and, from an examination of the brain, are probably not used. The muscles—and the parts of the brain associated with them—are poorly developed, and the skeleton is weak. The fish has no swim bladder, but probably stays buoyant because it weighs so little. Females are about 0.8 in. in length, and males 0.6 in. long.

The differences between these two bristlemouths typify the variations in life-style between fishes living in deep and very deep water. *G. denudatum*, which lives higher in the water, is built to be active. Since the rich upper waters contain plenty of food, it probably migrates vertically every day in search of prey that it identifies by eye. It is likely that its sharp vision and light-emitting glands also assist it in finding a mate.

Hatchets, vipers and dragons

More is known about the appearance of the many fishes that populate the mesopelagic zone than about their habits. The family of deep-sea hatchetfishes with its 27 species is an example. Growing to a maximum length of only 3 in., they have slender tails that resemble the handles of a hatchet, and deep, silvery, flat bodies that resemble the blades.

Some deep-sea hatchetfishes have tubular eyes, and many have large, almost vertical mouths. All have large clusters of light-emitting organs on their undersides. They are arranged in a pattern unique to each species, so individuals can recognize members of their own species from below. They live in all the world's oceans, usually at depths of 1650-5000 ft. Although deep-sea hatchetfishes are not as numerous

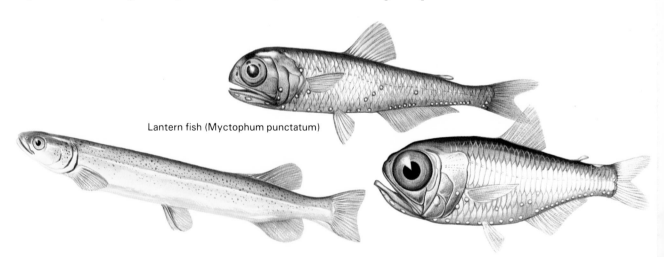

Lantern fish (Myctophum punctatum)

Galaxiid (Galaxias attenuatus)

Lantern fish (Electrona rissoi)

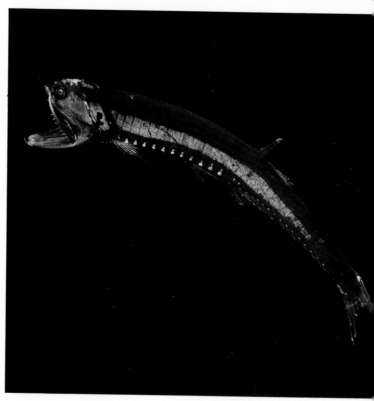

as the bristlemouths, they are a valuable link in the open-ocean food chain. They feed on tiny crustaceans, while commercial species, such as tunas, often prey on the deep-sea hatchetfishes.

The six species of viperfishes form a family that inhabits the Indian Ocean, Mediterranean, North Atlantic and parts of the South Atlantic and Pacific oceans. Each species prefers waters of a different salinity and temperature, so that two or more species are seldom caught together. Viperfishes are predators, migrating from the surface to a depth of 3000 ft. in search of their prey. They have well-developed eyes and various sets of light-emitting organs.

Viperfishes have long, snake-like bodies and fangs that curve back into their enormous mouths—both adaptations for swallowing large prey. The remarkable freedom of movement of their lower jaws enables them to deal with prey even larger than themselves. Viperfishes can open their mouths to more than 90 degrees by tilting their heads back and dropping their lower jaws.

Dragonfishes are similar to viperfishes in appearance and life-style, although their heads are smaller and their bodies narrower. Black dragonfishes have two distinguishing features: males and females differ markedly in appearance, and the larvae resemble neither the male nor the female adults. Adult females have long, slender bodies measuring 12-16 in. in length, pelvic fins, a long, luminous chin barbel, and teeth set in large jaws. They are black to dark brown in color, with white fins and light-emitting organs on their sides and behind their eyes.

Adult male black dragonfish measure a maximum of 2 in. long, they have no pelvic fins, no chin barbel, and no teeth. Their internal organs are shrunken and are probably useless, and their body cavities are completely filled with large testes. As adults, they probably only live for the couple of months needed to migrate to the deep waters, where they find mates.

The eyes of black dragonfish larvae are set at the end of long, cartilaginous stalks that may extend to more than a third of their body length. As the larvae grow, their eye stalks shorten. When the fish reach 1.2-1.6 in. in length, their eyes assume a normal position. Only when the young fish are about 1.6 in. long can their sex be determined.

ABOVE Popularly named because of their fine, needle-like teeth, bristlemouths resemble other deep-sea fishes in having a row of luminous organs along each flank. They are the most common fishes in the world in terms of numbers, and are trawled in tens of thousands from the bottom of all oceans each year. They also form an important part of the food chain, feeding on small invertebrates and in turn falling prey to larger fish, including their relatives.

Lizardfishes and lancetfishes

The 190 species of lizardfishes and their relatives are small, mostly large-mouthed predators with a single fatty, or adipose, fin situated between the dorsal fin and the tail. The majority live in the mesopelagic zone, although a few frequent coastal waters. The seven most primitive members of the order form a family that occurs worldwide in both deep and shallow water. *Aulopus filamentosus*, for example, is a bottom-dwelling inhabitant of the continental slope, at a depth of 1300-3300 ft. It is distinguished mainly by a very tall leading edge on its dorsal fin. The most colorful species in the family is the Sergeant Baker, which lives in shallow waters off the coast of Australia. Its name is said to derive from the soldier who first caught one, but there is no real evidence for this. All the members of the family are remarkably colorful, and some of them live as deep as 3300 ft.

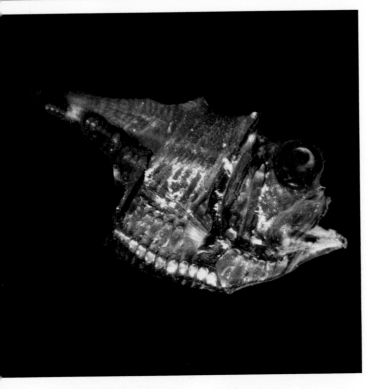

ABOVE The deep-sea hatchetfishes take their name from their unique body shape. They measure only 2.7-3 in. long and are eaten by many of the predators that hunt in the open water, rising to the shallower waters by night, and swimming deeper by day. They live in all the oceans of the world, feeding on tiny crustaceans and other small animals, and range from the surface to depths of over 11,500 ft. (although the majority are found between 3300 and 6500 ft.).

STOMIIFORMES CLASSIFICATION

The order Stomiiformes contains about 250 species, many of which are deep-sea fishes. They are grouped into 53 genera and nine families, and range throughout the oceans. The family Gonostomatidae comprises the 26 species of lightfishes or bristlemouths, including those from the genera *Gonostoma* and *Cyclothone* The 41 species within the family Sternoptychidae include the pearlfish, *Maurolicus muelleri*, and the deep-sea or marine hatchetfishes—most of which occur in the genus *Polyipnus*. The family Chauliodontidae comprises the six species of viperfishes from the genus *Chauliodus*, such as Sloane's viperfish, *C. sloanei*. The family Idiacanthidae consists of the four black dragonfishes from the genus *Idiacanthus*.

The greeneyes are fairly abundant in the North Atlantic. They are laterally compressed, silvery fishes with large eyes. They grow up to 12 in. long and live at depths of 650-2500 ft. In all species, the lateral line system is well developed and extends to the snout, head and gill covers, enabling the fish to detect the approach of small prey.

The tripod fishes inhabit muddy areas at great depths, between 1600 and 16,000 ft. deep. They have minute eyes set in a small, flattened head. In contrast, some of the rays on the leading edges of their pectoral, pelvic, and lower tail fins are immensely elongated, giving the fish a stilt-walking appearance.

Lizardfishes

Most of the lizardfishes are bottom-dwellers in quite shallow coastal waters, although a few of the 39 species inhabit the deeps, at 8500-15,500 ft. The members of this family resemble and act like lizards, from whom they derive their common name. Usually measuring about 12 in. long (some can reach 20 in.), lizardfishes have stout, pointed heads and long jaws, as well as heavy, shiny scales and large pelvic fins set well forward. When the fishes are at rest on the bottom, they lean on these fins at a slight angle. If a prey fish swims within range, the lizardfish will dart upward at great speed and swallow it with a single gulp. Lizardfishes are widely distributed in tropical waters.

Only the largest lizardfishes are considered edible by humans. One of them is the bummalow, a blunt-nosed and long-finned version of the lizardfish that is eaten in great quantities under the name of Bombay duck. Bummalows have large, sharp, curved teeth that they use to seize fish and invertebrates. They form enormous shoals in estuaries and are taken in vast numbers around the mouth of the Ganges.

Predators in the deeps

Giganturids exist in the extreme depths of the ocean. They rarely grow to more than 6 in. long and have silvery, cylindrical bodies and forward-facing tubular eyes. Their large, fan-like pectoral fins are set high on their bodies. They have no pelvic or fatty (adipose) fins, and their tail fins have extended lower lobes. They have enormous mouths, armed with teeth that can be pushed down, enabling prey to pass easily down their throats. They are voracious predators, attacking fish far longer than themselves. It is believed

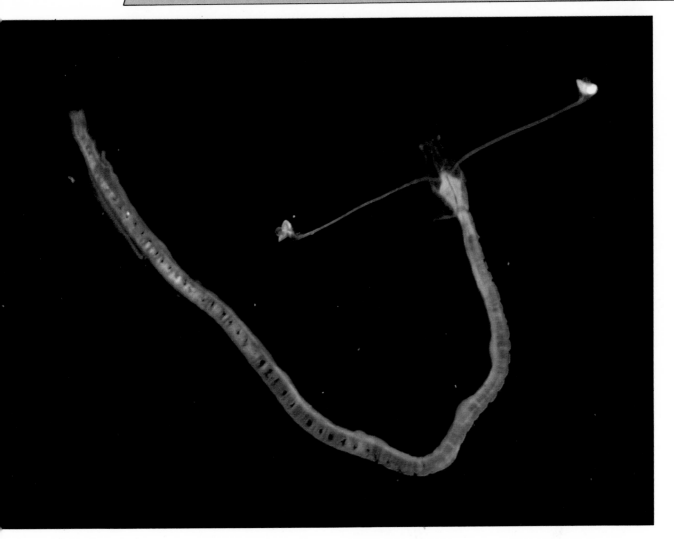

that the dense, black lining of their throats and their distensible stomachs prevent their prey's luminous organs from betraying the giganturid's position during the slow process of swallowing and digestion.

The barracudinas are larger, more common and widespread mesopelagic predators that form important middle links in food chains. The 50 species make up a family that is represented in all of the world's oceans, from the Arctic to the Antarctic. Barracudinas are slim fish with small, rounded fins and large heads. They grow to a maximum of 3 ft. 3 in. long, but are more common at less than 12 in. in length.

Records of barracudinas taken by a deep-sea research craft show them hanging head-up in the water. Barracudinas' eyes are designed to give the optimum field of binocular vision downward, so that when they swim head-up their line of vision is straight ahead. Barracudinas feed on small fishes and shrimps at depths of 10,000 ft.

ABOVE The larvae of the black dragonfish are transparent, with their eyes mounted at the end of long stalks. At this stage, they feed on diatoms and minute crustaceans, moving from deep water in their earliest days to surface water as they grow. As they mature, their eye-stalks shorten and the fish assume their adult form. Females are black and measure approximately 16 in. long, while males are light-colored and measure no more than 3 in. long.

The daggertooth or javelinfish is the only species in its family, and it lives in the upper layers of the ocean in the temperate and subpolar sea (not in the tropics). Closely related to the barracudinas, it is a long, slim fish, reaching 3 ft. 3 in. in length, and is among the largest of the mesopelagic fishes. Only one mature adult has been recorded. It was recovered from the stomach of a whale in the Antarctic and measured 29.5 in. long. Its stomach contained two barracudinas, measuring 10.6 in. and 7 in. long, both full of krill.

LEFT The enormously elongated fin rays are typical of the tripod fishes. These fishes live at depths of between 1550 and 18,500 ft. in tropical and temperate oceans. The exact function of their rays is unknown, but observations suggest that the lower rays act as a tripod when the fish "stands" on the muddy sea bed (giving the fish its name). They are also thought to be touch-sensitive, enabling the fish to search for food.

AULOPIFORMES AND MYCTOPHIFORMES CLASSIFICATION

The order Aulopiformes contains about 190 species of lizardfishes and their relatives, grouped in 40 genera and 12 families. Most occur in the deep sea throughout the oceans, but some live in coastal shallows. The seven species of aulopuses make up the family Aulopodidae. They include the Sergeant Baker, *A. purpurissatus*. The family Chlorophthalmidae, the greeneyes, comprises 38 species, including the tripod fishes of the genus *Bathypteris*. The 39 species of lizardfishes make up the family Synodontidae. They include the red lizardfish, *Synodus synodus*, and the bummalow or Bombay duck, *Harpadon nehereus*. The five species of giganturids form the family Giganturidae, and the 50 species of barracudinas make up the family Paralepididae. The daggertooth or javelinfish, *Anotopterus pharao*, is the only member of the family Anotopteridae. The three species of lancetfishes that form the family Alepisauridae include the longnose lancetfish, *Alepisaurus ferox*.

The order Myctophiformes contains 241 species grouped in 35 genera and two families. The 235 species of lanternfishes form the main family, the Myctophidae. Their genera include *Myctophum* and *Lampanyctus*, and the various species range through all the oceans.

The three species of lancetfishes are voracious mesopelagic predators with large stabbing teeth and stomachs that can expand to take in large prey. Although they are fish of middle water, they have no luminous organs. The lancetfishes' heads are large and their dorsal fins are long and high, and can be folded into a deep groove along their backs, making them invisible. Lancetfishes are fast swimmers and are large enough to prey on a wide variety of deep-sea life. A longnose lancetfish caught off the coast of California contained 42 fishes of five different species.

Lancetfishes are large for their oceanic zone and measure 5-6 ft. in length. Few fishes of this size venture to depths of more than 1600 ft. However, for all their length, they are not heavy fish, since they have thin skeletons, and large specimens weigh no more than 4 lbs. 6 oz.-5 lbs. 8 oz.

Lanternfishes

Many of the fishes that live in the mesopelagic zone possess light organs of various patterns and intensities. Perhaps the most common of these light bearers are the lanternfishes. Forming an order with 235 species, they range from the polar seas to the tropics. They are usually small fishes—less than 6 in. in length—with large eyes and blunt heads. At night, they migrate to between 164 and 328 ft. of the surface to feed on the plankton, so that their lights are well known to sailors. During the day, the fish retreat as far down as 3937 ft. But whether near the surface or in deep water, lanternfishes are preyed on by a variety of predators including tunny, bonito and angler fishes.

The lights of the lanternfishes are arranged in patterns that vary from species to species. In many of them, the light organs resemble small, luminous buttons running in rows along their flanks—and the light they give off may be yellow, green or blue. One lanternfish species even has light organs on its tongue. In addition to these lights, many lanternfishes have luminous patches on their heads that they can turn on or off.

MIGHTY BREEDERS

Few fishes are as fertile as the cods and their relatives. Each female lays more than six million eggs at a time—a figure that may account in part for the huge numbers of cod netted by the fishing fleets

ABOVE **Most members of the cod family hunt in the gloomy depths, using their sensitive chin barbels to locate crustaceans, worms and the larvae of other fishes on the sea floor. Cods are also voracious predators of smaller fishes, relying on their large eyes to find—and** large jaws to catch—such species as herring, haddock and sand eels. PAGE 1947 **Rockling are elongated fishes that lurk on the seabed and in rock pools where they prey largely on mollusks and crustaceans, seeking them out with their sensitive barbels.**

PERCOPSIFORMES CLASSIFICATION

The order Percopsiformes contains just nine species grouped in six genera and three families. All live in freshwater habitats in North America. The family Percopsidae consists of the two species of trout perches, *Percopsis transmontana* and *P. omiscomaycus*. The pirate perch, *Aphredoderus sayanus*, is the sole member of the family Aphredoderidae. Six species of cave fishes make up the family Amblyopsidae, including the southern cavefish, *Typhlichthys subterranus*.

The three orders dealt with in this chapter include the trout perches and the cods and their relatives, as well as the strange cave fishes, the rattails and the cusk eels.

The inland waterways of North America are the home of the trout perches and their relatives. Together they constitute an order containing three families: the trout perches; the pirate perch; and the cave fishes. The two species of trout perches take their common name from their perch-like first dorsal fin—which has two flexible spines at the front—and the trout-like adipose (fatty) fin lying in front of the tail. They have relatively large heads with low-slung mouths and sturdy, hump-backed bodies. The most common species, the 8-in.-long *Percopsis omiscomaycus*, is widespread in the lakes and rivers of North America, from the western coast of Canada to the Great Lakes and throughout the Mississippi-Missouri river system.

Trout perches are mainly silver in color with two rows of dark spots, and they have small scales bearing fine, comb-like spines on their free edges. They generally feed on aquatic invertebrates and small fishes. In spring, the trout perches usually move to shallow water to spawn, the females laying their eggs on the gravel or stony bottoms of the streams and lakes.

The pirate perch is the only member of its family. Measuring 6 in. long, it is a sluggish, dark-hued fish that lacks the adipose fin of the trout perches. Its diet consists mainly of insect larvae and other invertebrates. Occasionally, it will also prey on small fishes—the probable reason for its common name. In the breeding season, the pirate perch builds a simple nest to hold its eggs, and both parents guard the nest until they hatch.

Cave fishes

The cave fishes, or amblyopsids, comprise a family of six species living in the USA. Two species inhabit the swamps and streams of the Atlantic coastal plain. The other four, in contrast, are confined to a system of limestone caves that lie in Kentucky and neighboring states, between the Appalachian Mountains and the Great Plains. Here, they live in a world that is perpetually dark—an unusual way of life that is known as troglobiotic.

Small, pale fish measuring not more than 4 in. long, they are all spindle-shaped, have no scales on their heads, and have minute eyes. In common with

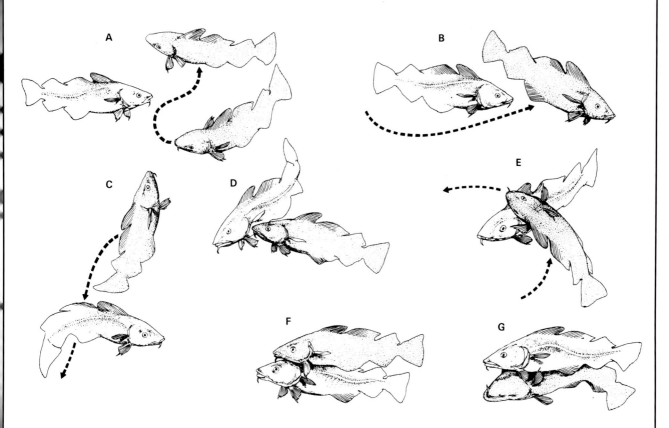

cave-living fishes of other orders, they have few scales on their bodies (those that they do possess are scattered at random on their flanks) and they have no skin pigment.

Most fishes have specialized organs known as lateral lines running along their sides that detect vibrations, movements or changes of pressure in the water. In the lateral line system, the tiny organs that pick up the pressure changes are known as neuromasts, each of which consists of small groups of sensitive cells with a projecting hair covered with a protective, jelly-like tissue. In the almost silent world of the caves, where food drifts in quietly from the outside world, cave fishes expose these neuromasts directly into the water, enabling them to find food. In some species, the neuromasts are mounted on tiny lumps (papillae) that are concentrated around the head, but they also occur elsewhere on the body. The sensitivity of the neuromast hairs was revealed in experiments with a 1.6-in.-long cave fish. The hairs responded to the pressure caused by a water flea measuring just 0.2 in. long that swam past at a distance of 1.4 in.

ABOVE **Stages in cod courtship: as the female cod enters the territory of the male, he bobs and weaves before her (A), then swims in a circle, undulating up and down (B). He may even swim backward (C) in his efforts to impress the** female. If she does not respond, he may tap her with his snout (D). Eventually, the male swims round into the mating position (E), and the two release eggs and sperm together, either one above the other (F) or belly-to-belly (G).

Cods and their relatives

The cods and their relatives (the haddock and common ling, for example) form one of seven families within an order that contains about 414 species. The cod family includes some of the most fertile creatures on Earth. A female Atlantic cod may produce over 6 million eggs each season (though 2 or 3 million are more usual), while a large female ling may shed up to 60 million eggs in a season. Indeed, the record for the greatest number of eggs produced by a vertebrate at one time is held by a ling that was found to be carrying 28,361,000 eggs in her body when she was caught. Such fertility has given the cod family great

ABOVE The haddock, a close relative of the cod, has suffered severely from overfishing in recent years. Despite this, seasons occur when an unusually large number of young survive to maturity, though the reasons for these fluctuations are not known. Haddock live on both sides of the Atlantic Ocean and in Arctic waters, feeding on bottom-dwelling crustaceans, sea urchins, worms and shellfish. They can be identified by their three dorsal fins and the dark patch on their flanks behind the gills.

powers of recovery, and has enabled the fish populations to withstand sustained onslaughts from the fishing fleets.

For years, an average of 400 million cod were caught annually in the North Atlantic alone, but recent developments in sonar (the echo-sounding devices that enable fishermen to locate shoals) and netting systems have led to overfishing, and a reduction in the tonnage of fish caught. Yet even today, the annual cod catch is exceeded only by the catches of herring-like fishes, whose market value per ton is much lower. Consequently, the cods and their relatives are among the most economically important of all fishes.

Fishes of cool waters

Cods usually measure 18-39 in. long and weigh about 10-11 lbs. (although some can measure 59 in. and weigh approximately 24 lbs.). They have large heads with a very long dorsal fin (that may be divided into two or three distinct sections), a pair of pelvic fins that are situated beneath the throat (often in front of the paired pectoral fins), and a long anal fin that may be split into two sections. They also have a fleshy barbel on the chin. Well supplied with touch and taste cells, cods use their barbel to locate food. With a few exceptions, cods are fishes of cold and cool seas of both Northern and Southern hemispheres. The Arctic cod, for example, lives near the surface among the drift ice at the edge of the polar icecap, while other species usually occur on or near the continental shelves (shallow seabeds that border the continents).

The Atlantic cod is probably identical to the North Pacific cod, giving the species a distribution in coastal waters throughout much of the Northern Hemisphere. In the Atlantic Ocean, cod live in distinct populations off Newfoundland, Greenland, Iceland and in the North and Barents seas, but individual fish continually migrate from one population to another. In this way, they prevent the genetic isolation of groups that leads to the development of separate subspecies.

A cod's coloring varies according to its habitat. In deep water, it tends to have a light-gray, mottled back and a pale belly, but if it lives among seaweed the light gray is replaced by a mottled reddish brown or yellowish green. The lateral line forms a conspicuous pale band that runs the length of its flank, rising and arching over the base of its pectoral fin. The three dorsal fins and two anal fins touch at their bases to make a continuous series of fins from head to tail.

As with the herrings, the economic importance of the cods has prompted a large amount of research into their habits. Soviet scientists, for example, have carried out detailed studies of the cod populations exploited by fishing fleets in the Barents Sea. From these studies, it appears that the cod's main breeding grounds are located near the northern coast of Norway, and particularly the Lofoten Islands. The fish from deeper waters migrate to this area to spawn in the shallower water from February to May, before returning to the open sea where they feed on the invertebrates (especially crustaceans and worms) and fishes that flourish in the cold, northern waters.

The female cod lays between 500,000 and 5 million eggs, depending on her size. After they have been fertilized, they float upward to drift in the plankton near the water surface where the currents scatter them. After two to four weeks, the eggs hatch into 1.6-in.-long larvae that continue to drift with the plankton, eating the microscopic, floating animals and being eaten in turn by other fishes. Of the several million eggs that each female produces, only a

ABOVE The whiting is a slender, silvery member of the cod family that occurs around the coasts of Europe, including the northern Mediterranean. It is an important food fish, accounting for almost half the total catch of cod-like fishes in European waters. Whitings are most abundant in shallow, inshore waters at depths of 100-330 ft., where they feed on young cods and herrings, sprats, sand eels and shrimps.

tiny percentage survive to become mature fish. The rest become food for the other inhabitants of the northern seas, including other cod.

Commercial relatives

The cods are not the only economically important members of the family. The group also includes several other edible species, such as the haddock. Immediately identifiable by a black patch on its flanks above the pectoral fin on each side of its body, the haddock has a high, first dorsal fin, large eyes and a short lower jaw with a very short chin barbel. The dark greenish gray on its back fades to silver on its flanks, and the fish has a white belly.

The haddock is mainly a North Atlantic species that has adapted to slightly warmer waters than the cod. Since it needs a higher water temperature for breeding (41-44.6°F), its range extends further south: on the

GADIFORMES CLASSIFICATION

Seven families make up the order, the Gadiformes, with a total of some 414 species grouped in 76 genera. Almost exclusively marine, they range from the shallows to the deepest parts of the ocean, and from polar waters to the tropics.

The cods and their close relatives form the family Gadidae, with some 55 species, such as the Atlantic cod, *Gadus morhua*; the Arctic cod, *Boreogadus saida*; the haddock, *Melanogrammus aeglefinus*; the pollack, *Pollachius pollachius*; the saithe, *P. virens*; the common ling, *Molva molva*; the whiting, *Merlangius merlangus*; the burbot, *Lota lota*; the greater forkbeard, *Phycis blennoides*; and the five-bearded rockling, *Ciliata mustela*.

The 16 species of merluccid hakes make up the family Merlucciidae. They include the North Atlantic hake, *Merluccius merluccius*, the Pacific hake, *M. productus*, and the stockfish, *M. capensis*. There are 260 species of rattails or grenadiers in the family Macrouridae, including *Odontomacrurus numax* and the roughsnout rattail, *Trachyhynchus trachyrincus*. The family Bregmacerotidae consists of the seven species of codlets such as *Bregmaceros macclellandi*.

ABOVE The tadpole fish is a short, thick-set relative of the ling and lives in shallow inshore waters just below the low-tide mark. It is a solitary species that lives on the bottom, usually among rocks, and feeds on worms and shrimps. Its body is protected by a thick skin encased in small scales and a layer of mucus.

American side of the Atlantic it occurs down the eastern coast of the USA, while on the European side it extends into the Bay of Biscay.

Jellyfish protector

One curious feature of young haddock is their habit of sheltering under the mantles of large jellyfishes, where the stinging cells in the jellyfishes' tentacles give them a measure of protection from predators. The young haddock feed on small, floating crustaceans, but once they are about 2 in. long, they swim close to the seabed where they begin their adult diet of bottom-dwelling mollusks, worms, brittle stars and the eggs and young of other fishes, such as herrings and sand eels. Haddock can grow to 3 ft. or more in length, but most are caught by fishermen before they can attain that size.

The pollack is a similar species to the haddock, but its lower jaw protrudes beyond its upper jaw and it has no chin barbel. The dark, greenish brown of its back fades to white on its belly, and it has a dark, arching lateral line. Pollack occur mainly in mid-water, rather than close to the bottom, although when young, they feed mainly on crustaceans, worms and bottom-dwelling mollusks. Mature pollack often swim in small shoals over wrecks and reefs, where they prey on other fishes such as sand eels, small herrings and young cod. In turn, large cod eat the young pollack.

Pollack spawn between January and April, in fairly deep water between 350 and 650 ft. The eggs and larvae drift with the current and gradually float inshore to the shallows, where young pollack are most commonly found. They often feed in shoals, in inshore waters, over sandy seabeds and in estuaries.

Trawlers regularly catch pollack, which have little commercial value compared with the cods. The saithe, a close relative of the pollack, is, however, an important food fish. It is usually marketed as "coley," a name derived from "coalfish" and referring to the dark color of the fish's back. It has a pale, straight lateral line and a silvery belly. The saithe is a widely distributed North Atlantic fish, usually found near the surface of deep water where it hunts in shoals, preying on other species such as sprats and herrings. Its breeding habits are very similar to the pollack's.

The lengthy lings

The three species of lings—members of the cod family—all inhabit the northeastern Atlantic Ocean. Resembling the eel in appearance, they are long, large-eyed fishes with a single barbel on their chins. Unlike many other members of the family that have three dorsal fins, the lings have two dorsal fins—a short one at the front and an elongated fin behind that extends along the length of the back to the tail. They also have an elongated anal fin beneath the belly and tail.

Lings usually inhabit rocks and sunken reefs in inshore waters, and rocky ground in deeper water (1000-1300 ft.). They are able to remain motionless for hours, pressing their bodies into crevices or curling themselves around stones. As with the conger eel, lings also seek shelter in wrecks, making them popular sporting fishes with anglers who specialize in fishing deepwater wrecks.

The common ling ranges from Iceland south to the Bay of Biscay. Growing to 6 ft. 6 in. in length and 66 lbs. in weight, the common ling is the largest member of the cod family. A secretive fish, it only ventures out when hunger forces it to hunt. Its diet includes a wide variety of smaller fishes, especially dab, haddock and mackerel.

TOP The five-bearded rocklings take their name from the five barbels or fleshy, sensory filaments that grow alongside their nostrils, on their upper lips and on their chins. Adults usually live in rock pools or in hollows in the seabed where they can find shelter among the rocks and seaweed. They usually measure approximately 8 in. in length.
ABOVE The three-bearded rockling grows up to about 20 in. in length and lives in coastal waters at depths of 35-400 ft.

ABOVE A fish of deep water, the greater forkbeard usually occurs over sand or mud at depths of 500-1000 ft. where it eats shrimps, crabs and the occasional fish. It grows to a length of 30 in. and has two distinctive pelvic fins that are visible as long, filament-like rays. The fish ranges from the western Mediterranean, where it is fished for local consumption, to the west coast of Britain—although it is rarer off Scotland.

Buoyancy at birth

Lings breed from March to June, or later in more northerly latitudes. Fertile fishes, they lay an extraordinary number of floating eggs, each one of which contains a globule of pale-green oil that gives the egg the buoyancy to rise to the surface. After they hatch, the young lings (fry) make their way to deeper water where they grow quite quickly. At first they develop long pelvic fins, but as the fishes grow, these disappear.

Freshwater predator

The burbot is the only member of the cod family to live in rivers and lakes. Although now extinct in Britain, it remains one of the most common predators of cold, northern freshwaters, ranging throughout North America, Europe and the USSR. Similar in appearance to the lings, it is eel-like in shape, and mottled-brown or occasionally gold in color. It has two dorsal fins: the first is short and barely reaches the long, second dorsal fin. Growing to 16 in. in length and 18 oz. in weight, the burbot is smaller than the lings, although specimens weighing 66 lbs. have been reported from Siberia.

Burbot often live at great depths; they have been caught at 656 ft. in some southern lakes. Largely nocturnal in habit, they only leave the refuge of boulders and undercut banks to forage for fish—for example, roach, perch and gudgeon—as well as for invertebrates. Burbot particularly enjoy fish eggs—a feeding habit that makes them highly unpopular with fish farmers.

Fish-meal candidate

The immediate relatives of the burbot are similarly of little commercial importance. The 43-in.-long greater forkbeard ranges from Norway to the Mediterranean Sea. It moves in shoals near the seabed at depths of 500-1000 ft. and is fished for processing into fish meal. It takes its name from the paired fins on its underside that are modified into long filaments.

The torsk lives near the seabed at depths of 650-1650 ft. off eastern Canada, Iceland, northwest Scotland and Scandinavia. Growing to a length of 16-36 in., it has a single, long chin barbel, thick skin with small scales and one elongated dorsal fin that joins up with the tail fin. In Scandinavia, the torsk is dried and sold as "stockfish." Similar in taste to lobster, the torsk is a popular, but rare, food fish.

The rocklings

Outwardly similar to the burbot, but sporting a variable number of sensory barbels on their upper lips, the rocklings are small to medium-sized members of the cod family. They range throughout the Northern Hemisphere and occur mainly in rock pools and around breakwaters. Varying in length from 7 to 28 in., they all have two dorsal fins and are usually red-brown in color with lighter markings.

The different species of rocklings take their names from the number of barbels they have. The five-bearded rockling is the most familiar species in the North Atlantic. Despite eating a diet of crustaceans, it is very unpalatable and does not grow to more than 8 in. long, making it of no commercial value. Its four-bearded, three-bearded and shore relatives are less common and live in deeper water.

RIGHT Like many of the deep-sea fishes seen only by scientists and fishermen, *Odontomacrurus numax* lacks a common name. It is a fairly typical member of the rattail or grenadier family. It lives on the continental slopes of most of the world's oceans, at depths that may exceed 13,000 ft. Most rattails have light-producing organs, and are able to make various sounds. BELOW RIGHT The rattail has a heavily armored head and large eyes, enabling it to see in the dim light.

Hungry hunters

The seven species of hakes are voracious and cannibalistic members of the cod family that live in shoals at depths of 1800 ft. The North Atlantic hake ranges from Norway to northwest Africa and into the Mediterranean. The silver hake, a similar fish, lives in the Atlantic Ocean off North America, and other species occur in the Pacific Ocean off North America and Chile. Commercially, the most important hake species is the stockfish, which occurs in shoals off the coast of South Africa. It is the single most valuable fish in that region, popular because of its well-textured flesh.

Hakes are deepwater predators that have streamlined bodies and large mouths armed with sharp teeth. Instead of having three dorsal fins (like many species in the cod family), hakes have two dorsal fins—a short one in the front and a long, second dorsal fin with a distinct notch in the middle. There are two main patterns of movement in the life of the hake. The first is a nightly migration up toward the middle and upper waters to feed (during the day, the hake rests on or near the bottom). The second movement is seasonal: during summer, the hakes migrate closer to the shore. In winter, hakes feed on blue whiting, other hake and squid, and in summer they add whiting, mackerel, herrings and other fishes to their diet.

Rattails

The family of rattails—members of the cod family—derive their common name from their long, tapering tails. Ranging throughout most of the world's oceans at depths of 300-6500 ft., they generally measure 12-36 in. long, have large, heavily armored heads, a single, tall dorsal fin that is often supported by a sharp, strong ray, and long, low dorsal and anal fins. They do not have tail fins.

Despite their abundance, little is known of the diet and habits of the rattails. They probably feed on a mixture of smaller fishes, shrimps and the tiny

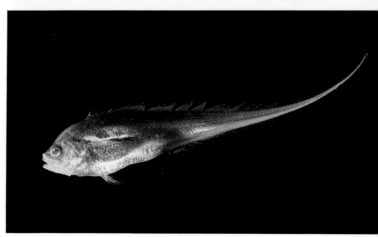

starfishes that inhabit the bottom ooze. Their downward-facing mouths can be pushed forward to root for food in the mud of their murky habitat, while the single sensory barbel on their chin helps them in their search.

Male rattails have muscles attached to their swim bladders that enable the fishes to produce loud drumming noises. The receptor centers in the brain that are associated with hearing are well developed, which may indicate that sound plays a role in courtship. Living in the dark ocean depths, rattails have large eyes that they probably use to recognize the light-producing organs of other rattails (or other species). They probably use their eyesight, too, during their migrations into shallower water. Their light

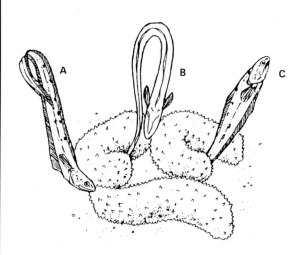

LEFT A young pearlfish attempts to shelter inside the body of a sea cucumber by forcing its head into the vent of the marine invertebrate (A). After curling its body to insert its tail (B), the pearlfish wriggles into the open vent tail-first (C). If the sea cucumber attempts to close the vent, an adult pearlfish will twist its long tail like a corkscrew to force its way directly inside.

organs are usually mounted on their bellies, where areas of scaleless skin allow the light generated by bacteria to shine through.

Elongated fins

The 164 species of cusk eels and brotulids form one of four families within an order that includes the viviparous brotulids and the pearlfishes and their relatives. The cusk eels and brotulids resemble rocklings in appearance, but their anatomy is sufficiently different for them to be placed in a separate order. They have elongated bodies with long dorsal and anal fins that often merge with the tail fin. Their thread-like pelvic fins lie beneath the lower jaw and may serve a similar purpose to barbels (as sensitive organs of touch), since the fishes trail them delicately along the bottom as they swim. Most cusk eels and brotulids are small, secretive fishes that burrow in crevices or hide away among rocks and coral.

Cusk eels rarely exceed 12 in. in length, with the exception of the kingklip, a 5-ft.-long giant that only occurs off the coast of South Africa. The spotted cusk eel lives in the eastern Pacific Ocean at depths of 650 ft. It burrows tail-first into sand and into crevices until it completely disappears. When it emerges, the fish adopts a vertical posture, anchoring the lower part of its body in the seabed. The brotulids have deeper bodies and broader heads than the cusk eels. Ranging throughout the world, they mainly occur in deep water.

The 85 species of viviparous brotulids are mainly marine fish, although a few species inhabit shallow water. They differ from their deepwater relatives in bearing live young, but share their secretive nature, shunning the light by hiding among rocks. Certain species of viviparous brotulids inhabit caves in the Yucatan Peninsula in Mexico and in Cuba. The caves are near the sea and contain brackish water of varying salinity. Freshwater viviparous brotulids give birth to live young whose coloration ranges from violet to dark brown.

The 24 species of the pearlfish family are slender fishes with long, pointed tails and transparent bodies. They are extremely secretive, often hiding in the bodies of sea cucumbers, shellfishes, starfishes and sea urchins. Indeed, their common name is said to derive from fish that have become trapped and entombed in pearl shells. Most pearlfishes inhabit shallow water in tropical and subtropical seas. The *Carapus acus* is a Mediterranean species that takes up residence in large sea cucumbers. The fish enters through the anus of its host tail-first, with a corkscrewing motion. During the day, it rests in the body of the sea cucumber, sometimes feeding on its sexual organs and gills, but ventures out at night to feed on crustaceans.

OPHIDIIFORMES CLASSIFICATION

The order Ophidiiformes contains about 294 species divided into 86 genera and four families. Most are marine, occurring in the Atlantic, Pacific and Indian oceans, but a few live in freshwater habitats. About 164 species belong to the family Ophidiidae, the cusk eels and brotulids. They include the spotted cusk eel, *Otophidium taylori*, the kingklip, *Genypterus capensis*, and the brotulid species, *Bassogigas profundissimus*. The other group of brotulids, the viviparous brotulids, make up the family Bythitidae. There are about 85 species, including the cave-dwelling fishes of the genus *Ogilbia*. The family Carapidae, the pearl-fishes and their relatives, consists of 27 species, including the pearlfish species, *Carapus acus*.

MASTERS OF DECEPTION

Camouflaged by flaps of skin resembling weeds or polyps, the anglerfishes loll motionless on the seabed waving their "fishing rod" lures to attract inquisitive fishes; when they approach too close, the anglerfishes snap them up in their jaws

ABOVE **The oyster toadfish lives on the bottom of shallow waters along the eastern coast of the USA. Although it averages less than 10 in. long, it is fiercely territorial, using its sharp teeth to attack intruders. It is especially aggressive during the breeding season in June and July when it is protecting its eggs. Like other toadfishes, this species** makes a variety of grunts, growls and whistles by moving the muscles that surround its swim bladder.
PAGE 1957 **The Atlantic goosefish—a member of the anglerfishes order—rarely leaves the sea floor, since its ungainly, flat body and pancake-shaped fins are more suitable for camouflaged life on the bottom than for swimming.**

The three orders of toadfishes, anglerfishes and clingfishes that appear in this chapter comprise largely marine fishes. Some of them—such as the deep-sea anglers—live in extremely deep water at depths of 3300 ft. or more.

The 64 species of toadfishes constitute an order that ranges throughout coastal waters in tropical and temperate seas. They are among the few creatures that benefit from the impact of human waste and litter on their environment. Inhabiting mainly warm, shallow waters, the toadfishes are sluggish bottom dwellers that often shelter in the cans and broken bottles that litter long stretches of the world's coastline. They are voracious predators, feeding on a wide range of food, including worms, shrimps, crabs and squid, all of which they can snap up in a single gulp. Because they only have three pairs of gills, their oxygen requirements are low, allowing them to inhabit polluted waters, especially around sewage outlets. Some toadfishes enter brackish water, and a few confine themselves to freshwater.

Named for their odd resemblance to toads, the 12-in.-long toadfishes are small and stocky in appearance and have eyes on the top of their heads. They are dark brown in color, and have very small scales embedded in their slimy skin. Usually, they have broad, flattened heads with wide mouths that are armed with blunt teeth. Tags of skin decorate their lower lips and parts of their faces. Many species adopt a coloration that matches their habitat. The recently discovered *Sanopus splendidus*, an 8-in.-long inhabitant of the waters off the coast of west Mexico, has a vivid decoration of blue spots and stripes, edged by brilliant yellow fins.

Foghorn fish

Toadfishes are solitary and highly territorial. Skulking among rocks, cavities and tunnels in the mud, they are reluctant to stray beyond the small areas that form their territories. If intruders threaten, they attack with their teeth, snapping and seizing the object in a determined grip. Toadfishes are also extremely vocal, using highly adapted swim bladders to produce a range of grunts, growls and whistles that have been compared to the noise of a rivet gun, the sound of a passing train and a distant foghorn. The noises play an important role in the ritual defense of territory and in breeding behavior.

Brightly polished buttons

The midshipmen, a genus of fishes inhabiting the Pacific and Atlantic oceans, belong to the same family as the toadfishes. They take their name from the hundreds of small, glowing light organs that supposedly resemble the polished buttons on a midshipman's

BATRACHOIDIFORMES CLASSIFICATION

The order Batrachoidiformes contains only the family Batrachoididae, the toadfishes. The 64 species in 19 genera live mainly in the coastal waters of the Atlantic, Indian and Pacific oceans, with a few species living in freshwater habitats. They include the oyster toadfish, *Opsanus tau*; the newly discovered species, *Sanopus splendidus*; the northern or plainfin midshipman, *Porichthys notatus*; and the Atlantic midshipman, *P. porosissimus*.

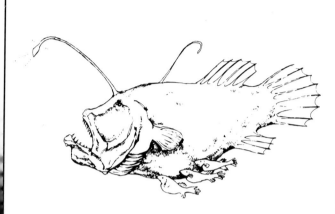

ABOVE The small-6-in-long males of the deep-sea anglerfish species *Ceratias holboelli* cling with their teeth to the belly of the massive 4-ft.-long female. Once they have fused to her body, they draw nutrients from her bloodstream.

RIGHT The deep-sea angler *Melanocetus johnsonii*, sometimes known as the black devil, lives at depths of over 6500 ft., and grows up to 5.5 in. long. It uses the thin, white stem above its jaws to attract prey, engulfing them as they approach.

jacket. The northern midshipman grows to 16 in. in length and lives on the Pacific coast of North America, while the Atlantic midshipman grows to 8 in. in length and inhabits the waters of the Atlantic coast.

Many fishes that are sedentary by nature and camouflaged for protection use spiny fins as a further form of defense. The toadfishes are no exception. They all have strong, sharp spines in the dorsal fins and on their gill covers, and certain species are also venomous. Poisonous toadfishes inject their venom from sacs through two large, hollow spines in their dorsal fins, and through similar spines on the upper edges of each gill cover.

Angling for food

The 265 or so species in the order of anglerfishes are generally small fishes that occur in deep water. The goosefishes are an exception. They are a bottom-dwelling family that range from the tidal zone to depths of 3300 ft. in the Pacific, Indian and Atlantic oceans. The Atlantic goosefish is the largest member of the family, growing to over 6 ft. in length and 66 lbs. in weight. Its body is superbly camouflaged, enabling it to ambush prey. The color of its upperparts varies from red-brown to dark green, while its underparts are white and camouflage the fish as it rests immobile

against rocks and seaweed. Its huge head is wide and flattened, and its enormous mouth is lined with prominent curved teeth in both jaws.

The body of the Atlantic goosefish is tiny in comparison to its head, tapering sharply to a rounded point with a small tail fin. It is decorated with warts and a variety of outgrowths, including flaps of skin. These are usually dull in color, helping to camouflage the outline of the fish as it rests half buried in mud or sand on the bottom. Goosefishes have jointed pectoral fins that they use in a similar manner to feet in order to move across the seabed in short jumps. Their pelvic fins also resemble feet, and lie on the undersides of the fishes.

Rod and line

A goosefish uses a "rod and line" to catch its prey of small fish. The rod is a modified spiny ray of the dorsal fin that rests on the upper jaw—the ray has a fleshy flap at the tip that resembles a marine worm. Using the flap as a lure, the goosefish waves the rod above its mouth to attract prey. As the prey closes in on the rod, the fish opens its huge mouth, and the victim is carried in by the sudden rush of water. Fishes are not the goosefish's only victims. It also takes sea birds such as diving ducks.

Goosefishes breed in spring and early summer, moving into the offshore waters at depths of over 3300 ft. The eggs form a single layer within a floating, jelly-like structure that measures about 29 ft. 6 in. long and 24-36 in. wide. Each ribbon-like mass contains up to 1.5 million eggs.

The deep-sea anglers

The majority of deep-sea anglers live in the darkness of the deep oceans at depths below 3300 ft. The 110 species occur worldwide, but are unevenly distributed. Rarely growing to more than 3 in. long, the deep-sea anglers lack pelvic fins. Because they inhabit deep water, they have developed an elaborate, luminous lure on the end of their "fishing rod." The lures can be retracted at will. Male deep-sea anglers are smaller in size than females, and often very different in form.

In the largest deep-sea angler, *Ceratias holbroelli*, the female reaches 4 ft. long, but the male grows to only 6 in. The male spends only a short time swimming freely when it is just 0.7 in. long. Even then, it has eyes but no digestive tract. Attracted to the female by her chemical secretions, the male grips her with his teeth, then undergoes a remarkable transformation. His eyes degenerate, his skin becomes spiky and his mouth fuses with the female's skin, leaving only a pair of holes for breathing. Eventually, his blood system joins hers, so that he relies on the female for nutrients. His internal organs continue to shrivel away until only his sex glands remain active and he becomes merely a "sperm bank," ready to fertilize the female's eggs during spawning time. The same reproductive techniques are common to many smaller anglerfishes, and the sizes of the male and female are similar in proportion.

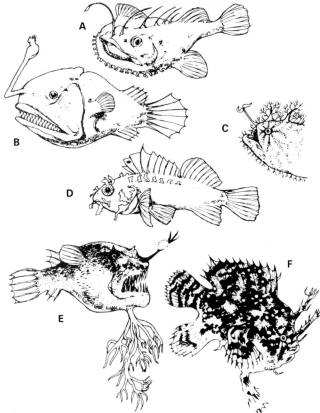

ABOVE LEFT **Two males of the species *Edriolynchnus schimidti* fuse themselves to the body of the larger female. Each male will lose most of his body systems and become little more than sacs for the discharge of sperm during fertilization. The bloodstream of the female both nourishes the fused breeding partners and controls the discharge of their sperm.**

LEFT **Anglerfishes have evolved a variety of shapes and lures for catching prey. The species include the Atlantic goosefish (A); one of the deep-sea anglers, *Chaenophryne parvonicus* (B); the frogfish *Phrynelox scaber* (C); *Iracundus signifer* (D); another deep-sea angler, *Linophryne arborifer* (E); and the frogfish *Antennarius marmoratus* (F).**

LOPHIIFORMES CLASSIFICATION

The order Lophiiformes, the anglerfishes, contains about 265 species in 64 genera and 16 families. They are all marine, and many inhabit very deep water around the world. There are 25 species of goosefishes in the family Lophiidae, including the Atlantic goosefish or angler, *Lophius piscatorius*. The 60 species of frogfishes make up the family Antennariidae. They include the split-lure frogfish, *Antennarius scaber*, the Pacific yellow angler, *A. moluccensis*, and the sargassum angler, *Histrio histrio*. The batfishes of the family Ogcocephalidae contain 57 species such as the redbellied batfish, *Ogcocephalus nasutus*.

Eleven families in the order are collectively known as the deep-sea anglers. They contain 110 species in all, including the species *Ceratias holbroelli*; *Linophryne arborifer*; *Chaenophryne parvonicus*; and the black devil, *Melanocetus johnsonii*.

Frogfishes and batfishes

The family of frogfishes are among the most elaborately camouflaged of marine creatures. Their patterns and colors vary according to their background and they always merge perfectly with the colorful floating weeds. The 60 species range in size from 1 to 14 in. long and inhabit tropical and subtropical oceans. They are stout, scaleless, warty creatures that are flattened from side to side, with loose flaps of skin enveloping their fins. The first ray of the dorsal fin is situated on the snout to form a rod and lure. Fishing lures in the frogfishes vary in design. That of the split-lure frogfish is a short, thin whip with a fleshy flap, while that of the Pacific yellow angler is long and bare.

The batfishes make up a family of 57 species that measure about 8 in. long. When viewed from above, their flattened bodies appear either triangular or circular. Their mouths are quite small, and their lures are retractable. They have pointed noses and wide heads, with large, elbowed pectoral fins. The largest species of batfish is the redbellied batfish, a 16-in.-long fish that inhabits the Caribbean Sea. Batfishes use their muscular pectoral fins, together with the pelvic fins below the throat, to shuffle along the seabed. They live in the deep water of all tropical seas.

TOP The mottled coloration of the sargassum anglerfish camouflages it among the drifting weed—especially sargassum weed—of tropical oceans. It uses its pectoral fins to grasp the weed and to creep through it.

ABOVE An 11-in.-long redbellied batfish rests on the sea bottom by leaning on its extended pectoral fins. It seldom swims up to the surface, preferring to use its fins to crawl about in search of shellfish, small fishes and worms.

The clingfishes

The clingfishes make up an order of 114 species. They live in areas where waves, currents or streams are strong. Yet, despite the tidal force of their habitats, the clingfishes survive without spending much energy. Their ventral and pelvic fins combine with a flap of skin to form a powerful sucker, enabling them to grasp onto boulders or seaweed in the zone between the tides or, in a few species, in fast freshwater streams. Clingfishes are small, tadpole-shaped fishes with flattened heads, and some are even distinctly duckbilled. They forage for a wide variety of crustaceans and worms, and some species, such as the tadpole clingfish, use strong teeth to seize limpets and mollusks from rocks.

The South African rock sucker is one of the largest species of clingfish, growing to 12 in. in length. Its sucker is so powerful that anglers who accidentally hook one often break their line before their catch releases its hold on the bottom. The amphibious clingfish from Chile is probably one of the most enterprising of fish in areas of strong surf. It forages on the miniature cliffs above the tide, eating algae and shellfish. Clingfishes spawn in bivalve shells or under stones and show varying degrees of parental care for their eggs.

ABOVE A shore clingfish *Lepadogaster lepadogaster* ventures out over sand in search of food. One of the four species of clingfishes to occur in British waters, it lives between and immediately below the tide marks, using its sucker (clearly visible under its throat) to cling to the undersides of rocks in the rush and pull of the waves. It grows to about 2.5 in. long. Clingfishes occur in shallow seas in most parts of the world.

GOBIESOCIFORMES CLASSIFICATION

The clingfishes and their relatives make up the order Gobiesociformes. The 114 species are arranged in 36 genera and two families, and occur in shallow seas in most parts of the world, with a few species occupying freshwater habitats. The family Gobiesocidae contains the 110 species of clingfishes such as the tadpole clingfish, *Arcos macrophthalmus*; the shore clingfish, *Lepadogaster lepadogaster*; the South African rock sucker, *Chorisochismus dentex*; and the amphibious clingfish, *Sicyases sanguineus*. The second family, the Alabatidae, contains the four species of singleslits from the genus *Alabes*.

GAUDY TROPICALS AND OCEAN GLIDERS

The many families of toothcarps include such colorful aquarium fishes as the guppy and molly. They belong to the same order as the flying fishes whose gliding displays are a familiar sight to ocean voyagers

The flying fishes and toothcarps belong to an order that also contains the needlefishes and four-eyed fishes. The second order in this chapter covers the silversides and rainbow fishes.

Fishes that leap out of the water provide one of the most spectacular displays in the marine world. It is not unusual to see whole schools of fish glide gracefully through the air at the same time, their wing-like fins outstretched to keep them airborne. The grace of this curious spectacle conceals a more serious purpose—escape from predation. The most well known of these fishes are the flying fishes, but the group also includes the needlefishes and halfbeaks.

Needle-sharp

The 32 species of the needlefishes range throughout marine and freshwaters in India, South America and Southeast Asia. Although the needlefishes grow to a maximum length of 38 in., they have slender bodies that rarely weigh more than 2 lbs. 10 oz. Their average size varies considerably within their range—the subspecies that occurs in the Black Sea is much smaller than species that inhabit the Atlantic Ocean. The Atlantic needlefish is the most common of the needlefishes. It is also called the garfish, but is no relation to the garfish of North America.

ABOVE Using its excellent vision, a needlefish hunts its prey in the surface waters of the ocean, pursuing small fishes and seizing them with its rapier-like bill. When attacked by larger fishes, the needlefish leaps clear of the water, displaying its affinity with the closely related flying fishes.
PAGE 1963 The sailfin black molly is not black in the wild, but acquires its dark color and elegant fin shape through selective breeding.

The needlefishes have sharply pointed bodies and raked-back tail fins that maximize their speed through the water. Their long, beak-like jaws contain numerous needle-sharp teeth with which they grip the small, fast-swimming fishes that form the main part of their diet—sprats and anchovies, young herrings and cod, as well as sand eels and squid. When hunted by predators such as tuna, a shoal of Atlantic needlefish will leap out of the water to escape from them.

Complete camouflage

The coloration of the needlefishes is typical of surface-living fishes. They have dark green-blue upperparts fading to silver on their flanks and underparts. Like herrings, the body color of the needlefishes provides good camouflage. Their silvery underparts make them almost invisible when viewed from below, and their dark upperparts prove difficult

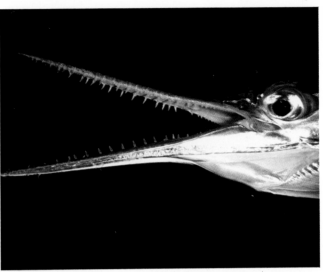

RIGHT A needlefish has greenish-colored bones and its bill is lined with numerous small, but extremely sharp, teeth. It uses its teeth to grip prey—small fish and crustaceans—and prevent them from escaping. Like all fishes, the needlefish never chews its food but swallows it whole.

to detect against the sea surface when viewed from above. Curiously, the needlefishes have green skeletons and green muscles caused by the bile pigment biliverdin. Although harmless, the green coloring limits their popularity as a food fish. Nevertheless, needlefishes are caught in large quantities, particularly in Scandinavian waters.

Needlefishes spawn in coastal waters in spring, although on occasions their breeding period may extend into late summer. The female lays 1000-35,000 eggs depending on her size. The eggs have long, sticky filaments that entangle in weeds or adhere to rocks. After five weeks, the 0.4-in.-long larvae emerge from their eggs. At birth, they lack the long bills of the adults, but as the larvae grow, their lower jaws begin to lengthen, followed by their upper jaws. When halfway through their development, the young fishes have a long lower jaw that projects far beyond the upper jaw, a feature that is characteristic of another family in the order—the appropriately named halfbeaks.

Half a beak

The halfbeaks are coastal and freshwater fishes that inhabit Southeast Asia and the Indian and Pacific Oceans. In all species of halfbeaks, the lower jaw is longer than the upper jaw. They use this curious facial structure to comb the water surface from below, searching for food such as mosquito larvae. The halfbeaks provide a valuable natural control over the serious insect pests.

Dermogenes pusillus is a halfbeak species that occurs in streams and pools throughout the Indo-Australian archipelago. Like several other freshwater species of halfbeaks, it has a more advanced breeding method than the other fishes in the order. After fertilization has taken place, the female retains the eggs inside her body until they hatch, thereby keeping them safe from predators. She later gives birth to live young.

Leaping to safety

The eggs of halfbeaks that inhabit coastal areas have long adhesive filaments and are similar in appearance

— CYPRINODONTIFORMES — CLASSIFICATION: 1

The order Cyprinodontiformes contains 845 species grouped in 120 genera and 13 families. They range through the Atlantic, Indian and Pacific oceans, and occur in freshwater habitats in many parts of the world, especially in tropical regions.

Needlefishes, sauries and halfbeaks

The family Belonidae contains the 32 species of needlefishes, such as the Atlantic needlefish or garfish, *Belone belone*. The sauries of the family Scomberesocidae number four species, the most widespread of which is the saury or skipper, *Scomberesox saurus*. There are about 80 species of halfbeaks in the family Hemiramphidae. These include the freshwater species, *Dermogenes pusillus*.

Flying fishes and ricefishes

The flying fishes make up the family Exocoetidae. There are 48 species in all, some of the most well known of which are the Atlantic flying fish, *Cypselurus heterurus*; the Californian flying fish, *C. californicus*; the margined flying fish, *C. cyanopterus*; the Mediterranean species, *C. rondeleti*; and the common tropical species, *Exocoetus volitans*. The seven species of medakas or ricefishes form the family Oryziidae. They all belong to the genus *Oryzias*, and include the Japanese medaka, *O. latipes*.

to the eggs of needlefishes. The filaments anchor the eggs to the seabed and prevent them from being swept away into the plankton, where the danger of predation is much greater. As with other flying fishes, the 18-in.-long halfbeaks are able to make occasional leaps from the water, and they can skitter over the surface at great speed. Because their beaks resemble driftwood, the halfbeaks swim at the surface, luring insects with the red spot on their snouts.

Food in Japan

The strictly marine families in the order include the four species of sauries, which are a valuable food fish in Japan. They occur mainly in the eastern and western Pacific—the species that occurs in the Atlantic, the saury or skipper, is of little economic importance. Sauries are open-sea fishes that are similar in appearance to needlefishes. Their distinguishing features include long, slender bills and rows of small finlets behind their dorsal and anal fins. Apart from the clear green color of their upperparts, they share the same coloration as needlefishes.

Sauries and needlefishes are similar in behavior and diet, but the sauries are smaller in size—reaching 16 in. in length. As a result, they feed on smaller prey such as shrimps and fish fry. The female usually lays

ABOVE A halfbeak—a juvenile needlefish—has jaws adapted for feeding on animals that float at or near the water surface. It has an elongated lower jaw that acts like a scoop to catch prey, and a short upper jaw that clamps shut to hold on to it.

Although it can bounce across the water surface, it does not glide through the air like its relative, the flying fish. The halfbeaks inhabit temperate and tropical waters, and also occur in the lakes and rivers of Southeast Asia and Australasia.

her eggs in the open sea. Instead of having long anchor filaments like those of needlefish eggs, the sauries' eggs just have short threads. As with the needlefishes, the jaws of the young grow at an unequal rate; the lower jaw lengthens more quickly than the upper jaw.

Flying fishes

The 48 species of flying fishes constitute a family that divides into two groups—the two-winged and the four-winged forms. The two-winged flying fishes only have enlarged pectoral fins, while the four-winged species have enlarged pectoral and pelvic fins. The most common flying fish species—the Atlantic flying fish—is two-winged. Four-winged species include the Californian flying fish, a coastal fish that often entertains visitors to Californian beaches with its dramatic aerial displays.

The flying fishes generally occur in the equatorial and tropical waters of the Indian and Pacific Oceans, but they also appear seasonally in the North Atlantic. The two groups of flying fishes contain species that inhabit both the open sea and coastal waters. Like the sauries, the eggs of flying fishes that inhabit the open sea have very short filaments and hatch while falling slowly through the water. Coastal species resemble the needlefishes in laying eggs that have long filaments that anchor themselves to coastal seaweed.

Blunt snouts

Apart from the shape of their eggs, flying fishes appear to have little in common with sauries and needlefishes. An adult flying fish has a cigar-shaped body rather than the slim needle-shape of its relatives. Growing to a length of 12-18 in., it also has short, equal-length jaws that form a blunt snout. The paired fins lengthen into "wings" for its gliding flight and are different from the insignificant fins of other fishes in the order. During their larval stage, the newly hatched flying fishes have small, paired fins similar in appearance to those of a mudskipper (some species also have a lower jawbone that extends to form a bill). These gradually decrease in size as the fishes grow, and vanish altogether by the time they reach sexual maturity.

ABOVE *Dermogenys pusillus* is a freshwater member of the halfbeak family that has abandoned egg-laying. During mating, the male introduces sperm directly into the female's body. The young develop within the female — protected by her during the larval stage when egg-laying fishes are at their most vulnerable — and they are born live.

The flight mechanism

For many years, zoologists debated whether flying fishes vibrated their wings while in flight or merely extended them so that they could glide. It now seems that the fishes do not actually fly through the air under the propulsion of their wing-like fins. They catapult themselves out of the water using powerful strokes of their tails, then glide until they lose momentum and plunge back into the sea. Of the two-winged and four-winged flying fishes, the latter are the most accomplished gliders.

A flying fish swims just beneath the water surface. When embarking on a flight, it darts directly toward the surface, powering forward with increasingly rapid, lateral strokes of its tail. As its body emerges above the water, the lower lobe of its tail vibrates rapidly from side to side at a rate of 50 beats per second. The pectoral fins unfold, stretching out at right angles to its body and the fish becomes airborne, gliding about 3 feet

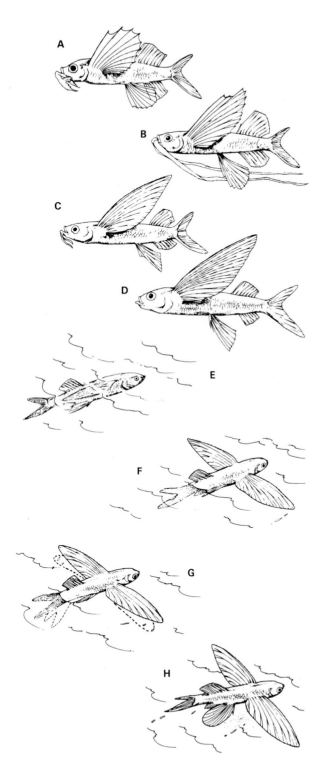

above the surface. On average, the fish remains airborne for a duration of 10 seconds and covers a distance of 150 ft. Astonishingly, the longest recorded flight lasted 42 seconds.

At the end of its flight, the flying fish folds back its fins and submerges the lower lobe of its tail fin into the sea. The tail may immediately begin to vibrate from side to side, so that the fish picks up speed and, if necessary, can make another leap into the air. Flying fishes usually "fly" in order to escape from predatory fishes such as tuna. Unfortunately, they often leap out of the jaws of the tuna only to fall prey to fish-eating sea birds.

Atlantic fliers

The most common species of flying fish in the Mediterranean is the 8-in.-long *Cypselurus rondeleti*, which also ranges into the Atlantic Ocean. Individuals that inhabit the Atlantic grow to a larger size than those that live in the Mediterranean. It spawns at the beginning of summer, and each egg is equipped with about 80 filaments. When the larvae hatch, they are about 0.2 in. in length and light blue in color. Their color becomes deeper as they grow, but once they achieve a length of about 2.8 in., it starts to fade again to the silver-blue body color of the adult.

The Atlantic flying fish is large: it exceeds 12 in. in length and is more tolerant of cold water. In the Mediterranean, it breeds from May to July. Its eggs bear about 20 filaments at most, one of which is always much longer than the others, and the eggs are always found adhering to floating objects. In young fish, the pelvic fins are longer than the pectorals, and all the paired fins are a distinctive blue-black color.

The toothcarps

The toothcarps form a group of families that includes the killifishes, the rivulines and the live-bearing toothcarps. Toothcarps are popular aquarium fishes because of their bright colors and fin shapes (both the consequence of selective breeding) and the ease with which they breed. Studies of the courtship, development and adaptations of toothcarps have cast light on the lives of many more inaccessible species. Because of their breeding behavior, the toothcarps have been classified into two basic divisions: those that lay eggs in the usual way and those that bear live young.

FAR LEFT Some flying fishes have long barbels in the juvenile stage. The post-larval margined flying fish has developing barbels (A). The juvenile has very long barbels (B) that later shrink (C). The barbels have disappeared by the time the fish matures (D). When pursued by a predator, the flying fish shoots to the surface (E), spreads its fins (F) and drives itself out of the water with its tail (G) to glide through the air (H).

ABOVE Flying fishes are widely distributed in tropical seas, but only one species, the Atlantic flying fish, inhabits colder northern waters. It spreads its wing-like pectoral fins to leap clear of predators and to glide to safety. Power for the leap comes from muscular movements of its hind body and tail. In some species, the pelvic fins are also modified for gliding.

PAGES 1970-1971 Selected breeding of guppies has produced a variety of ornate strains that have made the species the most popular of aquarium fish. The guppy is named after a Reverend Robert Guppy, who came across the fish in Trinidad in 1866.

1969

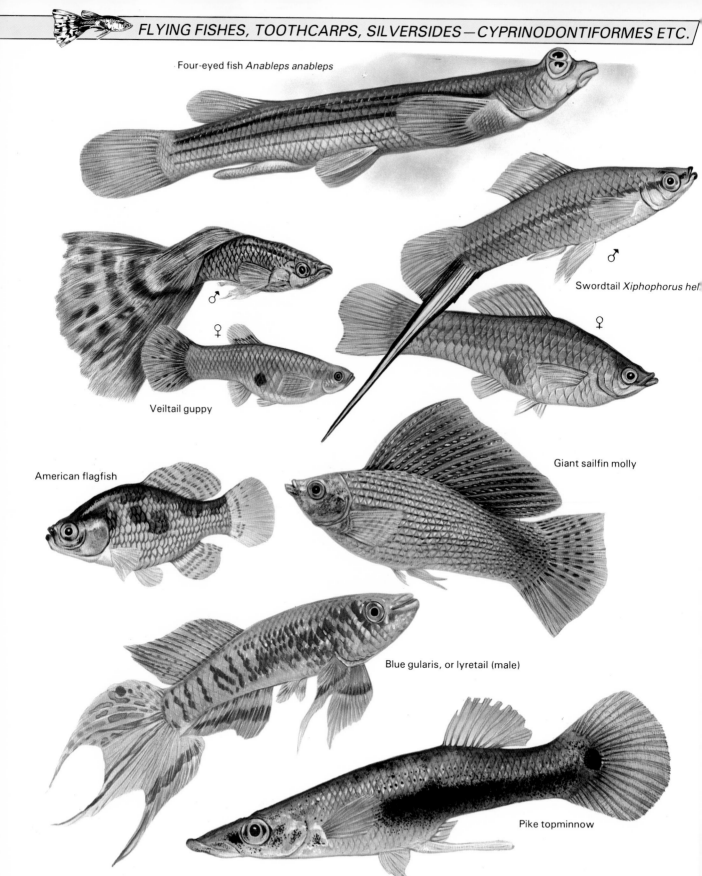

Four-eyed fish *Anableps anableps*

Veiltail guppy

Swordtail *Xiphophorus hel*

American flagfish

Giant sailfin molly

Blue gularis, or lyretail (male)

Pike topminnow

Egg-laying toothcarps

The 268 species of killifishes form a family that lives in pools, rivers and estuaries in a broad band from the Americas, across Africa and the Mediterranean, to the Middle East and Southeast Asia. Although usually confined to warmer waters, a few species occur in southern Europe. They prefer clear, shallow water with a good growth of water plants, although some killifishes have colonized very inhospitable places. For example, one species, the desert pupfish of California, tolerates temperatures of 125.6°F in hot springs, while the Devil's Hole pupfish can be found in just one pool in Death Valley National Monument in the southwestern USA. The pool lies 59 ft. below the surface of the desert floor.

Most killifishes dislike bright light, favoring small pools and streams with lush vegetation overhanging the water that provide shade. In the areas they inhabit, the water is often soft, while decaying plant matter makes it slightly acidic. Such an environment is also perfect for the growth of mosquito larvae, worms and water fleas—all of which killifishes eat. Their mouths are large and situated at the tips of their snouts, enabling the fishes to catch moving prey more effectively.

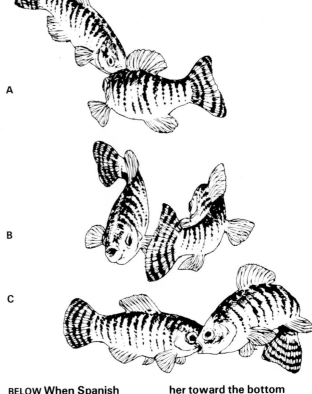

ABOVE **During territorial display and contact between two male Spanish killifish, the challenging fish spreads its fins** first (A). **Then both fish display and circle (B), and one tries to bite the other's fins in a flank attack (C).**

BELOW **When Spanish killifish mate, the male adopts a display posture (A), and then pursues the female (B), pressing** her toward the bottom **(C-D). After maneuvering into a mating position (E) and (F), he mates with her (G).**

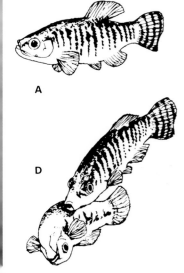

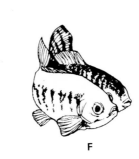

Killifishes measure 2-4 in. long and are brightly colored, often with shades of blue, violet and red decorating their nearly transparent bodies. Males and females differ in color and size—the females are smaller and less spectacular. Despite their size, killifishes do not lay many eggs—400 eggs would be a high figure for the most fertile of killifishes. Their mating behavior ensures that their eggs are accurately fertilized, and many of the fishes care for their young.

Coping with adversity

Parts of the tropical range of killifishes have distinct wet and dry seasons. Months of torrential rain are followed by long periods of drought during which many ponds, pools and streams dry out, killing the fishes that inhabit them. The 26 species of killifishes that live in South America and Africa have adapted their breeding—and indeed their whole life cycle—to survive these extreme conditions. Known as annual killifishes, their lives span less than a year, but their eggs can survive considerable periods of drying out. As the pools begin to shrink in the intense summer heat, the fishes indulge in mating rituals that end with them burying their eggs. The parents then die, leaving the eggs below the surface of the thin, dry mud. When the rains return, sometimes after months, the tough-skinned eggs break open to release the young—a process thought to be helped by bacteria in the mud. The newly hatched young fish take their nourishment from other simple organisms that live off the decomposing bodies of the previous season's fish.

A killifish of the Americas

The mummichog is a small species of killifish that lives in rock pools, tidal flats and estuaries along the coasts of North and South America. Males are dark green or gun-metal blue, striped with thin, silver bars and decorated with white and yellow spots. All these colors become more pronounced at breeding time.

TOP LEFT Typical of the egg-laying toothcarps, male and female African panchax have characteristic physical differences. The male has much larger fins than the female, with red and white spots on his dorsal and anal fins.

LEFT A male lyretail makes its way to the surface, where it feeds by sipping insects from the surface film, or by leaping after them. Its mouth is at the very tip of its head and angled upward as an adaptation for surface feeding.

The females are larger than the males, measuring 1.5 in. long, and are colored plain olive-green.

Mummichogs mate between April and August. At first, the couple swim together calmly with the female above and slightly ahead of the male. The male directs his mate with slight taps of the head on one or other of her flanks. As he becomes more excited, he swims above the female and directs her down toward an isolated place on the bottom. The female signals her acceptance by flashing her white underside. The couple then link their dorsal and anal fins while supporting themselves against a firm, upright object, such as a stone or a clump of weeds. With her head and belly pressed against the object, the female adopts an S-shaped posture, her tail facing outward and slightly upward. The male, meanwhile, rests his thick, stiff anal fin on the bottom. The fish maintain their positions and shake the rear halves of their bodies until both eggs and sperm emerge and mix. The presence of a male ensures that the eggs are fertilized immediately. If a female becomes overloaded with eggs, but no male is present, she still swims to the bottom where she takes up a mating position against a firm object. If a male does not appear, she forms the S-shape, shakes her tail and releases her eggs. A male may be attracted by the movements of her tail, and will fertilize the eggs; if not, the eggs will be wasted.

Quarrelsome males

During the breeding season, male mummichogs are quarrelsome. They issue a challenge by slowly approaching a potential opponent, stretching all their fins to their maximum extent to overwhelm the rival with their size and colors. The challenged male often takes up the same posture and launches himself violently at his opponent. Sexual maturity (revealed by brighter colors and a more aggressive approach) rather than size, decides the outcome of the conflict. Once beaten, a male seldom challenges again.

In the American flagfish, another species of killifish, the male takes care of the eggs. He fans them with his fins to ensure a constant supply of oxygen-rich water, and protects them from predators that include the female. The male may dig a small hole for the eggs, but in many cases they are scattered over quite a wide area. He then has to rush from place to place, alternately displaying at the female to drive her off, while frantically fanning each egg in turn.

ABOVE **The American flagfish cruises around in the water looking for food. It is unusually stocky for a killifish, and its pugnacious appearance reflects its nature. Among aquarists, it has a reputation as a fighter.**

BELOW **The North American mummichog adopts elaborate positions in order to fertilize its eggs accurately. After a mating display, male and female lock fins while leaning on something solid: seen from below (A) and above (B).**

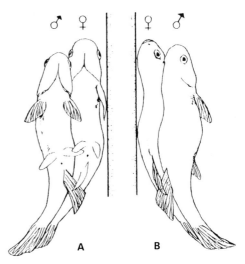

The rivulines

About 210 species of rivulines form a family that includes the Argentine pearlfish. Measuring 3 in. long, they are thick-set, muscular fish that live in the pools of eastern South America. Their coloration is variable, but males usually have dark blue backs, lighter blue sides and bright white spots on their heads, bodies and fins. The females are smaller and usually yellowish with dark bars across their bodies. Pearlfish are most active during the cool winter months (May to October), at the end of which they begin their mating rituals.

When a pair of adult Argentine pearlfish meet, the male courts the female by showing off his spectacular breeding colors, and by swimming around the female to expose his fins and flanks. He leads the female to the bottom of the pool and explores it for conditions that are suitable for egg-laying. The male then presses his flanks against the female and turns downward to make a hole in the mud. At this point, the female presses her flank against his and as she lays an egg, her mate immediately fertilizes it. One of the pair then carries the egg to the hole and buries it. The two fish repeat the process many times in the course of a day. Some of the adults die of exhaustion, others die when the pool dries out, but a few survive for months. When the rains return, the eggs hatch.

The rivuline species *Rivulus marmoratus* lives in tidal water meadows and brackish water across Florida and the West Indies. The female usually sheds eggs in the normal way, but she may keep them in her ovaries for some time. The species may have an organ that produces both eggs and sperm, enabling the fish to fertilize its own eggs.

Live-bearing toothcarps

The family of live-bearing toothcarps includes the guppies, swordtails, mollies and platys, all of which live in rivers and coastal waters in the southern United States, Central and South America, and some West Indian islands. They thrive best in quiet water among heavy vegetation and feed on both animal and plant matter. The pike topminnow, another member of the family, is an energetic, predatory fish eater that is a

BELOW The geographical distribution of the toothcarps and their relatives.
RIGHT Male (above) and female (below) swordtails display their elaborate fins and bright orange color acquired through selective breeding. In the wild, they inhabit springs, streams and swamps in Mexico and Guatemala, and are a drab, olive-green color with an orange side stripe. The male is distinguished from the female by the sword shape of his tail and the extension of part of his anal fin used for transferring sperm during mating.

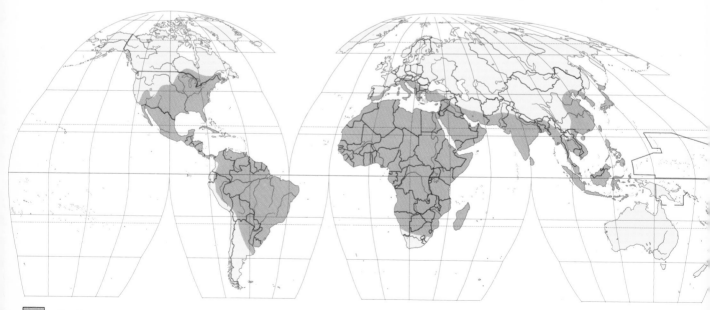

Toothcarps

ABOVE The female black-and-white variety of the sailfin molly is highly prized by aquarists. The finest species are bred in enormous outdoor farms in Florida. Unusually, the wild sailfin molly is perhaps more spectacular than those bred in captivity.

The eggs of live-bearing toothcarps develop in different ways according to the species: the female may keep them in her body until they hatch, a system known as ovoviviparity in which the young feed off yolk sacs; or the eggs may develop inside the female, receiving nourishment directly from her body through a placenta or a similar structure, rather than from a yolk.

Broody females

The females of some species use only part of the male's sperm and store the rest, so that they can use it to produce several consecutive broods from the single mating. The dwarf topminnow's sperm, for example, becomes embedded in the lining of the female's oviduct and is released in batches over a period of months to fertilize the eggs. The female gives birth about once every five days, and live sperm have been found in a specimen ten months after her last mating.

miniature (8-in.-long) look-alike of the familiar northern pike (though not a relative). Other members of the family range in size from the 0.4-inch-long mosquito fish to the giant sailfin molly, which averages 2-3 in. in length.

The different species of live-bearing toothcarps vary considerably in body chemistry, form and behavior. Males and females differ markedly in size, shape, color and fin arrangement. The males are smaller and more brightly colored than the females, which are thicker in outline and comparatively dull in color. In some species, the male's dorsal fin and tail are far larger and more elaborate than those of the female. In males, the anal fin is adapted—to varying degrees according to the species—into a special organ (a gonopodium) for introducing sperm into the female's genital opening. By using the gonopodium, the fishes can ensure that most, if not all, of their eggs are fertilized—unlike most other fishes whose many eggs are released into the water and get carried away without being fertilized.

__ CYPRINODONTIFORMES __ CLASSIFICATION: 2

Killifishes and rivulines

The family Cyprinodontidae contains the 268 species of killifishes. They include the Devil's Hole pupfish, *Cyprinodon diabolus*; the mummichog, *Fundulus heteroclitus*; the Spanish killifish, *Aphanius iberus*; and the American flagfish, *Jordanella floridae*. The family Aplocheilidae, the rivulines, comprises about 210 species, such as *Rivulus marmoratus*; the Argentine pearlfish, *Cynolebias bellotti*; the panchaxes of the genus *Aplocheilus*; and the lyretails of the genus *Aphyosemion*.

Live-bearing toothcarps and four-eyed fishes

There are about 150 members of the family Poeciliidae, the live-bearing toothcarps. Some of the best-known species are the guppy, *Poecilia reticulata*; the sailfin black molly, *P. latipinna*; the giant sailfin molly, *P. velifera*; the platys and swordtails of the genus *Xiphophorus*; the pike topminnow, *Belonesox belizanus*; and the mosquito fish, *Gambusia affinis*. The three species of four-eyed fishes that make up the family Anablepidae all belong to the genus *Anableps*.

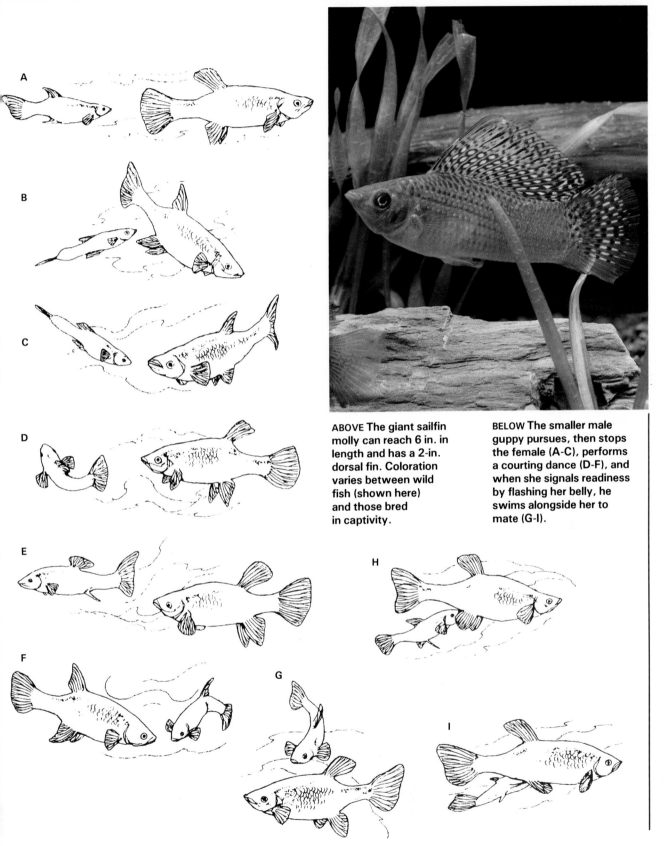

A

B

C

D

ABOVE **The giant sailfin molly can reach 6 in. in length and has a 2-in. dorsal fin. Coloration varies between wild fish (shown here) and those bred in captivity.**

BELOW **The smaller male guppy pursues, then stops the female (A-C), performs a courting dance (D-F), and when she signals readiness by flashing her belly, he swims alongside her to mate (G-I).**

E

H

F

G

I

The female dwarf topminnow can also maintain broods at various stages of development within her body—as many as nine broods have been recorded. The young are nourished by their yolks, as well as by a complex system of tiny blood vessels that form around the developing egg's compartment in the oviduct. There is no set gestation period, although it is shorter in warmer weather. The number of young carried by the female depends on the size of the fish. Young female guppies, for example, brood about six young, whereas larger, older females may brood 60 or more. Large swordtails, which can carry up to 200 young, also produce far more eggs than younger, smaller individuals.

Live-bearing oddities

One species of molly that lives in rivers and coastal waters from Texas to Mexico consists largely of females. In their breeding, they use males of different species (such as sailfin and common mollies) merely to stimulate fertilization and perpetuate the species. Sperm from these males penetrate the eggs of the female, but no genetic material is exchanged in the normal way. The sperm serve only to stimulate development of the eggs (a technique refined in modern bioengineering to produce clones) and the females then reject them. The result is that most of the

ABOVE Male veiltail guppies display their fins in a routine confrontation over space. A highly adaptable species, they inhabit many parts of South America. They have been introduced to other countries for mosquito control, since they eat the larvae. Wild guppy populations also occur in Britain and North America, breeding in warm canals and power station cooling outlets.

offspring are females (males are rare, perhaps one in 10,000) and the young inherit all the characteristics of the mother, looking and behaving in exactly the same way and having the same internal anatomy.

Medical scientists have studied the effects of cross-breeding species of toothcarps. When spotted platys breed with green swordtails, the offspring tend to develop lethal cancerous growths on their flanks, just forward of their tail fins. Since these tumors are strikingly similar to certain human growths, the fishes are used to study the mechanics of inheritable cancer.

To aquarists, one of the greatest attractions of the live-bearing toothcarps is the ease with which they can be crossbred. Attractive fishes can then be selected to establish new strains. Even within one species, the possibilities for decorative fish are endless. In addition, the whole family—unlike most other fishes—has no definite breeding season.

GAUDY TROPICALS AND OCEAN GLIDERS

Mosquito killers

Many of the live-bearing toothcarps feed near the surface. Their diets include large numbers of the mosquito larvae that hang from the surface film of the water. The mosquito fish, named for its diet, is a greedy consumer of mosquito larvae and pupae. Resembling the guppy, it occurs naturally in the southeastern United States and in the Caribbean islands. Black spots on the tail distinguish the female from the male, which is also duller. The fish's mouth is directed upward, and it spends its time cruising the upper waters for food. It can consume vast quantities of larval mosquitoes—a 2.4-in.-long mosquito fish can eat its own weight of larvae in a day.

Once the mosquito fish's ability to eat significant numbers of mosquito larvae became known, public health authorities throughout the world distributed the species widely, especially in warmer countries where mosquitoes carry malaria. It was also introduced into a freshwater bass hatchery in the USA to remove mosquitoes and to serve as prey for the bass. Scientists discovered, however, that its introduction had serious consequences: the mosquito fish ate so many bass eggs and young that the numbers of bass dropped sharply.

Four-eyed fishes

The position and structure of animals' eyes immediately indicate their way of life. Predators tend to have forward-facing eyes so that they can judge distances well, and prey species have eyes mounted on the sides of their heads for all-around defensive vision. Animals that live in low light often have large eyes. One family closely related to the live-bearing toothcarps—the four-eyed fishes—have large goggle-eyes that are adapted to a totally different life-style.

Averaging 8-12 in. long, the three species of four-eyed fishes live in freshwater from southern Mexico to northern South America. They spend most of their time swimming close to the surface of the water with only the upper halves of their eyes jutting above the surface. As a result, they can see above and below the water at the same time—giving them a far greater field of vision than most other fishes. A horizontal strip of skin-like tissue divides each eye into two sections—an

ABOVE A male swordtail cruises through the clean water and healthy plants of a well-kept aquarium. It could well have been a female a short while ago, since females change sex fairly frequently in this species. A female may give birth to a hundred young, change sex and grow the sword on the bottom of the tail, then go on to father another hundred young. In some varieties of swordtail, up to a third of the females change sex.

upper one for seeing out of water, and a lower one for seeing in water (each fish, therefore, has four sections or "eyes"—hence its name, four-eyed fish). Not only is the cornea (the transparent shield that covers the eye) divided in this way, but the image-receiving retina at the back of each eye is also divided. Light and images of objects seen by the fish underwater must first pass through the lower cornea so that it can be picked up by the upper retina.

Since lenses of different thicknesses are needed to see through air and water, the oval lens of each eye is thicker below for seeing underwater, and thinner above for seeing through air. The function of four-eyed fishes' eyes seems to be defensive, enabling these surface-dwelling fishes to watch out for aerial predators—as soon as they spy any movement, they leap away with astonishing speed. They are more vulnerable at night. Four-eyed fishes have not been seen to take

LEFT A female platy displays its yellow crossbreed coloration. The platy is a popular aquarium fish and has been widely bred to produce many new color varieties. Female platys are larger than the males, and have relatively colorless fins.
RIGHT A four-eyed fish's eyes are adapted so that the fish can see equally well both in and out of the water. Each eye is divided at the waterline by a barrier of tissue. The upper "pair" of eyes serve mainly to give the fish early warning of overhead predators, while the lower ones scan for food and predators in the water. Because fishes have no eyelids and their eyes must be kept wet, four-eyed fish bob their heads constantly at the surface.

insects from the air. They do, however, dive clumsily for food, before returning to their customary position at the surface.

Like the live-bearing toothcarps, the four-eyed fishes are viviparous—their eggs are fertilized within their bodies and the females bear live young. The males also possess a gonopodium, an organ for passing sperm into the female, but its movement is restricted. Some individuals can move it only to the right, others only to the left. The female has a side-mounted scale over her genital opening so that she can only receive the gonopodium from the left or from the right. As a result of this arrangement, only a "right-handed" male can mate with a "left-handed" female and vice versa.

Silversides

Sand smelts are commonly known as silversides to avoid confusion with the smelts, a group related to salmon. Silversides form a separate order, the Atheriniformes, consisting of about 235 species. They inhabit tide pools along the coasts and estuaries of tropical and temperate seas, with many species living permanently in freshwater.

Silversides are small fishes (the largest species is no more than 24 in. long) with separate dorsal fins, one spiny and one soft, and a broad, silvery band running the length of their bodies. They move in large shoals. Like the sand eels, they are a valuable source of food for other fish and for some humans.

Silversides are better known in the United States, where one species, the grunion, lives in shallow waters along the North American Pacific coast. The 6-7-in.-long grunion moves inshore and spawns high on the beaches, within the upper rush and wash of the waves.

ATHERINIFORMES CLASSIFICATION

The Atheriniformes number about 235 species grouped into 48 genera and five families. They range throughout the tropical and temperate seas, and many species occur in freshwater habitats. The largest family, the Atherinidae, contains the 160 species of silversides or sand smelts. These include the Californian grunion, *Leuresthes tenuis*; the European sand smelts of the genus *Atherina*; and the Celebes rainbowfish, *Telmatherina ladigesi*. The other large family in the order, the Melanotaeniidae, comprises another group known as rainbow fishes. There are about 50 species, including the black-lined rainbow fish, *Melanotaenia maccullochi*.

The mating behavior of silversides is unique, regulated by the monthly lunar cycle of the tides. Silversides spawn at night, following the highest of the spring tides, when the moon is full and the water reaches its highest point up the beach. The fishes assemble behind the waves and wait for high tide. As soon as the water starts to turn for the ebb, the females rush from the surf and hurl themselves as far up the beach as possible—near the top of the high-tide mark. They wriggle about in the sand to create a 1.5-2-in. pit in which to lay their eggs. The males follow, two or three males to a female, wrapping themselves around her and fertilizing her eggs.

With precision timing, the females wriggle out of their pits on the wash of the next wave. The eggs receive a coat of protective sand in which they can develop until the next time the water reaches them. It will not wash over them again until the new moon, two weeks later, when they hatch and the young are washed out to sea. European silversides are less flamboyant, and are content to lay sticky strings of eggs among weeds and flotsam.

1983

ABOVE A trio of Celebes rainbow fish in a fish tank. They are freshwater fish belonging to a large family containing the silversides, or sand smelts, most of which live in coastal waters and estuaries throughout tropical and temperate seas.

LEFT A pair of Californian grunions mate in the sand above the high-tide level. The fish leap from the water up the beach on nights with a full moon when the tide is at its highest. They then bury their eggs in the sand above the rush of the waves before returning to the water. The eggs hatch at the next spring tide, two weeks later.

SLIDING JAWS

The open sea is home to an order of fishes with unique upper jaws that slide forward. They include the richly colored opah and the rarely seen oarfish, known in Nordic mythology as "King of the Herrings"

ABOVE Flat and oval, boarfish measure about 6 in. long and inhabit rocky-bottomed waters in the Mediterranean and northeast Atlantic Ocean. They are deepwater fish, living at depths of 328-1310 ft., though upwelling currents sometimes carry them close to the surface. PAGE 1985 Squirrelfish inhabit coral reefs in tropical waters. Mainly nocturnal, these 24-in.-long predators hunt at night and hide in holes or under reef ledges during the day.

The order Lampriformes contains 11 families of scarce fishes that inhabit the open ocean. These include the opah, the oarfishes and the ribbonfishes. Some of them live in very deep water. They are often strange in shape and have dramatic coloration. Their jaw structures have a unique hinge that enables the upper jaw to slide forward and backward. None of the lampriformes have true spines in their fins.

The opah

The opah, or moonfish, is the only member of its family. It is a large fish with a deep, oval-shaped body. It may reach 6 ft. in length and over 198 lbs. in weight, and it has long pectoral fins that are mounted like flapping wings. The opah's markings are especially vivid. It has a steel-blue back, a silvery belly and brilliant white spots or flecks all over. Its soft-rayed fins are bright scarlet, and it has salmon-pink iridescent scales that change shade according to the angle of the light. The opah lives in all the world's oceans, but is most common in North American and Japanese waters. It appears to live in the middle waters of the open ocean at a depth of 328-1310 ft. Although its shape does not indicate that it is a fast swimmer, and its pectoral fins seem to be adapted to a gentle "flying" or "sculling" action, it includes some swift, agile creatures in its diet. Although toothless, it eats small fishes, octopus and squid.

The oarfishes

The opah's nearest relatives, the oarfishes, are long, ribbon-like fishes that may reach extraordinary sizes. They live in most temperate and tropical seas, but are rare. The largest of the two species of oarfishes may grow to 30 ft. in length. It is compressed laterally (from side to side) and is very thin; an 8-ft.-long fish is only about 12 in. deep and 2 to 2.5 inches wide. Its fins are red, and its dorsal fin runs the length of its back. The oarfish can erect the first 10-15 rays of its dorsal fin to form an impressive crest. Its pelvic fins consist of long, single rays with a flap of skin at their tips. The pelvic fins may serve as chemically sensitive probes that enable the oarfish to track down its prey. It has little or no tail fin. Its body is

LAMPRIFORMES CLASSIFICATION

The order Lampriformes (or Lampridiformes) contains 11 families of fishes of the open ocean, some of them living in very deep water. There are a total of 39 species grouped into 20 genera. The opah or moonfish, *Lampris guttatus*, is the only member of the family Lampridae, and the oarfish or king of the herring, *Regalecus glesne*, is one of only two species in the family Regalecidae. Eight species of ribbonfishes or dealfishes make up the family Trachipteridae, including the king of the salmon, *Trachipterus altivelus*, and the dealfish, *T. arcticus*.

white or silvery with a bluish tint and narrow dark longitudinal bars.

Only a small number of oarfishes have been caught and studied and most of these specimens have been damaged. Many captured oarfishes have been sickly fish taken at the surface, or dead ones washed into shallow water. It is believed that healthy oarfishes can outswim a net and that they swim at an angle of about 45 degrees to the horizontal, with their long red crests streaming out. They often have extensively damaged hind bodies, to the extent that large parts may be missing; it seems that this part of the body is disposable—it may serve as a defense mechanism.

Oarfishes probably live at 1000-2000 ft. in open waters, and have been recorded in all temperate and tropical oceans. However, they are more numerous in the waters around New Zealand. They are plankton eaters with small mouths, no teeth and up to 58 gill rakers that strain tiny crustaceans from the water as they pass over the gills.

One of the two species of oarfishes is also known in northern Europe as the "king of the herrings," and is said to lead the herring shoals on their seasonal migrations. Scandinavian fishermen used to maintain that to harm it would have disastrous consequences on the herring fishing.

Ribbonfishes or dealfishes

The family Trachipteridae contains eight species of ribbonfishes or dealfishes. They have long dorsal fins,

TOP The John Dory is one of the more unusual-looking fishes of the North Atlantic Ocean. The origin of its name is unknown, though some believe that "John" is a nickname given to it by fishermen, and that "Dory" comes from the French *dorée*, meaning "golden"—referring to the yellowish sheen of its flanks. It feeds on herrings, pilchards and sand eels, quietly stalking its prey and then quickly extending its large jaws forward to seize them.
ABOVE The opah or moonfish occurs in the Atlantic and Pacific oceans and is most commonly found at depths of 330-1300 ft. It catches prey with its small, toothless mouth and feeds mainly on squid, octopus and fishes, including hake.

but lack the crest of the oarfishes. Dealfishes have lost the bottom lobe of their tails, and the upper lobe has only a few rays. It is long and turned upward at almost 90 degrees to the body—like an open fan. The 8-ft.-long dealfish *Trachipterus arcticus* is the most common species and lives in the Atlantic. It is found at depths of 1650-3300 ft., sometimes in shoals, and feeds on fishes, squids and crustaceans.

The ribbon-like dealfish, *T. altivelus*, grows to 5 ft. 6 in. in length. It is a member of a separate family, and is

known in the Pacific as "king of the salmon." Its name derives from a belief that dealfishes had magical powers over salmon, and determined whether the North American Indians' salmon fishing would be successful.

A whale of a mouth

Whalefishes are grouped in three families: the redmouth whalefish, the barbourisid whalefish, and the flabby whalefish. Named for their enormous mouths rather than their size—they average only about 4-6 in. long—whalefishes live in the tropical oceans at depths of 6550-18,000 ft. There are about 16 species, some of which are known from only single specimens. Flabby whalefishes have no pelvic fins, no scales and extremely fragile, smooth skins. Their stomachs, however, can stretch enormously to accommodate large prey. The eyes of adult flabby whalefishes are small and provide poor eyesight. A close study of the eyes of their larvae suggest that the young can see fairly well while living near the surface, but lose this ability as they grow older and sink into deeper waters.

All whalefishes are acutely sensitive to pressure and vibration, using their lateral lines to detect minute changes in the surrounding water. A whalefish's lateral line is a massive, hollow tube that runs down each side of its body. It opens to the outside through a series of large pores. Since the whalefishes have no swim bladders, scientists believe that they keep their balance and buoyancy by relying on cone-shaped structures lying between the pores of their lateral lines. Like many deep-sea fishes, whalefishes emit light, but they do so in a fashion shared only by the gulper eels. They do not possess light organs, but secrete luminous mucus at the bases of their dorsal and anal fins. Whalefishes are brick-red or brown in color.

Squirrelfishes, alfonsinos and lanterneyes

Most of the 70 species of squirrelfishes live around shallow tropical reefs. They measure about 12-24 in. in length and are often bright red in color. If anything distinguishes them from the complex, bright crowd of coral fishes, it is their large eyes, their spines and their spiny-edged scales. They are strongly territorial and inhabit a small "home" patch of reef that they defend aggressively.

Squirrelfishes are able to make sounds, generated by muscles that vibrate against their large, hollow

TOP The 4-in.-long pinecone fish commonly occurs in the Indian and Pacific Oceans where it moves along the bottom in shoals at depths of between 130 and 650 ft. It takes its name from the thick, plate-like scales on its oval body that resemble the scales on a pinecone. ABOVE An inhabitant of shallow waters in the Indian and Pacific Oceans, the flashlight fish has a large light organ below each eye that it can turn on and off at will.

swim bladders (gas-filled bags in the gut cavity that enable certain fish to neutralize their weight in water at different depths). Their repertoire of clicks and grunts serves much the same purpose as bird song. It advertises their position and wards off intruders.

When squirrelfish eggs hatch, the larvae bear no resemblance to the adults—they are small, long-nosed, pointed creatures. The young join the plankton in the surface layers of the water and are carried over great distances by ocean currents.

The alfonsinos form a family closely related to the squirrelfishes. Living in deep water—typically at depths of 2000-2500 ft.—they have a remarkably long history. The fossil record shows that they were the first spiny-rayed fishes to occur, some 135-70 million years ago (during the Cretaceous period). The evolution of spiny rays proved something of a milestone for fish, and today is an important criterion for distinguishing between "primitive" and "advanced" fishes. Alfonsinos are brightly colored and differ from squirrelfishes in having shorter, stumpier bodies with elongated tail stalks.

The lanterneye family takes the squirrelfish's talent for communication one step further. As their name suggests, they have lights by their eyes. Many fishes have luminous organs of various kinds, but only lanterneyes can turn them on and off at will. The light is generated by luminous bacteria contained in a series

ABOVE At night, squads of striped squirrelfish patrol tropical and subtropical coral reefs. Normally territorial, these nocturnal fish use sounds and threatening displays to stake their claim to individual hunting areas.

They prey only on small fishes, which probably ensures that there is sufficient food to go around. Their large eyes, resembling those of the squirrels after which they are named, are typical of nocturnal animals.

of tubes forming a broad bar under each eye. A lanterneye regulates the light in two ways: it has a dark eyelid that can "shutter" the light (as in the flashlight fish of the East Indies) or it can rotate the whole gland (as in another member of the flashlight fish family, *Anomalops kaptoptron*, also from the East Indies). *A. kaptoptron* is a shoaling fish that measures about 12 in. long and lives in shallow water. It flashes its light on for about ten seconds, and off for about five. The fishes are active at night, and the lights may serve for communication, prey attraction, or even navigation.

The fishermen of the East Indies use the luminous gland, which may shine for hours, to good effect as an attractive bait.

Dories and boarfish

The ten species of dories and six species of boarfishes belong to two separate families within the same order. They all display similar features, such as

ABOVE **The soldier fish rarely separates from its shoal. Unlike its close relative the squirrelfish, it is a social species, and shoals are common over the coral reefs of the Indo-Pacific and the Red Sea.**

BERYCIFORMES AND ZEIFORMES CLASSIFICATION

The order Beryciformes contains 14 families, with a total of 164 species in 38 genera. They are found in seas throughout the world, and many of them inhabit the deepest waters. The family Holocentridae comprises the 31 species of squirrelfishes, such as the striped squirrelfish, *Holocentrus xantherythrus*, and the 30 species of soldier fishes, of which the most widespread is *Myripristis murdjan*. The eight species of alfonsinos belong to the family Berycidae. They belong to two genera, *Beryx* and *Centroberyx*. The lanterneyes belong to the family Anomalopidae, with only four species, including the flashlight fish, *Photoblepharon palpebratus*, and the species *Anomalops kaptoptron*. Three species of pinecone fishes make up the family Monocentrididae, and include the pinecone fish, *Monocentris japonicum*. The 16 species of whalefishes are split between three families—the Rondeletidae, the redmouth whalefishes; the Barbourisiidae, with only the species, *Barbourisia rufa;* and the Cetomimidae, the flabby whalefishes.

The order Zeiformes contains six families, with 36 species grouped in 21 genera. All are marine, occurring throughout the oceans, with many living in deep waters. The dories make up the family Zeidae, with 10 species including the John Dory, *Zeus faber*. The six species of boarfishes form the family Caproidae. They include the zulu or red boarfish, *Capros aper*.

spiny rays in the fins, deep, thin bodies and mouths that they can push forward. Most of them are deep-sea species. The John Dory is the best-known dory species. It inhabits the midwater zone of the eastern Atlantic Ocean, from Scotland to South Africa, as well as the Mediterranean Sea. Its body is so deep that it looks almost oval when viewed from the side, and it is also very narrow. The dorsal fin is tall and impressive, and consists of two parts: the front section is made up of nine or ten long spines that curve backward; the rear section has several shorter, more flexible rays.

The John Dory's body is mottled white and olive-brown with a yellowish, metallic sheen. On each flank it has a distinctive black spot encircled by a thin, yellow band. According to legend, the black spots are the finger and thumbprint of the New Testament apostle Peter, who is said to have taken a John Dory out of the Sea of Galilee in order to extract from it tribute money for the local tax collectors. For this reason, the John Dory is known in some places as "St. Peter's Fish." However, the story applies equally to the haddock—and neither fish is ever likely to have inhabited the Sea of Galilee.

Measuring about 25.5 in. long, the John Dory is a solitary fish, usually found from near the coast to a depth of about 650 ft. It sometimes occurs around floating rubbish or weed. It is not a strong swimmer, and stalks rather than chases the small fishes and crustaceans on which it feeds. When it comes within striking range of its prey, it thrusts out its extendible jaws and grabs hold of the animal in its toothless mouth.

Boarfishes

With their deep, narrow bodies and sharp dorsal spines, boarfishes are smaller, slightly more streamlined versions of the dories. They live at depths of about 230-1970 ft. in the Pacific, Atlantic and Indian oceans. The most familiar species in northern and tropical Atlantic waters is the zulu or red boarfish. It ranges throughout the Mediterranean and from Ireland south to Senegal (West Africa). Although it lives at depths of 330-1300 ft., ocean currents sometimes shift it from its home among the rocks and yellow coral into shallow waters. Specimens taken from deep water are brick-red in color, while those taken from the shallows are yellow. In the north of its range, the zulu feeds almost entirely on crustaceans, though its diet is wider in the Mediterranean, and includes worms and mollusks.

DILIGENT FATHERS

Male sea horses and pipefishes are famous for brooding their young in stomach pouches. Other devoted fathers include the sticklebacks, which defend their eggs against predators by displaying their blazing red undersides

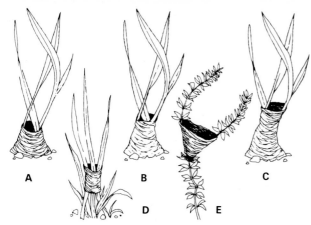

ABOVE **Sticklebacks are small fish that live in rivers, lakes and coastal waters across the Northern Hemisphere. The nine-spined stickleback measures two to three inches long and ranges across Europe, northern Asia, Japan and North America. In Britain it can also be found in brackish, weed-filled estuaries.**
LEFT **Male sticklebacks use aquatic plants to build** some of the most complex nests in the fish world. The first drawings (A–C) show three stages in the construction of one type of nest built by the four-spined stickleback of North America. The final drawings (D and E) show two other types of nests built by the fish.
PAGE 1991 **When they stop swimming, sea horses remain upright by wrapping their tails around seaweed stems.**

Renowned for their complex breeding behavior, sticklebacks inhabit cold and temperate zones in the Northern Hemisphere. The majority of the seven species live in fresh or brackish water, but the four-spined stickleback of North America and the 15-spined stickleback of Europe are mainly marine. The latter grows to a length of 9 in. and is the largest member of the order. All species of sticklebacks show a high level of parental care, but it is the male that builds the nest and guards the young after they hatch.

Growing to a length of 3 in., the sticklebacks are long and slim in shape with large eyes. The spines from which they derive their name (the Old English word *sticel* means "thorn") are sharp, freestanding rays of the first dorsal fin that vary in number according to the species. The second dorsal fin of the sticklebacks has soft rays, while the pelvic fin is reduced to a single sharp spine.

Because of their adaptability, the sticklebacks can survive drastic changes in their environment, including heavy pollution. As a result, they are quite common throughout their range. Perhaps the most familiar species is the three-spined stickleback. Inhabiting freshwater, saltwater and brackish water, this highly variable and adaptable 4-in.-long fish ranges throughout the Northern Hemisphere. In Europe, it occurs from the Mediterranean to the Arctic; elsewhere it ranges throughout Asia, Canada and the USA.

Bony body armor

In the northern parts of its range, the three-spined stickleback spends the winter in coastal waters but swims upriver to spawn. The adults in these northern regions have no scales—they have a complete row of bony plates along their bodies that act as armor and they are known as the "trachura" variety. In the extreme south of its range, the three-spined stickleback is usually a freshwater fish. Because the adults do not have these bony plates, they are known as "hologymnuras." Other forms of the three-spined sticklebacks have either three or four plates behind their heads, or have bodies only half covered in plates.

Sticklebacks are regarded as pests in countries that farm freshwater fishes. They compete for food with food fishes and eat their spawn. But they have a wide diet, eating other creatures such as fleas, freshwater shrimps, insect larvae, worms and small mollusks. Outside the breeding season, sticklebacks are quite sociable, forming large shoals in shallow water.

Building a nest in safety

As the breeding season approaches, the females congregate in shoals. The throats of the males turn a brilliant red in color, and the fishes become territorial around their chosen nesting area. Sticklebacks are among the few fishes that build complicated nests, a task that usually falls to the males. The 15-spined stickleback makes the simplest nest, binding together fronds of seaweed with sticky secretions from his kidneys. The nest of the male three-spined stickleback is a more elaborate structure. After digging a depression on the bottom of the ditch, estuary or stream where he lives, the male gathers and binds together fragments of weed. He then lifts the weedy mass up into the water and furrows a cavity through the center to form a hollow for the eggs.

After the male stickleback has finished his nest, he waits for a female to pass by. The appearance of an egg-laden female stimulates the male into an elaborate courtship display. He performs a zigzag dance before the prospective mate to entice her to lay eggs inside his nest. She is then driven off, allowing the male to guard and aerate the eggs. After hatching, the young remain under the protection of the male until they can fend for themselves.

Spiny defenders

The sticklebacks' entire breeding sequence takes place in fairly open water where the males' bright breeding colors make them especially conspicuous. But their excellent spiny defenses protect them during mating. Unsuspecting young pike and perch that attack sticklebacks for the first time soon discover that their spines are too painful to deal with and spit them out. After they have made several attacks on sticklebacks, with inevitably painful results, they learn to recognize and avoid them.

The nine-spined sticklebacks are among the smallest European freshwater fishes, only measuring up to 2.4 in. in length. Although they have

GASTEROSTEIFORMES CLASSIFICATION

The order Gasterosteiformes contains 10 species grouped in eight genera and three families. They occur in marine and freshwater habitats in many parts of the Northern Hemisphere. The most well-known family is the Gasterosteidae, which comprises the seven species of sticklebacks. They include the three-spined stickleback, *Gasterosteus aculeatus;* the four-spined stickleback, *Apeltes quadracus;* the nine-spined stickleback, *Pungitus pungitus;* and the 15-spined stickleback, *Spinachia spinachia.*

more spines than the three-spined species, the spines are not very stiffened and prove less effective as a defense against predators. The nine-spined sticklebacks inhabit densely weeded backwaters in northern areas of the Northern Hemisphere, occurring in the Black Sea, the Caspian Sea and the Aral Sea.

The nine-spined sticklebacks have dark olive upperparts and lighter sides that acquire a copper tint in brackish water. Unlike the vivid breeding coloration of other species, the male nine-spined sticklebacks develop a black coloring on their throats during the breeding season. The males construct their nests about an inch above the bottom, fastening them between the stems of thick weeds using secretions from their kidneys. Spawning takes place only in freshwater, and the males are just as conscientious as their three-spined relatives in caring for the young.

Inherited reactions

The sticklebacks clearly respond to certain stimuli. The male three-spined stickleback, for example, reacts to color when defending his nesting territory. If someone places a wooden model fish with brilliant red belly markings within his territory, he attacks it more fiercely than he would a real rival with duller coloration. The male also reacts to a particular stimulus during courtship. His courtship display is triggered by seeing a female whose belly is swollen with ripe eggs. The male will be more enthusiastic in courting a wooden model with a round belly than he will in courting an actual mate with a slimmer shape.

THE THREE-SPINED STICKLEBACK
— LOVING FATHERS —

Migrating colors

During spring and early summer, huge shoals of three-spined sticklebacks gather at the mouth of lowland rivers to begin their migration to spawning sites upstream.

While the migratory females from the sea retain their silvery body color, the males acquire a striking display coloration and become highly territorial in behavior. Their throats and underparts become red in color, their backs adopt a bright green sheen and their irises turn a brilliant blue. The intensity of these colors varies according to how excited the male is feeling—greater intensity will result from the proximity of a mating partner or an intruder.

Each male then claims a suitable spawning site in sandy ground in shallow water, preferably close to weeds. He will defend the site fiercely. If another male intrudes, the territorial male darts toward him with his dorsal fins erect and his mouth gaping. If this ritual defense display fails to deter the intruder, the male stiffens his pelvic fins and hovers with his head pointing downward—he is now ready to fight if necessary.

Walnut-shaped nest

After securing his territory, the male digs a shallow depression on the bottom with his pectoral fins. He then builds a nest, using sticky secretions from his kidneys to glue pieces of weeds and algae together. When the plant mass is complete, the male forces a rough cavity through the middle with his body, and lifts the nest into the water.

The appearance of females with bellies full of eggs stimulates the male to perform a zigzag dance pattern until one eventually swims directly toward him. At this point, the male swims round to the entrance of the nest and tempts the female to push her way in, until her head and tail protrude at either end.

To stimulate the female to begin egg-laying, the male hammers her side and tail with his snout. After the female has filled the nest with several hundred eggs, the male drives her away and fertilizes them. The process is repeated

with several females, until the male transfers his attention from mating to care of the eggs. He guards the nest closely—especially against hungry females—and constantly fans a current of well-oxygenated water over the eggs with his pectoral fins.

Protective custody

Depending on temperature, the young hatch after 5 to 12 days. They remain in the nest until they have used up their yolk sac supply of nutrients. If strays venture outside at this stage, the protective male gathers them in his mouth and spits them back into the nest. After two weeks, the young school take to the shelter of the weeds. The male loses his breeding colors and returns to the communal life of the shoal.

Such a bright display of colors and activity in open water can only be performed safely by a well-defended fish. The three-spined stickleback proves a formidable opponent to both perch and pike. It has three sharp, sturdy spines in front of the dorsal fin that stiffen by means of a jointed linkage. The joint prevents the spines from being forcibly bent downward during a fight and makes them formidable weapons.

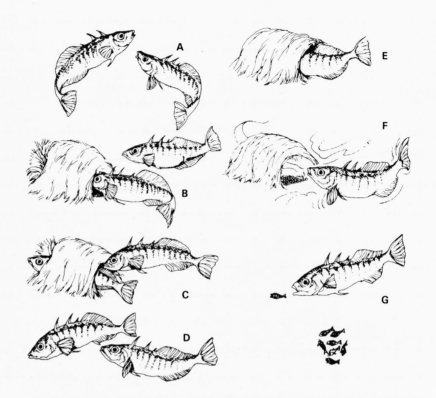

LEFT The usual habitat of three-spined sticklebacks is a debris-lined pond containing plenty of waterweed. Here they feed on tiny crustaceans, mollusks and insect larvae.

TOP RIGHT The stickleback breeding sequence: having built a nest, the male displays to passing females (A) until one can be encouraged to enter the nest (B) to lay her eggs (C). Once she has left (D), he enters the nest to fertilize the eggs (E). The male fans water over them with his fins to prevent them from developing fungal infections (F). Once the eggs hatch, he watches over them, catching strays in his mouth and returning them to the family group (G).

RIGHT During the spring breeding season, the three-spined stickleback displays a red underside and bright blue eyes.

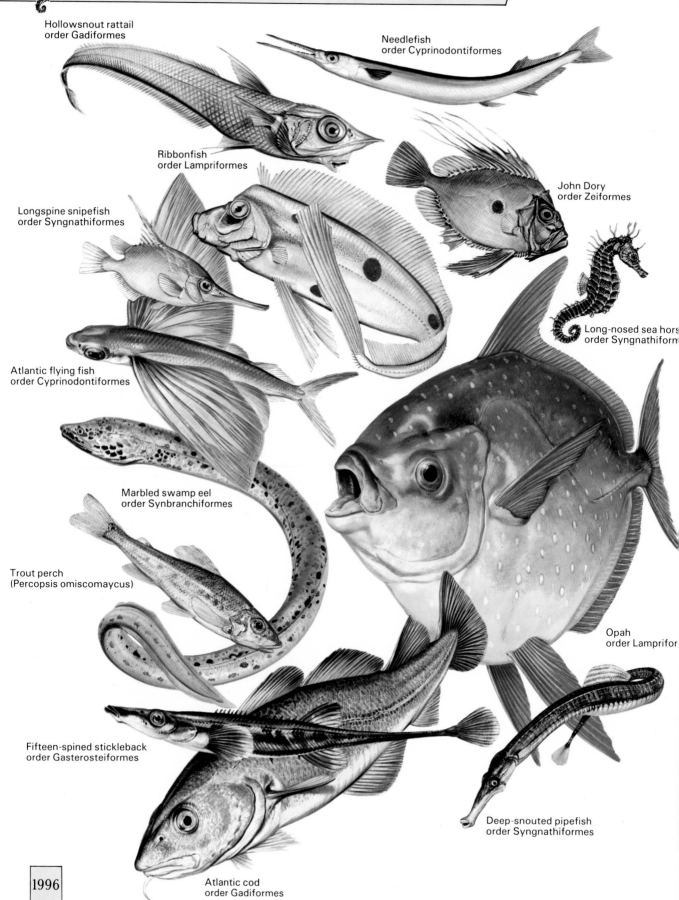

Hollowsnout rattail
order Gadiformes

Needlefish
order Cyprinodontiformes

Ribbonfish
order Lampriformes

John Dory
order Zeiformes

Longspine snipefish
order Syngnathiformes

Long-nosed sea hors
order Syngnathiform

Atlantic flying fish
order Cyprinodontiformes

Marbled swamp eel
order Synbranchiformes

Trout perch
(Percopsis omiscomaycus)

Opah
order Lamprifor

Fifteen-spined stickleback
order Gasterosteiformes

Deep-snouted pipefish
order Syngnathiformes

Atlantic cod
order Gadiformes

An oriental mystery

In 1929 a small, unusual fish was collected from Lake Indawgyi in Upper Burma. Measuring less than an inch in length, its peculiar physical characteristics earned the fish the scientific name of *Indostomus paradoxus*. Although its slender body is covered in bony plates similar to those of the pipefishes, and it has five short dorsal spines like those of the sticklebacks, it does not have enough features in common to place it in any existing order. It has therefore been placed in an order of its own.

Normally inhabiting heavily weeded, shallow water, the *Indostomus paradoxus* spends much of its time at rest, lying on the bottom at a slight upward angle. It has effective body camouflage, with a brown body, lighter patterns on the back and bars on the fins. Although this Burmese fish usually cruises slowly through the water by fluttering its pectoral fins, it can produce surprising bursts of speed when hunting.

The sea moths

The five species of sea moths range throughout a huge area—from the waters off East Africa to the Hawaiian islands in the Pacific Ocean. They are among the strangest of fishes in appearance. Their tubular snouts, which end in a tiny mouth, and the bony plates that encase their bodies give the sea moths a superficial resemblance to the sea horses and the pipefishes. However, their short bodies are broad and flattened from top to bottom, and their pectoral fins are wide and wing-like, giving them the moth-like appearance from which they take their popular name.

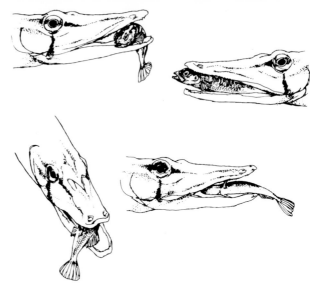

TOP The 15-spined sticklebacks live in the coastal waters of northern Europe, including the British Isles. Growing up to 7.5 in. long, they prefer areas thick in seaweed, though they sometimes inhabit estuaries in large numbers.

ABOVE A pike tries to find the best position to swallow a stickleback; the smaller fish's spines, however, make a prickly mouthful from any angle. Sticklebacks have a number of enemies including pikes, eels, kingfishers and grebes.

— INDOSTOMIFORMES AND PEGASIFORMES — CLASSIFICATION

The order Indostomiformes comprises the family Indostomatidae, with just one species—Indostomus paradoxus. A freshwater fish, it is native to Lake Indawgyi in Burma. The order Pegasiformes contains only the family Pegasidae, the sea moths. There are five species distributed through the Indian Ocean and the western Pacific. All belong to the genus *Pegasus*, including the winged dragon, *P. volitans*.

TOP Long and slender, the trumpetfish (named after its tubular snout) lives amid coral or plant-encrusted wrecks.
ABOVE RIGHT A trumpetfish lurks above a parrotfish browsing on coral. As soon as tiny fishes are attracted to the cloud of particles thrown up by the feeding parrotfish, the trumpetfish emerges from hiding and snatches the fishes.
ABOVE The sea moth, a fish of the warm, coastal waters of the Indian and Pacific oceans, grows to about 6 in. in length.

Trumpetfishes, pipefishes and sea horses

The order Syngnathiformes contains six families and 257 species. They include the trumpetfishes, pipefishes and sea horses. Their bodies are long and covered with bony plates that, in pipefishes and sea horses, form bony body and tail rings. Some species can swim backward as fast as they can forward, others can swim with their bodies held vertically. Certain species use other fishes as shields for camouflage.

The three species of trumpetfishes form a family that live in the coral regions of the Caribbean Sea and the reefs of the Indian and Pacific oceans. All have tube-shaped snouts that evolved from the gradual fusion of their elongated jawbones. They use the tubular snouts, which end in tiny, flap-like mouths, to suck in food. Their elongated bodies, measuring 24 in. in length, have up to 12 separate spines in front

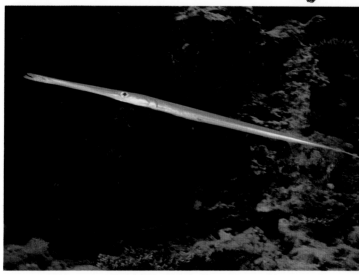

RIGHT The flutemouth or cornetfish measures up to 6 ft. long. An efficient predator, it floats through the water resembling a stick or piece of weed, and as soon as it encounters a shoal of fish, it strikes with surprising speed.
BELOW The map shows the geographical distribution of the sticklebacks.

of their dorsal fins. The second dorsal fins and the anal fins are short and set to the rear. Because the fins are almost transparent, their constant, rapid motion is difficult to see.

Hitching a ride

Despite being slow swimmers, trumpetfishes are always well concealed and they travel safely across open water by aligning their bodies with other passing fish. One trumpetfish was seen to shoot out of its haven among the coral and lie along the back of a passing parrotfish. Despite the protest maneuvers of the parrotfish, the trumpetfish remained where it was until they reached the next coral, when it swam into cover again. Trumpetfishes often align themselves with features of the coral and its associated growths, and also hang in floating sargassum weed. Such "position camouflage" is also used as cover to surprise prey.

The four species of cornetfishes, or flutemouths, are similar to the trumpetfishes but are distinguished by a long filament that extends behind their tails. They also lack the line of small dorsal spines found in the trumpetfishes. Cornetfishes are efficient predators in the tropical, shallow reefs of the Atlantic, Pacific and Indian oceans, often forming small shoals (especially among the young). They grow to a maximum of about 6 ft. 6 in., but have an extremely thin body—a 6-ft.-long red cornetfish was found to weigh only 7 lbs. 3 oz.

Floating sticks

The flutemouth is a 5-ft.-long member of the cornetfish family that lives in the Indian and Pacific oceans. It uses its long, thin shape to imitate floating sticks. On sighting an unwary shoal of prey fish, it drifts down on the tide and current into its midst, then strikes with swift accuracy. It has been seen to repeat this tactic several times on the same shoal.

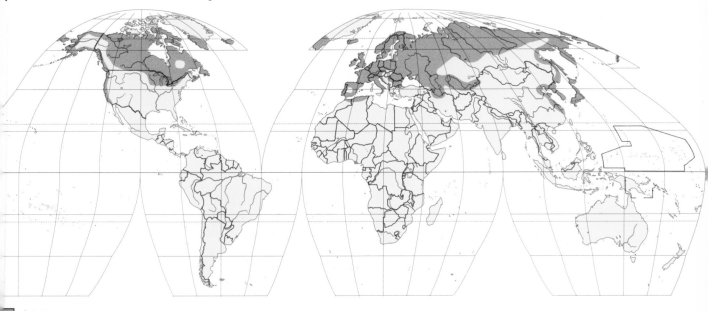

Sticklebacks

ABOVE The 6-in.-long longspine snipefish lives in the Atlantic Ocean and Mediterranean Sea. During the day, it stays at depths of about 328 ft., but at night it comes to the surface. The adults have distinctive tubular snouts and dorsal fins that have an extended second spine. There are 11 species of snipefishes; some can swim equally quickly backward or forward, while others have a habit of hanging in the water with their heads down.

Snipefishes

The family of snipefishes are deep-bodied, long-snouted inhabitants of the tropical and subtropical waters of the Atlantic, Pacific and Indian oceans, as well as of the Mediterranean Sea. The largest of the 11 species reaches 12 in. long, and all of them have a long, second spine on their dorsal fins. They live at depths of 330-2500 ft., and scientists know little about their lives in the open ocean. In aquariums, they have been seen to swim backward and forward with equal speed, and they sometimes hang head-down in the water. They also show a distinct taste for the eggs of starfishes and other animals in their tanks.

Shrimpfishes

The four species of shrimpfishes make up a small family living in the Indian and Pacific oceans. They spend most of their lives suspended in the water in a vertical position, only swimming horizontally when they are frightened and need to make a fast escape. Their razor-thin bodies do not have scales, but are covered instead with thin, bony plates (extensions of their spines) that meet on their bellies to form a sharp edge.

A shrimpfish is an unusual shape. Its back is flat and finless, and ends in a single, long, backward-pointing spine. The fins that would normally occur on the back

SYNGNATHIFORMES CLASSIFICATION

The order Syngnathiformes contains 257 species grouped in 63 genera and six families. They range throughout the seas, with some species also occurring in freshwater habitats. The three species of trumpetfishes from the genus *Aulostomus* make up the family Aulostomidae, while the four species of cornetfishes form the family Fistulariidae. The latter includes the red cornetfish, *Fistularia villosa*, and the flutemouth, *F. petimba*. The 11 species of snipefishes make up the family Macroramphosidae. They include the longspine snipefish, *Macroramphosus scolopax*. The four species of shrimpfishes from the genera *Aeoliscus* and *Centriscus* belong to the family Centriscidae, and the five species of ghost pipefishes from the genus *Solenostomus* make up the family Solenostomidae.

The largest family, the Syngnathidae, contains the pipefishes and the sea horses. There are about 200 species of pipefishes, including the greater pipefish, *Syngnathus acus*; the little sargassum pipefish, *S. sargassum*; the Florida pipefish, *S. floridae*; the deep-snouted pipefish, *S. typhle*; the snake pipefish, *Entelurus aequoreus*; the worm pipefish, *Nerophis lumbriciformes*; the weedy or leafy sea dragon, *Phyllopteryx taeniolatus*; and the blue-striped pipefish, *Doryrhamphus melanopleura*. The 30 species of sea horses all belong to the genus *Hippocampus*. They include the dwarf sea horse, *H. zosterae*, the long-nosed sea horses, *H. guttulatus*, and the spotted sea horse, *H. kuda*.

cluster beneath this spine, while the tail fin has been pushed out of its normal position at the end of the body to lie at a downward-facing angle. The snout is narrow and pointed and ends in a tiny, toothless mouth through which it sucks up its food.

Ghost pipefishes

The five species of ghost pipefishes constitute another family that occurs in the shallow waters of the Indian and Pacific oceans. The shape of their heads and bodies (which reach a maximum length of 6.3 in.) have much in common with the pipefishes and sea horses. They have long, tubular snouts and stout, armored bodies with elaborate fins. Ghost pipefishes

ABOVE **At 20 in. long, the snake pipefish is one of the larger European pipefishes. It lacks pectoral or anal fins.**

ABOVE RIGHT **The long snouts of the pipefishes reveal their close family links with the sea horses. Pipefishes have no teeth— they forcefully suck their prey into their mouths.**

RIGHT **Great pipefish measure up to 18 in. long and frequently live amid the forests of eelgrass that grow in temperate and cool waters. Apart from providing excellent camouflage for these thin fish, the weed is also full of the small prey, such as shrimps, on which the pipefish feed.**

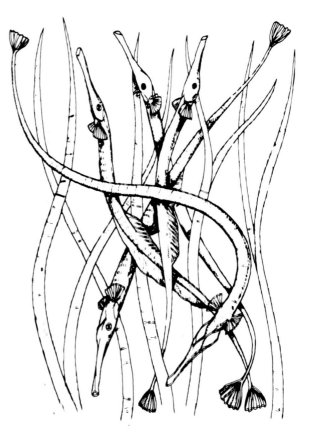

are not common and little is known of their biology, except that the females have a brood pouch in which the eggs develop—in contrast to the pipefishes and sea horses in which the males have the brood pouches.

Pipefishes and sea horses

The pipefishes and sea horses make up a family that is distributed throughout the shallow waters of the world's temperate and tropical oceans. Their bodies appear segmented by the bony armor plates underneath their skin. Their snouts are tubular and have small mouths set at the end, and the gills have tufted lobes (a characteristic shared with the ghost pipefishes). Their fin rays are soft, enabling the fishes to vibrate their fins extremely fast for maximum

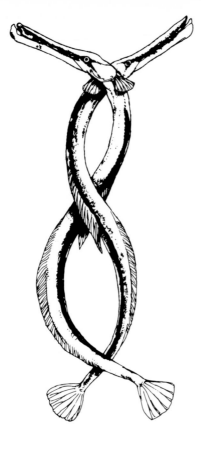

ABOVE **The deep-snouted pipefish is smaller than the great pipefish, measuring about 12 in. long. It was once a common inhabitant of eelgrass, but its fortunes turned when this plant suffered an epidemic of bacterial disease. All the pipefishes of one particular genus have brood pouches made of loose skin folds on either side of their bodies in which they incubate their eggs.**

LEFT **During a mating ritual, two pipefish intertwine their bodies. The female aligns her egg-laying organ with the male's brood pouch and lays a few eggs; the male wriggles to shake them down, and the female lays more eggs. The process is repeated several times.**

propelling power—a necessary feature in fishes whose rigid, armor-plated bodies contribute little to swimming.

The pipefishes number about 200 species, most of which live in the oceans, though a few occur in fresh and brackish water. They range in length from about an inch to 24 in. and show a wide range of coloration: various shades of brown and green, intricate mottling and dazzling zebra stripes.

In pipefishes (as in sea horses), the male carries the eggs throughout their development in a special brooding site on the underside of his body. It can vary in form from a simple, sticky patch to a fully developed pouch. Several grades of brooding sites can be identified in the pipefishes. The worm pipefish, a 6-in.-long species that lives along the coasts of

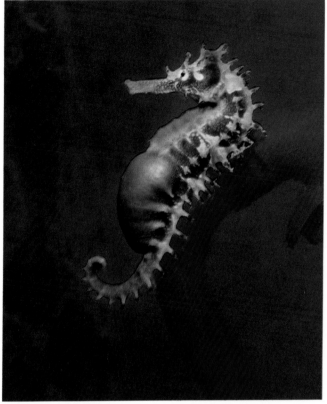

Europe, has a pair of simple grooves on its belly to which the eggs stick in a mass. The 18-in.-long weedy sea dragon of southern Australian waters keeps its eggs on a spongy flap of skin on the inside curve of its tail. Here, the eggs are separated from one another and firmly fixed in place.

An intricate courtship

The courtship of the Florida pipefish has been studied in some detail. The male and female adopt a vertical position and circle one another with the front sections of their bodies bent forward. When they are close enough, the male leans forward and rubs the female's belly with his snout. He then throws the front part of his body into excited corkscrew motions, and rubs her again. After a while, the pair move together so that their bodies form a sinuous double S-shaped pattern, with their heads facing. The female inserts her egg-laying organ (the ovipositor) into the male's pouch and lays a few eggs. The male wriggles around to arrange the eggs in the pouch, and the two pipefishes repeat the process several times until the male's pouch is full. About 10 days after hatching, the young emerge from the pouch.

Ocean thoroughbreds

There are about 30 species of sea horses, all belonging to the genus *Hippocampus*, a Latin name meaning "horse-caterpillar." They measure from 1 to 8 in. long, from the top of their heads to the tips of

ABOVE The male sea horse carries the young in his brood pouch for four or five weeks until they are ready to hatch. In the final stage of their development, the eggs increase greatly in size, forcing the male's brood pouch to swell up.

BELOW The leaf-like projections of Australia's weedy sea dragon camouflage it in seaweed (A). Before mating, a male and female court (B); then the female places her eggs in the male's pouch (C). The male gives birth to miniature sea horses (D).

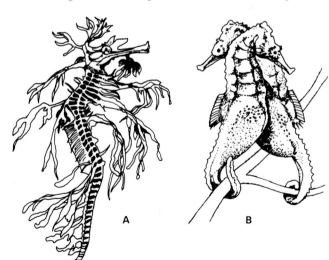
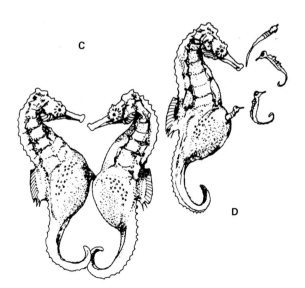

ABOVE The worm pipefish is one of the few pipefishes that can be found between the tidemarks, hidden among rocks and seaweed. Recognizable by its very short snout, it grows to about 6 in. long and is common on rocky coasts all around the British Isles.

ABOVE Although the pectoral fins of the flying gurnard are extremely wide, the fish cannot fly. It uses its fins in a threat display — if disturbed, it fans them out, increasing its apparent size and revealing bright markings that deter predators.

__ DACTYLOPTERIFORMES __ CLASSIFICATION

The order Dactylopteriformes contains just one family, the Dactylopteridae, with the four species of flying gurnards separated into four different genera. They range throughout the warmer regions of the Atlantic, Indian and Pacific oceans, and include the species *Dactylopterus volitans*.

their tails, and they have flexible tails that they wrap around seaweed and coral for support. Sea horses swim slowly in an upright position, moving forward by rippling their single dorsal fins and steering with the aid of their heads. They feed mainly on tiny crustaceans, sucking their prey in through their tubular snouts from as much as 1.6 in. away.

Unlike the pipefishes, all sea horses have fully developed brood pouches on their bellies. The mating procedure is similar to that of the pipefishes. In studies made on the species *Hippocampus abdominalis*, one female showed a definite preference for certain males; when the wrong males approached her, she withdrew and would not accept them even in the absence of the favored male. Once the acceptable male was reunited with the female, the pair linked tails and the male appeared to bow several times—probably to press out water from his brood pouch. The female then passed some eggs into his pouch through its enlarged entrance. The mating process was repeated 13 times, after which the entrance to the male's pouch closed to the size of a tiny pore. The eggs took 30 days to develop, after which 160-200 offspring emerged.

The flying gurnards

The four species of flying gurnards constitute a single family in its own order. When alarmed, the fishes suddenly spread their enormous pectoral fins to display patterns of brilliant blue spots on a red background—a defensive measure that enlarges their outline and shocks the intruder. Flying gurnards are relatively harmless, having only hard, blunt heads and a couple of non-poisonous spines on their gill covers. They live in the shallows of the warmer zones of the Atlantic Ocean where they feed on crustaceans and small fishes.

AIR BREATHERS AND VENOMOUS BEAUTIES

Swamp eels are snake-like fishes that can survive in muddy water by gulping in air from the surface. In another order, the zebra fish of the coral reef protect themselves with elegant, plumed fins bearing poison spines

ABOVE The cuchia is a species of swamp eel that lives in the swamps, ditches and canals of the Indian subcontinent. It grows up to 28 in. long, and is equipped with air sacs (in addition to gills) that function like lungs, enabling it to breathe air.

A sluggish fish, the cuchia hides by day in holes or beneath submerged logs, and hunts by night.
PAGE 2005 The elegant, feather-like fins of the zebra fish hide spines whose venom can bring on paralysis in humans.

Two orders of fishes are covered in this chapter: the order Synbranchiformes, which contains the single family of swamp eels; and the order Scorpaeniformes, a huge group of 20 families and over a thousand species including the scorpionfishes, gurnards and stonefishes.

Fishes that resemble snakes are often called eels, regardless of their scientific classification. They also tend to be associated with dark, often muddy, water. The swamp eels are an extreme example. They differ from the true eels in several respects: there are significant differences in their internal anatomy; most of them live in tropical and subtropical ditches and swamps; they can breathe air; and some of them estivate—they sleep during the hot season.

Although all 15 species of swamp eels have gills to absorb oxygen from the water, some species that live in stagnant, poorly oxygenated water can breathe in air from the surface through their mouths. The rice eel of Southeast Asia, the Philippines and Indonesia is found in rivers, ditches and swamps, and has been so successful in invading the flooded fields in which rice is grown that it has become an important source of food in some areas. It has also been introduced to the Hawaiian islands.

SYNBRANCHIFORMES CLASSIFICATION

About 15 species and four genera of swamp eels make up the family Synbranchidae, the only family in the order Synbranchiformes. Fishes of fresh and brackish water, they occur in parts of Africa, Asia, Indonesia, Australia and much of Central and South America. They include the rice eel, *Monopterus albus*; the cuchia, *M. cuchia*; and the species *Synbranchus marmoratus*.

The rice eel's three pairs of gills are small and simple—obviously of limited importance for taking in oxygen. The membranes of the throat and hind part of the gut, however, are well supplied with blood vessels, so the fish can approach the surface and take in oxygen directly from the air. In the wet months, the rice eel hunts at night for worms, snails and other small animals and fish, staying in deeper water by day.

Rice eels breed in the summer. The male builds a nest of mucus-covered bubbles at the surface. As the female lays each egg, the male picks it up and spits it into the nest. He then guards the eggs and young until they become independent.

Scorpionfishes and their relatives

Distributed throughout the world, the scorpionfishes and their relatives are predominantly shallow-water marine fishes, although some live in freshwater habitats. Most species are spiny, and have large armored heads—from which the order takes its popular name of mail-cheeked fishes. They are usually reddish in color, and the rays of their lower fins are often separate. However, the order contains a wide variety of fishes, and there is only one anatomical feature common to all of them—they all have a bone across each cheek, linking the eye socket and gill cover.

Scorpionfishes

The scorpionfishes (or rockfishes) comprise a family containing about 310 species living in every ocean except the Antarctic. Most species stay near the ocean floor, often using their large pectoral fins to rest or to propel themselves forward for a sudden attack on their prey.

One species, the redfish, lives in the cooler parts of the North Atlantic at depths of 150-1600 ft. It is a bright red, unattractive predator that reaches sexual maturity in its eleventh year when it is about 16 in. in length. It moves in shoals and feeds on oceangoing shrimps, arrowworms, some fishes' eggs and smaller fishes. The largest adult redfish will eat herrings and capelin.

Some of the scorpionfishes are among the most spectacular fishes in the world. The zebra fish (also known as the turkey fish or lion-fish) has separate, extended multicolored rays on all its fins (except for the tail fin), forming patterns of contrasting stripes. When the zebra fish makes its way through the reefs, its vivid colors warn potential predators of its approach. It also has sharp, slender spines that contain an exceedingly painful—but rarely lethal—venom.

Stonefishes

The stonefish is an unattractive member of the Synanceiid family (the 30 species of stonefishes and their relatives). It lives in the shallows of the Indian and Pacific oceans and the Red Sea, also inhabiting freshwater in some areas. It is a superbly camouflaged fish—almost indistinguishable from a weedy rock or lump of mud—and it contains a strong venom that is lethal to humans.

Gurnards

The gurnards (or sea robins) of the triglid family are both colorful and harmless. The 83 species are widespread in all the temperate and tropical oceans, ranging from the shallows to water about 656 ft. deep. The red (or cuckoo) gurnard, which is usually 12-16 in. in length, inhabits the shores of Europe, North Africa and Turkey. The slightly smaller gray gurnard is common on the east coast of Britain, and along the coasts of Iceland, Scandinavia, Turkey and the Black Sea.

Gurnards move in small shoals, communicating with grunts and clicks that they make with the muscles attached to their swim bladders. The first few rays of their pectoral fins move independently, and gurnards use them as feelers. The rest of their pectoral fins they use to "walk" over the seabed in search of the crabs, prawns and small fishes on which they feed. Many species (known as "unarrowed" sea robins) have casque-like bony heads and bodies covered with scales or long plates. A few (known as "arrowed" sea robins) have bodies encased entirely in heavy, spiny plates.

Flatheads

There are about 70 species of flatheads in the platycephalid family. Some are known as gurnards in their Indo-Pacific and tropical east Atlantic range, since they resemble flattened and stretched gurnards. Over 3 ft. in length, the shape of flatheads reflects their life-style—they bury themselves in sand or mud, often in estuaries.

The nine species of greenlings comprise a family that is common in the Pacific Ocean. They have no

SCORPAENIFORMES CLASSIFICATION

Twenty families make up the order Scorpaeniformes, with a total of about 1160 species placed in 269 genera. Most species are marine, and are distributed throughout the oceans, but some occur in freshwater habitats.

The family Scorpaenidae, the scorpionfishes or rockfishes, contains about 310 species. They include the plumed scorpionfish, *Scorpaena grandicornis*, and the redfish or ocean perch, *Sebastes marinus*. Another member of the family, *Pterois volitans*, is referred to by several different names including zebra fish, lion-fish and turkey fish. The family Synanceiidae contains about 30 species of stonefishes and their relatives, two of which, *Erosa erosa* and *Dampierosa daruma*, are among the most poisonous of all fishes. The gurnards or sea robins make up the family Triglidae. Among the 83 species are the tub gurnard, *Trigla lucerna*; the northern sea robin, *Prinotus carolinus*; and the red or cuckoo gurnard, *Aspitrigla cuculus*.

There are about 70 species of flatheads in the family Platycephalidae, with *Platycephalus* forming the largest genus. The family Hexagrammidae contains the nine species of greenlings, including the kelp greenling, *Hexagrammos decagrammus*, and the ling cod, *Ophiodon elongatus*. The family Cottidae, the bullheads or sculpins, contains about 300 species. These include the bullhead or miller's thumb, *Cottus gobio*; the long-spined sea scorpion, *C. bubalis*; and the shorthorn sculpin or bullrout, *Myxocephalus scorpius*. The lumpsuckers and sea snails (or snailfishes) make up the family Cyclopteridae. There are 177 species, the most well known of which is the lumpsucker, *Cyclopterus lumpus*.

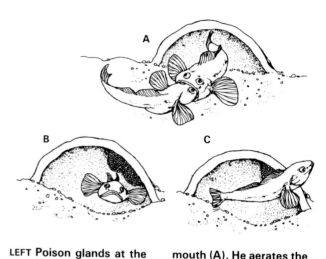

LEFT Poison glands at the base of its dorsal fins enable the long-spined sea scorpion to deliver an extremely painful sting.
ABOVE During spawning, the male bullhead grabs the head of the female in his mouth (A). He aerates the fertilized eggs with his fins (B) and guards them (C) until they hatch.
RIGHT The strikingly colored zebra fish usually spreads its poisonous, elongated dorsal spines to deter attackers.

spines or plates on their heads, and often have more than one lateral line—the specialized organ running along their sides that detects vibrations, movements or changes of pressure in the water.

The kelp greenling, a 20-in.-long species that inhabits shallow, rocky ground on the west coast of the USA, has five lateral lines. The largest species is the lingcod, which exceeds 5 ft. in length and 66 lbs. in weight. It is a slim fish, notable for its large teeth and the ferocity with which the male guards the pinkish egg masses.

Bullheads

There are some 300 species of bullheads (or sculpins) in the cottid family. They are small fishes—rarely more than 20 in. long—with flat, spiny heads. Their bodies often appear naked, even though many species have scales or small spines on the sides. The sexes often differ in appearance, and some males have an organ that can deposit sperm on the female's cloaca. Bullheads live in the Northern Hemisphere, with more species occurring in the Pacific than in the Atlantic. Bullheads may also inhabit freshwater. They are among the few fishes to live in the waters of the Arctic Ocean.

The shorthorn sculpin (or bullrout) is the most common representative of the bullhead family in northern Europe. It grows to about 12 in. off the coast of Britain and up to 24 in. farther north. Like many cottids, the shorthorn sculpin lives in the shallows to a depth of about 200 ft.—mainly in the seaweed zone of coastal waters. It is a voracious predator, eating crustaceans and the eggs and larvae of some fishes.

The bullhead (or miller's thumb) is a freshwater species. It takes its name from its broad, heavy head, which is thought to resemble a bull's head and the thumb of a miller, reputedly broadened from constantly rubbing grain against the fingers. Catching bullheads was once a popular sport among children, all the more exciting because of the fish's aggressiveness. Although a bullhead seldom grows to more than 4 in. in length, it attacks anything that intrudes on its shelter in holes and under rocks.

The bullhead lives in the shallows of clear, well-oxygenated but slow-moving streams, and around the shores of some lakes to a depth of about 30 ft. Highly sensitive to pollution, including the run-off of agricultural chemicals, it is now in steady retreat from its natural habitats. It is a nocturnal fish, lying under stones or in dense weeds during the day and feeding on a wide variety of crustaceans and small fishes at night. Although it shares its habitat with trout and salmon, it rarely eats their eggs.

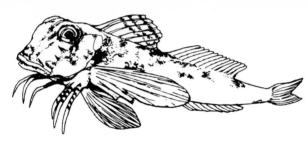

ABOVE Distinctive patterns and borders decorate the outstretched pectoral fins of the tub gurnard. It mainly occurs in the eastern Atlantic Ocean, where it crosses the seabed in search of the crabs, mollusks and small fishes that form its diet.
LEFT Most species of gurnards have a number of free rays on their pectoral fins that they use as sensitive feelers when creeping along the bottom in darker waters.

The bullhead spawns between March and April. First the male digs a hollow under a stone to use as a nest. Then as a form of courtship, he takes the female's head in his mouth. She enters the nest, and lays up to 250 sticky, yellow eggs—each about 0.08 in. in diameter—on the underside of the stone. The male fertilizes the eggs, drives off the female, and repeats the procedure with several more females. He guards all the eggs against predators and fans water over them with his large, broad pectoral fins. The young stay in the nest for a short while after hatching and then disperse. The male will eat any stragglers.

Lumpsuckers and sea snails

There are 177 species of lumpsuckers and sea snails (or snailfishes), making up the cyclopterid family. They live in the cold-temperate and polar seas of the north. Stocky, heavy fish, they often have a sucker on their bellies formed from the pelvic fins. Lumpsuckers have two dorsal fins, sea snails only one.

The most common species of lumpsucker, *Cyclopterus lumpus*, is found on both sides of the Atlantic, extending from the extreme northern USA and Canada to south Greenland, Iceland, Britain and Scandinavia. It lives in midwater and on the bottom, feeding on invertebrates and growing to about 24 in. in length.

In the breeding season, the female lumpsucker attaches her sticky orange eggs in loose clumps to rocks or seaweed close to the shore where they are often exposed at low tide. The male aerates the eggs with a current of water from his fins, and guards them even when the water recedes or the eggs move. Harmless and sluggish, the male can do little to protect the eggs against birds and rats at low tide.

A MULTITUDE OF FORMS

The 8000 species of perch-like fishes comprise the largest order of fishes in the world. Occupying most freshwater and marine habitats, they range from the 1750-lb. bluefin tuna to the colorful wrasse and coral-nibbling parrot fishes

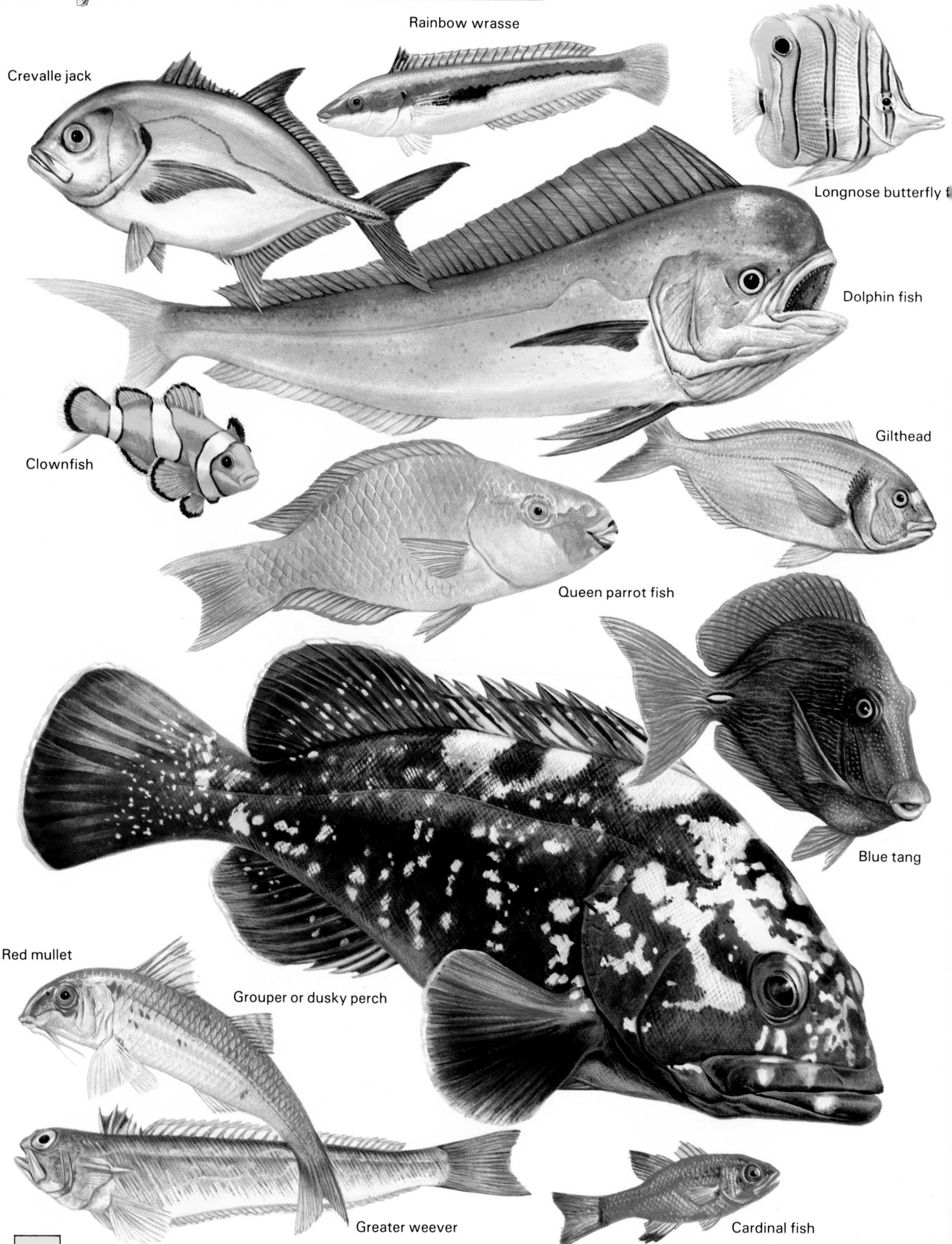

Rainbow wrasse

Crevalle jack

Longnose butterfly f

Dolphin fish

Clownfish

Gilthead

Queen parrot fish

Blue tang

Red mullet

Grouper or dusky perch

Greater weever

Cardinal fish

The huge and diverse order Perciformes—the perch-like fishes—consists of 8000 species arranged in 150 families, and contains a large proportion of the world's teleosts (bony fishes). They live in most waters (both sea and freshwater) except for the very coldest, and represent all extremes of shape, size, habitat and behavior.

At one end of the order Perciformes are the mighty bluefin tuna that may reach 13 ft. in length and weigh as much as 1750 lbs. While they roam the upper waters of the ocean, enormous crowds of bright, 4 in.-long cardinals haunt the coral reefs below. The Perciformes' methods of catching prey vary. Athletic silver sea bass chase their prey right into the white water of the surf, while weevers lurk, immobile and camouflaged, in the sand, waiting for prey to pass. Archerfishes shoot insects down from bankside foliage, and parrot fishes crunch on coral, while wrasse survive by picking parasites from fishes many times their own size. Breeding behavior, too, differs: perches simply abandon their eggs, while some cichlids incubate their eggs in their mouths.

The perches

The 146 species of perches comprise a family that lives in the freshwaters of North America and Eurasia.

ABOVE The sharp, spiny dorsal fins of the young perch provide an effective defense when they are erect. During the early stage of their development, all young perch protect themselves by swimming in small shoals of six individuals. Their barred color patterns provide excellent camouflage against the stems of water plants and weed beds in which they lurk, ready to ambush unsuspecting small fish.
PAGE 2011 A clown fish rests within the cup of a piece of living coral.

PERCIFORMES CLASSIFICATION: 1

With some 8000 species in about 1370 genera, the order Perciformes is the largest of all the fish orders. They have a worldwide distribution, covering both marine and freshwater habitats (over 1000 species inhabit rivers and lakes). They are divided into 150 families, among the largest of which are the Percidae, the perches; the Serranidae, the sea bass and groupers; the Labridae, the wrasse; the Pomacentridae, the damselfishes; the Cichlidae, the cichlids; the Echeneididae, the remoras; the Gobiidae, the gobies; and the Blenniidae, the comb-tooth blennies.

ABOVE The smallmouth bass of North America is highly aggressive, often attacking and killing fishes larger than itself. It is a compact-bodied, voracious predator, and hunts worms, frogs, crustaceans and fishes of all sizes. Because of its belligerent nature, the smallmouth bass is very popular as a sporting fish, and has been introduced into freshwater European alpine lakes. Unfortunately, the low temperatures in these lakes tend to stunt its size.

PERCIFORMES CLASSIFICATION: 2

Perches and sunfishes

Two very similar families occupy the northern freshwaters of North America and Eurasia: the Percidae, the perches; and the Centrarchidae, the sunfishes or freshwater bass. The family Percidae contains 146 species, including the perch, *Perca fluviatilis;* the yellow perch, *P. flavescens;* the zander, *Stizostedion lucioperca;* and the walleye, *Stizostedion vitreum.* The sunfishes family comprises 30 species, such as the largemouth bass, *Micropterus salmoides;* the smallmouth bass, *M. dolomieui;* the pumpkinseed, *Lepomis gibbosus;* the blue-spotted sunfish, *Enneacanthus gloriosus;* the banded pygmy sunfish, *Elassoma zonatum;* the Everglades pygmy sunfish, *E. evergladei;* and the black-banded sunfish, *E. chaetodon.*

One of the best-known species is the perch. Common in ponds, lakes and all but the fastest rivers, it lives mainly around such underwater objects as rocks, the legs of bridges, fallen trees and reeds. In the shadowed and dappled shallows, its barred coloration provides effective disruptive camouflage, and as the fish grows older, it makes increasing use of ambush as a feeding strategy. The diet and behavior of perch depend on their age and size. In ideal conditions—a large, deep lake with plenty of fish to eat—perch may reach 11 lbs. in weight, although anglers nowadays consider any individual of more than 2 lbs. to be large. In small, crowded ponds where competition for food is intense and numbers are high, perch may never exceed 3.5 oz. in weight.

The perch's mouth is small, but opens into a wide gape, and although its main sense is sight, it can also hear and smell. It starts life on a diet of animal plankton, supplemented by the insects, worms and freshwater shrimps that live near the bottom. Later, it feeds on fishes—including its own young—as well as the larger insect life that inhabits weeds and the middle and upper zones of the water. Small perch form quite large shoals that often venture into open water or patrol the bankside shallows for food. Although larger perch come to rely heavily on camouflage and ambush, they are not lazy. Perch hunt actively and are relentless in pursuit, snapping at their prey and engulfing it with surprising speed. In winter, the pattern of life changes. The perch slow down and retreat to the warmer, deeper waters and wait for their food to come to them. They can, if necessary, draw on oxygen in their swim bladders to breathe.

Perch spawn in April or May. Several males attend each female as she swims through the weeds or tree roots, shedding long ribbons of eggs. The ribbons become attached to water plants and one or more of the males then fertilize the eggs, which hatch in about 18 days (or 8-10 days if the weather is warm). Prospects for the majority of the young are poor, especially if there is a stock of larger perch in the water. Because of this, a large female may lay up to 200,000 eggs to compensate for the high number of losses.

A pike-like newcomer

The zander, another member of the perch family, is a comparative newcomer to western European waters. From its original home in the larger lakes and rivers of Sweden and central Europe, it has been introduced into a wide variety of habitats throughout the rest of Europe; it breeds quite freely in Britain. It grows quickly, perhaps reaching 12 in. in its first year, 16 in. in its second year and 28 in. in its third year. Zander of 4 lbs. 6 oz.-6 lbs. 11 oz. are common, but an individual may live for 13 years and in suitable waters they can reach a weight of 22 lbs. or more.

In many respects, the zander is perch-like in its behavior, but it is a more discriminating feeder. It also undertakes minor migrations of 15.5 miles or so to find shallow water at breeding time. Zander eat fish, but lack the gaping jaws of the perch, and their snouts are much more pointed. They bite, kill and turn their food around, rather than simply swallowing it with a single snap. In this respect, they resemble pike, and their alternative name, pike perch, may well reflect this habit (their elongated, sharp appearance is also pike-like). The zander is not, however, related to pike, which belong to a separate order of fishes, and it is a true species, not a hybrid.

The sunfishes

Both zander and perch have their American equivalents in the walleye and the yellow perch. But neither of these is as popular among anglers as the sunfishes (also called the freshwater bass), the larger species of which are keenly sought by fishermen. Most sunfishes are perch-like in outline, but have rounder

ABOVE The wide, protruding jaws of the largemouth bass enable it to engulf large prey as they swim at the surface. Although it prefers fishes, the powerful largemouth bass will snatch anything from frogs and water snakes to rats. It is ferocious by nature, and uses a combination of surprise, ambush and pursuit to catch its victims. During the breeding season, the male will attack its largest enemies, except perhaps the otter, in defense of its young offspring.

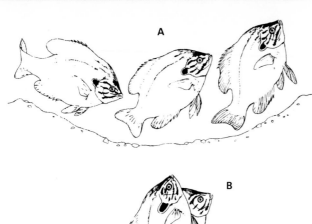

TOP **Pumpkinseed fish have black extensions on their gill covers known as "ears." When in direct sunlight, these fishes develop a brilliant sheen.** ABOVE **During nest building, the pumpkinseed (A) makes** a wide, shallow depression by beating its fins and tail while its body remains almost horizontal. The long-ear sunfish (B) adopts a more vertical posture and digs a deeper, sharper-sided nest.

profiles. Members of both the sunfishes and the perches families, however, sport an impressive array of spines on the front sections of their dorsal fins.

There are some 30 species of sunfishes, occupying most freshwaters throughout North America. They, too, have been introduced into areas far from their original homes—some because of their sporting value, others because they have been released from aquariums—and can be found as far afield as western Europe and southern Africa. The smaller types (generally known as the pygmy sunfishes) are tiny, hardy and brightly colored. A well-known example is the blue-spotted sunfish, a 2-in.-long inhabitant of the coastal areas of the eastern USA, from New York to Florida. Wide-eyed, deep-bodied and fringed by a fine spread of fins, it is reddish bronze in color and decorated by lines of spectacular iridescent spots. The banded and the mottled sunfishes are even smaller; they mature at only one inch long, and seldom exceed 1.2 in. in length. The black-banded sunfish, 3-4 in. long, has become so difficult to capture in its native stillwater ponds, lakes and river backwaters (in the eastern USA), that it is now imported for aquarists on a large scale from Germany.

The larger species of sunfishes are active hunters. The largemouth bass and the smallmouth bass, for example, are burly, muscular fish, with powerful tails and wide-gaping mouths. As adults, they eat a wide range of prey: young water birds, frogs and newts, as well as the usual diet of fishes, including the smaller members of their own kind. Both species originated in the northern parts of the American continent, from Canada to Florida. Since they are similar fishes and employ much the same ambush-or-pursuit methods of hunting, they have avoided competition by occupying different habitats. The largemouth bass prefers shallow, weedy lakes, ponds and muddy, lowland streams, whereas the smallmouth bass opts for clearer, cooler water in faster streams and rivers, and larger lakes.

Earnest nest builders

Sunfishes differ from the perches in that they build nests and care for their young. Mature males move into the weedy shallows in spring and early summer, establish small territories for themselves, and dig their nests. Each nest is a saucer-shaped depression in the bottom; the fish makes it by fanning the soft silt or mud with his fins and tail until it is washed away to a depth of about 1.5 to 3 in., leaving the floor littered with heavier bottom debris, such as sticks or stones. The nest measures 8-12 in. across, and varies in contours according to each species' method of digging. Sunfishes (bluegills and longears) that merely lash the mud or silt with their tails make small, deep holes with steep sides; species such as the pumpkinseed, that lash with their bodies and pectoral fins as well as with their tails, make wider, shallower depressions. All of them readily adapt the nests of other sunfish species, or even take over a nest from a weaker fish.

Once the male sunfish has completed his nest, he waits for a mature female to swim nearby and attracts her attention by swimming in circles around her. He displays with wide-open gills, and sometimes taps and nibbles her. The female then enters his nest and starts to swim in very tight circles around the rim, followed by the male. From time to time, she turns on her side and lays a few eggs that the male fertilizes. Other sunfish, more concerned with eggs than partners, may interrupt the breeding sequence, or the female may be attracted to another nest. In this way, the eggs of several females can end up in the same nest.

Once the female sunfish has laid her eggs, the male guards them closely until they hatch. He then watches over the fry for several days until they are mobile enough to fend for themselves among the weeds. Throughout this period, the male chases off all intruders—including fishes larger than himself—with a startling and spirited display of aggression. If any of the helpless fry drift too far from the nest, the male retrieves them by taking them in his mouth and spitting them back into the nesting area. The larger bass follow much the same pattern, although they dig their nests while in a horizontal position by vigorously fanning their fins and tails. They prefer to dig near to an object, such as a log.

The sea bass

Although the Perciformes have colonized freshwaters over a large area of the globe, their true strongholds are the shallow coastal regions. In coral reefs, for example, they occupy every available living space and display a wide array of life-styles.

In cooler, northern coastal waters, the Perciformes are represented by the sea bass—a group of fishes that

ABOVE The goldsinny wrasse normally occurs in small groups among rocky seaweed fields in coastal waters of the Mediterranean. It is an energetic fish, and usually feeds on snails, mussels and crabs. Spawning takes place in late summer, and the eggs float freely in the water, often turning up in tidal pools among rocks.

belong to two families. The first, the Percichthyidae, contains some 50 species. One of them is the sleek, heavy-scaled and muscular European sea bass that exploits its coastal habitat to the full, from the rim of the beach to the offshore tidal currents. It ranges from northern Britain and Scandinavia to North Africa, including the Mediterranean and the Black Sea. Although it may be found off most types of coasts, it seems to prefer sandy bottoms with rocky outcrops that face the prevailing wind, where the surf is strong. It also lives amid shallow offshore reefs and in tidal estuaries.

Sea bass thrive best in warm water; the northern limit of their summer distribution coincides with a water temperature of 57.2°F, and they cease to feed at less than 46.4°F. Around Britain and France, therefore, they appear between the warmer months of April and October, retreating to moderately deep waters during winter. They probably travel only a short distance from shore, because mild winter weather often brings them back.

THE CLEANER WRASSE
— COOPERATION BETWEEN SPECIES —

The mucus layer that covers a fish's skin provides it with important information about its world. A fish is sensitive to pressure all over its body and any break in its layer of mucus interrupts the fish's contact with its surroundings. Small wounds caused by parasites (tiny shrimp-like creatures and lice) are liable to infection by bacteria or fungus, often with fatal results. Consequently, fishes use a variety of methods to remove parasites from their skin.

Certain small fishes and some shrimps have made a specialty of cleaning large—sometimes enormous—fish, in a remarkable example of cooperation between species. The fish that does the cleaning obtains a meal, and the "customer" swims off with a clean, healthy skin.

Cleaning stations

Small members of the wrasse family were the first fishes to be observed cleaning other fish, and serve as excellent examples of the cleaning phenomenon. They are well qualified as cleaners, and their body form, behavior and color all play important parts. These wrasse are "pointed" fish, seldom more than 4 in. long. They use their sharp, tiny teeth to pick off parasites and dead skin with great accuracy. All wrasse are territorial, feeding in a particular area and returning to a home crevice or ledge at night. Cleaner wrasse go one step further; they make their home near a conspicuous item on the coral reef—perhaps a big coral head or a bright sponge—and instead of searching for food, they dance for it. The brightly striped blue and white fishes advertise their services in a vivid display as they dance over their home landmark.

As many as 300 fish have been seen waiting at one cleaner's station, some of them regular visitors from the nearby reef, while others will have swum inshore from the open ocean to be cleaned.

The large fishes cooperate completely with the cleaning attentions of the wrasse. As the cleaner works over the surface of the skin, it keeps up a constant motion with its fins, creating a current that the larger fish can feel. As

it approaches the gills, the larger fish opens them, allowing the wrasse to clean them, and when the wrasse reaches a fin, the larger fish holds it steady. Surprisingly, fish that are usually predators allow the cleaners inside their mouths and do not attack them. The cleaners nip off pieces of dead skin, remove food particles, and feed on the shrimp relatives and lice that parasitize all fish.

When the larger fish is clean, it shakes its whole body and the cleaner moves to the next customer. Many fish that are being cleaned assume a passive position—they roll on their sides, opening their gills and spreading their fins. Both this and the finishing shake are employed by most species of fish, in a rare example of communication between species.

A fish needing cleaning, however, must keep on its guard. An unscrupulous blenny, Aspidontus taeniatus, an unrelated fish of very similar size and coloration to the cleaner wrasse, sets traps for the unwary. It dances in a similar way to the wrasse and persuades its victims to assume the helpless posture adopted for cleaning. It then uses its predatory, knife-like teeth to snatch a chunk of fin or gill and bolt for cover before the shock wears off. Not surprisingly, it fools more young fish than older ones.

ABOVE RIGHT Large fishes, such as the surgeon fish, often gather in great numbers at specific coral reefs known as "cleaner stations." Here, they seek the attention of the blue streak wrasse, a cleaner fish that cleans parasites from their bodies in return for protection from attack.

RIGHT During its cleaning operation, the blue streak wrasse can enter the mouth and gill openings of fishes such as the coral trout without fear of being eaten.

FAR LEFT The vent of the twinspot wrasse is a prime site for parasites.

LEFT Cleaners sometimes work in pairs to clean larger fishes such as angelfishes.

Agile hunters

Sea bass have large mouths and will eat almost any marine prey. Although they do not feed in muddy water or in very rough weather, they are very active before a storm. It seems that no water is too shallow for hungry bass: they can be seen racing up estuaries with the tide, and even venturing onto the shallow flats that are under only an inch or so of water at the highest spring tides. They are at their most agile in the surf riding the hollows of the waves, then dashing in on a big breaker and retreating as the water recedes.

Sea bass spawn as early as January in the Mediterranean, and from late April to mid-June farther north. The females do not lay all of their eggs at once, but deposit them in batches in shallow, offshore areas where the tide is strong. The young emerge after four or five days and soon drift to sheltered inshore areas, such as the middle reaches of estuaries, tidal lagoons and backwaters—these are the shoals of silvery fry that often haunt clear, shallow pools and the water beside harbor walls in summer.

For several years, the shoals of young "school bass" behave like small perch in the tidal run of their estuary, snapping at all types of small food. Gradually, they disperse to join their elders along the coast; they mature at four to seven years in males, five to eight years in females. The females are larger than the males, and account for the majority of fish weighing more than 4 lbs. A typical bass of northern waters takes 12 years to reach about 22 in. in length, and up to 20 years to grow more than 29 in. Warmer waters promote faster growth, so their maximum weight may be 30 lbs. in the southern parts of their range, but nearer to 20 lbs. in northern parts.

The groupers

Most of the 370 species of sea bass in the family Serranidae live in warmer waters, and many of them are known as groupers. They are perch-like in shape and vary in coloration from dull gray to brightly patterned (they can change color within the space of a few seconds). Some species grow to a large size. The Queensland grouper from Australia's Great Barrier Reef, for example, reaches 13 ft. in length and weighs more than 1100 lbs. Groupers live in shallow seas and around coral reefs, and lead fairly sedentary lives.

Groupers are predatory, ambushing or patiently stalking their fish prey. When its prey is close enough, the grouper opens its enormous mouth and raises its gill covers, powerfully sucking the prey into its mouth, together with a large volume of water. The mouth shuts and the grouper forces the water out over its gills. The sequence is incredibly rapid and the prey disappears from sight instantly.

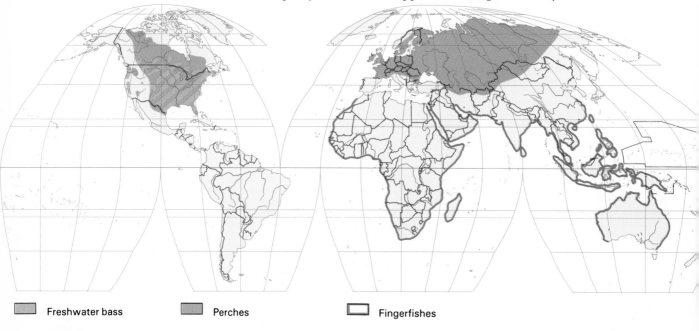

| | Freshwater bass | | Perches | | Fingerfishes |

——— PERCIFORMES ———
CLASSIFICATION: 3

Sea bass and groupers

The sea bass from tropical and temperate waters belong to two families—the Percichthyidae and the Serranidae. There are about 50 species in the Percichthyidae, some of which occur in brackish and freshwater habitats. They include the European sea bass, *Dicentrarchus labrax*, and the striped bass, *Morone saxatilis*. The family Serranidae contains 370 species, many of which are known as groupers. They include the Queensland grouper, *Epinephelus lanceolatus*, and the golden-striped grouper, *Grammistes sexlineatus*.

Wrasse and parrot fishes

The wrasse and parrot fishes range throughout the tropical and temperate seas, with most species in tropical waters. There are about 500 species of wrasse in the family Labridae (the precise figure varying greatly from one authority to another). They include the Maori humpback wrasse, *Cheilinus undulatus;* the Atlantic bluehead wrasse, *Thalassoma bifasciatum;* the rainbow wrasse, *Coris julis;* the goldsinny wrasse, *Ctenolabrus rupestris;* the cuckoo wrasse, *Labrus mixtus;* and the cleaner wrasse of the genus *Labroides*.

The parrot fish family, the Scaridae, contains 68 species. They include the queen parrot fish, *Scarus vetula,* and the rainbow parrot fish, *S. guacamaia.*

ABOVE The richly colored parrot fish uses its curious "parrot's beak" to bite off chunks of coral, grinding the pieces with the flattened teeth in its throat until it can swallow them. The specialized feeding habit of the parrot fish is gradually eroding the reefs.

FAR LEFT The worldwide distribution of some of the families in the Perciformes order — the freshwater bass, the perches and fingerfishes.
PAGE 2020 The rock cod, a member of the large grouper family, inhabits the Red Sea.

A changeable sex life

Biologically, the grouper genus *Serranus* is the most interesting, since these small fishes change sex. Sperm and eggs develop at the same time in some of them, although no naturalist has yet recorded any self-fertilization taking place. In other species of groupers, the organs for both sexes are present, but appear at different times in the fishes' lives. Thus, a striped serranid from the American coast is female for the first four or five years of life and male thereafter.

Wrasse

Even in the kaleidoscopic life of the reef, the wrasse stand out; their colors are brilliant, the combinations of them are extraordinary, and each fish changes color according to mood and conditions. Such is their variety that the usual estimate of 500 species in the family may be inflated by species that have been named more than once because early classifiers were fooled by age, sex or mood.

Wrasse average about 12 in. in length, although a few (such as the cleaner wrasse) never grow to more than 4 in. long. On the other hand, a few species achieve very large dimensions—the hump-headed Maori wrasse of the Indian and Pacific oceans is a lumbering giant that reaches 7 ft. 6 in. long, and can weigh 420 lbs. Wrasse live in all temperate, subtropical and tropical seas, but the majority live around coral. Unlike other families with a similar distribution, those that live in temperate seas are as brightly marked as their tropical cousins (which suggests that they have

ABOVE The angelfishes are popular aquarium fishes, prized for the attractive patterns and colors that decorate their flattened bodies. They are solitary by nature and normally shelter for days in rock beds or among seaweed, feeding on the sea anemones that form the coral reefs of their tropical water habitat. When a tiny polyp extends its tentacles and sack-like body from the hard skeleton surrounding it, the angelfish snatches and eats it with surprising speed.

few enemies), and they provide some of the most colorful species to be found off the European coasts.

Wrasse are usually solitary, territorial fishes, given to occupying a small area of broken, rocky ground or reef. They take life at a leisurely pace, swimming slowly with ripples of the dorsal fins and sculling motions of the pectorals, reserving the power of the tail for emergencies or displays. Most wrasse possess a formidable combination of teeth, well suited to a diet of hard-shelled animals. Their mouths are set at the very tip of their heads, where strong jaws contain long, sharp teeth, some of which are visible even when their mouths are closed. They use these teeth to tear food from its mountings—such as ripping mussels from rocks. Once swallowed, the destruction of even the strongest shells is assured by blunt, grinding teeth attached to the massive bones of the throat (the so-called pharyngeal teeth). Even hard, spiny sea urchins, which have few other predators, are not immune to wrasse attacks. Several species of tropical wrasse pick the sea urchins up, smash them against a rock, and sort through the spiky remains for the edible flesh.

Although wrasse tear off much of their food and swallow it whole, small wrasse can also pick at food with remarkable accuracy. Members of the genus *Labroides* advertise this ability with a territorial display to attract larger fish. They then offer a precision cleaning service: they eat the external parasites that plague all fish, and as a result even the largest and most ferocious predators do not attack them.

PERCIFORMES
CLASSIFICATION: 4

Angelfishes and butterfly fishes

The angelfishes and butterfly fishes make up two marine families, the Pomacanthidae and the Chaetodontidae, that are closely associated with coral reefs in warm seas throughout the world. The 74 species in the family Pomacanthidae include the imperial angelfish, *Pomacanthus imperator*, and the zebra angelfish, *P. semicirculatus*. There are 114 species in the family Chaetodontidae. These include the longnose butterfly fish or beaked coral fish, *Chelmon rostratus*, and the forceps fish, *Forcipiger longirostris*.

Damselfishes and catalufas

The family Pomacentridae contains about 235 species of damselfishes. Most inhabit tropical waters, but a few species range into temperate zones. They include the three-striped damselfish, *Dascylius aruanus;* the spotted damselfish, *D. trimaculatus;* the garibaldi, *Hypsypops rubicunda;* and the clown fishes or anemone fishes of the genus *Amphiprion*. The catalufas or big-eyes belong to the family Priacanthidae. The 18 species range through the tropical and subtropical seas and include the big-eye, *Priacanthus arenatus*.

Colorful blueheads

One of the most common fishes to inhabit the Caribbean reefs, the breeding biology of the bluehead wrasse has come under close scientific scrutiny. Blueheads exist in two quite different color phases: most of them are yellow on the top and sides, white below, with a dark spot on the top of the dorsal fin, but a minority have a bright blue head, a greenish body with two black "saddle" marks, and a crescent tail. The latter are all older males, and some scientists maintain that they are females that have changed sex. They certainly have a different breeding procedure, choosing an individual mate at spawning time, rather than spawning in large groups as the yellow-phase blueheads do.

The cuckoo wrasse ranges from Norway to the Mediterranean Sea. In the breeding season, the male—far more brightly colored than the female—digs a nest in the bottom by turning on his side and flapping his tail. He then turns white on the upper part of his head and trunk, and bullies females with a barrage of bites and bumps until one of them is persuaded to follow him and mate in the nest. The eggs hatch in 21 days, and the cuckoo wrasse lives to 17 years of age.

Parrot fishes

The parrot fish family contains 68 species. Their bodies are similarly shaped, they change color and

ABOVE **The brilliantly colored imperial angelfish uses its extensive fins to cruise slowly through coral and rocks, where it forages for small invertebrates.**

BELOW **The geographical distribution of some members of the order Perciformes—the archerfishes, butterfly fishes, angelfishes and leaf fishes.**

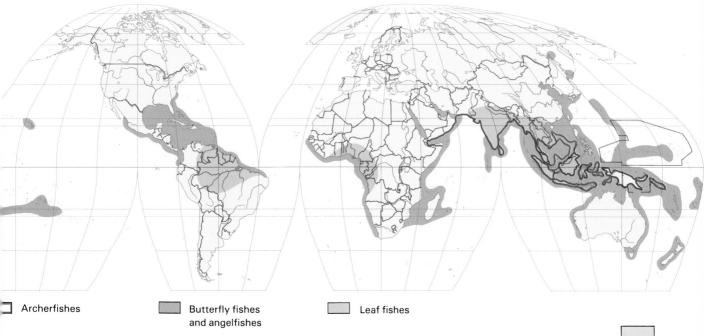

☐ Archerfishes   ▨ Butterfly fishes and angelfishes   ☐ Leaf fishes

their mouths and pharyngeal teeth are very strong. The name "parrot fish" derives from the adaptation of the teeth in the jaw; they are fused to form a beak capable of nipping off lumps of coral.

Parrot fishes are mainly vegetarian, grazing on the algae and weeds that grow on coral. They follow definite and habitual paths from a secure home (a cranny or overhang in the coral) to a pasture. They excrete undigested coral fragments, leaving them in special places along the route they follow to and from their caves. In some areas, parrot fishes are a principal cause of reef erosion, and over hundreds of thousands of years they must have been responsible for much of the fine sand that lies in between coral formations. Parrot fishes are noisy eaters and can be heard—even from out of the water—crunching their way across the reef.

The ability of many parrot fishes to change sex (and their basic coloration), makes any description of their reproduction difficult. The redfin parrot fish, or yellowtail, for example, has four sexual phases: primary males (those that are born male and stay male all their lives); secondary males (those that were female in early life and have changed sex); females; and females that are changing into males. Larger, older fish (the primary and secondary males) are much more brightly colored than the younger female fish.

Most of the younger parrot fishes spawn in groups. Males leave the feeding grounds to form great shoals several feet above the bottom in water that is 65-98 ft. deep. From time to time, small groups of parrot fishes move toward the surface, to be joined by a few females, and mating takes place. The larger fish court and mate in pairs, sometimes putting on elaborate courtship dances near the surface, and sometimes basing their rituals around territories on the bottom. In general, both pair and group matings take place on the outer fringe of the reef at high tide, or soon after. Strong currents then ensure that the eggs are widely scattered amid the offshore plankton.

Cocooned for the night

Both wrasse and parrot fishes move by day and sleep by night. Their choice of sleeping quarters varies: some bury themselves in the sand, some jam themselves into crevices, and some spin a cocoon of slime around themselves—a construction that takes half an hour to make in the evening and half an hour to remove in the morning. One study of the Hawaiian fish fauna found that, out of the 48 wrasse species observed, only one did not bury itself in the sand at night. Instead, it spun a cocoon of mucus around itself. Flaps at each end of the cocoon ensure that a current of water passes over the gills. Although the fish's body processes are slow in sleep, the cocoon

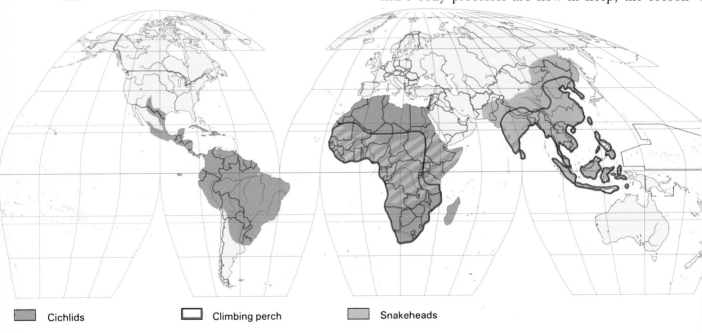

Cichlids   Climbing perch   Snakeheads

may help to prevent the gills from silting up while the fish rests on a sandy bottom. It may also mask the fish's smell or the vibrations its body creates in the current, both of which might betray the helpless sleeper to nighttime predators, such as moray eels.

Angels and butterflies

Angelfishes and butterfly fishes are Perciformes that are so specialized for life in coral waters that they are seldom, if ever, found away from the reefs. Small, usually solitary fishes, they are strikingly marked, with deep, thin bodies and often long snouts. Angelfishes and butterfly fishes belong to two separate but closely related families that together contain 188 species. They are very similar in appearance, though butterfly fishes can be distinguished by a strong spine on their gill covers. Most of these fishes measure 6-8 in. in length, although a few angelfishes reach 24 in.

Both angelfishes and butterfly fishes have short, fine teeth in mouths set at the very tips of their heads, or located at the end of snout-like extensions. Such arrangements are ideally suited to picking tiny creatures from cracks and crevices in the coral, or even eating the coral polyps themselves. Some species are content to browse on the mucus secreted by coral colonies, which is surprisingly rich in nutrients.

ABOVE The body of the beaked coral fish is perfectly adapted for life in the coral reefs. When feeding, it uses its elongated snout and tiny mouth to grasp minute food in the nooks and crannies of the coral reef. A dark false eye mark above the tail serves as a decoy for predators that can be deceived into striking at the wrong end of the prospective meal. The fish also specializes in a technique of swimming in a series of confusing zigzag patterns.
LEFT The geographical distribution of the cichlids, climbing perches and snakeheads, all members of the Perciformes order.

Although butterfly fishes and angelfishes are noted for their peaceful nature, the forceps fish—a member of the butterfly fish family—is highly aggressive toward its own kind. Its weapons are the spines on its dorsal fins. When confronted by an intruder, it swims close, turns on its side while erecting its fins, and tries to rake the other fish's flanks with the dorsal spines. In contrast, other butterfly fishes are noted for their curiosity—if a diver enters their living space, they edge away slowly, tilting from time to time to cast an eye backward, as if looking over their shoulder.

In general, angelfishes and butterfly fishes are not territorial. Only the species that rely heavily on coral polyps for food tend to defend this specialized resource. The rest of the species roam the reef in search of food, leading to breeding behavior quite

TENANTS IN DEADLY TENTACLES
— AT HOME IN AN ANEMONE —

Safe space is at a premium in the coral reefs, especially for small fish. Several species of damselfish, known collectively as clown fish or anemone fish, have solved the problem in a unique way. They make their homes among the tentacles of large sea anemones, colonial creatures armed with batteries of explosive and poisonous sting cells, despite the fact that these sea anemones feed on fish of identical size and shape as their colorful tenants. The relationship is close; each fish, or family of fishes, has a home anemone; if placed in another one, it would be paralyzed and eaten.

The exact mechanism of the clown fish's immunity to its host is not known, but it involves a period during which fish and sea anemone learn to recognize each other. If a clown fish and its anemone are separated then reunited, the fish darts to the anemone and circles it, then ducks under the tentacles to nibble the body several times. The fish does not swim in a normal manner at this stage; it makes curious vertical movements of the body. Whether this sets up vibrations recognized by the anemone, or whether it merely expresses the fish's nervousness about the following stage, is not known.

The fish then makes passes over the tentacles and eventually lets them brush its skin. The tentacles stick, showing that the stinging cells are in action. The fish jerks free, then repeats the procedure. Eventually, the tentacles stop sticking and the fish settles down in its living home, even seeking refuge in the anemone's stomach at night when the tentacles are retracted. The whole familiarization process takes about an hour.

To the clown fish, the advantages of the relationship are obvious; few predators are prepared to chase it into the painful nettlebed of a sea anemone, which can be as large as 50 in. in diameter. The advantages to the anemone are small but cumulative. The fish eats the anemone's waste materials and removes growths and debris from its skin. Some species of clown fish drive off butterfly fish that might make a meal of their home, or part of it, while others even feed the anemone prawns or pieces of fish. The fish's forays into the anemone's stomach

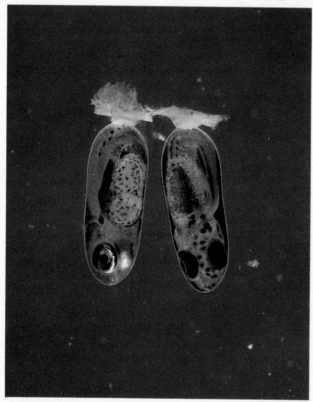

may also improve the anemone's oxygen supply.

Once past the poison barrier, day-to-day life in an anemone is ideally suited to a member of the damselfish family. Damselfish tend to be highly territorial, and many of them form close bonds with their breeding mates. Thus clown fish protect their precious—and sometimes scarce—home against intruders, and do not have to leave it in search of a mate. Few damselfish stray far from their home crevices, and the short forays for shrimps and algae undertaken by clown fish are similar.

Clown fish breed in the shadow of the tentacles, laying 600-1600 large, red eggs at the base of the anemone's stalk. The eggs are cared for by the male, who fans them with his fins and eats any that are infertile or infected with fungus. They hatch after 9 or 10 days, usually by night in bright moonlight, and the fry swim to the surface to join the plankton for a while. After a period of bottom life, hiding by day and feeding by night, they reach a length of 0.3-0.4 in. and go off in search of an anemone. The young seek the anemone Radianthus, a type avoided by adults, ruling out competition. As they mature, the clown fish graduate to the anemone Gyrostoma.

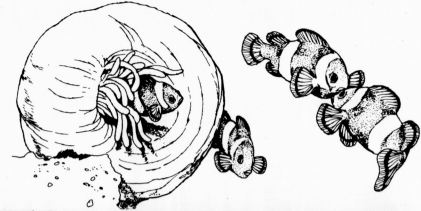

RIGHT A layer of mucus covers the body of the clown fish, making it immune to the venomous tentacles of the sea anemones and other marine invertebrates of the coral reefs.

ABOVE RIGHT A clown fish hides from predators among the tentacles of a sea anemone (A). They are protective of their territory and widen their pectoral fins in front of intruders in a territorial display that makes them look larger than usual (B).

FAR LEFT The sea anemone provides a safe nursery for the eggs of the clown fish, since the mucus covering the eggs is made of the same substance as the body mucus of the adult.

LEFT Only as larvae and tiny fry do clown fish leave the safety of the sea anemone to feed on plankton.

ABOVE **Despite being aggressive, the spotted damselfish often lives in shoals over coral reefs in tropical waters. It is a lively fish that darts for cover in the coral reefs at the slightest sign of danger.**

BELOW **The male damselfish circles for two or three minutes over some attractive object on the seabed — in this case, an empty cone shell — in a courtship display that is designed to attract a potential mate.**

unusual in fish; some species form breeding pairs that may be stable for three years or more.

Color in the coral

Reef fishes display a spectacular range of colors, though their function has been a source of guesswork for many years. The fishes in question are not especially poisonous or dangerous, possible reasons for the bright colors in some animal groups. In these non-poisonous fishes, the bright color schemes may help species to recognize one another, they may be a sophisticated form of communication, or serve as a form of defense. It has been suggested that the colors serve as camouflage, or that they disrupt the fishes' outlines against the brilliant background of the reef. However, butterfly fishes and angelfishes actually stand out prominently, as do a number of other species. Furthermore, much of the coral environment is dull and gray, making the fishes seem even more striking. More remarkably, some butterfly fishes employ a trick of coloration used by their insect namesakes (butterflies), as well as by other animals— they sport a distinctive, large "eye" marking on or near their tails. The false eye fools predators, confusing them as to which is the front end of the fish, and their attack may miss its target, or damage a less vulnerable area of the body. Angelfishes and butterfly fishes rely on alertness and agility to avoid predation, and they use their small size and narrow bodies to take swift refuge in nooks and crannies amid the coral.

Damselfishes

About 235 species of damselfishes form a single family. They are as territorial as the butterfly fishes are solitary, and may defend a coral outcrop or a patch of algae. They are small, often brightly marked fishes, usually about 6 in. long, although some reach about 12 in. They are not confined to coral, and some species inhabit temperate waters. The garibaldi, for example, is a brilliant orange species that grows up to 12 in. long and lives in the cooler waters of the northern Pacific Ocean.

Damselfishes are loyal to their coral colony. Marking experiments with three-striped damselfish have shown that they use the same coral for at least seven months, and that the spotted damselfish, a related species, extends this to two years. The size of a damselfish shoal is directly related to the size of the coral colony, and is limited by the amount of plankton there is to eat and the number of safe spaces there are within quick swimming range. Over small coral outcrops, three-striped damselfish groups show an interesting social hierarchy. The group is dominated by a larger male of perhaps 2.7-3.2 in. in length, with several females of 0.8-2.8 in. below him, themselves organized by size. The larger the female, the better her chances of mating.

The most famous damselfishes of all are those that have formed protective relationships with sea anemones. Known as clown fishes, they have territories consisting of the tentacles and bodies of giant sea anemones. For any other fishes of similar size, the sea anemone is a deadly enemy since it uses its stinging cells to kill fishes for food; the clown fishes, however, are immune. Ownership of an anemone is a family affair. The anemone fish *Amphiprion percula*, for example, lives in and around the anemone *Discosoma*. It lays its eggs near the base of its host, beneath a protective umbrella of tentacles. When the fry hatch, they soon take refuge among the deadly arms above.

Clown fishes normally form social units based on a mating pair and some individuals that have not yet reached sexual maturity. The larger female dominates the whole group, while the pair are superior to the juniors. They protect their home anemone with sound, fin displays and head butting, and often drive away larger fish. The anemone is the center of their world, and they seldom venture far in search of the planktonic organisms and algae that make up their diet.

Preserving a family unit

The bond between male and female clown fish is strong and may last for up to three years. The partners can recognize each other by sight, even in a large shoal of mixed species. If one partner's appearance is altered artificially, the other fails to recognize it and becomes aggressive. In some species, all the young mature as males, turning female only if the mature female disappears from the social unit. In this event, the "senior" male takes the place of his mate. The change-over is quick; an ex-male may be laying eggs within a month of his mate's disappearance, preserving the whole family unit.

Safety in numbers

In open water, fishes congregate where food is most

ABOVE Like most of the shallow-water members of its family, the bigeye normally feeds by night in large shoals. It occurs on both sides of the tropical Atlantic Ocean above coral reefs. Its large eyes enable it to see in the dark waters.

plentiful—either at or near the surface where plankton occurs, or on or near the bottom where debris, algae and a range of tiny creatures accumulate. Marine life also gathers between these levels—in shallow waters, usually around coasts, fish often find safety in numbers and form tightly packed shoals.

Croakers

Despite all the advantages of a shoaling life, shoaling fish that feed by night, or make a habit of entering murky water, face problems of communication. To stay in touch, a surprising number of them use sounds. Some shoals have a dawn chorus, like birds; others start making sounds in the evening, reaching a peak toward midnight and fading toward dawn. Many species become more noisy at breeding time. Of all fish shoals, few communicate with more volume and range than the aptly named croakers.

There are 210 species in the croaker family, mainly inhabiting the shallow waters of the tropics and the

temperate seas. Some of them enter brackish water, while the freshwater grunt lives permanently in freshwater in North America. Many live in cloudy water with only limited visibility. A few croakers inhabit northern European waters, and the meager, which grows to 48 in. in length, frequents the estuaries and sandy beaches of the European and African coasts and is occasionally found in the English Channel. It forms the basis of lucrative fishing industries off the coast of South Africa, where it is known as the kob, and all across the Atlantic, where it is called the redfish or channel bass.

In general appearance, croakers are typical members of the order Perciformes. They have two dorsal fins, which appear separate but are connected at the base, and snouts that are usually rounded. Their ear bones are well developed, and those of the freshwater grunt are common good-luck tokens in the United States. The size of the ear bones found by archaeologists reveals that grunts were far larger 2000 years ago, weighing up to 200 lbs. Nowadays, they reach a maximum weight of about 55 lbs.

Although American Indians revered a fish that they could hear clearly from their canoes, the croakers' habit of underwater broadcasting only became widely known when sensitive listening devices were developed

ABOVE Tropical goatfishes usually swim over the rough, algae-covered ground of shallow water in tight shoals. When feeding, they prefer the soft seabed, probing with two taste-sensitive barbels that hang from the chin and fanning up clouds of silt with their broad pectoral fins. They are known as red mullet in northern waters, where they enjoy great popularity as a food fish.

during the submarine battles of World War II. Hydrophone operators often mistook the croakers' repertoire of clicks, grunts, pops and synchronized drummings for the often more subtle noises made by propellers and other machinery of enemy vessels.

Croakers produce their characteristic sounds by vibrating their muscles, using their swim bladder as a resonator. In many species, the muscles are attached directly to the swim bladder; in others, they connect to the body wall. The volume of the sounds made by croakers ranges from being almost inaudible to loud enough for a person on the deck of a ship to hear from 66 ft. below the surface. The croaks are a highly effective, long-range means of communication.

Goatfishes

Many fish use small barbels under their chins to locate food. Sensitive to taste and touch, the barbels are a common adaptation to life on the bottom.

Within the order Perciformes, goatfishes (also known as red mullets) employ barbels to good effect. The goatfish family contains 55 species, all with elongated bodies, angular heads and a pair of long barbels that they can retract under their bodies. They are not large, averaging 10 in. in length, although a few species reach 24 in. In color, goatfishes tend to be shades of red, yellow and gold, changing hue according to their behavior and background.

Goatfishes inhabit all the warm-temperature and tropical seas. They forage on soft ground, often in small shoals, fanning the mud and silt with their wide pectoral fins and probing for small invertebrates with their barbels. They often dig holes as deep as their body length, sending up "smoke signals" of displaced mud and silt. The clouds of mud attract a variety of small fishes (for example, sea breams and wrasse) that join the goatfishes, waiting for scraps.

Dragonets

The dragonets form a family that shares both its range and habitat with the goatfishes, but dragonets spend more time closer to the seabed. There are about 130 species of these small, thin, slimy fishes. Reaching a maximum length of 15 in., they specialize in a "dart-

ABOVE Dragonets always live near the bottom, and camouflage themselves by wriggling their long, flattened bodies into sand or below stones until they are almost invisible. Their heads are large, flattened and almost triangular when viewed from above, and they have large eyes on the forehead that orient upward, enabling them to survey their immediate environment as they lie submerged.

PERCIFORMES CLASSIFICATION: 5

Croakers, goatfishes and dragonets

The family Sciaenidae contains the 210 species of croakers or drums, which range throughout the oceans. Some species also occur in estuaries and freshwater habitats. The family includes the freshwater grunt, *Aplodinotus grunniens*; the meager or redfish, *Sciaena aquila*; and the Atlantic croaker, *Micropogon undulatus*. There are 55 species of goatfishes in the family Mullidae, ranging through the warmer regions of the oceans. They include the yellow goatfish, *Mulliodichthys martinicus*, and the red mullet, *Mullus barbatus*. The family Callionymidae comprises the 130 species of dragonets—fishes that also range through the warmer seas. The most common species off the coast of Europe is the European dragonet, *Callionymus lyra*.

Sea bream, stargazers and weevers

The sea bream belong to the family Sparidae. The 100 or so species live mainly in warmer waters, with some occurring in freshwater habitats. They include the red sea bream, *Pagellus pagellus;* the dentex, *Dentex dentex*; and the musselcracker, *Cymatoceps nasutus*. The stargazers, which range widely through tropical and temperate seas, form the family Uranoscopidae.

The family Trachinidae contains just four (or five) species of weevers. They mainly occur in the eastern Atlantic, and the greater weever, *Trachinus draco*, is the best-known species. The 12 species of sand eels or sand lances make up the family Ammodytidae. Ranging through the northern seas and the Indian Ocean, they include the greater sand eel, *Ammodytes lanceolatus*.

TOP The slim, streamlined shape and powerful tail of the silver bream make it a fast-swimming predator. It hunts fishes using the rows of strong, grasping teeth that line its jaws to seize the victim. One of the larger sea breams, it inhabits the eastern Atlantic and Mediterranean.

ABOVE Two diagonal bands of color cross the body of the two-banded bream. One of many sea bream species to occur in the Mediterranean, it usually occurs in tightly packed, disciplined shoals. Like its relatives, the two-banded bream is a formidable predator.

and-rest" hunting technique on sand and gravel bottoms from the coastal shallows to quite deep water.

Five species of dragonets inhabit European waters, although the marked differences between males and females once led to the belief that there were many more. Males are spectacular both in color and shape, with bright blue spots and whorls decorating their enormous dorsal and pectoral fins. Their bodies are brown on top and yellow underneath. A male in full breeding colors is a sight reminiscent of clear, blue tropical water rather than the gray North Sea. The females are far more restrained in appearance, lacking the extravagant fins and bright markings.

The European dragonet feeds on shrimps, worms and mollusks such as cockles, usually at depths of up to 164 ft. but occasionally venturing as deep as 328 ft. It rests its head pointing up, on the bottom, and then flicks and glides to the next feeding spot, sometimes wriggling to cast a little sand or gravel over its body for camouflage.

Dragonets spawn after an elaborate courtship and mating. The male's colors achieve their full brilliance in spring and early summer, and he displays them to best advantage in courtship activity, when he rushes at females with all fins spread. After a curious face-pulling ritual in which the male pushes out his upper lip and nods, the female accepts him and they link fins and swim toward the surface. The rest of their mating movements are devoted to forming a groove between their bodies, into which they shed their eggs and sperm. The sperm fertilizes the eggs immediately, and they float to the surface where they hatch after about two weeks. The young stay in the upper layers of water until winter, when they descend to continue their lives on the bottom.

Stargazers

Some fishes grub around in the sand and mud of the seabed for their food. Many others conceal themselves in the mud while they wait for their food to drift, swim or walk into range. Such a way of life involves a range of adaptations that enable the fishes to burrow, breathe and find a defensive substitute for fleeing when danger comes too close. The stargazer family incorporates the full range of adaptations.

Stargazers seldom measure more than 25.5 in. from their massive heads to their tapered tails. Their mouths are set almost vertically on the front of their

heads, opening trapdoor fashion to anything passing above. Their eyes lie on top of the head, gazing directly upward when the fish is at rest. When, as rarely happens, the fishes swim above the bottom, their eyes bulge like those of frogs. Stargazers use their large pectoral fins as shovels, wriggling and shouldering their way to invisibility at the bottom. Their dull brown color, broken only by an irregular pattern of spots, helps to conceal them.

To breathe in their burrowing positions, a few species of stargazers have nostrils that connect directly to their mouths, an unusual but effective way of ensuring a constant stream of water over their gills. Their lips have a fringe of short, fleshy tentacles that may help keep sediment out, or tempt tiny, inquisitive fish in. The European stargazer employs a special lure for this purpose. It has a fringe of tentacles mounted on a stalk inside its mouth. When wriggled, the lure gives a passable imitation of a marine worm and tempts small fish close enough to be snapped up.

Stargazers have two defensive adaptations: electric organs and venom glands. The electric organs generate electricity through modified muscle fibers contained in a pouch behind their eyes, giving the fish positive polarity on the lower surface and negative polarity above. In an emergency, stargazers can generate 50 volts, probably enough to stun prey and actively discourage predators. They can also use an electric field to detect approaching prey in the murky conditions and to signal to prospective mates in the breeding season.

As a second line of defense, stargazers have spines just above the base of their pectoral fins; they are double-grooved to carry venom from glands at their base. The venom is highly toxic, and can be lethal. However, stargazers are unlikely to sting bathers in European waters since they prefer to inhabit water that is 10-50 ft. deep.

Weevers

The weevers, members of another family that burrows and lurks for concealment and food, also carry venom. The lesser weever lies head-up and half buried in sand in shallow water, its black dorsal fin and the spines on its gill covers loaded with venom for the unwary. There are only four or five species in the family, and they range from West Africa and the Mediterranean to Scotland.

ABOVE Coming to rest on the sea bottom, a stargazer starts to shovel gravel with its pectoral fins, before burying itself until only its eyes show. It then awaits passing fish, sometimes tempting them closer with a worm-like, fleshy filament inside its bottom jaw, before darting out and seizing them. Remaining motionless on the seabed holds no dangers for stargazers; they are armed with venomous spines as well as glands capable of discharging a paralyzing charge of electricity at around 50 volts.

The greater weever, which lives at depths of 100-330 ft., is the largest species, averaging 16 in. in length. The lesser weever measures about 4 in., with a maximum length of 6 in. Weevers spend the day in the sand, waiting for small crabs, shrimps and the many species of fry that share their habitat. They move up the shore at high tide in an active search for prey.

Sand eels

Sand eels are hunted by nearly every predator that shares their habitat. Unrelated to true eels, they are highly specialized members of the order Perciformes. In appearance, they have long, pointed bodies and large mouths. Their dorsal fins are long and soft, their anal fins roughly half as long, and their tails are forked and not connected to the fins.

There are 12 species of sand eels, living in habitats that range from the shallows, where they are

TOP The well-developed pectoral fins of the greater weever are excellent for digging into sand, where it lies buried with only its eyes and erect dorsal fin exposed, waiting to snap up prey as they pass overhead. Although mainly active at night, the greater weever also feeds by day, pouncing on shrimps and crabs. All weevers have poison glands at the base of their spiny dorsal fins, making them a hazard for barefoot paddlers on sandy beaches.

PERCIFORMES CLASSIFICATION: 6

Bluefish and horse mackerels

Three species of bluefishes form the family Pomatomidae. They range throughout the warmer oceans of the world. The horse mackerels or scads form the family Carangidae. The 140 species have a wide distribution and include the horse mackerel, *Trachurus trachurus*; the pilot fish, *Naucrates ductor*; and the crevalle jack, *Caranx hippos*.

Dolphin fishes and mackerels

The two species of dolphin fishes form the family Coryphaenidae. Widespread through the Atlantic, Indian and Pacific oceans, they both belong to the genus *Coryphaena*. The mackerels and tuna belong to the family Scombridae. There are about 48 species, occurring throughout the seas, with more species in the warmer zones. They include the Atlantic mackerel, *Scombrus scombrus*, and the bluefin tuna or tunny, *Thunnus thynnus*.

occasionally dug out of the sand between tides, to depths of 656 ft. Most sand eels are about 8 in. in length, although larger species grow to 14 in. They swim in large shoals, feeding on a wide variety of crustacean and mollusk larvae and fish fry. At the slightest disturbance, they dive into sand or gravel with surprising speed, burrowing in head-first, and emerging cautiously later. They spend a large part of their lives resting with their bodies buried in the seabed, with gills, mouth and eyes just visible above the surface.

Sand eels are an important ecological link in the chain of life in northern oceans. They eat planktonic and larval creatures, and larger fish such as cods, bass, herrings and flatfish eat them in turn. The fortunes of many birds also rest on the sand eels. Puffins, terns, guillemots and others rely heavily on sand eels to feed their young, and the birds breed less successfully when the sand eels fail to turn up in sufficient numbers. In 1988, for example, when sand eels were scarce in northern British waters, breeding among the sea birds of the Shetland Islands was catastrophically low. It has yet to be established whether the sand eels were undergoing a natural fluctuation, or suffering from pollution or overfishing.

The bluefishes

The three species of bluefishes are among the most energetic of predatory fish, roaming the upper waters of tropical, subtropical and warm-temperate oceans in pursuit of their prey. They are regularly caught off Portugal and in the Mediterranean. Along the Atlantic coast of North America, they follow the movements of the menhaden, a relative of the herring that forms massive shoals.

Bluefishes are blue in color and have a dorsal fin that splits into two sections—the first is low and spiny, the second is long and soft. There is a black patch at the base of each of the pectoral fins. The fishes usually weigh 4 lbs. 6 oz.-11 lbs., and seldom exceed 26 lbs.

What bluefishes lack in size, they make up for in ferocity. They are among the few animals that continue killing after they have fed. Slashing right and left through prey shoals, they leave a trail of blood, fluttering scales, and maimed fish wherever they go. The closely related cobia, a slimmer but larger fish that reaches 6 ft. 6 in. in length and more than 110 lbs. in weight, is less savage in its feeding. It is distinguished by three dark stripes on the side of the body.

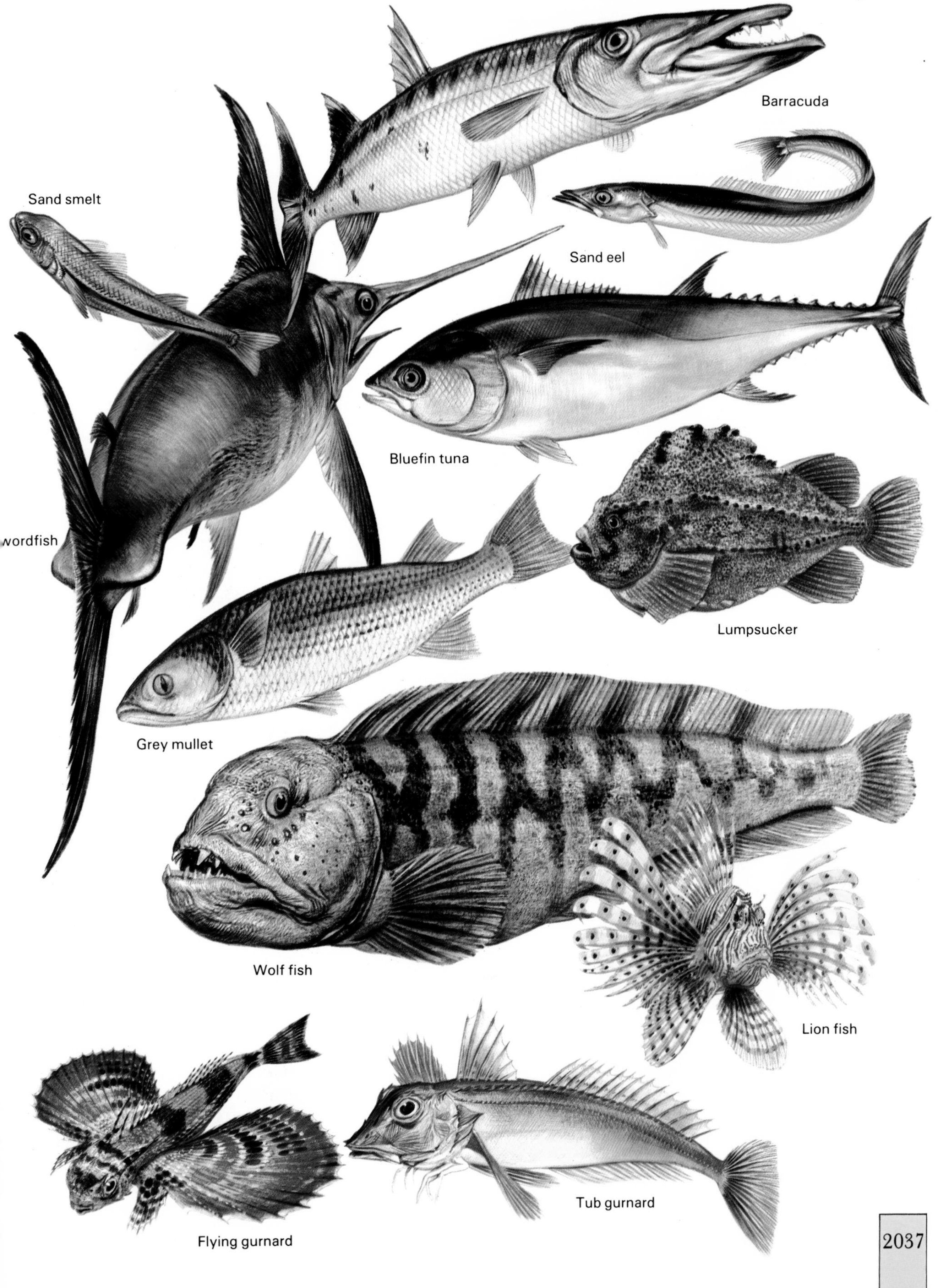

Barracuda

Sand smelt

Sand eel

Swordfish

Bluefin tuna

Lumpsucker

Grey mullet

Wolf fish

Lion fish

Flying gurnard

Tub gurnard

ABOVE In typical resting pose, a sand eel conceals most of its long, thin body below the gravel, leaving only its gills, eyes and mouth visible. Prey to most of the fish eaters in the northern seas, this fish's only defense is to burrow rapidly into the seabed. It wriggles in head-first and only bores its way out when the danger has passed.

Horse mackerels, jacks and pompanos

The horse mackerels (or scads), jacks and pompanos comprise a family of some 140 species and about 25 genera. The horse mackerels form a group of about six species, five of which occur along the Atlantic coasts of the Americas (though one species ranges right across the Atlantic to the coasts of West Africa and Europe); the remaining species lives in the Pacific Ocean. The jacks and pompanos are well known in waters around the USA. All the members of the family are heavy-headed and slim-bodied, and have a row of unmistakable heavy plates along their flanks. They grow to about 16 in. in length.

Members of the horse mackerel family generally travel in shoals that are sometimes very large, appearing to follow warmer water inshore in summer and returning to the deep waters in winter. They eat a wide range of fishes—particularly herrings, sprats, pilchard, anchovies and skippers—as well as invertebrates such as squid and shrimp species.

Horse mackerels breed in summer, and their 0.04-in.-long eggs drift in the upper layers of the water, buoyed up by goblets of red oil. The young take shelter among the tentacles of the common and blue octopus' jellyfishes, using them as bases from which they can venture out for food. In the relatively barren open seas, the young may also use the jellyfishes as mini-habitats, eating other creatures that have found similar shelter amid the tentacles. The young fish also nibble pieces of their hosts' tentacles or eat their eggs. When they have grown to a length of 14-18 in., they leave the jellyfishes and join the shoals of juvenile fish that feed in the animal plankton.

The pilot fish

Another member of the horse mackerel family— the pilot fish—is known for its association with ships and large objects at sea. According to tradition, the pilot fish guides whales and sharks as well as lost ships and lone swimmers. The opposite is, in fact, the truth, for it is the pilot fish that follows. As with other members of the family, it lives in the shadow of large objects such as ships, driftwood, slow-swimming turtles, sharks and whales and goes where they go.

Blunt, slim and rounded, the pilot fish is decorated with dark, vertical bands and grows to about 14 in. in length. Although it is reputed to feed on the parasites that infest the skin of its host, analysis of its diet shows that it prefers fish—which is more appropriate for such a predatory family. The pilot fish is common in warm seas and rarely occurs in northern waters.

Dolphin fishes

The two species of dolphin fishes form a family that also lives in the warm seas, and small shoals of them can be found around similar drifting objects. Here, however, the resemblance ends. Dolphin fishes are among the fastest and most active fishes in the world. They are also among the most beautiful, with backs that vary in color from turquoise to brilliant green, silver bellies and yellow lower fins. Their dorsal fins run the full length of their bodies, their tails are deeply forked, and the males have high, steep foreheads. Although this family shares a name with some marine mammals of the porpoise family, it bears no resemblance to them.

Dolphin fishes are fish-eating predators. One study recorded 32 species of fishes from 19 families in the stomachs of Atlantic dolphin fish. They hunt alone or in small shoals, relying on sheer speed—over 37 mph—to catch their prey. They occasionally hunt flying fishes, and may be responsible for some of the more spectacular speeds and flights recorded for them.

Dolphin fishes are popular sporting fishes, and large males may reach a length of 59 in. and weigh up to 88 lbs. Females are smaller, seldom weighing more than 35 lbs. Records from around the Hawaiian islands suggest an average weight of about 18 pounds. Hawaiians value them highly as a source of food; in the Philippines and along the tropical American coast, however, they are regarded as third-class fishes.

Mackerels and tuna

There are no doubts about the edibility of the members of the mackerel family. Wherever mackerels and tuna roam, the world's fishing fleets follow close behind. Sport fishermen, too, go to considerable lengths to catch them, whether taking greedy, 18-oz. mackerel from a dinghy in the North Sea, or trolling lines from an oceangoing launch in warmer waters in the hope of catching a 1100-lb. bluefin tuna.

For all their wide range of sizes, the 48 or so members of the mackerel family are remarkably consistent in form. The basic body shape resembles a pointed cigar, with a narrow tail stalk supporting a double crescent tail. Finlets decorate the upper and lower surfaces from the rear of the dorsal fin to the end of the tail stalk. They are unquestionably fishes built for speed, an impression confirmed by theory and practice.

The tuna's body shape comes closest to the mathematically ideal model for streamlined, underwater movements. It is no coincidence that each new generation of submarines is closer in design to the shape of the tuna. A tuna's skin is also very smooth, ensuring the least possible drag from turbulence at high speeds.

The tuna derives the power to push its body forward from its huge mass of muscle, and transmits it to a rigid, perfectly shaped tail. Nearly three-quarters of a tuna's body weight consists of muscle, compared with the two-fifths proportion of muscle in a moderately active fish, such as a goldfish, or the two-thirds muscle of any other very active fish, such as a trout.

The elegant crescent of the tuna's tail is a highly specialized propulsion unit that can be adjusted for both economical cruising and high-speed sprints. The muscles that drive it are similarly divided: blocks of red muscle sustain cruising, while white muscles come into play when the tuna needs extra speed. The enormous forces generated by these muscles are directed by strong, close-set fin rays in the tail that extend over the last few bones of the backbone, giving the fish great structural strength.

When the tuna is cruising, the tail acts like a highly efficient aircraft wing, its shape and cross-section generating maximum force at small angles to the water flow. In this mode it is driven by red muscle. When the fish sprints, it utilizes a system of "pulleys," made up of tendons that run over keels mounted on the sides of the tail stalk; this arrangement gives extra leverage and widens the angle at which the tail can cut the water. When the tuna accelerates, its tail takes bigger "bites" of water, thrusting the fish forward in propeller-like fashion. This helps the otherwise rigid fish to maneuver. After acceleration, the "aerofoil" function may take over again; a tuna or mackerel at full speed certainly beats its tail rapidly and at a shallow angle.

Tuna are capable of migrating thousands of miles, encompassing whole oceans in their travels. In 1951 two fish tagged off Florida were caught off Norway, some 4474 miles away, after only 120 days. If caught on rod and line in the course of such epic journeys, tuna sprint away at speeds of over 43 mph, and put up battles with their captors that may last for many hours.

Fast feeders

In most respects, the mackerel is a miniature tuna, and one of the most powerful fish in European waters. The familiar Atlantic species is green to blue on the back, has black, bent stripes running down the flanks and a silver belly. It averages 16 in. in length and 18 oz. in weight. Fishermen occasionally catch fish weighing 4 lbs. and ones weighing up to 7 lbs. 8 oz. have turned up in American waters.

Mackerels start their year in enormous shoals, moving toward coastal spawning grounds between April and June. The British populations breed around the south coasts of England and Ireland, at water temperatures of 51.8°-57.2°F. The females lay about a quarter of a million eggs that initially float on the surface but sink to midwater levels after two days. They hatch after six days; the fry join the surface plankton at first, then swim into shallower water.

Mackerels grow rapidly, reaching 9 in. in length in the first year, and maturing at about 12 in. in their second year. Once the adults have bred, the shoals break up into smaller ones and range through the upper waters in summer months, feeding with the energetic, indiscriminate abandon that makes them such favorites of amateur anglers and professional fishermen. They follow shoals of small fishes—

ABOVE **Schools of horse mackerel occur throughout the open waters of the Atlantic. They are blue-green fishes, with distinctive silvery underparts and a black spot on their gill covers. They feed on young herring-like fishes, sand lances, and small crustaceans, and often take shelter under marine invertebrates, such as coelenterates, where they pick off everything, especially the genital organs. Although horse mackerels are not eaten in northern Europe, they are a popular food fish in the Mediterranean.**

herrings, sprats and sand eels—and when these are driven to the surface, a characteristic "boil" occurs, in which the mackerels beat the water to a froth as they leap over each other in hungry eagerness.

As the colder months approach, the mackerels retreat to deeper water, resting in the banks and gullies of the continental shelf in a state of virtual hibernation. On waking again in the spring, the cycle begins again, with the fishes feeding on planktonic organisms and marine crustaceans on their breeding migrations.

Tunnies, albacores, Spanish mackerel and skipjacks follow similar patterns on a far more massive scale, although many of their breeding grounds have yet to be identified, and they take to deeper water without hibernating. All members of the family roam the warmer waters of the world, with the gigantic bluefin, or tunny, reaching farthest north.

The magnificent bluefin

Bluefin tuna follow their prey—mackerels, whitings, sprats, sand eels and squid—by schooling just below the surface in summer, deeper in winter, according to the size of the tunas. The larger the fish, the smaller the school. The titans, arguably the largest of all bony fishes, are solitary. Bluefins certainly reach a length of 13 ft., and there is little reason to doubt claims for fish measuring 14 ft. long and 1984 lbs. in weight.

Most of the bluefins caught in Europe commute between Spanish waters, or possibly the Mediterranean, and the North Sea off Norway and Germany. Where deep water lies close to shore, traditional trap-net fisheries catch bluefins. For some years in the 1960s, the Germans and Norwegians maintained a lucrative fishery for bluefins, but the far northern fish have since disappeared, possibly because of direct over-exploitation or over-fishing of their prey species. The ever more sophisticated technology of fish detection and netting endangers stocks of tuna and mackerels, too, and pollution may also have played a part in reducing their numbers.

A MULTITUDE OF FORMS

The swordfish

The swordfish is the sole member of its family. It is closely related to the mackerel family and is similar in appearance to the family of billfishes—the sailfishes, spearfishes and marlins. The most distinctive feature of the swordfish is its "sword," which is long and flattened and sometimes extends to as much as a third of its total length. By contrast, sailfishes, spearfishes and marlins have swords that are rounded and shorter.

Ranging the temperate and warm-temperate oceans of the world, the swordfish occasionally reaches northern European waters in late summer and autumn when the water is at its warmest. A solitary fish, it forms groups only when lured by a plentiful supply of food. Although the swordfish usually swims in the upper layers of the oceans, it regularly descends to 2000 ft. or more, and seems to show a preference for the entrances of underwater canyons. It feeds on other fish, and its deep dives may be in quest of squid.

The swordfish shares many of the adaptations for speed that characterize tuna. It is a large creature—about 16 ft. in length and more than 1100 lbs. in weight—and an active predator with little to fear from anything in the ocean. However, a shark can catch and eat it, and humans—its ultimate predator—have had extensive fisheries in the Mediterranean for thousands of years.

If tradition is to be believed, swordfish make a regular habit of ramming boats at high speed. Pieces of their bills have been found deeply embedded in wooden hulls, but such incidents are not common, and the stories reflect popular confusion between broadbills and billfishes. The exact purpose of their "beaks" has never been established. It has been suggested that the fishes use them to lash through shoals of prey, returning to pick up stunned fish at leisure, but this is unlikely. In fishes so uniquely adapted for speed, the bills probably serve a streamlining or control function.

Billfishes

The billfishes—sailfishes, spearfishes and marlins—form a family of about 10 species, all more confined to the tropics and the subtropics than the tuna or swordfish. Their bills are rounded in cross-section, their tail stalks have two sets of side keels, and their

ABOVE When a shoal of tuna meets a shoal of small fry, it is seized by a feeding frenzy. Each member of the tuna shoal charges forward, twisting and turning among the fry and occasionally breaking the surface to leap into the air. The commotion usually attracts the attentions of sea birds, such as the lesser frigate, which pounce on the fry as they are driven towards the surface. Young tuna largely feed on crustaceans but will eat herring and mackerel as they grow.

dorsal fins are long and many-rayed—and particularly high in sailfishes. Billfishes vary in size from the Pacific shortbill, which reaches a maximum of about 6 ft. 6 in. in length and 66 lbs. in weight, to the Indo-Pacific black marlin, which grows to about 16 ft. in length and 1550 lbs. in weight.

Often regarded as the fastest swimming fish, sailfishes have been recorded at well over 62 mph. The blue marlin offers close competition, however—it is one of the few fishes that can swim fast enough to make a regular meal of tuna species. The marlins are among the most popular game fishes, but their numbers are dwindling in the face of intensive commercial exploitation.

Barracudas

Most open-water predators inspire respect rather than fear. For all their speed and size, they are far from dangerous. The barracuda is a terrifying exception. Seldom enormous—even the largest species grows to no more than 6 ft. 6 in. in length—its sudden, fierce attacks are feared far more than those of sharks in some tropical waters. Eighteen species of barracuda inhabit the tropical and warm-temperate oceans of the world, with the 59 in. European

ABOVE When hunting in shoals, barracudas often herd shoals of smaller fishes into a confined space, preventing their escape by patrolling the edges of the shoal. The barracudas then dart separately into the middle of the shoal, feed at their leisure, and emerge with a victim in their jaws to resume their place on guard. Larger barracudas become solitary in behavior as they grow and eventually abandon the shoal.

barracuda, or spet, reaching the Mediterranean and eastern Atlantic.

Not unlike pike at first glance, barracudas are long, slim fishes. All members of the family have underhung jaws armed with impressively sharp teeth, long cylindrical bodies and rear-set fins. They are all fish-eating predators, moving in shoals while young, and becoming more solitary with age. They live in a variety of habitats and are common over reefs and continental shelves and in estuaries.

Barracudas make a specialty of feeding on shoaling, plankton-feeding fish, assaulting them in a headlong rush, snapping to right and left. They do not, however, lack strategy: groups of barracudas herd shoals of prey into easily charged masses, or shepherd them to shallow water as a living larder to be consumed at leisure.

Barracudas are sight feeders, which may contribute to their evil reputation in areas where waters are murky. When they find a target difficult to identify or an intruder's size impossible to estimate, they may attack out of fear or mistaken identity. Unless provoked, however, barracudas seldom attack. Whether or not they attack seems to depend on their location. For example, the great barracuda, an inhabitant of the western Pacific and both sides of the Atlantic, is considered safe in Hawaii but a fearsome danger in the West Indies. A typical attack consists of a single, massive bite.

Gray mullet

Gray mullet inhabit the waters between estuaries and the coastline. They make the transition between salt and brackish water with ease, sometimes venturing considerable distances up rivers. They are all similar in shape, which has made classification difficult. According to recent estimates, there are about 95 species of gray mullet.

Mullet are elongated, blunt-headed, thick-bodied fishes with one small, spiky dorsal fin set far apart from the soft one behind it. Their mouths are set at the tips of their heads, and their lips are often distinct and sometimes quite thick. They reach a maximum size of about 3 ft. 3 in. and 15 lbs. 6 oz. in weight. Abundant from the temperate seas to the tropics, mullet follow one another, moving in shoals.

ABOVE The jutting lower jaw and long, sharp teeth of the barracuda make it one of the most feared and dangerous predators along the coasts of tropical zones. It hunts primarily by sight, and undertakes a single, swift attack, taking its prey cleanly with a snapping bite. The barracuda orients toward anything that catches its attention, particularly the glow of a fishing bait, and anglers describe fearsome struggles waged with this fierce predator.

They feed on minute plant and animal matter, either filtering it from the mud with their sieve-like gill rakers or taking in organisms with mouthfuls of mud and spitting out the particles they do not want to swallow. Some species—for example the thin-lipped mullet—are reputed to prey on small fishes as well.

Like many plant eaters, mullet have very long intestines—often twice the length of the fish—that are divided into compartments for processing as well as digestion. The first part of a mullet's stomach forms a muscular gizzard, not unlike those found in some birds, with a lining that is tough enough to grind the small shellfish that they pick up with algae and mud.

Mullet often swim around in water that is thick with sewage or dairy by-products, and near harbor walls and piers where algae are abundant. Living close to the coast, mullet are a popular target for fishermen—despite their unappetizing diet, they make fine eating.

PERCIFORMES CLASSIFICATION: 7

The swordfish and the billfishes

The family Xiphiidae contains just one species, the swordfish, *Xiphias gladius*, which ranges through the warmer reaches of the oceans. The billfishes make up a separate family, the Istiophoridae. Occurring in tropical and subtropical seas, the 10 species include the Pacific sailfish, *Istiophorus platypterus*; the Pacific shortbill, *Tetrapterus angustirostris* (one of the spearfishes); and the blue marlin, *Makaira nigricans*.

Barracudas and gray mullet

The barracudas of the family Sphyraenidae number 18 species that inhabit the warmer seas of the world. All belong to the genus *Sphyraena*, including the European barracuda, *S. sphyraena* or spet and the great barracuda, *S. barracuda*. The family Mugilidae, the gray mullet, contains about 95 species that haunt coasts and estuaries from temperate regions to the tropics. They include the striped mullet, *Mugil cephalus*.

ABOVE **Gray mullet usually wander through the rich seabeds of tidal zones, sucking plankton, snails and mussels from the bottom as they swim by. They position their bodies** at an angle of 45 degrees from the seabed with their small mouths pointing downward. They usually occur in the warmer waters of the Mediterranean Sea.

PERCIFORMES CLASSIFICATION: 8

Archerfishes, leaf fishes and scats

The six species of archerfishes from the family Toxotidae live in coastal waters, swamps and rivers from India through Southeast Asia to Polynesia. The most widespread species is the archerfish, *Toxotes jaculator*, which is found from India to Australia and the New Hebrides. The 10 species of leaf fishes make up the family Nandidae. They are divided into seven genera and occur in freshwater in South America, West Africa and tropical Asia, and include the Amazon leaf fish, *Monocirrhus polyacanthus*, and the African leaf fish, *Polycentropis abbreviata*. The four species of scats belong to the family Scatophagidae. They usually inhabit estuaries and coastal waters in the eastern Indian Ocean and the western Pacific, although some can live in freshwater. They include the scat, *Scatophagus argus*, and the striped scat, *S. tetracanthus*.

However, mullet jump and leap well, and a frequent problem for fishermen is that when one mullet jumps out of the net, all the rest follow. Mullet breed in shallow water, and their young are common in tide pools.

Where the rivers end

The dense, overhanging vegetation of brackish, backwater mangrove swamps and freshwater rivers provide an unusual source of food for two families of the order Perciformes. Archerfishes knock insects from the leaves and stems of riverside plants by spitting water at them, while the leaf fishes imitate dead leaves from overhanging branches, enabling them to approach their prey undetected.

The six species of archerfishes are remarkable in that they use adaptations of the mouth and tongue to spit water with considerable force and accuracy. Measuring 12 in. long, they are deep-bellied fishes with lateral compressions and large dorsal and anal fins set well back on their bodies. They inhabit coastal waters, swamps and rivers of India, Southeast Asia, Australia and Polynesia.

Rate of fire

The most well-known member of the family is the archerfish, which ranges from India to the New Hebrides in the Pacific Ocean. Like its relatives, it can squirt water at insects in overhanging vegetation from a distance of up to 5 ft. If it misses, the archerfish adjusts the angle of fire and squirts several more jets in succession. At the moment of shooting, the archerfish forms a groove in the roof of its mouth by pressing its thick, fleshy tongue against the upper palate. It then compresses its gill covers powerfully to drive water from its gills into the groove. The flexible, whip-like tip of the tongue acts as a stopper, controlling the release of each jet of water.

Because light rays bend or refract as they enter water, the archerfish's prey are in a different position than they appear when viewed from below the surface. Remarkably, the archerfish compensates for the refraction by swimming forward until it is almost directly below its target. It then appears to take aim but, at the moment of firing, jerks its body upright until it is almost in a vertical position. By looking straight up out of the water as it fires, the archerfish reduces the effect of refraction to a minimum and sees almost the exact position of its insect target. It usually

shoots down spiders and insects on overhanging vegetation, but also takes insects that are trapped in spiders' webs.

Leafy deception

The leaf fishes have made remarkable adaptations that enable them to exploit the overhanging vegetation in their habitat. The 10 species of leaf fishes range through northern South America, western Africa and Southeast Asia, and are masters of camouflage. The Amazon leaf fish, a 4-in.-long inhabitant of freshwaters in northern South America, disguises itself as a dead leaf by changing its color and its shape. It has a fleshy barbel on its lower jaw that resembles a leaf stem, and changes its color between yellowish green and brown to camouflage itself against dense plant growths or the sandy bottom of clear water. Although such camouflage has a protective role, the fish uses it to best effect in hunting.

The Amazon leaf fish prefers shaded, slow-moving or still waters. Usually it appears near the shore, drifting motionless in the current with its head down to resemble a dead leaf. When it is within range of its prey, the Amazon leaf fish sucks them into its mouth with its protrusible jaws. Spawning occurs over leaves and stones, and the male guards the eggs. Although it is a popular aquarium fish, the ferocity and appetite of the Amazon leaf fish mean that its company must be chosen carefully.

Dung eaters

The four species of scats in the scat family inhabit the Indian and Pacific oceans. They are mainly marine fishes but can inhabit fresh and brackish waters (they can adapt remarkably quickly to water of different salinity). Normally scats grow to a length of 12 in., and have disk-shaped bodies with attractive

TOP LEFT AND RIGHT The archerfish has evolved an elaborate form of marksmanship to catch its prey. Prowling below the surface of mangrove swamps, it produces a jet of water to shoot down prey from overhanging foliage. It can knock down an insect at a range of 6 ft. 6 in.

ABOVE A specialist in assassination by stealth, the leaf fish uses its uncanny resemblance to a dead leaf to creep up on its prey. It drifts head-down in the current of its home stream, its chin barbel adding the final touch to the deception by resembling a leaf stalk.

PERCIFORMES CLASSIFICATION: 9

Remoras

The remoras make up the family Echeneididae. Ranging through most of the Atlantic, Indian and Pacific oceans, they number eight species, including the remora, *Remora remora*; the sharksucker, *Echeneis naucrates*; the slender suckerfish, *Phtheirichthys lineatus*; and the whalesucker, *Remora australis*.

body markings. As well as inhabiting estuaries and coastal waters, they occur in all major Southeast Asian ports. They are omnivorous eaters and gather in huge shoals around sewage outlets in the sea to feed on decaying organic matter (their family classification *Scatophagus* means "feces feeder"). Despite their diet, the scats are a popular food fish.

The professional passengers

The remoras, also known as sharksuckers, would be unremarkable fish were it not for their first dorsal fin. It is modified into a sucking disk that the remoras use to attach themselves to larger animals such as sharks—hence their common name. They have even been known to attach themselves to ships, thereby expending very little energy as they travel the warmer oceans of the world.

Remoras have slim, elongated bodies with the long second dorsal fin and the anal fin mirroring one another above and below at the rear. Their heads are pointed, with the lower jaw longer than the upper. Their tail fins are small and weak—not a surprising feature in fishes that let others provide their transport. There are eight species of remoras, ranging in size from the 6.7-in. *Remiropsis pallidus*, which often clings to

ABOVE LEFT The scat is an easily kept and lively aquarium fish. Its common name is an abbreviation of *Scatophagidae*, which translates as "feces feeder," and reflects its reputed habits. In the wild, the scat inhabits Indo-Pacific coastal sewage outlets and has a reputation for eating feces.
LEFT Popular with aquarists, the diamondfish is found in both fresh and saltwater throughout the tropics.

tunas and the swordfish, to the 35 in. sharksucker, *Echeneis naucrates*, which attaches itself to many species of sharks, turtles and large rays.

The remora has a sucking disk that is a remarkable departure from the original form and function of a fin. The hard rays of the first dorsal fin, typical of the fishes in the order Perciformes, lie alternately right and left, forming flaps across an oval disk on the top of the remora's head. The fish brings the disk into contact with the surface of a larger fish, and creates a vacuum by adjusting the flaps (or ridges) of the sucking disk, rather like the movement of slats in a venetian blind.

The flaps of the remora's sucking disk are also equipped with tiny, backward-pointing spines. These help the fish to maintain its grip on a host without expending extra energy keeping its muscles tense. Even when dead, a remora is difficult to remove from its host. In an experiment in the New York Aquarium, a fishing line attached to the tail of a 25.5 in. remora was used to lift a 24 lb. bucket of water. Fishermen in many parts of the world make use of the remora's gripping ability: attaching a line to its tail, waiting for it to attach itself to a fish or turtle, and then capturing the host.

Little more is known about the life of the remoras. They may pick up scraps from the meals of their hosts,

TOP The remora often uses its suction disk to catch a ride on the upperparts of the nurse shark. Although the shark may thrash around with considerable force to dislodge its unwanted guest, the remora alone can free itself.

ABOVE The first dorsal fin of the remora is modified to form a large suction disk with raised edges and diagonal ridges across its surface. When the remora attaches itself to an object, a vacuum is created in the gaps between the ridges.

or clean parasites from their skins. Some remoras appear to have a distinct preference for certain host species. For example, the slender 29.5-in.-long suckerfish, *Phtheirichthys lineatus*, usually attaches itself to barracudas and groupers, while the 20-in.-long whalesucker, *Remora australis*, is found exclusively on cetaceans—whales, dolphins and porpoises. *Remora osteochir* enters the gill chambers of billfishes, sharks and ocean sunfishes, and has been known to take up residence on the roof of a shark's mouth.

The relationship between remoras and their hosts remains unclear. It may be one of mild parasitism, in which the remoras create energy-expending drag and give nothing in return. On the other hand, it may be symbiotic (mutually beneficial), with the remoras cleaning parasites off their hosts in exchange for transport. Although many sources maintain that the hosts never eat their uninvited guests, this may be due to inaccessibility rather than inclination; one sand shark's stomach contained several sharksuckers.

Cichlids

The cichlid family is one of the largest of the order Perciformes, with about 84 genera and 680 known species. Most live in freshwater, a few in brackish areas and one or two in coastal waters. Hardy and attractive, some species have been reared in pools for thousands of years. The ancient Egyptians kept and harvested them for food, and the Mozambique mouth brooder and several species of freshwater angelfishes from the Amazon are still cultivated today.

The majority of cichlid species are found in Africa—especially in Lakes Victoria, Nyasa (formerly Lake Malawi) and Tanganyika—and Madagascar. They also inhabit all but the coldest parts of Central and South America, extending as far north as Texas, and some are found in the West Indies. The genus *Etroplus* is found in the coastal areas of India and Sri Lanka.

Strong jaws

Small and colorful, most cichlids have deep, laterally compressed bodies with strong jaws and large lips. Some are longer and slimmer, with a few predatory species of the genus *Crenicichla* even taking on a pike-like form. The largest species is probably the 31-in.-long *Boulengerochromis microlepis* from Lake Tanganyika in East Africa.

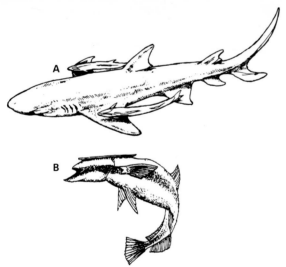

TOP White edges decorate the fins of the sharksucker's slender body. Although it is a good swimmer, the sharksucker often uses its oval-shaped sucker to adhere to the bodies of passing sharks, bony fishes and sea turtles.

ABOVE Remoras commonly attach themselves to sharks (A). They attach themselves by pressing the suction disks on the top of their heads against the body of the shark (B), and can only release themselves by swimming forward.

PERCIFORMES CLASSIFICATION: 10

Cichlids

The family Cichlidae is the second largest in the order Perciformes, with about 680 species. They live in fresh and brackish waters in Africa, Central and South America, and coastal parts of India. Some of the most well-known species are the ram cichlid, *Apistogramma ramirezi*; the marble cichlid, *Astronotus ocellatus*; the zebra Lake Nyasa cichlid, *Pseudotropheus zebra*; the jewel cichlid, *Hemichromis bimaculatus*; the barred cichlid, *Cichlasoma festivum*; the Jack Dempsey, *C. biocellatum*; the mouthbrooders such as *Haplachromis burtoni*; the freshwater angelfishes of the genus *Pterophyllum*; the tilapias of the genus *Tilapia*; and the discus species from the genus *Symphosodon*.

The cichlids' fin patterns are typical of the Perciformes, but they have a single nostril on each side of their heads. Other freshwater members of the order have double nostrils. The cichlids' lateral line is unusual for Perciformes. It starts below the gill cover in the normal fashion, but breaks below the middle of the dorsal fin and continues at a lower level to the tail.

Evolution in action

Many species of cichlids live in still or slow-moving water, seldom far from cover. They tend to be predatory, and some are territorial and quite belligerent. However, the cichlids of the great lakes of East Africa have adapted to a wide range of diets. Their teeth and jaws vary in shape according to whether they hunt, browse, or filter their food, and their body shapes vary according to their habitat and way of life.

Diversity within the cichlid family has its basis in Africa's geological past, and provides an insight into the speed and nature of fish evolution. The lakes of East Africa are much older than any of the European lakes—in existence for millions rather than tens of thousands of years. Moreover, they are enormous. Lake Tanganyika has an area of over 12,300 square miles and reaches a depth of 5000 ft. (second only in depth to Lake Baykal in the USSR). Lake Nyasa is only slightly smaller, and

ABOVE **The ram cichlid, a lover of sunlight and high temperatures, originated from the freshwaters of Venezuela. It is now a popular aquarium fish.** BELOW **A fish's shape often reveals its way of life.**

Among the cichlids, *Sarotheradon galileus* is a typical bottom feeder (A), *Telmatochromis vittatus* dwells in crevices (B) and *Rhamphochromis longiceps* is typical of a predator (C).

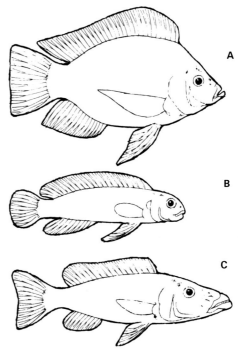

Lake Victoria is even larger than Lake Tanganyika, covering an area of 26,850 square miles, although it is shallower.

Isolated lakes

For most of their history, the freshwater lakes of East Africa have remained isolated from the rest of the world. The fish that live in them—with the cichlids as the dominant family—have been free to adapt to all available habitats, sources of food and life-styles without outside competition. As a result, there are more than 200 species of cichlids in Lake Nyasa, compared with 42 species from other orders; in Lake Victoria, there are 170 cichlid species and only 38 non-cichlids; and Lake Tanganyika has 126 cichlid species, with 67 non-cichlids. Undoubtedly there are more species waiting to be discovered.

So diverse are the cichlids of the East African great lakes that they include a representative of nearly every basic form of fish. Tall-bodied, slow-moving types, such as several species of *Tilapia*, grub for invertebrates in the lake bottom, while torpedo-shaped predators such as *Rhamphochromis longiceps* use speed and agility to hunt other fishes. In the open waters, silvery-sided and countershaded species sift for plankton (*Haplochromis*) or hunt fish (*Diplotaxodon*). In the shallows, well-camouflaged, striped species move between the light and shadow of the reeds and weeds.

Varied diets

Other physical differences in cichlid species relate to their varied dietary preferences. Several species of *Tilapia* use filaments on their gill arches to filter the plant plankton that they find both in the open water and in the rich sediment on the lake bottom. *Pseudotropheus tropheops* uses its rows of tiny teeth to scrape off the algae that coat the rocks in sunlit water. *Tilapia rendalli*, *T. zillii* and *Haplochromis similis* use a combination of pointed, gripping and blade-like shearing teeth to graze on the leaves and stems of water plants.

Among carnivorous species, *Haplochromis placodon* has blunt, fused pharyngeal teeth for crushing mussels and snails. *Macropleurodus bicolor* has strongly muscled, short jaws and conical teeth for the same purpose. By contrast, *Lapidochromis vellicans* has long, curved, crossing teeth for picking insect larvae and crustaceans out of crevices and weeds, and large eyes for identifying its prey.

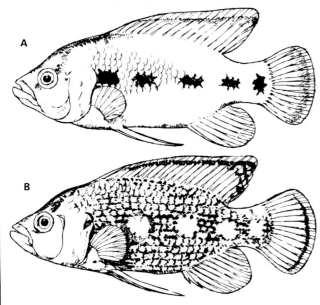

A

B

TOP The marble cichlid, originally from South American freshwater, has a distinct juvenile coloration. As it grows, its scales will become less obvious, giving it a suede-like appearance.

ABOVE Two marking phases of the 12 in. African banded jewel fish: outside the breeding season, it has dark markings on a pale background (A); its breeding colors reverse the pattern (B).

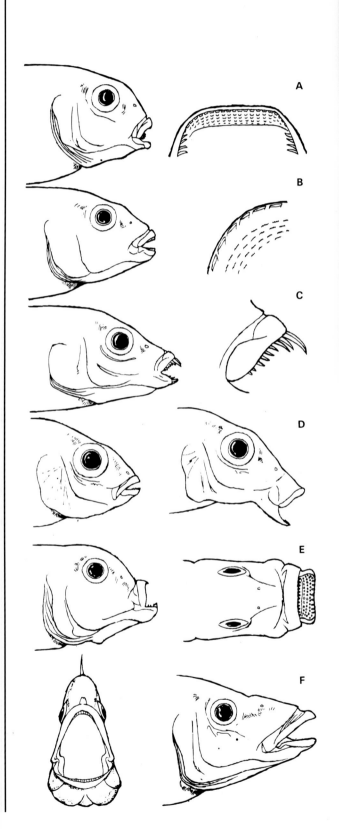

LEFT African cichlids have adapted to a wide variety of diets, revealed by the way their teeth and mouths have evolved. *Pseudotropheus tropheops* (A) eats encrusting algae; *Haplochromis similis* (B) eats plants; *Labidochromis vellicans* (C) picks up shrimp-like organisms from the bottom; *Lethrinops brevis* (D) sifts through the sand; *Genyochromis mento* (E) pulls out other fishes' scales; and *Haplochromis polyodon* (F) is a predator. ABOVE The zebra Lake Nyasa cichlid, named for its contrasting stripes, is a colorful addition to any fish tank, but has a habit of eating the smaller fishes. It is a mouthbrooder that grows to 4 in. in length, and has a reputation for defending its territory aggressively.

Cichlid predators range from slim, large-mouthed species that stalk and sprint, to creatures with undeniably bizarre habits. *Haplochromis welcommei* pulls the scales off slower cichlids; *Docimodus johnstoni* uses its sharp cutting teeth to remove neat chunks from other fishes' fins; and *Haplochromis compressiceps* supplements its diet of small fishes and insect larvae with the eyes of other fishes, which it tears out using its long teeth and jutting lower jaw.

Haplochromis livingstonii (known locally as "the sleeper") resorts to trickery to catch its prey. It lies on its side near the bottom of the lake, imitating a dead fish. Its coloring—irregular dark patches on a gray

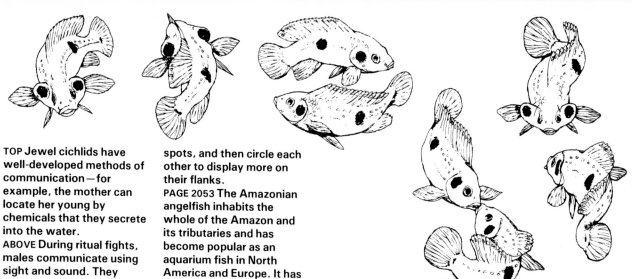

TOP **Jewel cichlids have well-developed methods of communication — for example, the mother can locate her young by chemicals that they secrete into the water.**

ABOVE **During ritual fights, males communicate using sight and sound. They raise their gill covers to show off a pair of eye-** spots, and then circle each other to display more on their flanks.

PAGE 2053 **The Amazonian angelfish inhabits the whole of the Amazon and its tributaries and has become popular as an aquarium fish in North America and Europe. It has a flattened body and reaches 10 in. in length.**

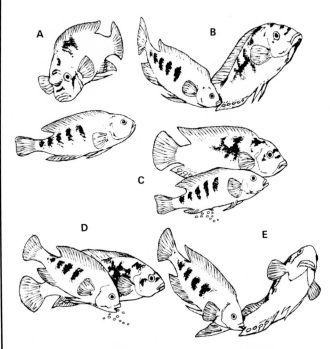

ABOVE The mating behavior of *Haplochromis burtoni*, a mouthbrooding cichlid: the male approaches the female (A) and shows her the false egg markings on his anal fin which the female tries to pick up (B). The female lays her eggs (C) and picks them up in her mouth (D). She tries to gather the male's false eggs, at which point he fertilizes the real ones (E).

background—resemble decomposing patches on a dead body and enhance the effect. When a scavenging fish investigates, "the sleeper" devours its prey with lightning speed.

Courtship, nesting and mouthbrooding

Most species of cichlids are highly territorial, closely guarding their eggs and young. African species tend to be mouthbrooders, with the females carrying the eggs, and many species take both eggs and young into their mouths for protection. With few exceptions, South American species deposit their eggs in nests or on specially cleaned sites on rocks and then guard them from predators.

African species often migrate to sandy areas to build their nests, often forming elaborate patterns that the males create by scraping, biting and pushing the sand. Congolese populations of *Tilapia macrochir* virtually fill their territories with a shallow depression about 59 in. wide. The depression has a low mound at the center, connected by channels to its raised rim.

Some species create a simple depression; others form extremely elaborate nests.

Among species of the genus *Tilapia*, mating is a rough procedure. The male *Tilapia karomo* builds a nest and waits for a female to swim within courting distance. He cannot stray far, since he must constantly defend the perimeters of his territory against rival males. Resplendent in fully heightened breeding colors, he flashes his flanks in front of a prospective mate until she follows him to the nest. Once there, they join mouths and the male shakes the female violently for up to half a minute. Then the male cruises over the nest, using the ripples of the soft parts of his dorsal and anal fins to stimulate the female to lay her eggs, which she immediately takes into her mouth. The male presumably leaves sperm behind in his excited sorties over the nest, and the female takes it in when she breathes.

Elaborate fertilization methods

Among mouthbrooders, fertilization can be an elaborate process. The male in one species, *T. macrochir*, leaves a thread of sperm hanging from the dome at the center of his nest, and the female eats it before she lays her eggs. The female *Haplochromis burtoni* picks up her eggs as soon as she lays them—before the male has a chance to fertilize them. The male has markings near his genital opening that resemble more eggs. By moving his fins, he reveals the markings to the female. When she tries to pick up the false eggs, he fertilizes the real ones in her mouth.

The female keeps the eggs in her mouth for 10-15 days, depending on the water temperature and species. By moving her jaw carefully, she rubs the eggs together so they do not acquire fungus and are fully exposed to the flow of water over her gills. The female does not feed during this period. Once the eggs hatch, however, some species leave the fry to fend for themselves. Others care for them closely, still using the mouth as a safe refuge.

The two species of South American discus in the genus *Symphosodon*, prized as aquarium fishes, are not mouthbrooders. In their unique method of feeding, the fry hang all over the body of one of their parents, feeding on nutrient slime produced from between the scales. When one parent's immediate supply is finished, it shakes itself to force off the fry, and they immediately attach themselves to the other parent. In an aquarium, this form of feeding goes on for up to a month, but few have witnessed the event as both species of discus are highly sensitive to environmental conditions and tend to eat their young when under stress.

Cod icefishes and plunderfishes

The family of cod icefishes constitute over half of the 100 species of fishes that inhabit the Antarctic. They have a confusing common name, since they are not related to the icefishes and bear little resemblance to the cods. All species have single nasal openings on each side of their large heads, with slim, tapering bodies and long dorsal and anal fins. Their pelvic fins lie under their throats before their pectoral fins. The pectoral fins both propel the fishes during swimming and provide stability when they are at rest.

The largest species of cod icefish is the Antarctic toothfish, which can grow up to 5 ft. in length. It has a cartilaginous skeleton, hollow vertebrae and ample body fat, enabling it to float in middle waters at 65-750 ft. below the surface. Some species of cod icefishes live below the sea ice and have a substance in the blood (called a glycoprotein) that acts as a form of antifreeze, allowing them to survive the severe conditions.

The family of plunderfishes range throughout coastal waters off islands north of the Antarctic—the Falklands, Kerguellen and Macquarie. The 19 species include the *Harpagifer bispinis*, a 4-in.-long inhabitant of Antarctic and sub-Antarctic regions. It lives in very shallow water under and around clumps of algae on the sea bottom. It has a blunt, large head and bears a striking resemblance both in form and behavior to unrelated species of bullheads that occupy a similar habitat in the Arctic—a remarkable example of convergent evolution.

Crocodile icefishes

Because the waters of the Antarctic are extremely cold and well oxygenated, cod icefishes require a lower level of oxygen-bearing red cells in their body. The 24-in.-long crocodile icefishes have discarded red blood cells altogether, and consequently do not possess hemoglobin—the chemical in red blood cells that transports oxygen from the gills. The crocodile icefishes compensate for the absence of red blood cells in a number of ways, most obviously through reduced activity. They also have a higher heartbeat rate and a larger volume of blood than other fishes.

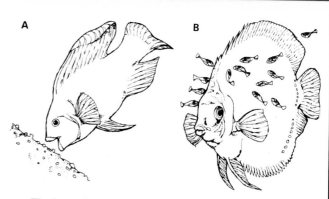

TOP The barred, or flag, cichlid shares its freshwater Amazonian habitat with the Amazonian angelfish. It is a shy species that prefers to shelter among weeds and rocks.

ABOVE A female Jack Dempsey clears a place on the bottom to lay her eggs (A). The fry of the South American discus feed on the layer of mucus secreted on the parent's skin (B).

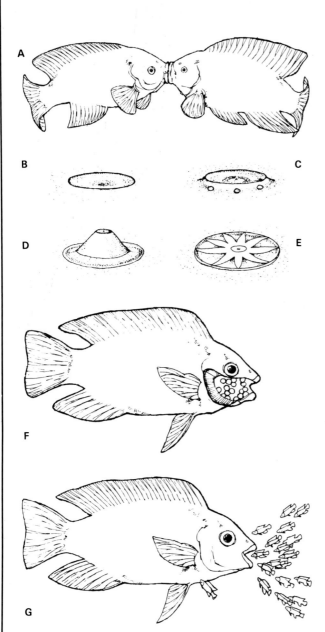

ABOVE The drawings show various aspects of behavior in *Tilapia*—a genus of cichlids. Mouth-to-mouth combat takes place between males of the same species (A). Various species build characteristic nests. The nest of *T. andersoni* (B); the nest of *T. variabilis* (C); the nests of *T. macrochir* (D and E).

Mouthbrooding is typical of *Tilapia*: a cutaway shows where the eggs are kept (F); the young retreat to the mother's mouth in times of danger (G).
ABOVE RIGHT The viviparous blenny—a member of the eelpout family—is one of the few blenny-like species to give birth to live young (rather than eggs).

PERCIFORMES CLASSIFICATION: 11

Cod icefishes, plunderfishes and crocodile icefishes

The southern polar seas are home to several families within the order Perciformes. Three families that occur only in these seas are the Nototheneiidae, the cod icefishes or Antarctic cods, with 50 species that include the Antarctic toothfish, *Dissotictus mawsoni*; the Harpagiferidae, the plunderfishes, with 19 species including *Harpagifer bispinis*; and the 16 species of crocodile icefishes from the family Chaenichthyidae.

Eelpouts, pricklebacks, gunnels and wolf fishes

Most of the 150 species of eelpouts from the family Zoarcidae occur in the cooler seas of the Northern Hemisphere. They include the ocean pout, *Macrozoarces americanus,* and the viviparous blenny, *Zoarces viviparus*. Three other families are restricted to the North Pacific and North Atlantic. The family Stichaeidae, the pricklebacks, contains about 60 species, including the longsnout prickleback, *Lumpenella longirostris*, and the Atlantic warbonnet, *Chirolophis ascanii*. The family Pholidae comprises the 13 species of gunnels, such as the rock gunnel or butterfish, *Pholis gunnellus*, while the seven species of wolf fishes or catfishes form the family Anarhichadidae. They include the Atlantic wolf fish, *Anarhichas lupus*, and the spotted wolf fish, *A. minor*.

Eelpouts

Eelpouts make up a family of 150 species, most of which live in the cold-temperate regions of the Northern Hemisphere. They are long, slim fishes with small pelvic fins that lie before the pectoral fins. The dorsal and anal fins merge into the tail fins, forming a continuous ribbon from the pectoral fins around to the vent of the fish. Eelpouts live at varying depths from the intertidal zone to 6500 ft. The largest species is the ocean pout of North America, which reaches a maximum length of 3 ft. 3 in.

Most eelpouts lay eggs, but some bear live young. The most familiar eelpout in European waters is a live-bearer known as the viviparous blenny. Breeding usually occurs in August and September, and fertilization takes place internally. The eggs remain attached to the ovary walls during incubation and hatch after 20 days. They remain in the mother's body for a further three months until they are 1.6 in. in length.

Pricklebacks

Pricklebacks owe their name to the unbranched spiny rays on their long, dorsal fins. They resemble the eelpouts, and prefer the shallower areas of the colder northern oceans (although the longsnout prickleback of Alaska occurs at depths of 1500 ft.).

The Atlantic warbonnet is the only member of the prickleback family to live in northern European coastal waters. It usually grows to a length of 10 in. and has a yellow-brown body with dark bars. Like its Pacific relative, the Atlantic warbonnet has large tentacles around its eyes—these tentacles become fringed in adults. They range from the coast of Norway to the southern North Sea, where they feed on mullusks, worms and marine invertebrates.

Gunnels

Gunnels have very long, sinuous bodies with lateral compressions, and their dorsal fins are long and contain only unbranched rays. The rock gunnel, a colorful 8-in.-long inhabitant of tidal pools, is typical of the family. It has a prominent line of decorative dark eyespots under its dorsal fin on its brown body. Normally, the rock gunnel lives among seaweed on the rocky bottom of tidal zones to a depth of 32 ft. Its popular name is the butterfish, a reflection of the extreme slipperiness of its skin and the

ABOVE **The broad mouth of the spotted wolf fish (a deepwater fish) is armed with powerful teeth. It uses the large, pointed teeth at the front to grasp shellfish and crabs, and the thick, flattened teeth on the palate to crush them.**

surprisingly swift and strong wriggling movements it makes when caught.

The rock gunnel breeds between September and March, laying its eggs in rock crevices and under empty mollusk shells. The parents show a high level of parental care, particularly the female. She winds herself around the clumps of eggs to form balls some 0.8-1.2 in. in diameter. Both parents then guard them until the 0.4-in.-long larvae hatch after a period of two months.

Wolf fishes

The seven species of wolf fishes range throughout the cold and temperate seas of the northern Atlantic and Pacific oceans. They are larger than their relatives, the gunnels—the Pacific species may reach 8 ft.—and have distinctive strong, rounded, sharp teeth that overhang their lips when their jaws are shut.

The wolf fishes resemble their inshore relatives, although they lack pelvic fins. The most common species in European waters is the Atlantic wolf fish, which lives at depths of 350-1000 ft. of water and usually feeds on sea urchins, brittlestars, crabs, whelks, mussels and other shellfish.

Breeding occurs during winter, and the female lays up to 24,000 yellow eggs in large, spherical masses on the seabed. The parents may guard the eggs, which hatch after two months. The fry are generally pelagic (living in the middle waters of the sea), but young fish sometimes appear among inshore seaweed.

ABOVE The butterfly blenny displays the distinctive large dark spot that adorns the front portion of its tall dorsal fin. Although not strictly territorial outside the breeding season, butterfly blennies have a strict "pecking order" determined by size. A butterfly blenny will drive smaller rivals from its sheltering holes among stones and tunnels, but will give way to larger ones.

Blennies

Blennies are among the most numerous fishes in the intertidal zone and occur in most of the world's oceans. There are about 680 known species contained in six families and 127 genera. Most blennies are small fishes—their average length is 6 in. However, the giant kelpfish—a related species that occurs along the Pacific coast from Baja California to central California—reaches a maximum length of 24 in. Blennies are well-camouflaged fishes with large heads, steeply sloping foreheads and delicately branched tentacles above their eyes. Their bodies taper away evenly, usually to a distinct tail fin.

Combtooth blennies

The family of combtooth, or scaleless, blennies occur in all warm and temperate seas and include some of the most common fishes of the European seashore. The most numerous species in Europe is the shanny, which lives above rocky bottoms in tidal zones. When the tide is low, the fish shelters under stones, in seaweed or in small rock pools. The shanny is distinguished from other blennies by the absence of any tentacles above its eyes. It feeds on a wide variety of food, including algae, barnacles, small crabs, mollusks and shrimps, which it finds while browsing in the tidal pools. Its basic coloration is olive-green to yellow with black spots or stripes, varying according to its habitat and mood.

The shanny lives according to a tidal rhythm, resting at low tide and becoming active at high tide. It devotes a considerable amount of energy to feeding and social behavior. Shannies maintain a "pecking order," or ranking system, according to size.

The shanny breeds between April and August. The male stands guard over the oval or pear-shaped eggs, often laid in batches on the undersides of rocks or in crevices. He fans the eggs with his pectoral fins to maintain a current of oxygenated water, and attacks any intruders. The eggs hatch after six to eight weeks.

The scaled blennies

The family of scaled blennies, or klipfishes, inhabit the intertidal waters of South Africa and Australia. Although very similar in form and behavior to their

PERCIFORMES
CLASSIFICATION: 12

Blennies

There are six families of blennies, which together range through the temperate and tropical seas, with most species inhabiting warm, inshore waters. A few species enter brackish waters. The largest family is the Blenniidae, the combtooth blennies, with over 300 species. They include the butterfly blenny, *B. ocellaris*, and the tompot blenny, *B. gattorugine*. The family Clinidae contains the scaled blennies or klipfishes. The 75 species include the giant kelpfish, *Heterostichus rostratus*. There are 102 species within the family Labrisomidae, including the hairy blenny, *Labrisomus nuchipinnus*; the marble blenny, *Paraclinus marmoratus*; and the sarcastic fringehead, *Neoclinus blanchardi*. The pike blennies or tube blennies make up the family Chaenopsidae, with 56 species including the bluethroat pike blenny, *Chaenopsis ocellata*. The remaining two families are the Tripterygiidae, the 95 species of threefin blennies, and the Dactyloscopidae, the 41 species of sand stargazers.

TOP The blennies have an inquisitive nature and often swim among honeycomb coral to investigate its holes and crevices. When disturbed, they dive into the holes, poking their heads out to check whether the danger has passed.

northern relatives, they have scales all over their bodies. Most of the males have large organs extending from their genital pores and fused to the last ray of their anal fins.

Most species of blenny lay eggs although one species bears live young, and is called the viviparous blenny. In many species, fertilization takes place internally. But in *Clinius testudinarius*, for example, fertilization of the eggs is external. The female attracts a male to her nest in a tuft of seaweed by swimming into it and shaking her body violently. When the male swims in she turns on her back and the male's sperm (milt) fertilizes the eggs externally. The male often protects the eggs at several stages of their development since, during his vigil, he may be visited by several more females.

The hairy blenny belongs to a family of stout, prickly fish. It occurs on both sides of the tropical Atlantic and is the most common member of its family in the Gulf of Mexico and the West Indies. It has short, branching tentacles above its eyes and on the back of its neck. Another member of this family, the marble blenny, lays its eggs in the cavities of the tubular sponge *Verongia fistularis*, which can grow to more than 19 in. in length. The eggs are attached by sticky filaments and benefit from the continuous water flow maintained by the sponge for its feeding. The sarcastic fringehead, an 8-in.-long inhabitant of Californian coastal waters, derives its name from the expression made by its cavernous mouth.

Pike blennies

The pike blennies have similarly large mouths. They have long, eel-like bodies, a dorsal fin that runs from head to tail, and no scales. Living around the coasts of America, they are colorful fishes that often live in the empty tubes left by marine worms or boring mollusks. The 5-in.-long blue-throat pike blenny uses a colorful and daunting display to defend its tube home. The male erects his dorsal fin to reveal a bright orange spot, at the same time gaping his large jaws and flashing his bright blue throat and gill supports at the intruder.

PERCIFORMES CLASSIFICATION: 13

Gobies and sleepers

The family Gobiidae is the largest in the Perciformes, with a total of well over 1500 species (some authorities estimate there may be more than 2000). They range through tropical and subtropical regions, occurring in marine, brackish and freshwater habitats. They include the pygmy goby, *Pandaka pygmaea*; the roughtail goby, *Evermannichthys metzelaari*; the neon goby, *Gobiosoma oceanops*; the Californian arrow goby, *Clevelandia ios*; the blind goby, *Typhlogobius californiensis*; the common goby, *Pomatoschistus microps*; the crystal goby, *Crystallogobius linearis*; the tank goby, *Glossogobius giurus*; the bumblebee goby, *Brachygobius xanthozona*; the rock goby, *Gobius paganellus*; the mudskippers of the genera *Periophthalmus* and *Periophthalmodon*; and the eelskippers of the genus *Scartelaos*. The sleepers of the family Eleotrididae are closely related to the gobies, sharing similar habitats and with a similar distribution. The 150 species include the guavina or bigmouth sleeper, *Gobiomorus dormitor*, and the goloveshka, *Percottus glehni*.

Myriad midgets

The family of gobies is the largest of the marine fishes. It includes over 1500 species that range through marine, brackish and occasionally freshwater in tropical and subtropical areas; some species are even land-based, such as the mudskipper. Gobies are also the most abundant freshwater fishes on oceanic islands, and have developed into diverse habitats during the course of their evolution. It is likely that many more species of gobies have yet to be identified. Estimates suggest that the family will eventually number 2000.

The gobies are small fishes that average 0.8-2 in. in length. They include the 0.43-in.-long pygmy goby, which is the smallest vertebrate in the world, and the 0.4-in.-long female of the *Trimmatom nanus*, a scaleless, saltwater fish from the Chagos Archipelago in the Indian Ocean.

Members of the *Evermannichthys* genus of gobies often make their home in the tubes and hollows of

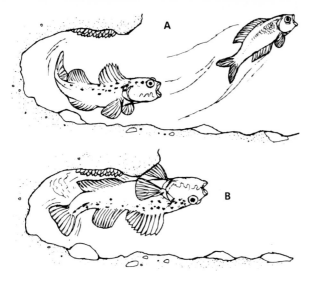

TOP The dappled body markings of the rock goby provide camouflage against the weed-covered rocky shores of its coastal habitat. On the underside of the fish, the margins of the pelvic fins join to form a sucker, allowing the rock goby to cling to the bottom in tidal pools.

ABOVE Male gobies become territorially aggressive during the breeding season, staunchly defending their eggs against intruders with furious threat displays (A). They prevent the build-up of fungus and bacteria on the eggs by pushing a current of water over them with their fins (B).

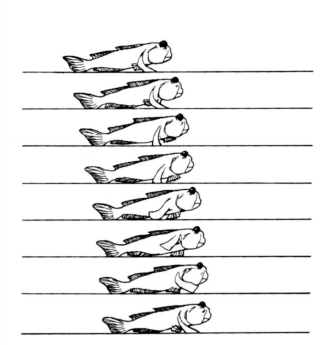

living sponges. For example, the roughtail goby, a slim, pale fish from the Caribbean Sea, commonly inhabits the loggerhead sponge. The edges of its scales on the rear and middle part of its body are elongated to form spines, enabling this 1.2-in.-long goby to maintain a grip in the hollows of the sponge.

Cleaner fishes

Certain species of gobies form close, interdependent relationships with other underwater animals. The neon goby from the Caribbean Sea cleans parasites from the bodies of larger fishes in exchange for protection from attack. Several forms of neon goby also form partnerships with shrimps, which build and maintain a burrow for the neon goby in return for protection. The fishes of the goby genus *Smilogobius* in the Indian and Pacific oceans position themselves at the entrance to the shared burrow and take shelter inside when danger threatens. Their companion, the shrimp, follows, and seldom emerges before the fish has checked whether the danger has passed.

The Californian arrow goby uses the U-shaped burrow of the innkeeper worm as a shelter and often shares the burrow with a pea crab. At high tide, the fish actively scours its coastal or estuary home for food, and retreats into the burrow at low tide.

The blind goby of the Indian and Pacific oceans has

ABOVE Bumblebee gobies are popular aquarium fishes because of their attractive coloration—the three species differ in the number of black stripes on their yellow bodies. Alternating between periods of stillness and energetic activity, the bumblebee gobies inhabit rivers and estuaries in Southeast Asia.

ABOVE LEFT The mudskipper "crawls" in dry mangrove swamps by swinging its pectoral fins forward while resting its weight on its pelvic fins. It then presses its pectorals down and propels itself forward before returning the weight to its pelvic fins.

become dependent on its crustacean partner, the mud lobster. When young, the blind goby is dark in color and has functional eyes. But once it moves underground, skin grows over its eyes and it remains in burrows that the mud lobster digs around tidal zones for the rest of its adult life.

Although many species of gobies live in cramped surroundings, the *Parioglossus taenitus* moves in large shoals through the open seas of the Indian and Pacific oceans, hanging above coral reefs and sheltering in coral branches if threatened.

The mudskippers

The mudskippers are extraordinary, land-based gobies that have assumed an amphibious way of life.

THE MUDSKIPPERS
— FISHES OUT OF WATER —

With intense competition for space in the intertidal zones, some six species of gobies have become adapted to living out of water for much of their lives. Known as mudskippers, these 4-8-in.-long fishes live in brackish waters and mangrove swamps mainly along the shores of the Indian Ocean, from Africa across to Australia, and the islands of the southwestern Pacific Ocean.

Mudskippers can live on land as well as in water since they carry oxygen-rich water in their enlarged gill chambers and absorb the gas through their mouths and throat linings. Their reserves are limited so they have to return to the pools left by the outgoing tide, both to renew their water supplies and to keep their skins wet.

Mudskippers must keep their eyes moist, too. Because they lack tear glands, they pull their eyes back into their heads at intervals to wet them. Their eyes can move about in all directions and have lenses that focus best in air. Their retinas (light-sensitive tissues) have some areas that can detect movement, and others that provide color vision, enabling mudskippers to interpret color signals during territorial disputes and breeding.

Skippers and hoppers

Mudskippers are divided into three groups according to how far they venture out of the water. The eel-skippers of the genus Scartelaos seldom move far from the water's edge, grouping in the soft mud. The mudhoppers of the genus Boleophthalmus live on the borders of mangrove swamps, venturing a short way under the trees. Lacking all-around vision, they turn their heads from side to side as they search for food.

The agile mudskippers of the genera Periophthalmus and Periophthalmodon belong to the third group. Living all over the banks and mangroves, they grow up to 12 in. in length and feed on insects, crabs, worms and even smaller mudskippers. Using their muscular pectoral fins as limbs, they can "walk" and skip across the mud with fast twists of their bodies.

One species, Periophthalmus chrysopilos, can climb vertical trunks

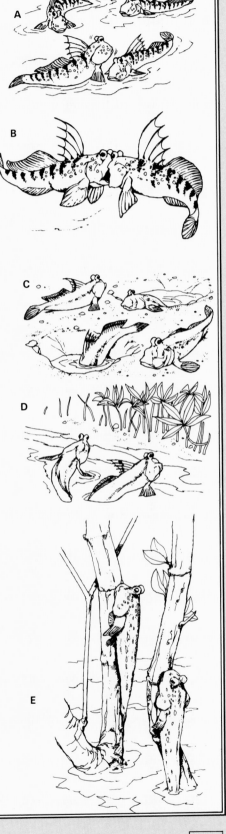

and shoots using the sucker created by the fusion of its pelvic fins. Another species, P. kalalo, lacks the sucker, and can only clamber up rough mangrove roots that project from the mud.

Signals in the mud

All mudskippers are highly territorial and use a variety of signals to advertise their presence. Eelskippers perform quick "tail-stands," flashing their silvery flanks as they throw themselves upward, and appearing to balance on the tips of their tails for an instant before flopping back.

Mudskippers build burrows by scooping the mud out with their mouths and spitting it onto the surface to form turrets or ramparts. The burrow entrance is often at the base of a dish-like depression that may be 24 in. wide. In the breeding season, the male mudskipper displays his heightened breeding colors to lure the female inside his burrow.

FAR LEFT When out of the water, the mudskipper *Periophthalmus papillio* breathes by extracting oxygen from water held in its enlarged gill chambers. It must return constantly to the swamp to renew the supply of water and to splash water over its drying skin.

ABOVE When the tide falls, mudskippers remain on the exposed mud, breathing air through the membranes at the back of their mouths. They move over the mud by swinging their pectoral fins.

RIGHT The mudskipper *Boleophthalmus boddaerti* defends its territory by raising and lowering its dorsal fins and giving a nodding display (A). If this fails to deter the intruder, it engages in a mouth-to-mouth pushing match (B). Scooping out mud with his mouth, *Periophthalmus chrysopolis* digs a burrow and tries to attract females inside for breeding (C). *Periophthalmus* species range all the way into the mangrove swamps (D); some have a sucker formed by their pelvic fins that enables them to ascend vertical twigs and shoots (E).

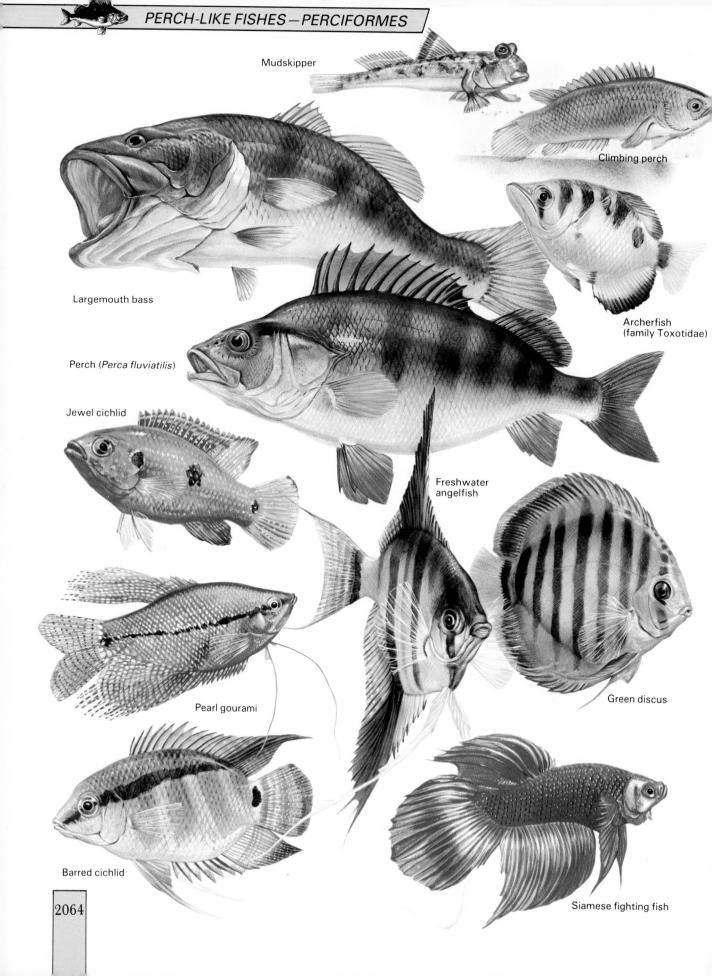

Mudskipper

Climbing perch

Largemouth bass

Archerfish
(family Toxotidae)

Perch (*Perca fluviatilis*)

Jewel cichlid

Freshwater
angelfish

Green discus

Pearl gourami

Barred cichlid

Siamese fighting fish

They grow to a length of between 4 and 12 in. and inhabit mudflats and mangrove swamps along the Indian and Pacific oceans. When the tide falls in the mangrove swamps, they remain on the exposed mud and use their arm-like, elongated pectorals to haul themselves rapidly along dry land. They have enlarged gill chambers that carry a supply of water when on land, and they also breathe air through the back of the mouth and throat.

Although the mudskippers can remain on land for long periods, they must keep their skin continually moist and renew the supply of water in their gills. The eyes of these curious gobies rest on the upper part of their heads to detect movement in all directions.

The common goby is 2.7 inches in length and has a dark gray body with minute spots on the flanks and bands on the fins that vary in number between the male and female. It normally inhabits the sandy and muddy bottoms of estuaries and coastal bays.

The common goby breeds during summer, and the female lays her eggs under the empty shells of mussels, cockles and other mollusks. The male guards the eggs until the 0.1-inch-long larvae hatch after 14 days. Adult common gobies die after breeding.

Open-ocean gobies

Two species of gobies inhabit the open ocean in northern waters. The crystal goby and the transparent goby have translucent bodies, apart from their pigmented eyes and a silvery swim bladder. They are slimmer, more agile fishes than their bottom-dwelling relatives, and have large eyes and sharp teeth. Normally growing to 2 in. in length, they occasionally congregate in vast shoals to feed on inshore plankton.

The sleepers

The family of sleepers are close relatives of the gobies, although they are larger in size and have separate pelvic fins. They inhabit all tropical seas and occasionally appear in brackish and saltwater. The guavina is one of the largest sleepers, reaching 24 in. in length. It ranges throughout coastal waters, rivers and lagoons from Texas to Brazil. Sleepers derive their common name from their habit of lying motionless on the bottom, but a few members of the family are active and inhabit open sea.

ABOVE The deep-bellied, oval-shaped body of the surgeonfish *Acanthurus dussumieri* is richly colored to camouflage it against the purple coral of the Great Barrier Reef, off the coast of Australia. Its eyes are placed relatively high on its strong skull, and it has a small, slightly protruding mouth with a single row of teeth on each jaw, which it uses to scrape algae from the coral.

Surgeonfishes

The surgeonfishes, or tangs, make up a family of 77 species living in the tropical oceans; they are especially numerous in the Indian and Pacific oceans. They are named after the pair of razor-sharp spines mounted on their tail stalks. These defensive weapons can inflict considerable damage to a predator—or a careless fisherman. In most species, the blade drops into a groove, like a pocketknife, and faces forward when it is erect, ready for defensive action. The unicorn fishes of the genus *Naso* have two immovable spines on each side of their tail stalks.

Distinctive larvae

Surgeonfishes' breeding habits have not been closely studied, but some Polynesian species (*Ctaenochaetus striatus*, *Zebrasoma scopas* and *Acanthurus triostegus*) have been seen to gather in dense groups around the gaps in reefs that connect lagoons with the open sea.

Surgeonfishes vary in color among individuals, and this is thought to be linked to the breeding season, although it may reflect the different habitats.

Closely related to the surgeonfishes is the Moorish idol. It is a 7-in.-long, dish-shaped fish of such outstanding beauty that it has become a symbol of the coral reefs. Curiously enough, relatively little is known of its natural history. It occurs in the tropical Indian and Pacific oceans, from East Africa to Hawaii.

It has broad, black and white stripes covering its body and tail, and its white dorsal fin is extremely long and high. Although it has no tail spines, a young Moorish idol has a spine over each eye, which is replaced by a lump in the adults. Because of these differences, the adults and young were often described as separate species; the young were known as *Z. canescens*.

Rabbitfishes

The rabbitfishes, or spinefoots, take their name from their rounded snouts and small mouths. They make up a small family that is closely related to the surgeonfishes, but should not be confused with the rabbitfishes or chimaeras (both are relatives of the sharks and rays). A few species penetrate into freshwater, and several live in estuaries. Most of them are similar in appearance, having various patterns of

ABOVE The Moorish idol, the most spectacular of the surgeonfishes, lives in shallow waters over the tropical coral reefs. It uses its protruding mouth to graze on algae in even the tiniest of crevices. Its unique shape and colors are unmistakable in the adult fish, although the young are so different that they were considered a separate species.

spots or maze-like reticulations, and all can change color quickly. One exception is the fox face, an 8-in.-long species that is quite common in the western Pacific. It has a concave forehead and a tubular snout, and might easily be mistaken for a surgeonfish. Rabbitfishes were among the first fishes to adapt to the massive changes in salinity in the Suez Canal, which connects the rich fish fauna of the Red Sea with the comparatively poor one of the Mediterranean. *Siganus rivulatus* and *S. luridus* are now resident in the Mediterranean.

Cutlassfishes

The cutlassfishes, also known as snakefishes or hairtails, make up a small family of distinctive predators. They live in open water from the surface to about 3300 ft. deep in tropical and temperate seas worldwide. They are unmistakable: their heads are almost pike-like, and they have formidable teeth, while their bodies are long, thin, and topped by a dorsal fin

that runs from their head to their tail. Their tail fins are either small or absent, and they do not have pelvic fins. They grow to over 6 ft. in length.

Rarer in the north but still common to all the tropical and temperate oceans of the world, the snake mackerels, or escolars, make up another family of elongated, open-water predators. They, too, have impressive teeth; their jaws are even better equipped to hold fast-moving, slimy prey than those of the cutlassfishes. They resemble stretched tunny or mackerel in appearance, having several isolated finlets between their long dorsal fins and their tail fins. Some snake mackerels are of commercial value, but their flesh is very oily. The deeper-bodied oilfish ranges throughout all the world's oceans, and its flesh has been used as a purgative. It grows to about 6 ft. and occurs as far north as Britain. *Nesiarchus nasutus* also occurs in northern European waters.

PERCIFORMES CLASSIFICATION: 14

Surgeonfishes and rabbitfishes

Widespread in the shallows of tropical oceans, the surgeonfishes belong to the family Acanthuridae. There are 77 species, including the tangs of the genera *Acanthurus* and *Zebrasoma*, the unicorn fishes of the genus *Naso*, and the Moorish idol, *Zanclus canescens*. The family Siganidae, the rabbitfishes, contains some 25 species. Most species, such as the foxface, *Lo vulpinus*, occur in the tropical shallows of the Indian and Pacific oceans, but two species, *Siganus rivulatus* and *S. luridus*, have spread into the eastern Mediterranean.

Cutlassfishes and snake mackerels

The cutlassfishes (also known as snakefishes or hairtails) belong to the family Trichiuridae. There are 17 species that range throughout the oceans, including the cutlassfish, *Trichiurus lepturus*, and the black scabbard fish, *Aphanopus carbo*. The snake mackerels or escolars make up the family Gempylidae, which also have a wide distribution but are more common in warmer regions. The 22 species include the oilfish, *Ruvettus pretiosus* and the species *Nesiarchus nasutus*.

TOP The *Ctenopoma ansorgi* floats motionless in mid-water as it prepares to snap at prey below. It is one of the smaller African climbing perches, and actively hunts among heavy vegetation in tropical freshwater habitats.

ABOVE The long, very mobile pelvic spines of the dwarf gouramis are clearly visible as they hover near cover on the bottom. These rounded, secretive fishes from India have particularly long, richly colored dorsal and anal fins.

Labyrinth fishes

Labyrinth fishes are particularly well adapted to survive in water that contains little or no oxygen. When necessary, they take oxygen from the air at the water surface. Numbering some 70 species, the labyrinth fishes comprise four families: the climbing perches, the gouramis, the kissing gourami, and the giant gourami.

Like most fishes, the labyrinth group breathe with their gills. However, they have an additional breathing apparatus—the so-called labyrinth—which is contained in an extension to the upper part of each gill chamber. Derived from the first gill arch, the labyrinth comprises hard plates covered in a complicated layer of skin, folded and wrinkled to give an extensive surface area that is well supplied with tiny blood vessels.

To breathe, a labyrinth fish rises to the surface, fans its gill covers to expel waste gases from the labyrinth, and then takes in some air. Air enters the labyrinth through the first gill arch, which a valve then closes.

The climbing perches

There are some 40 species of climbing perches. They have blotchy green or gray markings, long, spiny first dorsal and ventral fins, and spikes on their gill covers. Except for one Asian species, they all live in the tropical freshwaters of Africa. With their efficient breathing mechanism, they can leave the water and travel on land for some distance.

ABOVE The paradise fish was the first tropical fish to be brought to Europe. Originally a native of China and Southeast Asia, it is a hardy and aggressive fish that withstands temperatures as low as 59°F and tolerates low oxygenated water (because of its gill adaptations).

The best known and most typical member of the climbing perches family is the species known as *Anabas testudineus*. Ranging from India to the Philippines, it inhabits canals, rivers, ditches and ponds. It was the first species to be given the name "climbing perch," after a Dutch naturalist reported finding one 5 ft. up a palm tree.

To move over land, the climbing perch balances on its pectoral fins and the spiny edges of its gill covers, and bends and pushes its tail. When it comes to the crest of a slope, it simply rolls down the other side. Its movements may be clumsy, but on level ground it can progress at a rate of about 10 ft. a minute.

Little is known about the breeding habits of climbing perches, but it appears that their eggs float on the surface of the water. The adults either ignore or eat both eggs and fry. Climbing perches grow to a maximum of about 10 in. in length, and feed on plant matter and a wide range of crustaceans and insects.

The gouramis

The 28 species of gouramis form a family whose members are similar in appearance to the climbing perches but differ slightly in gill-bone structure and in lacking teeth on one of the palate bones. Gouramis live in freshwater habitats from China and the Philippines to India and its associated islands.

One species of gourami, the paradise fish, has a long history of selective breeding in its native Southeast Asia, where it inhabits ditches and rice fields. It was probably the first species to be kept in Europe purely for decoration. In the wild, the 3.5-in.-long paradise fish is quite drab, but aquarium-bred forms are an exotic contrast.

The fighting fishes

The seven species of fighting fishes are, despite their name, comparatively docile members of the gourami family. In the wild, the fishes only fight to establish and maintain territory and to prove dominance. Conflicts are brief, rarely lasting for more than 15 minutes—and they are seldom fatal unless wounds become infected.

In captivity, two male fighting fish placed side by side in a small container will swiftly launch into battle, biting one another's fins and nipping off scales and flesh. A fight may last from one to six hours, at the end of which one fish usually dies.

The most widely known of the seven species is the Siamese fighting fish. In the wild, the 2.4-in.-long Siamese fighting fish is dull green or gray, with darker stripes running the length of its body. Selective breeding has led to forms that are green, iridescent blue, bright red and almost black.

Like most members of the gourami family, fighting fishes build bubble nests at breeding time. The male takes in bubbles of air at the water surface, coats them with sticky mucus secreted in his mouth and throat, and then blows a couple of bubbles to the surface. He repeats the process carefully for several hours until he has built up a floating bubble raft about 4 in. wide and 0.8 in. deep.

Once the male fighting fish has completed the nest, he begins to court the female. He swims past her, displaying his fully expanded fins and colors and nibbling off a couple of her scales or even a piece of one of her fins. At the end of the courtship, the male pushes the female to the nest, where he turns her upside down and wraps himself over her to fertilize the first batch of eggs with his sperm.

The female fighting fish lays 7-20 eggs at a time. As they slowly sink into the water, the male darts after

ABOVE The long, pelvic rays of two richly colored pearl gouramis float below them as they rest among bottom vegetation. Males use sensory cells on their pelvic rays to brush approaching females during the courtship ritual.

After fertilization, they collect the eggs in their mouths and spit them into a large nest of tiny, mucus-covered bubbles. Pearl gouramis inhabit freshwaters in Malaysia, Thailand, Borneo and Sumatra.

them, taking them into his mouth and spitting them into the mass of bubbles that form the nest. The pair may devote five hours to egg-laying and fertilization, and the male wraps himself around the female up to 70 times. During this period they take breaks of between one and eight minutes.

Among the seven species of fighting fishes, the Java and Borneo fighting fishes are "mouthbrooders." As the female lays her eggs, the male gathers them up in his mouth and keeps them there until they hatch. Courtship starts when the female attracts the male's attention by pushing a ball of algae toward him. He returns it, and the "game" continues for some time before they mate.

The kissing gourami

The kissing gourami is the only species in its family. It lives in Borneo, Sumatra, Java, Thailand, Malaysia and Sri Lanka, inhabiting waters with heavy vegetation and slow currents. It is yellow in color with transparent fins, grows to about 12 in. in length, and

ABOVE LEFT A spectacularly colored Siamese fighting fish displays the brilliant red color of its massive fins. The belligerent nature of the males leads to ferocious confrontations when they are confined in small spaces.

ABOVE A male Siamese fighting fish guides a female toward the large bubble nest that he has built. The breeding partners wrap their bodies around each other and the female releases her eggs below the nest.

PERCIFORMES CLASSIFICATION: 15

Labyrinth fishes

Four families among the Perciformes are collectively known as the labyrinth fishes. They number about 70 species in all, and range through much of Africa, southern and eastern Asia and Indonesia, living in freshwater and brackish habitats.

The family Anabantidae contains the climbing perches (also known as the walking fish or climbing gouramis). The 40 species include the species *Anabas testudineus* and *Ctenopoma ansorgi*. The family Belontiidae contains the 28 species of gouramis. These include the pearl gourami, *Trichogaster leeri*; the dwarf gourami, *Colisa lalia*; the paradise fish, *Macropodus opercularis*; and the Siamese fighting fish, *Betta splendens*. The family Helostomatidae contains only one species—the kissing gourami, *Helostoma temmincki*—while the sole member of the family Osphronemidae is the giant gourami, *Osphronemus goramy*.

eats both animals and plants.

Like some of its relatives, the kissing gourami is a valuable source of food in Asia. In the West, however, it is popular as an aquarium species. Timid and peaceful, it has the charming and mysterious habit of "kissing" a partner with its thick, protruding lips. The two fish face one another and lock lips for a while. It probably has more to do with defending territory than displaying affection.

The giant gourami

Like the kissing gourami, the giant gourami is the only species in its family. It is believed to have originated in Java, Borneo and Sumatra, but is so valued as a source of food that it has been introduced into freshwaters in China, Southeast Asia, India and Sri Lanka.

The adult giant gourami can grow up to 24 in. long. It has a flattened, heavy body that is dark brown in color crossed by a few darker, vertical bars. Its anal fin is so long and deep that it sometimes appears to fuse with the tail fin, and its second dorsal fin is set well back on its body. Females have rounded dorsal and

anal fins, while those of the males are pointed.

The giant gourami has one feature that is characteristic of many species in the gourami group—a pelvic fin ray so long that it trails behind the fish. It may serve as an organ of touch in dark, muddy surroundings. Older fish develop steep, concave "foreheads" and the front parts of their bodies thicken.

As with fighting fishes, the giant gourami builds a nest of air bubbles at breeding time. Unlike them, however, both males and females share in the task of construction, mixing fragments of water plants with the bubbles to strengthen the nest. Only the male guards the eggs and the young. Young giant gouramis are more brightly colored than the adults, and are popular aquarium fishes.

The pikehead

The pikehead—the only member of its family—is a slim, elongated predator with a jutting lower jaw that gives it a passing resemblance to a pike. Growing to about 7 in. in length, it is reddish brown above, with dark flanks that give way to irregular white spots below. Its fins are yellow, and there are dark spots on its tail.

Although the pikehead has a breathing apparatus similar to, but simpler than, that of the labyrinth fishes, the families differ in certain important respects. The most obvious difference is the pikehead's underslung jaw, which can extend up to a third of the length of the fish's head.

Snakeheads

There are about 12 species of snakeheads, living in tropical Asia and Africa. They are elongated fishes with cylindrical bodies that become laterally compressed

ABOVE Two kissing gouramis approach each other, apparently about to kiss with their broad lips. Despite the affectionate appearance of this "kiss," it is probably a display to establish territorial dominance and to settle disputes during courtship. A lone kissing gourami will repeat the threat display to any species of similar size that enters its immediate tropical freshwater habitat.

toward the tail. Their heads are broad and snake-like, and their jaws are wide and underslung. The snakeheads' anal fins are about three-quarters as long as their dorsal fins, which usually run the length of their backs at an even height.

Snakeheads have uneven colors. Depending on the species, they may have brown to green blotches on a light background, bars, chevrons (V-shaped marks) or spots. The species also vary in size. *Channa africanus*, a V-marked West African species, is about 12.5 in. long, while *Channa micropeltes* from Southeast Asia reaches over 3 ft. in length and 45 lbs. in weight.

Lung-like pouches

Snakeheads have simpler breathing organs than labyrinth fishes, comprising tiny, lung-like pouches in the skin of their throats. Well supplied with tiny blood vessels, these pouches enable the snakeheads to live for long periods out of water, and even to crawl overland should the need arise. In hot, dry weather, they bury themselves in the mud.

Parental care

Snakeheads are attentive parents. *Ophicephalus striatus*, a common Asian species, moves into the shallows to breed. Both parents clear a breeding area by biting off vegetation in a rough circle. Then they deposit their eggs and sperm in the clearing. The

2071

ABOVE The spiny eel *Mastacembelus erythrotaenia* is found in Thailand. Living in a variety of habitats, spiny eels usually burrow into the ground during the day, or hide between plants or in rock crevices. They have distinctive coloration, often with zigzag bands running the length of their bodies.

PERCIFORMES CLASSIFICATION: 16

The pikehead, snakeheads and spiny eels

The family Luciocephalidae contains just one species—the pikehead, *Luciocephalus pulcher*. A freshwater fish, it occurs in Malaysia and Indonesia. The family Channidae comprises the 12 species of snakeheads from the genus *Channa*, including the Asiatic snakehead, *C. asiatica*, and the species *C. africanus*. The 63 species of spiny eels make up the family Mastacembelidae. Freshwater fishes of tropical Africa and Asia, they include the peacock-eyed spiny eel, *Mastacembelus argus*, the species *M. armatus* and the elephant-trunk fish, *Macrognathus aculeatus*.

fertilized eggs float to the surface of the water, but remain in the cleared area. After a couple of days, they hatch. At five weeks, they start to explore the bottom, and after nine weeks they live there permanently. The males keep a close guard on the eggs and the newly hatched young. One species from India, *Ophicephalus punctatus*, is said to weave water plants together to make a bowl-shaped nest, after which both parents care for the eggs and young.

Secretive spiny eels

Because they bury themselves in the sand or hide among plants and other concealed sites, little is known about the family of spiny eels. There are 63 species, the majority of which inhabit fresh and brackish waters in tropical Africa, Syria and southern and Southeast Asia. One species, *Mastacembelus brichardi*, lives in the torrential waters of the lower Zaire rapids in West Africa, where it shelters in the lee of rocks on the bottom and feeds on prey carried downstream by the currents.

Spiny eels have the remarkable ability to absorb oxygen from air by drawing the air over a film of water covering the gills. As a result, they can live in still, deoxygenated water and survive short-term drought in shrunken, muddy puddles that would barely support most fishes. They are long, laterally compressed fishes that have characteristic freestanding dorsal fin spines

and a fleshy appendage at the end of their snouts.

Spiny eels are not particularly large fishes (the biggest species, *Mastacembelus armatus*, grows to a maximum length of 35.5 in.). The Indian spiny eel, a 6-in.-long, eel-like fish, is typical of the group. It has small scales on its body and a long snout that extends into a mobile proboscis containing the tubular nostrils; its mouth and gill openings are very small.

Continuous fin

Like many bottom dwellers, the olive-green body of the Indian spiny eel is not striking in color. It lacks pectoral fins, and the spiny dorsal fin (made up of 20-40 free spines) and second soft-rayed dorsal fin merge into the tail and anal fins.

Most spiny eels live in ponds with muddy or sandy bottoms. They are nocturnal in habit and spend the daylight hours among weeds or buried in the bottom mud with only their nostrils protruding. During darkness, the spiny eels emerge to scavenge for the bottom-dwelling worms, insects and crustaceans that form their diet. They use their sensitive, elongate snouts to seek out prey, which is swallowed whole. During mating, the female lays her eggs among aquatic vegetation, where they are fertilized by the male. The parent fishes then abandon the eggs, which remain entangled in the weed for 36 hours before hatching into free-swimming larvae.

FLAT ON THEIR SIDES

Flatfishes, such as plaice, flounders and soles, begin life as ordinary shaped fishes with an eye on each side of their heads and horizontal mouths—but their features soon twist dramatically so that they can lie flat on the seabed

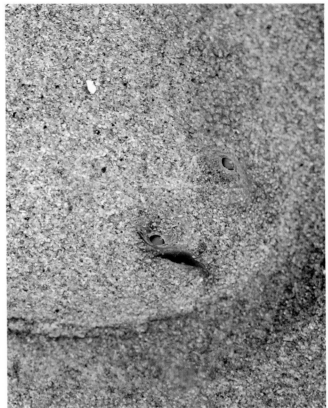

ABOVE During metamorphosis, the Dover sole adapts to life on the seabed by undergoing a peculiar transformation in shape. One eye migrates from one side of the body until both eyes are on the same side—the new upper side of the body.

ABOVE RIGHT A sole covers its body with sand by rippling its fringing fins until only the eyes remain clearly visible.
PAGE 2073 The mouth of the Müller's topknot gapes open as it lies camouflaged against the rocky bed of the eastern Atlantic.

The 538 species of flatfishes are masters of camouflage, and range throughout all seas, especially in warm and temperate zones. Although they share the flattened, broad bodies of other orders of bottom-dwelling fishes, their adult shape is an adaptation to life on the seabed.

The free-swimming larvae of the flat fishes resemble the larvae of all other fishes. But, as metamorphosis begins in open water, they change shape completely. The bones of their heads and jaws shift, twisting their mouths until they lie sideways, and one eye migrates across the head until both eyes lie on the same side. The side with the eyes becomes the new upperpart of the body, and the "blind" side becomes the underside.

The transformation of larvae into broad, flattened adults enables them to begin an exclusively bottom-dwelling existence. They lie on their new undersides when on the seabed, and their upperparts develop pigment cells in the skin that enable them to adopt the color of the seabed over which they swim. The cells (chromatophores) are controlled by the nervous system and give the flatfishes protective camouflage.

The flatfishes' eyes migrate to the left or right side of their heads depending on the family, although some species have both right-eyed and left-eyed forms. For example, the eyes of the primitive family Psettodids in the Indian and Pacific oceans migrate from either the left side or the right side. Although most species in the family Pleuronectidae are "right-eyed" fishes, the starry flounder varies according to area. In the coastal waters off California, more than half the population of starry flounders are left-eyed, a proportion that increases to 60 percent in waters off Alaska and to over 95 percent off Japan.

Successful adaptation

The origins of the flatfishes' curious adaptations are unknown but they are undoubtedly successful. The different species of flatfishes inhabit all the world's oceans and support enormous commercial fisheries. They mainly range through warm and temperate zones, but a few species also inhabit the Arctic and the borders of Antarctic waters.

PLEURONECTIFORMES CLASSIFICATION

Flatfishes

Six families containing a total of 538 species in 117 genera make up the order Pleuronectiformes, the flatfishes. The family Pleuronectidae contains 99 species that range through the Atlantic, Pacific and Arctic oceans. They include the plaice, *Pleuronectes platessa*; the flounder, *P. flesus*; the summer flounder or northern fluke, *P. dentatus*; the dab, *Limanda limanda*; the lemon sole, *Microstomus kitt*; and the Atlantic halibut, *Hippoglossus hippoglossus*. There are about 212 species in the family Bothidae, distributed throughout the oceans. Some of the best-known species are the turbot, *Scophthalmus maximus*; the brill, *S. rhombus*; and the topknot, *Zeugopterus punctatus*.

Tongue soles and true soles

The tongue soles or tongue fishes of the family Cynoglossidae number 103 species. Fishes of tropical and subtropical seas, they include the West African tongue sole, *Cynoglossus senegalensis*, and the Caribbean tongue fish, *Symphurus arawak*. The true soles make up the family Soleidae. There are 117 species, most of which live in coastal waters around the world, with a few occurring in freshwater habitats. They include the Dover sole or European sole, *Solea solea*, and the hogchoker, *Trinectes maculatus*.

Brackish waters

Flatfishes occur mainly on the bottom of shallow, coastal shelves, and rarely appear at a depth greater than 5000 ft. Certain species also penetrate brackish and freshwater—the flounder, a species that ranges along the coast of Europe from the White Sea to the western Mediterranean, often migrates over a mile upriver from coastal bays. Flatfishes are commonly small in size, and range from the 5-in.-long little sole to the enormous Atlantic halibut, which grows to an average length of 71 in. in the male and 90.5 in. in the female. In rare cases, specimens of Atlantic halibut measuring 10-13 feet have been caught.

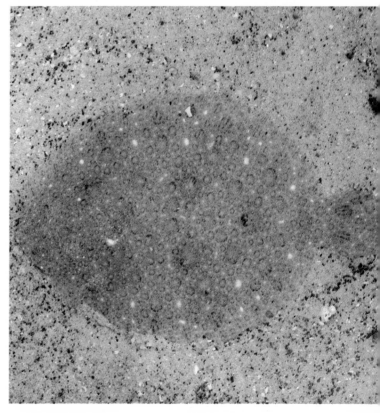

ABOVE A brill changes color for camouflage by adjusting the proportions of colored pigments in the branching cells beneath its skin—the colored pigments required to blend the fish against the sandy bottom fill the branches, and unnecessary pigments remain in the center of the cell. The process is indirectly controlled by the response of the eyes to the fish's surroundings.

Plaice, flounders and halibut

Many of the 99 species that form the family Pleuronectidae have been the mainstays of commercial fisheries for many years in the Atlantic, Pacific and Arctic oceans (plaice, halibut, flounder and dab are all food fishes). The plaice occurs in the northeastern Atlantic and along the coast of Europe from the White Sea off the northern coast of the USSR to the Mediterranean. Measuring 31.5 in. in length, it is the most extensively caught and marketed species of the family. It has smooth, brown upperparts with brilliant red spots and a pale white underside. A prominent line of four to seven bony knobs extends across its head from the eyes to the start of its lateral line. Unlike the flounder, it does not have prickles at the base of the dorsal and anal fins.

During the spawning season, the spots on the upperparts of the plaice become particularly vivid. The female can lay up to 500,000 eggs in a single

THE PLAICE
— AN UNDERWATER TRANSFORMATION —

The plaice is one of the best-known flatfishes, and one of the most important commercially. It is commonplace in European waters and is easily recognizable because of its familiar flat shape. The plaice's shape represents a unique adaptation to life on the bottom of the sea. Plaice, like all flatfishes, start life as larvae of "normal" shape. As they begin to grow, changes take place that involve a complete twisting of the structure of the head. As a result of these changes, both eyes of a plaice end up on the top of its body, rather than on either side.

Plaice live in the European Atlantic from northern Norway and Iceland to the Mediterranean and in northwest Africa. They spend the summer in shallow water and the winter in the deep, down to 660 ft. Breeding usually takes place in the spring—as early as February in the English Channel—although the dates vary depending on the environment.

The fish mate in mid-water. The male and female fishes lie on top of one another. The female releases a stream of eggs and the male emits the milt to fertilize them. Females shed around 250,000 eggs per 2 lbs. 3 oz. of their body weight, although the number of eggs laid ranges from 50,000 to 520,000, depending on the size of the female.

The eggs of most flatfishes contain oil droplets that enable the eggs to float near the sea surface. Plaice eggs are unusual in that they do not contain oil, and are only able to float if there is enough salt in the water. To ensure this, spawning occurs only in areas with a high enough salinity level (at least 10-12 parts salt per 100 of water). The eggs float with the plankton and are prey to the tide, the wind and predators—many thousands of eggs are eaten before they can hatch. The eggs hatch after 10-20 days, depending on the water temperature, into 0.3 in. larvae, with black and yellow spots. At this stage, they look like any other newly hatched fish, with round bodies and yolk sacs. The yolk sacs are absorbed after about a week, and the larvae then feed on the microscopic crustaceans in the plankton

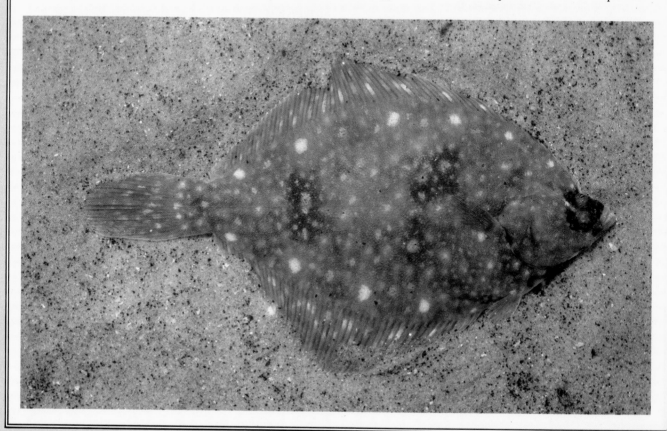

and on minute worm and snail larvae. After several weeks, the changes that will turn the larva into a miniature flatfish begin to take place.

Life on the seabed

As a young plaice develops its body deepens and flattens from side to side and it starts swimming on its side. The eye on the left side of its body moves across its head to lie alongside the other—this happens because the skull grows more quickly on one side than the other. The cartilaginous bar of skull separating the eyes is absorbed, the nostril simultaneously migrates to the eyed side, and the mouth twists into the same plane as the eyes. After about 40 days the metamorphosis is complete. While these changes are taking place, the young fish sinks to the bottom, settling on its left side, so its right side and both eyes are uppermost. Flatfish do not have a swim bladder, so they remain lying near the bottom where they continue their lives.

As with other flatfishes the growth rate of plaice is largely dependent upon temperature, the amount of food available and population density. They reach a length of 2.4-3 in. in their first winter, 4-5 in. by their second, and 6-8 in. by their third. At four years and 10-10.6 in. long, most of them have moved back into deeper water. They then grow a further 1.5 in. a year until they are nine years old, and 0.5 in. a year thereafter.

LEFT Grains of sand camouflage the smooth, orange-speckled upperparts of the plaice against the seabed.
RIGHT The plaice uses its twisted mouth to suck mussels and crustaceans onto its large, powerful throat teeth.
TOP RIGHT During metamorphosis, the body of the flatfish larva (A) becomes deeper (B), one eye migrates to the other side of the head and the jaws twist (C). By the time the young flatfish is 0.4 in. long, its eyes lie on the top of its head (D).

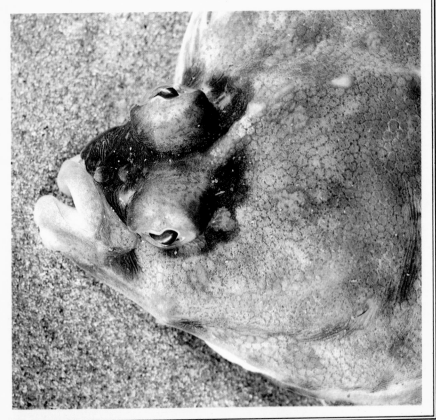

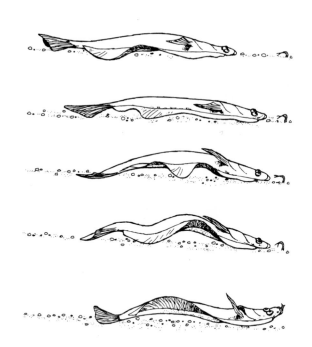

ABOVE The peacock flounder, a left-eyed flounder that inhabits the waters off Bermuda, has distinctive blue rings on its upperparts.
ABOVE RIGHT When the summer flounder of North America stalks a tube worm, it approaches its prey with care since its victim is sensitive to **water movements. Coiling its body ready to strike, the flounder leaps powerfully forward to snatch the end of the worm in its mouth.**
FAR RIGHT The bottom-dwelling dab is similar in appearance to the plaice but has a rougher surface on its green upperparts.

spawning, depending on her size. Although the plaice spends the free-swimming larval stage in the tidal zones near beaches, after reaching adulthood it moves to depths of 80-250 ft. over sand, gravel and mud along the continental shelf.

Thriving dab

The plaice is outnumbered in the northeastern Atlantic by its relative the dab, which measures 10-12 in. in length and weighs 15 lbs. 6 oz. The upperparts of the dab are pale yellow to dirty brown in color and lack the brilliant body markings of the plaice; the underparts are pale. It has toothed, tiny scales on its upperparts, and the lateral lines along its sides arch over the pectoral fins. Like the plaice, the dab is of considerable commercial value.

Normally, the dab lives at depths of 65-130 ft. along the sandy or muddy coastal seabed of Europe, from the Baltic Sea to the Bay of Biscay. In the main spawning season from March to May, a female dab produces up to one million eggs, which drift with plankton in the southern North Sea. The size and age at which an adult dab reaches sexual maturity varies between different regions.

Rough skin

The 20-in.-long flounder is a well-known species of flatfish that ranges along the coast of Europe from the White Sea to the western Mediterranean. Like the halibut, plaice, lemon sole and dab, its eyes usually occur on the right side of its body. In some areas, however, as many as one-third of the flounder population are left-eyed. The flounder is often confused with the plaice at certain stages of its growth, but it has a distinctive rough skin and thorny scales both along the base of the dorsal and anal fins and above the lateral line.

Its body is usually slate-gray in color and has numerous red or orange spots. The underside is dull white. The flounder penetrates further upriver into freshwater than any other flatfish in Europe, but returns to coastal, salty waters to breed from February to May. Young flounder are particularly vulnerable to seals and marine birds at low tide.

The largest member of the family Pleuronectidae is the Atlantic halibut, with a maximum length of 15 ft. 5 in. and a weight of 727 lbs. 8 oz. Usually it grows to 6 ft. 6in. in length, but commercial overfishing has reduced its average weight to almost 100 lbs. as increasingly young Atlantic halibut are caught. The Atlantic halibut inhabits sand, gravel and mud sea floors at depths of 330-5000 ft. Often, it hides in gullies between boulders and underwater canyons.

TOP The greenback flounder adopts the coloration of its background on the seabed to camouflage itself. The initial stimulus to change color comes from its eyes, which it can move from left to right and up and down.

ABOVE A flounder is superbly camouflaged against the gravel on the seabed. In Britain, the term "flounder" is given to the species *Platichthys flesus*, but in North America it may be applied to nearly any flatfish, regardless of its family.

Turbots

The 212 species of the turbot family are more commonly known as the left-eyed flounders because their eyes occur on the left side of their bodies. They are a large, colorful family that includes the American Atlantic peacock flounder, which sports large, spectacular blue rings and spots on its brown body. The males and females of certain species also differ in shape, a condition that is unusual among flatfishes; the pectoral fins of the female scald fish from Australian waters in the Indian Ocean extend to the tip of the tail, while those of the male are shorter.

Perhaps the best-known species in European waters is the 31-ft.-long turbot, which occurs in the northeastern Atlantic and along the coast of Europe from the Baltic to the Mediterranean. It has a thick, rounded body and a large mouth. The eye side of the body has many bony hooks that develop from modified scales. Like the sole, the turbot has the ability to change its brown coloration according to the sand, shell gravel and gravel of the seabed. It is a daytime predator that lives on the coastal shelf to a depth of 260 ft., hunting sand eels, sprats, pilchards and a wide range of other species.

The turbot is notable for the extraordinary number of eggs that the female lays during the spawning season (an 18-lb. female will lay almost 9 million eggs). Like its relative the brill, the turbot is a valuable food fish. The brill has smooth, scaled upperparts rather than the hard, bony upper body of the turbot.

Soles and tongue soles

Members of the sole family are important food fishes that range from North America and Europe east to Japan and Australia. They have oval bodies and blunt, elongated snouts that protrude over their twisted mouths. The soles are right-eyed fishes with poor vision, forcing them to rely on scent for detecting prey. During the day, they remain buried for protection and only emerge at night to hunt. They generally inhabit temperate and tropical marine waters, crawling as well as swimming across the bottom of the sea.

Tongue soles are generally marine creatures, although certain species, such as the tongue sole of West Africa, regularly move into large estuaries and rivers to spawn. They are large, left-eyed flatfishes that usually inhabit shallow waters in tropical zones.

BRISTLING WITH DEFENSES

In an order of fishes protected by thick skin, bony plates, spines, locking spikes and poison, the pufferfishes and porcupine fishes have one extra defense: they can inflate themselves with water or air to resemble spiky balloons

Curious body shapes, sedate movements and elaborate defenses are all typical of the Tetraodontiformes order, a diverse group of fishes from the warmer seas. Most of them are small fishes, with scales adapted to form spines, shields, or plates, often lending their bodies a stiffness that prevents efficient swimming. Many of them, such as the pufferfishes and the porcupine fishes, expand their bodies as a defensive mechanism, either by filling themselves with water or air (or both), or by adjusting their pelvic bones to extend a flap on their bellies. Others, like the triggerfishes, are generally small-mouthed, with strong teeth often forming a powerful beak. Nearly all the Tetraodontiformes are marine, although a few species of puffers penetrate freshwater. Many are able to produce sounds, either by grinding their teeth or by vibrating their muscles, and their swim bladders amplify the sound.

Porcupine fishes and pufferfishes

Porcupine fishes and pufferfishes share the ability to pump themselves full of water—or, if forced to, air—turning their bodies into balls several times their normal size. Since many pufferfishes and all porcupine fishes are very spiny, this serves as an effective deterrent from predators. Both types of fishes have an elastic stomach, or an extension to it, with a muscular flap at the entrance that serves as a valve. On being disturbed, the fishes quickly inflate. Deflation takes longer, and a pufferfish that has filled itself with air floats at the surface for long periods of time.

The porcupine fishes have long, deeply rooted spines all over their bodies. Some species add an extra "bluff" in the shape of two life-like eye markings that are revealed when they inflate. They are found in all the tropical oceans, in a wide variety of habitats. The 20-in.-long balloonfish, for example, may be found in the creeks of mangrove swamps, over reefs, or in sandy bays. The porcupine fish *Diodon hystrix* is the largest in the family. It grows to a maximum length of 35 ft., and ranges farther north than the balloonfish.

ABOVE LEFT Its long spines peacefully aligned with its body, a porcupine fish swims through a reef with fanning movements of its large pectoral fins. If disturbed, it inflates its body by pumping water into its stomach until it is nearly spherical and its spines stick out vertically. When inflated, the fish floats upside down at the surface where it is easy prey to sea birds and other predators.

TETRAODONTIFORMES CLASSIFICATION

The order Tetraodontiformes contains 329 species grouped in 92 genera and eight families. The porcupine fishes of the family Diodontidae range throughout the oceans. There are 15 species including the porcupine fish, *Diodon hystrix*; the balloonfish or shiny pufferfish, *D. holocanthus*; and the striped burrfish, *Chilomycterus schoepfi*. The pufferfishes of the family Tetraodontidae number 118 species. They range throughout the tropical and subtropical seas, and include the blowfish, *Tetraodon fluviatilis*, and the sharp-nose puffers of the genus *Canthigaster*.

The triggerfishes or leatherjackets of the family Balistidae number about 135 species. They range throughout the oceans, and include the queen triggerfish, *Balistes vetula*; the scrawled filefish, *Alutera scripta*; and the Picasso fishes of the genus *Rhinecanthus*. The family Ostraciidae contains the 30 species of boxfishes, cowfishes and trunkfishes from the tropical seas of the world. They include the buffalo trunkfish, *Lactophrys trigonus*; the cowfish species, *Lactoria diaphana*; and the blue-spotted boxfish, *Ostracion tuberculatus*. The family Molidae contains the three species of molas or sunfishes, which mainly inhabit the warmer seas of the world. The best-known species is the ocean sunfish, *Mola mola*.

Triggerfish
Odonus niger

Porcupine fish

Spiny eel

Triggerfish
*Oxymonachanthus
longirostris*

Pufferfish

Boxfish

Ocean sunfish

Halibut

Batfish

Turbot

Dover sole

Goosefish

2083

Porcupine fishes can retract their spines while swimming, but the closely related burrfish have permanently erect spines. The striped burrfish, a western Atlantic species that grows up to 10 in. long, adds jet propulsion to the gentle action of its fins by blowing strong jets of water through its tiny gill openings. The main difference between the porcupine fishes and the pufferfishes lies in their teeth. The porcupine fishes' teeth are completely fused to form powerful beaks. The pufferfishes' teeth have a gap in the middle on both the top and bottom rows so that they appear to have four teeth, as their family name, Tetraodontidae, indicates. Both groups feed on mollusks and corals using their beaks to crunch their way through their hard-shelled prey.

Both the porcupine fishes and the pufferfishes have poisonous internal organs (and occasionally flesh), making their defenses very impressive. However, the unfortunate porcupine fishes are sometimes used by humans to make unusual lightshades for the tourist trade, while Japanese gourmets sacrifice a few every year for *fugu*—eating the non-toxic flesh of several species of pufferfishes. The gut, liver, blood, and gonads of these pufferfishes still contain tetrotoxin, a

LEFT When irritated, the pufferfish inflates itself by pumping water into a sac in its stomach. It keeps the water in the sac by contracting valve muscles on each side of it. The pufferfish also pushes spines out of the pores in its stomach to make it appear more menacing and prickly. The pufferfish will only expel the water and return to its normal shape when its muscles become fatigued.
ABOVE The pufferfish *Arothron nigropuncatus*, a particularly richly colored inhabitant of tropical reefs, has a long, pointed snout with distinctive black nostrils protruding from each side. Above each nostril it has a gill opening that stretches as far as the middle section of its pectoral fins.

deadly nerve poison. All cooks who prepare *fugu* must be specially trained in the safe preparation of these fishes. Research into the medicinal properties of tetrotoxin is largely a Japanese enterprise.

Many of the pufferfishes are brightly colored, and the sharp-nosed species of the genus *Canthigaster* are small enough to be kept in aquaria, as they reach a maximum length of just 4.7 in.

Armor plate and horns

Boxfishes', trunkfishes' and cowfishes' bodies are covered with large, bony plates that make their weak

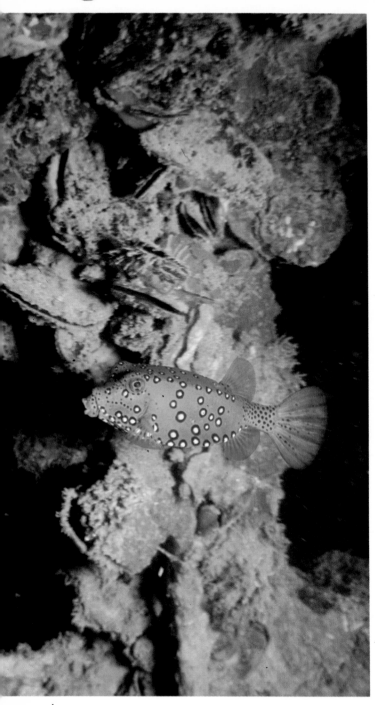

ABOVE **The blue-spotted boxfish is found throughout tropical waters where it inhabits coral reefs and rocky crevices. It investigates an algae-encrusted shellfish colony for the crabs and smaller shellfish that make up its diet.**

Its head and body are encased in an inflexible armor of fused, thick, six-sided plates. The armor reduces the flexibility of the fish's tail and fins, allowing them only to fan gently and row. As a result, it is a slow swimmer.

swimming movements seem like the mechanical movements of a cheap toy. Only their fins and tails protrude from the armor that makes their bodies three-, four-, or five-sided in section. These are fanned swiftly to enable the fishes to maintain their slow progress. The undersides of these fishes are flat, and many of them have horns and spikes. The 10-in.-long cowfish, *Lactoria diaphana*, from the Indian and Pacific oceans derives its name from a pair of horns above its eyes. Most of this group are very brightly colored and live on reefs and sea-grass beds, with a couple of species that live in quite deep water. They usually have small mouths and feed on a wide range of bottom-living invertebrates, including tunicates and sponges, as well as some marine plants. Few of them exceed 12 in. in length, although the 18-in.-long buffalo trunkfish is large enough to be considered worth eating in some parts of its western Atlantic range. The plant element in the diet of many of this group enables them to transmit ciguatera, a poison thought to be derived from populations of certain marine algae. In a more direct form of poisoning, some species, such as the trunkfish *Ostracion lentiginosum*, secrete a poison (called ostracitoxin) into the water around them. Presumably a defense mechanism, it is probably derived from tissues in their mouths and may even prove fatal to its bearer in confined quarters.

The locking spike

The triggerfishes make up a large and distinctive family. They are distinguished by bodies that look diamond-shaped or oval when viewed from the side, and almost blade-thin when viewed from the front. They are usually approximately 18 in. in length, and are named for their strong, sharp, spike-like dorsal spines, usually situated above or just behind the eyes. When erected, the front spike is locked by the second one, and cannot be retracted until the latter releases it. Triggerfishes have sharp, separate teeth in small jaws mounted at the very tip of their snouts. The teeth are implanted in sockets in their jaws, an unusual refinement in fish, and are strong enough to make holes in shellfishes and crabs. Some triggerfishes also eat other fishes. If alarmed, triggerfishes seek a hole or crevice that they can lock themselves into with their spines, and they defend themselves by snapping their jaws. There are about 40 species, which are usually found in the tropical shallows, although a few species live in the open oceans, and there are some that wander into temperate seas.

The gray triggerfish lives in the Atlantic Ocean from West Africa north to Portugal and from Argentina north to Nova Scotia. It regularly occurs in British waters, especially during hot summers. Triggerfishes' colors vary from being garish and conspicuous to the extremely cryptic and, combined with their body shape and behavior, provide them with an extremely effective camouflage. The Picasso fishes, *Rhinecanthus aculeatus* and *R. rectangularis*, represent the former group, resplendent in purple-blue, yellow, black and white stripes in patterns appropriate to their namesake. They are said to sleep on their sides at night, and, if disturbed, make a whirring noise by rubbing together the bones that support their pectoral fins.

Closely related to the triggerfishes, the filefishes are thinner in body section, with their dorsal spine usually placed farther forward. They are named for their hard, rough scales. Filefishes share the triggerfishes' distribution, and usually grow to about 10 in. in length, although the scrawled filefish reaches a maximum length of 35 in. They have small mouths and feed on encrusting organisms and other bottom-living invertebrates as well as some plants.

Sunfishes

The three species of marine or ocean sunfishes are also known as molas (taken from the Latin word *mola* meaning "millstone," alluding to the fishes' almost circular shape). They are the wandering giants of the world's temperate and tropical oceans, quite unlike any other fishes in shape, and are probably the heaviest bony fishes of all. The ocean sunfish is the largest, measuring a maximum of 14 ft. from head to tail. Reports of its maximum weight vary; a specimen rammed by a ship in 1908 was towed to Port Jackson, Australia, and found to weigh 4910 lbs. Less exceptional specimens probably average about 3 feet long and weigh about 100 lbs. The marine sunfishes are remarkable in appearance. They are almost circular in shape with tall, triangular dorsal and anal fins and no pelvic fins. Their tail fins join the dorsal and anal fins together, and vary slightly in shape according to the species. The 10-ft.-long sharptail sunfish has a pointed lobe on its tail fin, just above the center, while the smaller (31-in.-long) slender sunfish has a fringe-like tail fin.

ABOVE The bones in the upper jaw of the triggerfish *Pseudobalistes fuscus* have fused to form a beak, which produces a strange grinding noise when rubbed against the lower jaw. Its teeth are very efficient at chewing food with mineral structures such as mollusks and crustaceans, and it will also feed on fishes and echinoderms that are not preyed upon by many other fishes.

Although ocean sunfishes appear at the surface regularly, apparently basking in the sun, many naturalists consider these fishes to be sick and behaving abnormally. Most ocean sunfishes that have been examined have had empty stomachs, but the remainder seem to indicate that they eat anything that they can suck into their comparatively small mouths. Small jellyfishes, comb jellies, shrimps, young fishes, even the leptocephalus larvae of eels, have all been recorded as food. Healthy fishes probably live between the surface and about 1300 ft. deep. Little is known about sunfishes' breeding habits, except that the female lays an immense number of eggs; it was estimated that one female measuring 4 ft. contained 300 million eggs. The sunfishes' larvae are spiny. Although no spawning grounds have been found, nor any larvae caught, pea-sized post-larval individuals have been caught in the open ocean.

SEA SQUIRTS
AND
LANCELETS

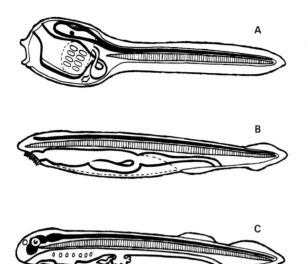

ABOVE The notochord (shaded with vertical lines in the diagram) is a characteristic feature of the chordates. In the sea squirt larvae (A), this primitive form of spinal column supports the muscular tail but vanishes when the invertebrate becomes an adult. The notochords of the lancelet (B) and primitive vertebrates such as the lamprey (C) extend the length of the body from the tail to the head. PAGES 2088-2089 The sea squirt *Didemnum molle*, which grows in colonies among turtle weeds and white soft coral off Australia, has an orange body with green-fringed siphons.

SEA SQUIRTS AND LANCELETS CLASSIFICATION

The phylum Chordata is divided into three subphyla.

The most familiar of these is the subphylum Vertebrata, which consists of the fishes, amphibians, reptiles, birds and mammals. As mammals humans are also vertebrates and therefore chordates.

The second subphylum is the Urochordata or Tunicata, which consists of the sea squirts of the class Ascidiacea, and the salps and pelagic tunicates of the classes Thaliacea and Larvacea. There are about 2000 species in all.

The third subphylum is the Cephalochordata or Acrania, a small group of some 20 species known as the lancelets.

Mammals, birds, reptiles, amphibians and fishes all have well-defined spinal columns and are therefore all vertebrates. For the majority of these creatures, the most prominent feature of the spinal column is a series of vertebral bones that make up the backbone. However, a more basic feature is the single, hollow nerve cord that runs inside the entire length of the animal's spine.

Some primitive vertebrates—notably the hagfishes—do not have backbones in the conventional sense, but they do have spinal nerve cords. The nerve cord is a delicate organ that is supported, but not enclosed, by a strong flexible rod called a notochord. The notochord exists in more advanced vertebrates, but since its function has been superseded by the bony vertebrae, it has become redundant and degenerated into a series of fragmentary remains.

Chordates.

The nerve cord and the notochord are features that exist in a number of other animals too primitive to be classed among the vertebrates. Instead they are included in the great phylum of creatures known as the Chordata, or chordates. This phylum includes the vertebrates and two other groups—the sea squirts and their relatives, also known as the urochordates, and the lancelets, or cephalochordates.

Most urochordates have a spinal chord only at the larval stage, and then only in their tail end. Adults look quite different from larvae, and appear to have no chordate characteristics. Cephalochordates have a dorsal chord that runs the entire length of the body from head to tail tip and is retained throughout the adult stage.

Simple mouths

Another structure shared by vertebrates, urochordates and cephalochordates is a cavity or pharynx formed from the top of the digestive tract. In humans and other mammals, the pharynx has divided into the nasal and mouth cavities, but in fishes it remains a single cavity, with the mouth and gullet at either end and gill apertures at the sides.

In primitive chordates and in many fishes, the gill mesh that fills the apertures has a dual function—as a respiratory organ, and as a filter for straining fine food particles out of the water. The animals breathe and feed by "inhaling" water, absorbing oxygen, trapping

suspended food particles in the gill network, and then expelling the spent water through the gill apertures.

Although vertebrates, urochordates and cephalochordates are very different in their adult forms, they display great similarities in the early phases of their development. Their embryos are almost identical, each with a distinct nerve chord running down their backs.

ABOVE During its development into adulthood, the sea squirt attaches itself to a rock or outcrop on the bottom of its ocean habitat. The circular inhalant siphon at the top of the sea squirt pumps water in through the throat and across a mesh of gills, and a similar external siphon at the side discharges the water. The material that makes up the thick outer tunic of the sea squirt resembles cellulose, the main constituent in the structure of plant cell walls.

The urochordates and cephalochordates probably resemble the distant ancestors of the vertebrates in many respects. The cephalochordates are very like hagfishes and larval lampreys, and could have given rise to the primitive fishes. Conversely, their similarities with other invertebrates show how they themselves could have developed. Altogether, these unspectacular animals represent a key phase in the evolution of the vertebrates.

Sea squirts and salps

Adult sea squirts are most unlikely members of the group of higher animals known as the chordates. Superficially more like plants than animals, they have soft, jelly-like, largely hollow bodies that are anchored to rocks, plants or the shells of other marine animals. Their relatives, the salps, are free-floating but equally plant-like. For many years, they were thought to be related to mullusks such as mussels and oysters since they live in much the same way—drawing in water through siphons and filtering out the food particles. However, there are fundamental differences in the way their bodies are organized.

A typical mature sea squirt is shaped like a teapot without a handle. It draws in water through a lid aperture—the inhalant siphon—and strains it through a gill network that forms a basket suspended within the main part of the "pot." After filtering out any food and absorbing the oxygen it needs, the sea squirt draws the water down and expels it through a small spout at the side—the exhalant siphon. The process is continuous: tiny, mobile hairs in the gill network drive a steady current of water through the animal, and a sticky fluid retains food particles and passes them into the gut for digestion.

A pot and spout

The principal organs of the sea squirt—the gut, heart and sexual organs—are located in the "pot" beneath the gill basket, and waste products of digestion are excreted through the spout. Sea squirts are

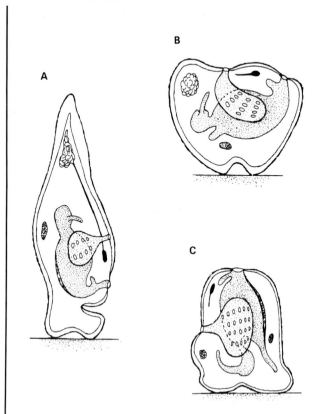

A

B

C

ABOVE LEFT The *Ciona intestinalis* processes food in a coiled gut that is clearly visible through the leathery surface of the outer tunic. It will expel waste through its lower

exhalant siphon.
LEFT The three stages of metamorphosis in the *Ciona intestinalis* from the free-swimming, larval stage (A) to adulthood (B and C).

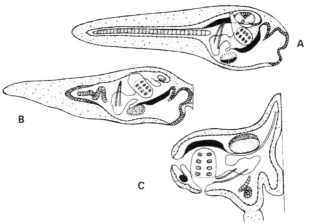

LEFT The transparent bodies of the *Clavelina* sea squirts are divided into the thorax, abdomen and post-abdomen. They usually occur in dense colonies on the bottom of open seas.

ABOVE During its three stages of metamorphosis, the free-swimming larva of the *Clavelina* (A) attaches itself to a rock (B) and develops into sexually mature adulthood (C).

hermaphrodites, so each animal produces both eggs and sperm, and expels them through the spout, too.

Most species deposit their eggs in the water to be fertilized by the sperm of other individuals, but some retain them in the spout. The eggs are fertilized by sperm drawn in from the surrounding waters, and they develop inside the animal, improving their survival rate. The larvae swim free as soon as they hatch. Colonial sea squirts can also reproduce asexually by growing new individuals as "buds." These individuals are genetically identical to the parent, so the sexual phase is essential to introduce new genetic material and allow the species to evolve.

Headless adults

An adult sea squirt has no head, and no trace of a spinal nerve cord or notochord, so it does not appear to be a chordate. In its larval form, however, the sea squirt is very different. Instead of being anchored to a rock, it swims freely in the water. It is a tadpole-like creature with a distinct head and tail, and it has a nerve cord, stiffened by a tough notochord, running from the middle of its back right down the length of its tail. The sea squirt "tadpole" has a number of adhesive pads at the front of its body. When it is ready for metamorphosis into an adult—within days or even

hours of hatching—it attaches itself to a rock, shell or plant and begins to change shape. The metamorphosis takes place in several stages that involve almost total regression of the tail and the growth of several new structures. Among them, an outer casting or "tunic" is formed from a material that resembles cellulose—the tough, fibrous substance that forms a main constituent of plant cells. The whole life cycle usually lasts about a year.

Complex colonies

There are about 2000 species of sea squirts, ranging in length from 0.1 in. to about 8 in. Many are brightly colored. They are exclusively marine animals, found throughout the world, mainly in coastal waters at depths ranging from a few feet to 160 ft. There are a few deep-ocean species. Nearly all sea squirts have a free-swimming larval stage and a sedentary adult stage, spending most of their lives permanently moored to rocks or plants.

Growing colonies

Many sea squirts are basically solitary, but some form colonies, often simply untidy aggregations enlarged by asexual reproduction. As buds form on each individual, the colony becomes denser and

ABOVE The cushion-like colonies of *Distomus variolosus* occur in lower coastal zones. They develop from a single, free-swimming larva, which anchors itself to a rock or frond of algae. Each larva reproduces itself asexually to create new individuals or "buds," which in turn generate a cluster of sea squirts on the common base. These will remain within the existing structure or drift away to form new colonies.

denser. In the transparent *Clavelina lepadiformis*, for example, an established colony looks a little like a tuft of grass, where each stem is a single animal that has budded off the original parent. *Distomus variolosus* forms cushion-like colonies that, close up, resemble piles of soft leather flasks in a pinkish red color.

Sharing a tunic

In some species the relationship between individual colony members is more complex, and the animals cannot survive on their own. In the case of *Distaplia rosea*, single animals join together to form a globe-like structure encased in a common outer tunic. The outer tunic is perforated with numerous holes corresponding to the siphons of the animals within. A similar type of organization is displayed by *Aplidium proliferum*, which forms mushroom-like colonial masses attached to rocks by a common stalk, and by

Diazona violacea, where the individual animals join up to form very extensive mats in which the animals are free at their top ends but attached to a common base.

Among star sea squirts, such as *Botryllus schlosseri*, there are even closer relationships and more complex interactions. Individual animals are arranged in flat rays around single longitudinal exhalant siphons, on a common base. The rays are often vividly colored, giving the effect of a series of small flowers embedded in jelly. The individual animals obtain their own supplies of food and oxygen through their own inhalant siphons, but share a common waste-disposal system.

Solitary sea squirts nearly always reproduce sexually. Their offspring swim away and become attached elsewhere, and so they rarely occur in groups. There are many examples of solitary sea squirts in the Pyurid family. The red sea squirt, or *Halocynthia papillosa*, is a common Mediterranean species. It is a beautiful creature with a velvety red tunic and long pinkish yellow siphons adorned with striking brown bristles round their edges. The peculiar-looking sea egg, or *Microcosmus sulcatus*, has a tough tunic with numerous folds that provide safe hiding places for a multitude of tiny creatures, such as sea anemones, tubeworms, algae and other sea squirts. *Microcosmus claudicans*, common in coral reefs, usually covers its tunic with a layer of sand grains.

Most sea squirts attach themselves to solid objects such as stones, seashells or the fronds of seaweed—but some do not. The small *Psammostyela delamarei* is typical of sandy seabeds, where it anchors itself to the bottom by means of numerous small filaments that bind the sand grains together like the roots of a plant.

Far more curious are the sea squirts of the family Octanemid, a recently discovered group of species that inhabit tropical seas at depths of 13,000 ft. or so. Rather like small starfish in appearance, they do not attach themselves to rocks, plants or even sand. Instead, they move about freely, and are probably able to crawl and swim.

Home builders

Sea squirts have vertebrate-like features when they are young, but lose them as they mature. However, the animals in one class of urochordates—the Larvacea—retain their tadpole-like appearance into maturity, and are able to breed while still in the "infant" state. Known as neoteny, this phenomenon allows a group of animals to make a great stride in development. If the larval form proves more suitable to its way of life, it can simply grow sex organs and retain its juvenile body. The alternative is to gradually modify the adult body form until it resembles that of the larva—a long-term, haphazard process.

In their basic body form, larvaceans resemble sea squirt larvae. Their bodies consist of an oval front section containing the viscera, and a long tail with a dorsal nerve chord and strengthening notochord running down its whole length. There are about 70 species, distributed throughout almost all the oceans of the world, although more occur in warm-temperate seas. They float in the plankton in the upper layer and feed on other floating microorganisms.

All larvaceans are tiny creatures, rarely exceeding 0.1 in. in length, but they appear to be much larger because they live within extraordinary gelatinous "houses" constructed from a special mucus-like substance secreted by the body. These constructions can be large compared with the size of the animal within; in some species, they are as large as walnuts.

Transparent home

Larvaceans of the genus *Oikopleura* build transparent spherical or oval houses, and inhabit a chamber in the middle. Like sea squirts, they are filter feeders, taking in and expelling water through a mesh-like gill network that absorbs the oxygen and retains food particles.

Larvaceans are minute in size, so their food consists of the smallest microorganisms. Ingeniously, they use their "houses" to screen out inedible material. Each entrance has a protective grid of interwoven filaments, which keeps out debris and food particles too large for the animal to eat. The larvacean moves its tail rhythmically inside its chamber to create a fast flow of water through the entrance. As water approaches the animal, it passes through a series of ever finer filters that reject all particles except the tiny nanoplankton, which larvaceans can eat.

Flushing the filters

Sometimes the filters become blocked, but this poses no problem. The animal simply reverses the water flow every so often to flush debris out of the filters, then carries on as before. If the structure of the "house" is damaged in any way, it is replaced in its entirety, since it is not an integral part of the animal.

ABOVE **Star sea squirts form a colony by arranging themselves radially around a common exhalant siphon. They maintain their position by embedding themselves in jelly. Each star sea squirt has its own inhalant siphon or aperture with** tiny tentacles along the fringes.
BELOW **The red sea squirt clings to marine vegetation in a shallow-water rock crevice. The vivid coloration of this large, solitary creature becomes jet black at depths below 50 ft.**

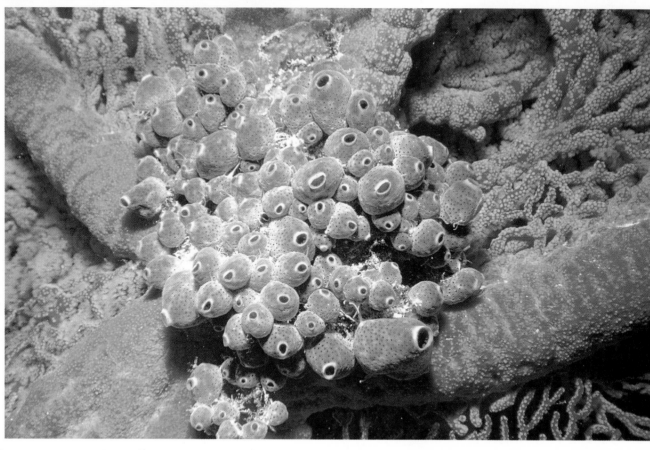

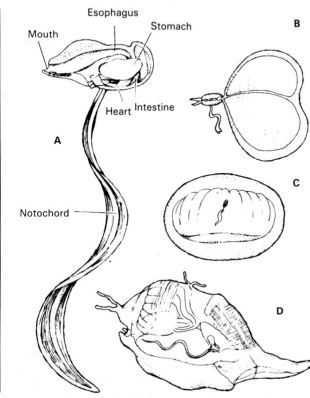

Labels: Esophagus, Mouth, Stomach, Heart, Intestine, Notochord, A, B, C, D

ABOVE Colonial sea squirts grow attached to the body of a gorgonia sea fan.
LEFT When removed from its protective outer tunic, the sexually mature *Oikopleura albicans* (A) resembles the larval form of the sea squirt in appearance. The tunics of these neotonous adults occur as a large filter around the mouth (B), a simple spheroid (C) or — in the case of *Oikopleura* — a multifiltered structure (D).
PAGES 2096-2097 A dense colony of *Clavelina* sea squirts grow among fronds of algae in the Mediterranean Sea.

In different larvacean families, the structure and function of the houses vary somewhat. In the family Fritillarid, the houses do not completely surround the animals' bodies; instead, they are restricted to small mucus spheres around the mouth. Among members of the family Kovalevskiid, the houses cover the whole animal, but they do not have obvious filters; instead, food is probably screened by the house walls.

Larger species of larvaceans can filter about a gallon of water every day through their houses, and trap 600,000 or more floating microorganisms. Their houses also help the animals to float in the plankton and provide them with a degree of protection against predators.

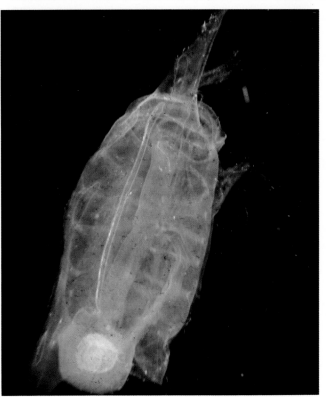

Salps

Salps, or thaliaceans, are typically gelatinous tubular or sack-shaped organisms that float in the waters of warm seas. They are rather like free-floating adult sea squirts in that neither adult nor larva has any trace of a dorsal nerve chord or notochord. However, a small cell mass of uncertain function, known as eleoblast, has been found in the larvae of some species and tentatively identified as a rudimentary spinal chord. It suggests that salps have evolved further along the route pioneered by the sea squirts—indeed they are considered by some biologists to be the most highly evolved of the urochordates—but this has taken them further away from the basic chordate body plan that probably gave rise to the vertebrates.

Jet propelled

Although they look passive and plant-like, most salps are capable of independent movement using the powerful muscle bands that are arranged in rings around their bodies. When the muscles contract, they expel water violently from the cloacal siphon, and this thrusts the animal forward through the water by jet propulsion. At certain times of year, or if stimulated, many salps become phosphorescent because their bodies carry light-emitting bacteria.

Most salps live in colonies, floating through the water in great aggregations or long chains. Salps of the Pyrosomid family build cylindrical colonies that are hollow inside and open at one end. Individual animals are arranged with their mouth siphons facing outward and their anal siphons opening inward. The continual flow of water through the animals, into the central cavity and out of the rear aperture, helps to push the colony along.

Vast chains

Some colonies in the Mediterranean species *Pyrosoma atlanticum* are distinguished by an intense yellow or blue luminescence and can grow to 24 in. in length. The colonies of *Pyrosoma spinosum*, typical of warm seas, often grow to over 13 ft. long. Among species of the family Salpid, common in the Mediterranean, colonies consist of hundreds of barrel-shaped individuals that line up alongside one another to form chains that can be more than 82 ft. long.

Other species in the family do not organize themselves into colonies, but swim freely on their

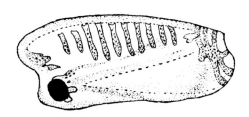

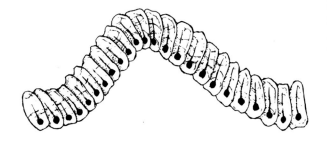

TOP The gelatinous, sac-like salps resemble larvae in appearance. They normally drift in colonies through the deep waters of the oceans, although some free-swimming individuals do occur. Like adult sea squirts, they do not have a spinal chord.

ABOVE The *Salpa maxima* is the largest salp in the Mediterranean. Although generally free-swimming, individuals will unite to form a chain-like colony up to 82 ft. long

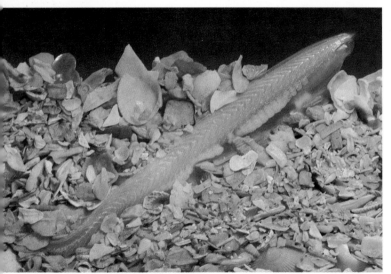

ABOVE The long, blade-like body of the lancelet has a strong, reinforcing notochord that runs from its head to its tail. It also has powerful blocks of muscle along its flanks, and a fin-like membrane that it uses to propel itself through the water. It has no head, and lacks the brain, sensory organs and jaws normally associated with vertebrates.

own. Free-swimming species are larger than the colonial types—about 6 in. long compared to 0.2-0.3 in.—and have bodies bounded by several faces (polyhedral) equipped with two long filaments instead of front and rear body extensions.

The family Doliolid includes a few small species that rarely grow longer than 0.4 in. and are normally restricted to warm seas. Typically, their bodies are barrel-shaped and pigmented in delicate shades of pink, violet and blue. Some species occur quite frequently in the Mediterranean.

Asexual reproduction is common among colonial species, alternating with sexual reproduction from one generation to the next. An individual that hatches from a fertilized egg can only reproduce asexually—producing a long ribbon that gives rise to new individuals. Asexually produced individuals can only reproduce sexually, producing eggs and sperm that combine to form a larva in the usual way. The sexual stage introduces new genetic material and allows the species to evolve, but its main function is to disperse the species and create new colonies.

The cephalochordates

The cephalochordates, or lancelets, are the organisms that most resemble vertebrates. Superficially eel-like creatures, they have lance-shaped bodies that are reinforced by a strong notochord running the whole length of the body—not just in the tail. A tubular dorsal nerve cord runs above and parallel to the notochord, but it does not terminate in a thickened bulb in the head area as in juvenile sea squirts.

In higher animals the thickened bulb is developed into a brain. Not only do lancelets lack a brain, or even the beginnings of one, but they have no real head. They have no cranial casing—for there is no brain to go inside it—and no eyes, scent receptors or jaws. The front end of the lancelet's body is simply an aperture, like the inhalant siphon of a sea squirt. It is surrounded by an eye-catching circular crown of long filaments, or cirri, which double as sense organs and primary water filtration devices.

The mouth aperture opens into an elongated gill basket or pharynx, like that of a sea squirt, and acts in the same way—absorbing oxygen and trapping food particles from water passing through the animal. Filtered water passes down the outside of the gill basket within the sleeve formed by the lancelet's body wall and finds its way out through an aperture known as the atriopore, which corresponds to the exhalant siphon of the sea squirt. Filtered food particles are collected in a sort of gutter on the floor of the pharynx, mixed with mucus and passed into the gut. Waste is ejected through a separate anus.

House designs

Although lancelets operate in much the same way as sea squirts, they bear a strong resemblance to primitive fishes such as lampreys. Both groups have well-defined muscle blocks along the sides of their bodies and fin-like membranes along their backs and undersides. Lancelets are free-swimming, although in practice they spend most of their time embedded in sand or mud close to the shore, with only the head end of their bodies protruding into the current to take in plankton-rich water. Lamprey larvae also bury themselves in the seabed and feed by filtering the water for microorganisms. The main difference between the two is that lamprey larvae have proper heads, with eyes and a brain.

Among cephalochordates, reproduction is always sexual. Eggs hatch into larvae covered in hair-like cilia. The cilia beat rhythmically, propelling the creatures through the water in the plankton layer where they live until they sink to the seabed and metamorphose into their final form.